Excitement and praise for a landmark work

"*Bi Any Other Name* is one of the most comprehensive, well-edited anthologies I have ever read. At roughly 380 pages, it may be deemed the Bisexual Bible." —*Lambda Book Report*

❖

"These urgent testimonials lead us to a sexually whole society where, with our varied queernesses, we are all welcome. This is a necessary book." —Judy Grahn

❖

"Young voices speak next to old, lawyers next to factory workers, blacks next to whites next to Asians; single people and people in group marriages are given equal time. After reading even part of this thick book, bisexuality seems so natural that the reader begins to wonder what all the fuss is about. And that's the beauty of *Bi Any Other Name*." —*Philadelphia City Paper*

❖

"*Bi Any Other Name* will change and/or validate more lives than any other volume published this year by a feminist or gay or lesbian small press." —*Bay Area Reporter*

❖

"This ground-breaking anthology deserves a place not only on the *bisexual* shelf of every bookstore, but among the classics of sexual minority literature." —*Out on Campus*

❖

"Everyone should read this book. At long last we are telling our stories and telling them with pride." —*Equal Time*

❖

"My capsule review of this book, in ten words or less: Yes. Yes, yes, yes, yes. And about bloody time, too." —*San Francisco Bay Times*

❖

"There are seventy-five authors in all, diverse in race, class, gender, able-bodiedness, age, and lifestyle. I certainly recomend it to anyone who wants to develop an understanding of bisexuality." —*Labyrinth*

❖

"A ground-breaking collection of seventy-five powerful voices articulating bisexual identity, pain, and pride, *Bi Any Other Name* is a landmark book for bisexual people and the bisexual movement." —*BiFocus*

BI ANY OTHER NAME
Bisexual people speak out

edited by
Loraine Hutchins
and
Lani Kaahumanu

Boston • Alyson Publications, Inc.

The following have generously given reprint permission:

Lesbian Contradictions, Seattle/San Francisco, for the excerpt of Jane Litwoman's "Some Thoughts on Bisexuality," pp. 4–5; and Dajenya's "Sisterhood Crosses Gender Preference Lines," appearing in its entirety, pp. 247–251. Both reprinted from the Winter 1990 issue, #29.

North Bi Northwest, the Seattle Bisexual Women's Network newsletter, for the "Biotypes" cartoons by Beth Reba Weise and Claudia Smelser, appearing on pp. 3, 31, and 72. Also for permission to reprint "Can Bisexuals Be Monogamous?" by Lenore Norrgard, pp. 281–284.

Gay Community News, 62 Berkeley Street, Boston, MA 02116, for the cartoon "Bisexuality Insurance," appearing on p. 224, from their 1983 April Fools issue. (Subscription rates: 1 yr., individual, $39; 1 yr., institution, $55; 6 mos., $25.)

"Room For You," copyright © 1983 by Betsy Rose.

"Myths/Realities of Bisexuality," p. 12–13, copyright © 1989 by Sharon Forman Sumpter, Los Angeles, California.

Photo credits: pp. 93 and 364 by Efrain Gonzalez. Back cover photo of co-editors by David Hamilton.

Typeset and printed in the United States of America.

This is a trade paperback original from Alyson Publications, Inc.,
40 Plympton St., Boston, Mass. 02118

Distributed in England by GMP Publishers, P.O. Box 247, London N17 9QR England.

First edition, second printing: October 1991

Library of Congress Cataloging-in-Publication Data

Bi any other name : bisexual people speak out / edited by Loraine Hutchins, Lani Kaahumanu. — 1st ed.
   p.   cm.
   ISBN 1-55583-174-5 (alk. paper) : $11.95
   1. Bisexuality—United States.   I. Hutchins, Loraine, 1948– .
II. Kaahumanu, Lani, 1943– .
HQ74.B5 1990
306.7'65'0973—dc20
                                      90-45816
                                        CIP

For my daughter,
Dannielle
the great
—L.K.

&

for us,
beautiful bisexuals,
we love you!
—L.H.

Juliet: *O Romeo, Romeo!...*
Deny thy father, and refuse thy name;...
O! be some other name:
What's in a name? that which we call a rose
By any other name would smell as sweet...

Romeo: *With love's light wings did I o'er-perch these walls;*
For stony limits cannot hold love out,
And what love can do, that dares love attempt.

Shakespeare's tragedy, *Romeo and Juliet,* is about lovers whose warring families prevent their love. We bisexuals are also caught between our heterosexual and homosexual families. We're called by *every* other name but bi, and still we dare attempt our love. Thus, the title for our book.

Contents

Preface

We walk silent among disputes and assertions,
but reject not the disputers, nor any thing that is asserted;
We hear the bawling and din — we are reach'd at by divisions,
jealousies, recriminations on every side,
They close peremptorily upon us, to surround us, my comrade,
Yet we walk unheld, free, the whole earth over,
journeying up and down,
till we make our ineffaceable mark upon time and the diverse eras,
Till we saturate time and eras, that the men and women of races,
ages to come, may prove brethren and lovers, as we are.
                                   —Walt Whitman, *Leaves of Grass*

We are Lani and Loraine, two very different bisexual women in our forties. Lani has lived on the West Coast most of her life, in the San Francisco Bay Area. Loraine has lived on the East Coast most of her life, in Washington, D.C. Lani was married and is the mother of a grown son and daughter. Loraine has never married or had children. Lani comes from a Hawaiian, Japanese, Irish Catholic background. Loraine's roots are mixed-European Protestant, from generations of educated Yankee women who married southern, blue-collar men. Lani identifies more with the lesbian and people-of-color communities. Loraine identifies more with the Left and with all sexual minorities. We're both radical feminists and bisexual activists, locally and nationally.

West Coast roots: Lani
As a bisexual coming out of a lesbian closet in 1980, I needed books that did not exist. I wanted to walk into my favorite women's bookstore and find an anthology of bisexual coming-out stories. I wanted to find a book on sexual theory with a thoughtful feminist analysis that included bisexuality to answer my questions, to push my thinking, to add my voice. I wanted to walk into the bookstore and find a section (however small) labeled

> BISEXUAL
> BISEXUAL HISTORY
> BISEXUAL CULTURE
> BISEXUAL WOMEN OF COLOR

BISEXUAL POLITICS
BISEXUAL SEXUALITY
BISEXUAL SPIRITUALITY.

I wanted to walk in and feel at home, feel welcomed. I didn't walk into my favorite women's bookstore because I knew what I wanted and needed did not exist.

My lover Bill and I decided to co-author a book that would end the invisibility, break down the stereotypes, give voice to a bisexual feminist movement. While we organized, I scoured the media for anything that would break my lesbian-identified, bisexual isolation. Finally, in the Summer 1981 edition of Denver's *Big Mama Rag,* I found Kim Woman-tree's essay. I must have read her "Nothing to Lose But Our Illusions ... The Politics of Feminist Bisexuality" a hundred times. Her words touched me, made me laugh and cry out loud. "I am a radical feminist, a lesbian for five years and now bisexual," she stated.

> I am writing this article to sort out for myself the issues bisexual feminists face. I will go deep into the problems bisexual feminists have with the women's movement because I have a unique perspective on the lesbian/ straight split, and I think understanding bisexual problems could lead to compassion, tolerance, and an eventual healing of this split. I don't think that it is important that every feminist try being bisexual. I don't think that bisexuals are necessarily better feminists. The idea that sexual preference can of itself lead to being a stronger liberationist has led to too many problems already.

I no longer felt so isolated. My sense that there *were* others (somewhere) was confirmed. Five years later, after many adventures and life changes, Bill and I parted as friends. I carried on with the book idea.

East Coast roots: Loraine

In the late sixties and early seventies I was awakening to all the possibilities of my life. I fell in love with people, not genders. It was part of the times. We were all tripping and cooking together and taking care of each other. If sex happened it was part of it; if it didn't that was fine too. We weren't interested in distinctions except us/them back then. Us was everyone peaceful and colorful. Them was everyone killing the Vietnamese abroad and the blacks here at home or beating and tear-gassing us as we demonstrated in the streets.

I knew from the start that I was attracted to energy, and only later did I sort out whom that energy belonged to and how I would act on it. That meant I could fall for a man with long hair and undulating hips on a dance floor, thinking him female, and still love him when I discovered him male. It meant his girlfriend could crawl into bed with us in the morning and we could include her in our cuddling too. We played and cuddled with one another for years before the analysis of feminism, gay liberation, race, sex, and class all came through. That's important. The feelings came first; the language and labels came afterwards. Naming can limit as well as empower.

In 1972, I wrote "Loving Women: Bringing the Dreams into Life," one of the first articles on lesbianism in the women's news journal *off our backs*. I lived in a commune with twelve other men and women, gay-identified and straight, all stimulating neglected aspects of ourselves by being around one another. I came out to my parents and at the youth services agency where I worked. I never stopped relating to men entirely, but I did stop relating to most men, particularly straight white men. I helped found Amazon Nation, a commune of lesbian, straight, and bisexual women. For several years I related to newly lesbian women, becoming many a woman's first woman lover, but never finding the right woman to stay with for a long time. Feelings of failure and shame overwhelmed me.

I worried about my personal makeup or conditioning. Was I incapable of greater intimacy with women? Finally I just said, Fuck the tyranny of lesbian-feminist correctness, and accepted myself as the 70-percent straight person I probably really am. I have had to constantly fight to have the 30-percent lesbian side not be ridiculed or misunderstood. The judgment cuts so deep. I have been silent far too long. In the early eighties I served as sexual-minorities rep for the National Network of Runaway and Youth Services. From that point on I began to speak out confidently as a bisexual, for the rights of sexual-minority youth and sexual-minority staff working with these youth. During the eighties I finally began to meet open, unafraid bisexuals. We formed support groups in Washington, D.C., up and down the East Coast, and nationally — from whence came the inspiration for this book!

Coast meets coast
We first met when Loraine visited San Francisco for the 1985 Lesbian/Gay Freedom Day Parade and ended up marching in BiPOL's[1] contingent. Loraine dressed as Janis Joplin, carrying a sign featuring Joplin's famous quote, "Don't compromise yourself, it's all you've got!" Other contingent members dressed as famous bisexuals, or made costume representations of puns that played upon the bi word — Bi Cuspids, Bi Focals, Bi All Means. Lani was Bi and Large. We held up wooden BiPhobia Shields to the sidewalk crowds whenever they booed us for being bold enough to proclaim ourselves bi in a gay crowd.

Lani planted the book project in Loraine's imagination then. Two years later she stayed at Loraine's home for the March on Washington for Lesbian and Gay Rights and the October 1987 opening of the Names Project Quilt on the Mall. The toll that AIDS was taking on our bisexual and gay community filled us with a sense of urgency, grief, and rage. Before going to the airport, Lani left Loraine a note: "Let's write the book we've been longing to read. Let's trust our own sweet selves to do it!"

Note

1. BiPOL is a San Francisco–based bisexual, lesbian, and gay political action group whose history is explained more in section IV, on politics.

Acknowledgments

Desiring a bisexual community and driven by feminist passion and politics, we built this book from many people's shared vision and inspiration, far too many for us to name. Some did their personal best, however, to make this book the reality it is today. We acknowledge their generosity and courage below.

Shirley Nakamura produced and designed our "Come Out, Come Out Wherever You Are" flyer in 1988, calling for contributions from bisexual feminists. Efrain Gonzalez recorded the beautiful bisexual community whose faces appear in this book, as photographed at the 1990 National Bisexual Conference in San Francisco.

As the stories began to arrive on both sides of the country we each had many friends who typed, proofread, gave sound advice, edited, argued, and affectionately gave us insights that furthered our progress and soothed our sometimes frazzled edges.

Lani individually thanks:
Ann E. Bailey, Karen Barnes, Jim Frazin, Rebecca Herman, Cherie James, David Lourea, Debra Markowitz, Pati McDermott, Tom Mossmiller, Carol Queen, Claudia Smelzer, Clare Thompson, Naomi Tucker, Dana Vinicoff, Merry Winslow, and my Asian Pacifica sisters Julie Mau, Pat Souza, and Willywoman Wilkinson for these gifts and services.

She also gives her heartfelt mahalos for the following special contributions:

♦ For computer access and limousine service above and beyond what I could have dreamed before I started: Kim Corsaro, Megan Costello, Bill Francis, Judy Francis, Jim Frazin, Perry Fry, Cherie James, Laurie James, David Lourea, David May, Vicki McGuire, Dannielle Raymond, and Mattie Key;

♦ To my date from hell Jim Rivaldo, who gave me much more than just the FAX, and to Walter Caplan, who opened his office to support a book whose subject doesn't exist;

♦ To Marcy Sheiner, whose gutzy inspiration, laughter, and skilled editing made for less drama in my life;

♦ To Diane Sabin, who adjusted the computer curvature of my neck and spine — I could not have comfortably continued to sit at the computer day after day without her loving hands, generous spirit, and healing energies.

◆ Several people supported me financially with loans and contributions during the final deadline months — Michael Ambrosino, Diane Estrin, Judy Francis, Joan Hill, Arlene Krantz, David Lourea, Vicki McGuire, Jay Paul, Dannielle Raymond, Karla Rossi, Seattle Bisexual Women's Network, Claudia Smelser, Than Sperry, Naomi Tucker, Beth Reba Weise, Mattie Key, and Tori Woodard.

◆ I want to recognize my coaches, whose love and laughter blessed my life: Rich Aranow, Karen Barnes, Megan Costello, Viktoria Faktor, Ron Fox, Lynne and Chris Frawley, Lynn R., Dannielle Raymond, Karla Rossi, and Merry Winslow.

◆ Becoming friends with Judy and Bill Francis was the surprise gift of this project. They generously opened their home, hearts, and a wealth of modern technology and assistance to me. Many of our conversations inspired new ideas, provided me with a different perspective, and gave a clearer sense of the possibilities of bisexual community.

◆ Professors and friends Sally Gearhart and Dorothy Haecker, my lesbian mentors, opened my eyes, my heart, my soul to a woman-identified reality; inspired radical-feminist possibilities; nurtured my lesbian identity, and four years later, my bisexual coming-out process. Dorothy told me I had important work to do in the lesbian community and encouraged me to reclaim bisexuals within the lesbian and gay history books. Sally gave me the courage to trust myself in difficult situations, to be open to new information, and above all to remain flexible. Her steady encouragement, humor, inspiration, and advice kept me in touch with what I wanted to say and my right to say it.

◆ And to Bill Mack, soulmate of many lifetimes, who successfully solicited crucial loans in the final weeks, and who has always encouraged me to be all I can be.

◆ In loving friendship and struggle, my son has supported this work for five years, doubting at first, then encouraging me to go for it.

◆ And to my mother, Aileen Helani Migliaccio, a writer and artist, whose talent and creative imagination, sense of humor, and unfailing love have inspired me for many years.

Loraine individually thanks:
◆ my muses Annie Sprinkle, Betty Dodson, Jim Gordon, Billy Jones;
◆ my computer doctors Rob Costa, Rozanna Scalzo, and Sandy Clagg — who left this world March 1990 as I worked on the book;
◆ my humoring housemates, both The Bad Girls of Fairmont Street, and Amy and Sly of Takoma;

◆ my wonderfully bi-positive sister, Becky, and parents, Adele and Tom, who courageously support me, whether I embarrass and challenge them, or make them proud;

◆ friends who helped type, proof, and read text — Tasha Belfiore, Colevia Carter, Rob Costa, Judy Davis, Jude Heimel, Heather Harts'horn, Ethelbert Miller, Liz O'Lexa, Carol Queen, Travis Smith, Suzin, Len Tirado, and Joy Wolfram;

◆ all the girls at Lammas Bookstore who put up with my frequent appropriation of their resources;

◆ and my D.C. support system — Bob, Charles At Last, Melinda DeLashmutt, Gunnel Ehrnford, David Hamilton, Juicy, Janet Shenk, Richard Spector, Dan Studenberg, Nancy Troll, and Vee.

Both of us thank all the contributors who didn't make it into the book as well as those who did (we learned much from all of you). Thanks to Sasha Alyson — who believed it was time we spoke for ourselves — and to us, LORAINE AND LANI — who birthed the book we longed to read.

Bicoastal introduction

*It would be a great boon to all of us if there were more social
space for self-defined bisexuals. This would mean that we would
all be a little freer from exclusivist and essentialist definitions. Of
course, because our society is rigidly gendered and is heterosexist
in structure, it would be utopian to imagine that bisexuality
could exist in a haven beyond gender and beyond gay oppression. But even a bisexuality with all the contradictions imposed
on it by our society can help to challenge the sexual status quo.
Contradictions, after all, are the moving force of history.*
— Mariana Valverde, *Sex, Power, and Pleasure*[1]

Why this book?

Bisexual people — by any other name, by every other name — have
lived and loved since the beginning of time. Yet we're told we don't exist,
that we're really heterosexual or really gay, that nothing exists except
these two extremes. Though usually not talked about or acknowledged,
our lives (and those of many who regard themselves as gay or heterosexual) manifest a wealth of experience and behavior between these
extremes. It is time for bisexuals to speak out, in our own voices, no
longer filtered by experts' interpretations of who we are.

In this book bisexual people tell the stories of our lives, name our
experiences, and take pride in ourselves. *Bi Any Other Name* is a primer
for the bisexual co.nmunity and movement, and for everyone who seeks
to understand. The voices in this book break our silence, and initiate
dialogue with the diverse communities we call home.

Bi Any Other Name is presented in four parts:

I. Psychology: Facing ourselves
II. Spirituality: Healing the splits
III. The bisexual community: Are we visible yet?
IV. Politics: A queer among queers.

Each section begins with an overview that introduces the themes of
the coming-out stories and analytical pieces within it. More than seventy
bisexual people — of all races, ages, classes, abilities, creeds, and
identities — speak in these sections.

The book ends with a brief resource list of bisexual organizations
and glossary of commonly used words.

Why now?

Why have the bisexual organizational rumblings that were just below the surface all through the eighties finally burst "out" locally, nationally, and internationally? A combination of many things, including the fact that the bisexual movement and community have reached critical mass, has forced us out. What seems sudden is actually the result of years of isolated grassroots organizing through social support groups and political caucuses within larger coalitions. Before AIDS, the prejudice against us, our very existence, was easily minimized or denied. The increase in homophobic attacks (caused partly by AIDS hysteria and partly by gay people becoming visible, vocal, and strong — demanding civil rights and respect) has forced society to look at the permeability of the "walls" between gay and straight. There are no walls.

Though awareness of AIDS may depend upon how personally we have been affected, one thing is clear — bisexuals are particularly affected. We were, and are, among those first and most severely affected (gay and bisexual men). We exist in that limbo land where people secretly venture but then are afraid *we* (who identify as bisexual) spread the disease among *them*.

Recent reports indicate that AIDS is now increasing most rapidly among IV drug users (and their babies), particularly people of color. These people are not all heterosexual, as is sometimes assumed. According to several panelists at the 1989 International AIDS conference, "Ethnic and racial minorities seem to have higher incidences of bisexuality," yet don't necessarily identify as bisexual, "thus creating special concerns for those directing AIDS education campaigns."[2]

Are we still a "special concern," not part of every planner's basic consciousness and understanding? Unfortunately yes. And it is clear, from the many different communities we span, that we function as bridges between opposed camps (gay and straight, women and men, of color and white). We are not to be blamed for this. Safe-sex educators say that unsafe practices, not certain groups of people, spread AIDS. In other words, it's *what* you do, not *who* you do!

The Kinsey Institute recently conducted a study showing that 46 percent of (self-labeled) lesbians reported having sex with men since 1980. Many of these men had had sex with other men. Often safe sex was not practiced. (Remember, these are *not* women who identify as straight or bisexual, these are women who label themselves lesbian.)[3]

While the AIDS crisis has forced recognition of bisexuals on the public, being listed in disease statistics is not the kind of acknowledgement we need or deserve. The bisexual community is just beginning to organize, under the light of public scrutiny. We cannot back down now or be intimidated by discrimination, misunderstanding, or fear. We must come to terms with our identity as bisexual people in the world.

Some gay publications and writers are beginning to recognize bisexuality as a valid part of the sexual minority community.[4] More and more lesbians and gay men are examining and openly exploring their bisexual behavior, as are some bisexuals within heterosexual closets. This is due, in large part, to the public lesbian- and gay-identified bisexual pioneers who began the work of bisexual pride in the early 1980s. As more of us come out, we challenge stereotypes, and our increasing visibility expands the space in which we live, move, and create.

As the writers in this anthology show, the bisexual community and movement is a strong, growing, viable force for coalition between groups. Bisexuals are a part of many different struggles. This diversity is certainly our challenge. It is also our unifying strength.

Why multicultural feminist bisexuality?
When any minority whose experience has been denied or trivialized by the dominant society takes pride and names their own reality clearly — for the first time, or for the hundredth time — it challenges the status quo and breaks down stereotypes. The feminist practice of consciousness-raising has shown us that sharing personal experiences on common topics is key to positive growth and change. An inclusionary multicultural feminist politic recognizes the complexity of sex, race, and class oppression, and how each affects and depends upon the others to survive.

Some have a difficult time with feminism. "Why not a human liberation movement?" they say. The answer is that the power differences between the sexes, races, and classes are still so extreme that invoking humanism, at this time, dangerously denies that fact. "Those in power always speak of humanism," says Robin Morgan, "and accuse those who have been made powerless and categorized as 'other' of divisiveness. This is done, however, only when the powerless recognize and name their already divided state, and begin to articulate their longing — for union. The fear is not that we are different. The fear is that we are the same."[5]

If mankind of course includes women (as we're told it does), why is it so difficult to identify with feminism as an inclusive term? Is it because it exposes the power imbalance from the other side and shows how things are organized, hierarchically, for the benefit of a few, at the expense of many? Yes!

Heterosexuality *needs* homosexuality, to be reassured that it is different. It also needs the illusion of dichotomy between the orientations to maintain the idea of a fence, a fence that has a right (normal, good) and a wrong (abnormal, evil) side to be on, or fall from. To the extent that we collaborate in seeing homosexuality as an opposite polarity (not part of a diverse range of human sexuality), we perpetuate this unhealthy, unrealistic, hierarchical dichotomy.

The dichotomies are absolutely
either/or
right/left
light/dark
male/female
masculine/feminine
hetero/homo
white/of color
upper class/working class
middle class/homeless
young/old
able-bodied/differently abled.

No room
for all points
in between

No room
for the perfect
Kinsey 2,3,4,5[6]

for
both/and
middle ground
dawn/dusk
transsexual
transvestite
bisexual
mixed race/culture/class
middle age
temporarily abled/hidden disability

absolutely
no room
for all points in between.

But reality is not
this or that
it is
all of this
and
all of that

and
they meet/merge/mingle
in between.

Most of our lives are played out on the middle ground. To recognize this doesn't mean it is better or worse. This space in between gives us valuable information and, when recognized in relation to the absolute extremes, it helps communicate our various realities to each other. As those of us who don't believe in the walls and fences join forces and speak out about our lives, the middle ground reminds everyone that we are part of a whole. And yes, this whole contains important extremes, but it is the vast expanse of gray areas where most of us live.

Life is both/and; there are male, female, and transsexual people. *All* these people can appear to be masculine and/or feminine since these fairly rigid traits are created by a polarized sexist reality. Think about it — who says what is masculine or feminine, what is sissy or tomboy, what is butch or femme? Transvestites, for instance, play out a broad range of possibilities within this dichotomy, whatever their sexual orientation.

What we see happening now with the bisexual liberation movement is a new audacity that, as Robin Morgan states,

> would dare to affirm the ultimate radical politics reflected in and reflective of the universe itself: radical integration. Integration of the self with the self (literally: integrity), and the integration with each other and our vision and all of life ... radical integration ... sacrifices nothing except false categories and burned-out strategies.[7]

It's not that separatism, or separate organizing on the part of any group, isn't an empowering tool for change. It is the best way for any oppressed people to recover their own sense of themselves and their oppression; a way to build a power base and become more effective as a group in the world at large. But for many, lesbian and gay separatism during the seventies and eighties became a chauvinistic, holier-than-thou way of life, a power-over tool that gave us a rigid party line by which to police one another for political correctness. In 1970 Ti-Grace Atkinson coined the phrase "Feminism is a theory, lesbianism is a practice."[8] As the movement developed, it was translated into "Feminism is *the* theory, lesbianism is *the* practice." This reinforced the us/them dynamic of politically correct thought and behavior, discounting and excluding many experiences. In reality, bisexuals were some of the first men to write gay manifestos and to initiate the men's anti-sexist movement and some of the first women to build the lesbian feminist movement.

In *Sappho Was a Right-On Woman,* lesbians Barbara Love and Sydney Abbott assert that some women might be

> moving into and developing a true bisexuality [and that very little is] known in the movement about the bisexual's views. It may be true, that numbers of women will develop into true bisexuals, or who are true bisexuals — that is, able to enjoy total relationships with both men and women — are

today calling themselves Lesbian, since despite all the controversy there is a theoretical basis for it as well as an aura of radical chic surrounding Lesbians in the women's movement ... bisexual women who have been caught on both sides and in the middle of the heterosexual/homosexual argument have a unique contribution to make to open discussion on sexuality ... [and may well be] the most important group to speak up in the women's movement on the whole topic of sexuality ... it is amazing that there is no bisexual caucus in the women's movement ... [It is probably] that bisexual women bring out fears of homosexuality in straight women and also fears of heterosexuality in women who live as Lesbians.[9]

(It is amazing that there is no bisexual caucus in the gay men's liberation movement or among anti-sexist men either.) *Sappho* was published almost twenty years ago. It's high time to get beyond these polarizations, hesitations, and fears!

"Women and men working together for a change"[10]

"Why include men?" We ourselves went back and forth, swayed by arguments, re-evaluating our own thoughts on the subject. Several women's presses told us they were not interested in a book that included men, because it was important to focus their limited resources on women. However, since this would be the first book of its kind, we wanted it to represent and unite the whole bisexual experience. There has been enough division. The bisexual community and movement includes women and men.

Feminism initially gave women a language and an analytic framework within which to understand their sexuality and sexual oppression. As a result, their voices in this anthology are more numerous and mature. The men's pro-feminist, anti-sexist movement is at least a decade behind. Men's thinking on bisexuality hasn't yet caught up. But this would be a poorer, different book without both sexes represented, without the combinations and contrasts of the experiences and different perspectives shared. We build from this point.

Notes

1. Mariana Valverde, *Sex, Power, and Pleasure,* New Society Publishers, 1987, p. 120.

2. Ronald J. Sanchez, "Angry Participants Commandeer AIDS Conference Session," *Washington Blade,* August 18, 1989.

3. J.M. Reinish, S.A. Sanders, and M. Ziemba-Davis, "Self-Labeled Sexual Orientation, Sexual Behavior, and Knowledge about AIDS: Implications for Biomedical

Research and Education Programs," in *Proceedings of NIMH/NIDA Workshop on Women and AIDS: Promoting Healthy Behaviors,* ed. S.J. Blumenthal, A. Eichler, and G. Weissman, Washington, D.C.: American Psychiatric Press (in press).

4. See for instance the recent "lesbians who sleep with men" articles: Kim Corsaro, "Lesbians Who Sleep with Men: An Interview with Susie Bright," *San Francisco Bay Times,* Sept. 1989; Jan Clausen, "My Interesting Condition," *Outlook,* Winter 1990; Jorjet Harper, "Lesbians Who Sleep with Men," *Outweek,* February 11, 1990. Also see the writings of bi-positive lesbians, such as Joan Nestle, *Restricted Country,* Firebrand Books, 1987; Valverde, *Sex, Power, and Pleasure;* and the recent *Lesbian Contradictions* article cited in the Psychology section overview, as well as various writings in the San Francisco magazine for the sexually adventurous lesbian, *On Our Backs.*

5. Robin Morgan, *The Anatomy of Freedom: Feminism, Physics, and Global Politics,* Anchor Books/Doubleday, 1984, p. 205.

6. See the glossary for an explanation of the Kinsey Scale.

7. Morgan, *The Anatomy of Freedom,* p. 301.

8. From her 1970 speech at Columbia University, New York City, as quoted in Sidney Abbott and Barbara Love's *Sappho Was a Right-On Woman: A Liberated View of Lesbianism,* Stein & Day, 1972, pp. 119–121.

9. Abbott and Love, *Sappho Was a Right-On Woman,* pp. 156–157.

10. This was the double entendre slogan used recently for a San Francisco benefit gala.

I.
Psychology:
Facing ourselves

Overview

*Bisexuals' lives provide new psychological and social under-
standings of sexuality and closeness, highlighting the mechanics
of sexual decision-making as potentially self-determined action.
Research is needed about all areas of the bisexual experience,
including studies of common qualities of bisexuals, therapeutic
case studies, and longitudinal studies of bisexuals' relationships.
The bisexual experience calls into question traditional definitions
of the nature of sexual identity development. Fluid, ambiguous,
subversive, multifarious, bisexuality can no longer be denied.*
                                            —Rebecca Shuster[1]

Defining bisexuality

As Kate Millett once said, "Homosexuality was invented by a straight
world dealing with its own bisexuality."[2] So it is not surprising that
looking up the word *bisexual* in the dictionary is like blinking into the
distorted mirror of Western society's ambivalence over sexuality.

The prefix *bi* means two, or dual. Therefore the word *bisexual* is
used to refer to things involving both sexes. However, this can mean
an individual who possesses physical organs of both sexes, or it can
mean some event or setting that involves both sexes at once. *Bisexual*
can also refer to individuals of either sex who are attracted to both
sexes. In this book, we use this last meaning. But our common frame
of reference is loaded with the combination of all of these definitions
together and how they affect our understanding of what is meant when
one says "bisexual." These multiple and contradictory meanings limit
our ability to discuss the subject clearly. For instance, someone who
possesses both male and female qualities, either psychologically (as in
being androgynous) or physically (as in being an hermaphrodite[3]), is
not necessarily attracted to both male and female people. To further
complicate matters, the definitions of *androgynous, bisexual, hermaphrodite,* and *homosexual* all overlap in many dictionaries and reference
books. For instance, the first definition of *bisexual* in Webster's *Collegiate Dictionary* is "hermaphrodite." Yet the same dictionary defines
the actual word *hermaphrodite* as "1 ... b. homosexual. 2. something
that is a combination of diverse elements."[4] Are homosexuals physical

YOUR LESBIAN FRIENDS	YOUR STRAIGHT FRIENDS	YOUR MOTHER
"Internalized homophobia won't allow you to accept your lesbianism."	*"Your interest in women is an attempt to avoid your fear of intimacy with men."*	*"You're sick."*

Reprinted with permission from *North Bi Northwest,* newsletter of the Seattle Bi Women's Network.

hermaphrodites? Not usually. Are they bisexual? Not necessarily. So, what "diverse elements" are combined?

Are we going round in circles? Perhaps what's really got us spinning are the contradictory, confusing definitions of sexual orientation manufactured by this heterosexist, sex-negative society. Unraveling *this* conditioning is the key.

Coming out bisexual, as Shuster's opening quote attests, truly does affect everyone. It breaks the conspiracy of silence, as gay people have also done. But it also challenges current assumptions about the immutability of people's orientations and society's supposed divisions into discrete groups. Bisexuals' coming out challenges other people's understanding of them*selves*. Our bisexuality reflects on society as a whole, threatening the monosexual[5] framework that heterosexism needs to survive.[6]

Since bisexuality threatens how society is organized, bisexuals often become the targets of discrimination, stereotyping and jokes. We are considered more sexual, more confused, more fickle than others,[7] whereas in reality all disempowered groups are sexualized in a hierarchical, sex-phobic society — as a way to divide and maintain fear of The Other.[8]

As the stories in this book show, we have the same hopes, fears, problems, and experiences as monosexuals do in relationships. But we are the target for the projected fear of being "other," from both the gay and the straight sides of humanity.

Bisexuality is much more than, and different from, the sensationalized "third choice," "best-of-both-worlds" phenomena it's made out to be. Bisexuality is an inclusive term that defines immense possibilities available to us, whether we act on them or not. It opens doors and accepts all the in-betweens, including the more conforming "accepted" ways we've identified in the past or will in the future. We have gay and heterosexual experience. We socialize with both, and we go back and forth interpreting each to the other, whether this service is appreciated or not. This will be recognized as more of us come out and take pride in the identity we were told is impossible. But first we must face ourselves. Declaring oneself bisexual means trusting one's own experiences. As Loraine has stated, "Unpredictable is not the same as unreliable. Integrating and balancing opposite parts of oneself is not 'confused' or 'unreal.' It might not be your cup of tea, which is fine, but it's a life-long creation I'm dedicated to and enjoying..."[9]

This is difficult, since so many people are confused by and concerned with the (so-called) fluid nature of bisexuality. But think about it. When we examine our lives, they are not neat, well-packaged scenarios. Life is vital and multifaceted, complex. As Adrienne Rich puts it:

> Truthfulness anywhere means a heightened complexity. But it is a movement into evolution ... This is why the effort to speak honestly is so important ... Does a life 'in the closet' — lying, perhaps of necessity, about ourselves, to bosses, landlords, clients, colleagues, family, because the law and public opinion are founded on a lie — does this, can it, spread into private life, so that lying (discretion) becomes an easy way to avoid conflict or complication? Can it become a strategy so ingrained that it is used even with close friends and lovers?[10]

Bisexual ways of being

Individual bi identities span many communities. Within this book you will find a wide range of bisexuals. We are bisexuals of all ages and colors. Some of us identify with the gay and lesbian communities, some of us identify with the heterosexual community, some of us identify primarily with other bisexuals. Some of us identify primarily with people of color or with other sexual minority communities such as S/M, cross-dressers, or transsexuals.[11]

Because our society is so polarized between homosexuals and heterosexuals, the bisexual closet has two doors. Both need to be opened. Coming out to the straight world and coming out to the gay world are not the same. Coming out bisexually is also affected by one's gender, one's race and culture, one's class, one's religion, and one's physical abilities or state of health. Once you've read a number of the coming-out stories you'll begin to have a better idea what we mean about how different, and yet how universal, we are.

In the quote that follows, Jane Litwoman expresses one particularly different and unique view of why she herself does, and does not, identify as bisexual:

> The sexologist Kinsey has created a 0–6 scale in which people are rated as to their homo/heterosexuality.[12] I think of myself as off the scale. To me, the Kinsey scale has as much relevance as if everyone were evaluated on a spectrum of whether they were more attracted to people with brown

eyes or green/blue eyes. Gender is just not what I care about or even really notice in a sexual partner. This is not to say that I don't have categories of sexual attraction, that I judge each person as an individual — I have categories, but gender isn't one of them. I'm erotically attracted to intelligent people, to people with dark/colored skin and light eyes and hair, to people with a kind of sleazy, sexy come-on, to eccentrics. In some of those categories I am homo-erotic (i.e., I'm intelligent and eccentric), in others I am hetero-erotic (i.e., I have light skin and dark eyes and hair). To be perfectly frank, I can barely imagine what it's like to be a lesbian or a straight woman, to be attracted to women because they are female — and that is sexy — or to men because they are male. In that way I feel like both of them share a common perception which I will never know — that I am color blind or tone deaf to a gender-erotic world.

I can relate more easily to people who are not primarily gender-erotic, but who are what is commonly referred to as fetishistic. At a gut level I can imagine what it might be to be erotically attracted to frilly lingerie or leather or the smell of the sea. The clearest way for me to understand lesbians and straight women is to accept them as fetishists. From my viewpoint straight women are malegender-fetishists and lesbians are femalegender fetishists who are so culturally supported in their sexual attractions that most of the time they hardly understand my different reality.

Of course I live in a world in which gender is a much more powerful concern than leather or the smell of the sea. Gender, along with race, class, ethnicity, and age, is one of the most profound social status determinants in our society. I could choose to only act on my attractions to female persons for political/social concerns. However, I instinctively resist straight-jacketing my sexual feelings for political reasons...

I don't define my sexuality so much by what I might or might not like — women, men, orgies, masturbation, romantic music, intimacy, anonymous sex, cunnilingus, etc. — but by honest exploration of my sexual desires. What I am sexually is sovereign.[13]

Yet, responsible scientific investigation into the kinds of issues raised above by Litwoman and Shuster is woefully lacking! Even sociologists such as Philip W. Blumstein and Pepper Schwartz, who have done extensive research on bisexuality, say that "little research has investigated the route bisexuals take to this identity or any of the common qualities of those who identify themselves as bisexual."[14] Still, so that we may better understand from where we start, a brief survey of the bisexuality research that *does* exist is in order.

Research based on a monosexual framework = Biphobia

Dividing people for purposes of study into only two groups, "heterosexual" and "homosexual," which is done most of the time, and defining all people at gay dances or all men found in gay bars as "homosexual," has the effect of lumping bisexuals into these groups and makes interpretation of the results extremely difficult. —Dr. F. Klein, *The Bisexual Option*[15]

Bisexuals are continually being studied, mostly by non-bisexuals, who base their research on a monosexual framework and then claim that we don't exist, or are rare, or are perverted, or are really on our way to something else. And, as with homosexuality, many of the studies on bisexuality are done from the heterosexual assumption that we're unnatural or sick to begin with. These researchers seem to forget they're only studying clients who come to them for counseling. What's important is that these studies, therefore, rarely distinguish between healthy and distressed bisexuals. The researchers have no sense for what is really intrinsic to being bisexual. Therefore, biphobia — the irrational fear of bisexuality in oneself or others and the distrust and discrimination practiced against us because of this fear — has permeated almost all existing research up to this point.

In the seventies, with the unfolding of the women's and gay liberation movements, an explosion of articles and studies on bisexuality appeared in the popular press. Most of them sensationalized us according to the myths mentioned earlier. Even the better books, like *The Bisexual Option*[16] and *View from Another Closet*,[17] rely heavily on the case-study method of interviews and surveys and the voice of the expert authority. The only first-person account, *Barry and Alice: Portrait of a Bisexual Marriage*,[18] is out of print.

Another problem with current studies on alternative sexuality is that they focus on married couples almost exclusively, and within these couples usually only one partner is gay, or bisexual.[19] Not only are single bisexual people ignored, no surveys of the many bisexuals leading closeted lives in the gay and lesbian communities are available. Gay people in heterosexual relationships are mentioned only within the research framework that there is no such thing as a bisexual, and that their homosexuality is their only true sexuality.

Klein's *The Bisexual Option* is especially good in pointing out how invisibility perpetuates research errors. He quotes noted sex researchers claiming that true bisexuality doesn't exist, and then catches them in their own errors.[20] On the gay research side of the myopia surrounding bisexuality, books such as John D'Emilio and Estelle Freedman's *Intimate Matters: A History of Sexuality in America*, assign less text and index space to bisexuality than to "bestiality."[21] Bestiality is mentioned three times in their index, bisexuality not once. And their book is not unusual.

What has been written *about* bisexuals is also not grounded in a feminist analysis of sexuality and power. Therefore, this kind of information provides an incomplete, distorted picture, and tends more to perpetuate myths about us than to dispel them.

Budding bi-positivism: Some signs of change

I do not in the least underestimate bisexuality ... I expect it to provide all further enlightenment. — Sigmund Freud[22]

"There are not two discrete populations, heterosexual and homosexual ... Only the human mind invents categories and tries to force fact into separated pigeon holes ... The sooner we learn this ... the sooner we shall reach a sound understanding of the realities of sex." — Alfred Kinsey[23]

"What is new is not bisexuality, but rather the widening of our awareness and acceptance of human capacities for sexual love. Today the recognition of bisexuality in oneself and in others is part of the whole mid-20th century movement to accord to each individual, regardless of race, class, nationality, age or sex, the right to be a person who is unique and who has a social identity that is worthy of dignity and respect ... Even a superficial look at other societies and some groups in our own society should be enough to convince us that a very large number of human beings, probably a majority— are bisexual in their potential capacity for love ... We will fail to evolve in our understanding of human sexuality if we continue to see homosexuals merely as "heterosexuals-in-reverse," ignoring the vast diversity actually represented by society's many varied expressions of love between people. — Margaret Mead[24]

Even with these few positive attitudes quoted here, the biological and environmental origins of sexual identification are still hotly debated today. Authorities don't agree on what causes what, much less on what part bisexuality plays. And incredible hostility and misunderstanding is still directed toward bisexuals and bisexuality. However, a number of bi-positive writers and researchers are beginning to speak against the phobic tide.

In a 1985 article,"Bisexuality: Reassessing our Paradigms of Sexuality,"[25] Dr. Jay Paul — one of a handful of "out" bisexual psychologists writing professionally on bisexuality — identifies current research errors on bisexuality:

There is far more variability and fluidity in many people's sexual patterns than theoretical notions tend to allow, suggesting that researchers have imparted an artificial consistency to an inchoate sexual universe.

It is not that science has ignored the indisputable fact that the sexual biographies of many include sexual experiences with both men and women, but rather the theoretical meanings given to those experiences. The tendency is to deny the legitimacy of one's erotic responsiveness to either males, or females; thereby, one assumes that all people are either basically heterosexual or homosexual. This refusal to allow for an equivalent basic bisexuality in some portion of the population leads to a variety of explanations for bisexual patterns.

(And, we might add, few of them adequate or good.)

Hansen and Evans, writing in the same journal, cite the common misinterpretation or misuse of the Kinsey scale, stressing that it describes only genital behavior patterns, not identity.[26]

In another article in the same issue, Dr. Gary Zinik[27] points out that in the forties and fifties the country was shocked by Kinsey's discovery of high rates of homosexual behavior among men and women. But what was even *more* overlooked was that "significantly higher percentages of people exhibit bisexual behavior than exclusively homosexual behavior." He explains that this is because a "conflict model" of bisexuality (in research circles, in researchers' minds) assumes that homosexual interests eradicate heterosexual responsiveness — that they can't exist peacefully side by side. But this isn't true for a significant number of people. In fact, the notion that "one drop of homosexuality indicates latent homosexuality in a straight" theory sounds suspiciously like the "one drop of black blood makes you black and you can't go to our schools" racist attitude in U.S. public schools last generation.

Zinik instead proposes a "flexibility model," where "indeed men and women are not considered opposite sexes so much as variations on a theme."

After all, what is the theme? The theme is life, in all its diversity. We are trained from birth to think of ourselves as either/or — female or male — and indoctrinated in sex-role conditioning under what Adrienne Rich calls "compulsory heterosexuality," based on and rooted in male supremacy. But if these things change, would we men and women really be so different, so opposite, so far apart?

Some feminists would have us believe so, saying that men's biology dooms them to violence (and thus women to be their inevitable victims and servants, as well as their prized possessions on pedestals). But other lesbian and feminist writers disagree. For example, French writer Elisabeth Badinter has caused great discussion in Europe with her book, *The Unopposite Sex: The End of the Gender Battle,*[28] where she argues that men and women are growing more and more alike in the modern age and that the basic bisexuality of all of us will be more and more revealed.

From the gay research angle, on the other hand, it is interesting to note that *The Many Faces of Homosexuality*[29] — a 1986 cross-cultural, anthropological study of homosexual behaviors in various times and places — clearly illustrates that much homosexual behavior is *actually* bisexual behavior, and that our modern U.S. Western model of who gay people are does not apply cross-culturally at all. Two modern gay writers who would agree are Warren Blumenfeld and Diane Raymond, whose highly readable book, *Looking at Gay and Lesbian Life*,[30] features a section called "The Homosexual/Bisexual/Heterosexual Continuum." They discuss the many aspects of gay and bisexual behavior versus identity, physical diversity among all sexual minorities, and what part of our behavior is chosen, what part innate.

Some of the best studies on bisexuality come from outside the U.S. The late-seventies publication *Bisexuality: A Study,* by British author Charlotte Wolff,[31] is still unsurpassed in its feminist understanding of all sexuality, though it is somewhat outdated now in the age of AIDS. More recently, a group of bisexuals living in and around London published a small anthology, *Bisexual Lives,*[32] that served as one inspiration for this book.

The debate and this present polarized state of affairs will go on. However, since AIDS has put sex and sexuality in the public eye more than ever before, we can no longer afford to deny the many issues it exposes, including the current rigid monosexual framework overlying the fluid nature of sex. We need new mediating approaches. Bisexual liberation is one of them. But for a more whole, peaceful way to come into existence, we must face ourselves — name our own bisexual potential— first.

Notes

1. Rebecca Shuster, "Sexuality as a Continuum: The Bisexual Identity," in *Lesbian Psychologies: Explorations and Challenges,* ed. Boston Lesbian Psychologies Collective, University of Illinois Press, 1987.

2. As quoted in *Bisexual Lives,* London: Off Pink Publishing, 1988. This quote was originally from Millett's book *Flying,* now reprinted by Simon & Schuster, 1990.

3. Noted sex researcher Dr. John Money of Johns Hopkins University estimates that there may be as many as one hermaphrodite born per thousand births, but that we cannot know accurately at this time. Doctors do not report such statistics to any national database, and often perform surgery on such children's "in-between" genitals shortly after birth to make them one sex or the other.

4. *Webster's New Collegiate Dictionary,* Springfield, Mass.: Merriam, 1977, p. 536.

5. *Monosexual* is a term coined by the bisexual movement to mean anyone (gay or heterosexual) who is attracted to just one sex, their own or the opposite one.

6. For definitions of *heterosexism* and many other words, see the glossary.

7. For more on this, see "Myths/Realities of Bisexuality," following these notes.

8. When society is dominated by one race, sex, or class of people, the groups not in power are seen as Other. White-male-dominated society, for instance, has portrayed women as more sexually insatiable and unclean than men; people of color as more immoral and sexual; and gays as child molesters. Actually it's mostly straight men who molest, and women and people of color, as groups, certainly do not have the negative characteristics that have been projected upon them as Other.

9. Loraine Hutchins, "Biatribe: Towards a Politic of Feminist Bisexuality," *off our backs,* February 1988.

10. From *Women and Honor: Some Notes on Lying,* Pittsburgh: Motherroot Publications, 1977.

11. See the glossary for definitions of any of these terms.

12. See the glossary for a definition of the Kinsey Scale.

13. From "Some Thoughts on Bisexuality," *Lesbian Contradictions,* Winter 1990.

14. Philip Blumstein and Pepper Schwartz, "Bisexuality: Some Social Psychological Issues," *Journal of Social Issues* 33 (Spring 1977): 30–45.

15. Dr. Fred Klein, M.D., *The Bisexual Option: A Concept of One Hundred Percent Intimacy,* New York: Berkley Books, 1980, p. 152.

16. Ibid.

17. Janet Bode, *View from Another Closet,* New York: Hawthorn Books, 1976.

18. Barry Kohn and Alice Matusow, *Barry and Alice: Portrait of a Bisexual Marriage,* Prentice Hall, 1980.

19. See, for instance, *The Bisexual Spouse* by Ivan Hill, McLean, Va.: Barlina Books, 1987; and *Uncommon Affairs: Gay Men and Straight Women,* by Catherine Whitney, New American Library, 1990.

20. Klein, *The Bisexual Option.* See in particular pp. 126–128 and 139.

21. John D'Emilio and Estelle B. Freedman, *Intimate Matters: A History of Sexuality in America,* Harper & Row, 1988. Billed as the "first full-length study of the history of sexuality in this country," this book contains much fascinating information. However, its fourteen-page index lists three references for bestiality, six for cross-dressing, and eleven for sexual revolution (including feminists, gay liberation, singles life, youth rebellions, and sexual vulnerabilty of women), but not

one mention of bisexuality! You would think our experience is rarer than any of the above and that we played no part in the entire sexual revolution they chronicle over the past twenty to two hundred years.

22. Sigmund Freud, "Three Essays on the Theory of Sexuality," in *Readings in Human Sexuality,* ed. Samuel T. Wilson, Richard L. Roe, and Lucy E. Autrey, pp. 71–79, New York: West, 1975. And as discussed by Christine Downing, a lesbian Jungian, in her *Myths and Mysteries of Same Sex Loving,* Continuum, 1989. (*Myths and Mysteries* is also of interest because its Jungian author discusses her own heterosexual marriage, her current long-term partnership with a woman, and her sexual, loving relationships with gay men.)

23. *Bisexual Lives,* op. cit.

24. Margaret Mead, "Bisexuality: What's It All About?" *Redbook,* January 1975, pp. 29–31.

25. F. Klein, M.D., and Timothy J. Wolf, Ph.D., eds., *Bisexualities: Theory and Research: Journal of Homosexuality,* vol. 2, nos. 1/2, Haworth Press, 1985, pp. 21–22.

26. Ibid., p. 3.

27. Ibid., pp. 7–11.

28. Elizabeth Badinter, *The Unopposite Sex: The End of the Gender Battle,* Harper & Row, 1989. (First published in English in Great Britain by Collins Harvill under the title *Man/Woman: The One Is the Other.)*

29. Evelyn Blackwood, ed., *The Many Faces of Homosexuality: Anthropological Approaches to Homosexual Behavior,* New York: Harrington Park Press, 1986.

30. Warren Blumenfeld and Diane Raymond, *Looking at Gay and Lesbian Life,* Boston: Beacon Press, 1988.

31. Dr. Charlotte Wolff, *Bisexuality: A Study,* London: Quartet Books, 1979.

32. *Bisexual Lives,* op. cit. (See note 2.)

Myths/realities of bisexuality

Sharon Forman Sumpter

Sexuality runs along a continuum. It is not a static "thing" but rather a process that can flow, changing throughout our lifetime. Bisexuality falls along this continuum. As Boston bisexual activist Robyn Ochs says, bisexuality is the "potential for being sexually and/or romantically involved with members of either gender."

MYTH: Bisexuals are promiscuous/swingers.
TRUTH: Bisexual people have a range of sexual behaviors. Some have multiple partners; some have one partner; some go through partnerless periods. Promiscuity is no more prevalent in the bisexual population than in other groups of people.

MYTH: Bisexuals are equally attracted to both sexes.
TRUTH: Bisexuals tend to favor either the same or the opposite sex, while recognizing their attraction to both genders.

MYTH: Bisexual means having concurrent lovers of both genders.
TRUTH: Bisexual simply means the *potential* for involvement with either gender. This may mean sexually, emotionally, in reality, or in fantasy. Some bisexual people may have concurrent lovers; others may relate to different genders at various time periods. Most bisexuals do not need to see both genders in order to feel fulfilled.

MYTH: Bisexuals cannot be monogamous.
TRUTH: Bisexuality is a sexual orientation. It is independent of a lifestyle of monogamy or non-monogamy. Bisexuals are as capable as anyone of making a long-term monogamous commitment to a partner they love. Bisexuals live a variety of lifestyles, as do gays and heterosexuals.

MYTH: Bisexuals are denying their lesbianism or gayness.
TRUTH: Bisexuality is a legitimate sexual orientation which incorporates gayness. Most bisexuals consider themselves part of the generic term "gay." Many are quite active in the gay community, both socially and politically. Some of us use terms such as "bisexual lesbian" to increase our visibility on both issues.

MYTH: Bisexuals are in "transition."
TRUTH: Some people go through a transitional period of bisexuality on their way to adopting a lesbian/gay or heterosexual identity. For many others, bisexuality remains a long-term orientation. In-

deed, we are finding that homosexuality may be a transitional phase in the coming-out process for bisexual people.

MYTH: Bisexuals spread AIDS to the lesbian and heterosexual communities.
TRUTH: This myth legitimizes discrimination against bisexuals. The label "bisexual" simply refers to sexual orientation. It says nothing about sexual behavior. AIDS occurs in people of all sexual orientations. AIDS is contracted through unsafe sexual practices, shared needles, and contaminated blood transfusions. Sexual orientation does not "cause" AIDS.

MYTH: Bisexuals are confused about their sexuality.
TRUTH: It is natural for both bisexuals and gays to go through a period of confusion in the coming-out process. When you are an oppressed people and are constantly told that you don't exist, confusion is an appropriate reaction until you come out to yourself and find a supportive environment.

MYTH: Bisexuals can hide in the heterosexual community when the going gets tough.
TRUTH: To "pass" for straight and deny your bisexuality is just as painful and damaging for a bisexual as it is for a gay. Bisexuals are

not heterosexual and we do not identify as heterosexual.

MYTH: Bisexuals are not gay.
TRUTH: We are part of the generic definition of gay (see Don Clark's *Loving Someone Gay*.) Nongays lump us all together. Bisexuals have lost their jobs and suffer the same legal discrimination as other gays.

MYTH: Bisexual women will dump you for a man.
TRUTH: Women who are uncomfortable or confused about their same-sex attraction may use the bisexual label. True bisexuals acknowledge both their same-sex and opposite-sex attraction. Both bisexuals and gays are capable of going back into the closet. People who are unable to make commitments may use a person of either gender to leave a relationship.

It is important to remember that *bisexual, gay, lesbian,* and *heterosexual* are labels created by a homophobic, biphobic, heterosexist society to separate and alienate us from each other. We are all unique; we don't fit into neat little categories. We sometimes need to use these labels for political reasons and to increase our visibilities. Our sexual esteem is facilitated by acknowledging and accepting the differences and seeing the beauty in our diversity.

Susan Carlton

This poem can be put off no longer

1.

You don't exist. He used to say it
to my face: You don't exist.

2.

You're what? What's that?
Oh.
Can I watch sometime?

Yeah, I've heard that that's trendy right
now. You're just trying to be cool. You're just trying to be
politically correct.

You're a fence
sitter. We're all waiting
for you to come out
come down. We're all waiting
for you.

Which one are you more, really? Who makes you come
the most?

You just take it
wherever you can get it, don't you?

We're here to talk today about everybodyexceptyou. We're
working for the rights of everybodyexceptyou. The oppression of
everybodyexceptyou has got to end.

Don't worry, you'll grow out of it.

But you're one of us. You can't be one of us and
one of those, too.

I could never sleep with you.
I could never sleep with one of you.
I might get dumped might get thrown over for one of them might
get AIDS might die might lose all
of my friends.

Oh, so is that why you always
have such a hard time coming?

Yeah, I know that some people feel that way, but
why do you always have to
talk about it so much?

You can't ever be monogamous/get married/have kids/
have a stable relationship, can you?

You're just oversexed
horny desperate confused. Why, you'd sleep with anyone,
wouldn't you?

Is this your way of telling me
that you want to go to bed with me?

I went through that phase too. It lasted 2
minutes 2 months 6 months 2 years 10 years, but I
saw the light
eventually.

I feel that way too, but that doesn't make
me
one of you.

3.

WE KNOW THAT IT IS VERY DIFFICULT. WE KNOW EXACTLY HOW YOU FEEL.
WE CAN HELP YOU. JUST STEP OVER HERE TO THIS
NICE LITTLE BOX WE HAVE FOR YOU. THAT'S IT, STEP INSIDE. COZY,
ISN'T IT? THERE NOW, WE'LL JUST PUT ON THIS LID NICE
AND TIGHT. IF YOU BREATHE REAL
SHALLOWLY, THERE SHOULD BE JUST ENOUGH AIR
TO LIVE ON.

NOW, DOESN'T THAT FEEL BETTER?

4.

and there is always that morning
fourteen in Foster City,
I woke up from what was not a dream
in which the two of you had taught me the meaning of a
new word

epilogue[1]

"WE NEED TO HAVE THIS MEETING
AT THIS TREE
AIN' EVEN BEEN
PLANTED
YET"

Note

1. From June Jordan, "Calling All Silent Minorities," in *Naming Our Destiny,*
Thunder's Mouth Press, 1989.

Carol A. Queen

The queer in me

I've been worrying about my sexual orientation lately, which is nothing new.

I have several different Kinsey ratings, and even more on the Klein scale.[1] Any sex therapist would tell me in an instant that I'm bisexual, but I'm not sure what that means. A lot of bisexuals I know seem straight, others gay, and some you can't tell — are they the *real* ones? It seems somehow important to have a sexual orientation, and when I meet people who question this I explain it in terms of having a community, a culture and outlook shared with others. Yes, I know Foucault[2] says there was a time before the concept of sexual orientation was invented, and presumably no one had one then. But we have them now, identities based on the genders of those we love and desire, and they're useful, like knowing whether a new acquaintance is a Scorpio or a Democrat. Further, our sexual orientation serves to affirm us in our sexuality, something I certainly want to have affirmed.

Before I became sexual with women, I was worried about calling myself bisexual. Now I'm worried because it seems so imprecise. I deal with it by saying "lesbian-identified bisexual" (or, when I'm feeling perverse, "faggot-identified lesbian"), but then almost no one understands.

I want to be able to express the truths of my life, and my sexuality, in a language that does not obscure. The word choices available now restrict me. I am not tolerant of these restrictions, of a world view that consigns dissidents to limbo. I want some place to belong, a name to be called.

At sixteen, I went to Germany as an exchange student, in flight from a precocious affair with my schoolteacher — a man twice my age with a wife and kids to boot. So I left town to spend my days at a girls' school and my nights under curfew. By the time I left Germany I had fallen for a wild, cat-eyed young woman who looked like she never slept at home, a baby-dyke who tutored me in French, my boyfriend's sister, a woman I saw on the bus every day, and a schoolteacher from England who befriended me.

Back home, too, none of my schoolmates was safe from my gaze. I already knew about eroticizing difference — that was what having crushes on boys was all about — but nothing prepared me for the impact of this difference-in-sameness. Instinctively I knew the territory I had entered. I did not say a word to anyone about the tumult in my heart — until a new teacher came to town, a gay man. He gave me the education of an old-style faggot, complete with stacks of Oscar Wilde and vintage male erotica. It was enough to confuse, but not deter me, in my nascent lesbianism, enough too to forever bond me to gay men. The erotica turned me on wildly, as did he, in a way other men never had; there was that sameness-in-difference again, in a wholly new way. I could almost forget his gender in the precious community of two we formed in that tiny town.

I went away to college and fell in love with a beautiful young woman. I told her I loved her; I was coming out. She was pleased to have the attention, as long as I continued to fuck men and didn't make sexual demands on her (that was no problem; I didn't know *how* to make sexual demands). She said she knew she would be very happy with me, if only I were a man. But the kisses she deigned to give me had a stronger effect than even Oscar Wilde: holding her, kissing her with more passion than I'd known was in me, yearning to make love to her (she never allowed it), my instincts told me I had every skill I needed to see her arch back and cry out. I knew I had lesbian blood.

So why did I continue to fuck men? For fun, for one thing — for the near effortless heat of it. And it was always easier than contending with the immobilizing passion for women I hadn't yet learned to express or control.

I joined a bisexual women's group. The only woman I felt close to there was a lesbian. I took a gay studies class and got a little support for my bisexuality, and a lot of support for getting past it — "a phase" I was going through. It was the beginning of the end of the stars in my eyes, a furtherance of all the confusion. I helped start a group for gay teens and fell in love with a new roommate, whose relationship with me was a blip on an otherwise very heterosexual life-path; our sexual relationship was much, much briefer than our time together. More confusion: maybe I wasn't cut out to be a lesbian after all, in spite of the passion I felt.

For more than two years, when I had sex at all, it was with sweet young faggots, on the sly. When I talked about bisexuality, the boys laughed nervously. It hardly seemed worth pursuing in light of the everyday gay dramas facing us: teens thrown out of their homes, dumped by their older lovers, an occasional suicide attempt — or occasional success. The stolen kisses were an expression of our community and our love for each other, even if we felt we had to downplay them ... and they were at least as illicit as the fantasy kisses of girls' school, for I was internalizing a new set of mores, the rules of a world where girls *don't* kiss boys.

The confusion increased when I finally found a *real* lesbian to love. We made love wildly for some years; we both had other lovers, and I even brought out a woman or two.

And I *still* fucked men. Sporadically, to be sure — "Once every couple of years, just to remind myself what it's like" — and, amazingly, the more comfortable I became with being a dyke, the more fun I had having sex with men!

My lover was liberal. "You're not bisexual," she'd assure me, "you're just a lesbian who sometimes sleeps with men." The rest of our community, I knew, would not be so understanding — I had a fetching crew cut, wore jeans and tank tops, and didn't shave; I was passing, but my secret escapades would get me in as much trouble in my lesbian world as I'd find if I could time-travel, lesbian blood hot, back to my old girls' school. I had to face it: I was just a pervert. I began to take a certain pleasure in it.

It is abundantly clear to the traditional dyke, as it was to medieval church fathers, that the seed of all insurrection lies in the femme. I bought my first brassiere in thirteen years. I grew my hair; I wore skirts; I put on lipstick. The white lace that I'd squirreled away for my lover's delectation when we did (of course!) schoolgirl scenes began appearing in public. I mixed it with leather. My lovers began to get nervous. I hoped to become so outré that no one would notice, or care, what I did.

First, of course, I had to get over the fact that *I* cared; that I was rebelling against the lesbian and gay community's rules, risking being thrown out of my heart's home, for being different. I'd been a gay community leader for some time, one of few publicly gay faces in my small city, and I was worried about being caught in bed with a faggot (or worse!). The only thing a queer can do in the face of fear of exposure, of course, is come out. Yet I moved toward that self-empowerment slowly, and with more fear than I'd ever felt leaving the dysfunctional heterosexual fold fraught with danger, games, and outmoded roles. The worst of it was — I didn't know if I had a place to come out *to*.

I *do* know that I am not alone, and that's why I tell my story. We are not divided into straight and gay peoples. Visualize Kinsey's famous het–homo continuum. Bisexuality begins the minute we step off the zero, heterosexual end. We don't hit unambiguous dry land again until we get to Six, at the other side of the ocean, where gold-star gays and lesbians dwell. Some of us, to be sure, swim right to it. For the rest of us, perhaps the journey, not the destination, is the thing.

I hate hearing "You just can't make up your mind." I make a decision each time I have sex. I choose to honor the purr in my cunt that says "Gimme." I choose the thrill of attraction and the promise of pleasure, the clit, the cock, the fire in the eyes.

My partner now is a gay man, and no, Mom, we're not just friends. A dyke and a faggot being lovers — is that a *gay* relationship? But when people ask me if I'm bisexual I still jump — ridiculously, like the "straight" men my partner picks up because they want to get fucked.

I've been thinking about this stuff constantly for fifteen years. Nobody makes it easy; I belong to and identify with a community whose values were forged in reaction to homophobic fire — a community that, finally, could proclaim, "Gay is good," but that found bisexuality too difficult, too close to heterosexuality, too *confusing* to embrace. The bisexuals huddle nervously in the middle, like kids listening to their parents (the gays and the straights) fight. We protest — we're basically all the same, sex is really just sex, doesn't much matter with whom — a little utopian choir in a war zone.

But utopia is not at hand; the war goes on. Many bisexually identified people I meet now that I've moved to the big city have a limited understanding of homophobia, coming as they often do from a place of expanding on a heterosexual identity. I rarely feel at home with them. It is the bisexual people who have carved out a home within the gay world, who understand homophobia and have stood up to heterophobia, who seem to be my people.

To address biphobia we have to be able to analyze both homo- and heterophobia first. We have to realize that gay people have had to thrash and fight to escape a mold that didn't fit, and that many remain defensive about it, full of fear and anger.

We must also realize that to homophobic straights, queer is queer. They're right! Proximity to a cock doesn't undo what I know as a lesbian, doesn't make me one iota less subversive, doesn't even dilute my lesbian blood. Far from trying to tell anyone that the New Age is here right now and we're all just alike, I use my bisexual wits to cross boundaries, crack codes, and bring back a store of secret information that society would like to use to keep us *all* in thrall. We won't have a chance at overcoming the barriers we were born into — female–male, gay–straight, class, color — without this kind of knowledge.

It is the queer in me that empowers — that lets me see those lines and burn to cross them; that lets me question the lies we all were told about who women are, who men are, how we may properly interact ... what nice girls do and don't do. The queer in all of us clamors for pleasure and change, will not be tamed or regulated, wants a say in the creation of a new reality.

Gazing at my classmates in the girls' school, desire and objectification mingling with identity, was just the beginning of a way of looking at the world for which none of my culture's teachings left me truly prepared; the heterosexual requirement that the Other is the love object went out the window. The fluidity of roles in relationships with women raised another question: why not take this information, this way of being, into connections with men? Who made the rules that we shouldn't? Why should we, who have other experiences to draw on, play by those rules?

Lesbian-feminist assumptions about who women are and how we may behave make sense to me, but I don't see myself engaging in heterosexual relationships even when my lover is a man. Conversely, I don't buy the mythology that men are just too different to relate to intimately, since that suggests a "men-and-women-are-opposites" dialectic that seems heterosexual to me. *All* our differences *and* similarities are vast and rich — their interplay is the fabric of all relating. It's hard to invent rules out of such complexity; we improvise as we learn about each other.

I want to honor and share our emerging secrets. If a bisexual community can form with no need to define itself in relation to its "opposite," perhaps there I will have my coming-out place. Until then, home is not a place, but a process.

Notes

1. Both scales are used to rate sexual behavior and orientation along a range, from heterosexual to homosexual.

2. Michel Foucault, *The History of Sexuality*, New York: Random House, 1978.

Ninety-three people = 100% acceptance

As a young man I was upset and ashamed of my same-sex preference. I liked girls, but I also liked boys. I went through college carrying this burden, then attended graduate school, securing an M.A. that qualified me to teach history in high school. When I could not obtain teaching positions because of the Great Depression, I eventually secured a fellowship to a school of social work, where I received another M.A. and satisfactory employment. I was successful in my work, but I was still worried and anxious because of my continuing same-sex preference. At that time homosexuality was considered to be a psychological illness, and I felt much pressure to get married and have a family, as all my brothers were doing.

I sustained two gay relationships over fairly long periods of time. I fooled myself, however, because I was fairly passive in each relationship, being acted upon rather than acting. I felt a fondness for my partners, enjoyed what they did for me, yet did little to give them a similar satisfaction. In the second relationship, things were more mutual and I cared a good deal about this man, but I can't say I loved him. By this behavior I fooled myself into thinking my problem was not so bad. I refused to be fucked and did not suck though they sucked me to my delicious satisfaction. Passive, I felt less homosexual.

I finally sought help to overcome this "serious malady" through psychoanalysis. I found the analysis incredibly helpful, not only personally but professionally as well. I became an expert counselor; I did not give up liking sex with men.

I met the woman who was to become my wife when I was about two years into my analysis. After a period of courtship we began a sexual relationship that was very satisfying to us both. I was proud of my virility, sometimes having two or three orgasms in one evening, and repeating this performance night after night. The only catch was that I still enjoyed and sought sex with men. I had no lover; these men were mainly "one-night stands."

Eventually I married my girlfriend, and we established a home. After a year of marriage we began trying for children. We produced two offspring. Lovely children they were, and we were good parents. I continued having same-sex encounters when I could manage it. My wife and I continued having good sex, though less frequently than before marriage. I felt guilty about my double life, but stop? — NO.

Our children grew up and married. They had children, making us loving and devoted grandparents. By the time our children were adolescents, I was drinking heavily. My sexual ardor with my wife declined. Under stress at work, combined with heavy smoking and drinking, I developed high blood pressure. In turn, the medication I took for this condition adversely affected my sexual potency, which was a great blow to my self-esteem. After a series of bad nosebleeds I gave up smoking. A year later I gave up hard liquor cold turkey. My nosebleeds and high blood pressure stopped, but my potency did not return, much to my chagrin and my wife's unhappiness.

When my wife died in 1978, I was sixty-nine years of age. I began seeking outlets in the gay community without much success. I did join Unitarian Universalists for Lesbian and Gay Concerns and here found friends with whom I could speak openly and freely. I experienced some short episodes with a few lovely and beautiful, sensitive men. I eventually established a friendship with a man somewhat younger, and this developed into a mutually satisfying and sharing relationship.

I entered into this relationship so fully that I learned the joy of freely loving a man. With this rich experience I began to think of coming out. My lover and I seemed about to make a commitment. As he got closer to it, however, he decided he could not leave his marriage. He was also fearful of, if not losing his job, at least reaching a point of no more promotions. I was sad but I was not angry. I was thankful that I had experienced the love of another man.

As I continued with UULGC I received much support, and after an international convocation in San Diego in 1986, I felt loved enough that I decided to "come out." I first came out to my San Diego friend of fifty years whom I was visiting at the time. He was very accepting of this news, and then I had dinner with a niece also living there. I came out to her, and she was very loving and accepting. In the past I had rationalized not coming out because I had few friends in the gay and bisexual community; if I came out to my straight friends and lost them I would

• 23 •

be bereft. With these initial coming-out experiences I no longer worried about this.

I came home and wrote letters to my children, coming out to them. I then proceeded to come out to my straight friends one, two, or three at a time. I kept track until I came out to ninety-three people with 100 percent acceptance, including my children and their spouses. Now I wonder what I worried about. Most of those to whom I came out gave me a hug and kiss and thanked me for trusting them enough to share something so personal with them.

Amanda Yoshizaki

I am who I am — A married bisexual teacher

I am married and monogamous. Not much of a bisexual you say. Yet my bisexuality influences my perception and my decisions. More than having sexual relations with both genders, bisexuality is a mind frame, a reference point from which to view the world. Being bisexual has more to do with potential than actuality. I happened to meet a man with whom I am compatible. He could have been a she. I do realize I am lucky. My husband is bisexual too, and consequently we share an understanding of experience most couples cannot.

Every Christmas I buy my husband a calendar with scantily clothed men in it. I spend quite a while going from bookstore to bookstore, trying to choose the one I think he'll like best, the one with guys who are kind of young (but not babes), who are healthy (but not Schwarzenegger), who are in artsy poses (but still erotic) — hell, it's not an easy task! But certain traditions must be kept up. (Most people who visit think he bought it for me.)

Being married puts me in an odd situation when it comes to the gay community. After all, I "enjoy" heterosexual privilege — I can stroll down the street arm-in-arm with my sweetie and no one will blink an eye. I can say I am married and have my relationship validated by the approving nods of great aunts. I am not sorry I am married. I am sorry that these privileges are not extended to same-gender relationships. I am sorry the world is not more accepting of variety.

Being a married bisexual also gives me a certain responsibility and freedom. I can educate in ways someone who is not in a "conventional" relationship cannot. I can bring up issues of homophobia, biphobia, and AIDS without fearing that I will be labeled or ostracized.

I can question those who express prejudice and intolerance with impunity. And I do.

Since I am a teacher, this role of educator is especially important to me. I remember one time I had my students brainstorming situations that would cause stress between parents and teenagers. The students were sitting in groups of five or six, and I was wandering from group to group eavesdropping and helping out when they got stuck. A girl in one group said if you were bisexual it could cause difficulty with your parents. The other students squirmed in their seats and made disgusted faces. The boy who was recording the group's information didn't write down her idea.

They were about to discount it and move on, when I stepped in. All I had to say was that she had made a good point, and for a lot of people in that situation it is difficult to talk to their parents about their lives and partners. The boy wrote down her idea. At least then it was open to discussion. This may seem like a trivial situation; however, what if she or another member of the class were bi, gay, or lesbian? How would she or he feel if I let that group ignore this girl's concerns? At least I cracked the door to discussion on gay, lesbian, and bisexual issues.

I know I walk a fine line when I question students' phobic beliefs. Many of these students' parents are homophobic and racist, and the students mimic their parents' values. Yet, my job is to get them to think about their assumptions and to make their own decisions.

I also know that if I were open about my sexuality I might be fired or harassed. So in my work I am closeted, cloaked by my seemingly traditional marriage.

I found I have to choose my battles and then fight them with fierce determination.

Alan Silver

Worth the balancing

Until about fifteen years ago I had only come across the term *bisexual* once and I certainly didn't consider myself one, even though I was married and having sexual relations with men.

My early years were spent in a post–World War II, black working-class family that aspired to the middle class, and that was, of course, very heterosexually focused. In college I became politically aware and joined campus groups, marched in protest of the Vietnam War and against domestic repression. I also got involved doing support work for various groups in the black community.

When I left college, I married. Not too long after that my wife and I became parents. My sexual focus was still heterosexual, although, during my marriage, I had my first male-to-male sexual experience. I was feeling curious and sexual and had an idea of what might happen, so I went for a massage. I was not seduced, nor was it an accident.

After that encounter, I sought to repeat the experience. I found partners in the personal ads of gay newspapers. I didn't consider myself gay or bisexual — I was just a married man having sex with other men. This random, near-anonymous mode continued for a couple of years. I never met with the same man more than once or twice since I was wary of a man becoming more interested in a long-term relationship or "blowing my cover" and disrupting my marriage.

Then I responded to an ad and met Gary. Although the primary focus of our getting together several times was sexual, we had similar interests in terms of politics, sports, and involvement in the larger community. Our relationship came to an abrupt end one night when he confessed how he felt toward me. Even though he knew I was married, he wanted me to move in with him. It was too much for me to even conceive of — move in and live with another man? Me? I told myself this is crazy, I'm married, I love my wife. I'm not gay. There followed a period during which I was not bisexually active, but I was in emotional and psychic turmoil. How could Gary love me when we were both men? Didn't just heterosexuals feel that kind of devotion? Weren't male–male relationships just sexual?

Through much angst and self-exploration I reached a point where I did consider that two men could share an emotional, mental, and physical relationship just as a man and a woman ideally could. I began to slowly re-examine my concepts of emotional attachments and acknowledge and accept my feelings for both men and women at this point.

After several years I met Gary again. He restated that he had had a crush on me. I shared with him that he had helped me to expand my view of sharing one's self and my sexual identity. Although he knew about my marriage, Gary always used the term gay when acknowledging my sexuality. To me this was limiting, because I liked women. I didn't see myself as gay or part of the gay community.

As a bisexual man of color, I not only have to struggle against the biphobia from the larger gay, lesbian, and heterosexual communities; I have to deal with the biphobia of my own community too. It seems that although there is a general level of homophobia in the black community, the level of biphobia is higher. The men and women who may be bisexual are closeted and classified as either gay or lesbian. I feel this biphobia and homophobia is due in part to the very strong influence of religion in the black community. I think this is unfortunate because as an oppressed community we need to recognize all social groupings and not further divide ourselves.

One reason I have become less closeted about being bisexual is the degree of nonacceptance, misinformation, and stereotyping that denies bisexuals the right to decide how to frame our sexual identities. Yes, it is possible to love men and women emotionally with or without sexuality. It is not a confused form of sexual identity or undecided sexual leanings, but men and women relating to men and women, from a less restrictive psychological framework, to shape relationships.

At this point in my life, with a marriage behind me and a couple of grown offspring, I hope to use some of my energies to bring about a greater acceptance and visibility of bisexuals — as people who are sometimes also parents and have hopes, fears, and share fun and caring ... just like all people.

Ann Fox

Development of a bisexual identity

Understanding the process

College was an intense time of growth, of coming into my independence from family and establishing myself as a vibrant and sexual being. As a seventeen-year-old freshman, I had a hunger for life even more powerful than my thirst for knowledge. I shared these years with my college roommate, and she became my best friend. The passion we shared for adventure and experience gave rise to feelings of closeness and love, and that love spilled over, under, and through the fence of social acceptability that women are supposed to wrap around our feelings for other women. I couldn't deny that I was in love with her and didn't understand why I should even try.

Since that time, I have loved other women. I have loved women in the same deep and romantic ways that I have loved some of the men in my life. I have loved them as friends, as lovers, and as possible life partners. For me, there has never been a question as to whether my feelings for women were more or less real than my emotional ties to men. They are simply (and complexly) different. I can no more deny the depth of my ability to love people of both genders than I could the fact of being, myself, a woman.

My curiosity has been to try and understand myself in the language of psychology, my chosen language of self-discovery.

As a bisexual feminist psychotherapist, I have spent many years trying to understand my own growth and development process and learning how to translate and apply those understandings in therapy to facilitate that process in others.

The process of claiming a bisexual identity in some ways paralleled the path I traveled in coming to define myself as a feminist. In both instances, I came to these ways of naming important, central aspects of myself through a journey which was sometimes gentle and sometimes difficult, but very gradual and cumulative.

Reflecting on my transformation, I have been able to identify a number of elements in this process. I will explain some of the issues I see affecting the development of bisexual identity, describe the identity formation process as I have experienced it, and discuss what I consider to be essential conditions necessary for the development of a clear, positive bisexual identity.

Issues affecting the development of bisexual identity

Development of a bisexual identity is a very individual process, but one that by definition involves the need to come to terms with, and accept, both the heterosexual and homosexual aspects of one's feelings, attractions, and desires. Further, it requires the ability to integrate homosexually and heterosexually oriented aspects of self into a cohesive sexual orientation, which can then be experienced as a congruent, affirmative aspect of one's self-concept. While understanding how heterosexual and positive gay identities are formed may be somewhat illuminating; forming a self-affirming bisexual identity is uniquely complex, involving both of these tasks and additional processes specific to the formation of bisexual identity.

The complexity of forming a bisexual identity emerges from the nature of the bisexual identity itself, barriers to forming a positive bisexual identity, and the virtual absence of a bisexual community. Each of these factors contributes to the complexity of the process, and each implies conditions necessary for such development to occur in a healthy, identity-enhancing way.

Factors intrinsic to the bisexual identity

Developing an identity as a bisexual woman or man requires a person to recognize, acknowledge as valid, and work toward the acceptance of her or his feelings of sexual and affectional preference for people of both genders. The majority of self-identified bisexuals probably form an initial heterosexual or homosexual identification and view themselves as belonging to one of these two socially recognized categories of sexual orientation.

Bisexual feelings and experiences may, however, date from early childhood too. The existence of early and recognized affectional and sexual attractions to people of both genders may undermine, in subtle or not so subtle ways, the conviction with which we adopt an initial identity label.

Other bisexuals may never have experienced these kinds of early attractions. They may first become aware of such feelings well into

Reprinted with permission from *North Bi Northwest*, newsletter of the Seattle Bi Women's Network.

adolescence or adulthood. Bisexual identity can develop at any point in a person's life cycle that feelings and attractions to the initially non-preferred gender surface. The key difference between being bisexual and developing a bisexual identity is that in developing a bisexual identity one decides to consciously acknowledge both the homosexual and heterosexual aspects of her or his experience and desire, recognizing and accepting a bisexual orientation.

The development of bisexual identity therefore involves redefining our sexual orientation in accordance with a decision to validate and give importance to previously disregarded, undeveloped, or newly emerging sexual and affectional feelings and behavior. Developing this identity, therefore, first involves re-evaluating and discarding an existing self-definition in which we have developed a degree of investment.

Barriers to forming a positive bisexual identity

Barriers to developing a self-affirming bisexual identity include intra-psychic, interpersonal, and societal obstacles. As with the development of a positive gay or lesbian identity, internalized homophobia is a serious impediment to the development of a positive bisexual identity. If we have initially identified ourselves as heterosexual, we may be paralyzed by homophobic fears about loving people of our own sex in this society that denigrates and terrorizes gays and lesbians. If we have initially identified as homosexual, there may be confusion and fear in realizing that sexual and emotional feelings are occurring toward people of the opposite sex. We may also feel fearful of exploring and acting upon the fact that we have feelings for persons of *both* genders. This "biphobia" is rooted in the homophobia of our society and may be further defined as fear of bisexuals, or an attitude of discrimination against people who are bisexual.

Homophobia and biphobia — and their consequences — create both internal and social impediments to the free exploration, consideration, or adoption of a self-affirming bisexual identity. Those of us whose internal feelings and life experiences are clearly bisexual in nature must come to terms with the fact that both our self-concept and our position in our community are likely to change as a result of the decision to adopt a bisexual identity.

Interpersonal barriers associated with taking on a bisexual identity include the necessity of reconsidering and possibly renegotiating existing intimate relationships to include this expanded self-definition. The decision to come out to friends, family, co-workers, and others in the community necessitates considerations of the same type as those associated with coming out as a gay or lesbian. Existing relationships may be significantly changed, and possibly lost, as a result of the decision to disclose. We who choose to limit our disclosure (for any number of reasons) may later be accused of "passing" or considered traitors to both gay and heterosexual acquaintances if we choose to share our identity at a later time.

Absence of a bisexual community

A final factor contributing to the development of a bisexual identity is the virtual absence of a bisexual community. A few groups of bisexually identified men and women have emerged in a number of the larger urban areas, and the number and size of these organizations is gradually increasing. More commonly, bisexual individuals meet and network through attendance at the occasional workshop or support group offered which is specific to their needs. In general, the bisexual community develops as an informal and largely invisible subculture within the women's movement, the gay community, or other sexually alternative communities. Bisexuals in less urban areas may network with urban organizations through correspondence, or access the minimal but growing body of literature and research dealing with the topic.

In general, however, bisexual women and men are isolated and difficult to identify or find in most communities. When we are involved in same-sex or opposite-sex relationships, we may tend to involve ourselves with the community or culture associated with the gender of the individual with whom we are involved. This, in combination with internalized homophobia and biphobia and externally experienced discrimination, contributes to the problem of establishing an ongoing, visible bisexual presence in gay and straight communities. One means of increasing our visibility is through sharing our stories.

Bisexual identity development: One woman's process

I would like to offer my understanding of this process as I lived it and describe some of the phases I went through in developing a clear bisexual identity. Naturally, this process varies considerably from one person to another and is affected by variables of gender, ethnicity, class, age, and the value orientation of our original religious, family, and cultural environment. I describe my own process — that of a white, Jewish, middle-class woman raised in an intact nuclear family in a suburban environment.

My first experiences of romantic intimacy occurred with boys, though even at that time I was aware of deep feelings for my best girlfriend and an attraction toward pretty girls. Without any real consideration, I adopted a heterosexual self-concept and the majority of my fantasies and experiences were connected to boys and men.

Gradually, I became more aware of my feeling toward girls and women. I would sometimes develop crushes on particular girls and find myself wanting to be close to them physically as well as emotionally. In a limited and tentative way, I sought out opportunities to explore my feelings of sexual and romantic attraction toward girls.

I was aware that these feelings were socially unacceptable and most of the time I was too afraid to act on them. I wondered if finding myself attracted to women in sexual and romantic ways meant that I was a lesbian. This was a frightening thought because I'd internalized society's homophobia in a very general, but powerful way.

In my college years, I began to openly acknowledge my attraction to women. I fell in love with my college roommate and through this began to experience the depth and intensity of my love feelings for women. While feeling awkward and shy about acting on these feelings, I became aware that existing labels of "straight" and "gay" were inadequate to embrace all of what I was experiencing. I knew I couldn't be a lesbian (as I understood lesbianism) because I knew that I definitely had sexual and romantic feelings for men. I believed lesbians didn't have those feelings and that they did not relate to men in sexual and romantic ways.

In college, I first met a woman who considered herself to be bisexual. I had never heard the term before, but the sense of discovery I felt was immediate and powerful. Upon hearing her description of what being bisexual meant to her, I experienced a profound sense of relief, excitement, and self-recognition. I now had a way to understand all of me.

From this point, my development was a matter of gradually working through my confusion, questioning, fear, and internalized homophobia. I came across some of the first writings about bisexuality and gained more exposure to feminism and lesbianism. I began talking to other bisexual women and participating in the women's community through my involvement with the rape crisis center. Later, I joined a bisexual women's support group offered through our local women's center — a truly empowering experience!

I have come to know intuitively that, for me, my romantic feelings can never be a matter of having to choose. In experiencing validation and support for my feelings for women, I realized them to be as real and as important as my feelings for men, though I have always felt more awkwardness about expressing those feelings toward women. My confidence about the validity of my experiences and clarity of self-definition alternated with periods of considering myself as heterosexual. Then too, I sometimes thought that my primary identity might be lesbian. However, the excitement about my loving feelings for women were compromised at times by fear, homophobia, and my resistance to feeling I must renounce heterosexual feelings and desires to achieve acceptance in the lesbian community.

Gradually, I experienced the emergence of a full, clear, and confident sense of my identity as a bisexual woman. I could say with confidence, "No, I am not 'indecisive.' I am bisexual. My feelings for both men and women are mine, are real, and are valid bases for acting to establish relationships." Over time I have developed my own value system about loving women, loving men, and having relationships congruent with my identity as a bisexual woman. I have had to struggle with issues of coming out, monogamy vs. nonmonogamy, the relationship between my bisexual and feminist identities, my relationship to heterosexual society and the gay and lesbian communities, and my desire for a community supportive of my bisexual identity.

Conditions for developing a positive bisexual identity
Developing a clear and positive bisexual identity is clearly not an easy task, but the payoff is a sexual self-image consistent with our broader sense of who we are. Many people consider themselves bisexual, but label themselves heterosexual or gay in order to avoid dealing with the negative social consequences of coming out as a bisexual. Others adopt a bisexual self-definition but feel a sense of shame or inadequacy for their failure to fit neatly into the prescribed categories of straight or gay.

What does it take, then, for someone not only to self-identify as bisexual, but to do so with a sense of pride and self-affirmation? The essential ingredients are: permission, recognition, validation, support, and (ideally) community acceptance.

Permission is fundamental. Permission means allowing myself to experience all of the sexual and emotional feelings I have in response to a given person or situation. Ideally, permission also means that whomever is important to you in your life also allows you to experience these feelings without denigrating or discounting you or your experiences. (Without a sense of permission, bisexual feelings may never break the surface of thoughtful consciousness, coming into awareness only as intrusions of thought or arising unbidden in dreams and fantasy.)

Recognition means naming our feelings and experiences for what they are, and then placing them in a context of inclusion. While my feelings of sexual attraction toward a man may or may not occur concurrently with feelings of attraction for a woman, I recognize that those sexual and emotional feelings don't belong to different "selves" (a homosexual self and a heterosexual self) but rather to my one, evolving self.

There may be differences in the intensity or quality of my feelings toward women and men, but in both instances I am experiencing feelings which are sexual and romantic. My recognition is both the recognition of the sexual and romantic nature of my feelings, and my decision to view my feelings for women and men as cut from one cloth.

Validation is probably the single most important factor determining whether an achieved bisexual identity can be positive. Validation can occur from within, but few of us are strong enough to establish and maintain a positive sense of identity alone. Validation from others affirms our feelings and recognizes that our experience of loving is what we say it is.

Further, validation is telling ourselves or being told by another that what we are experiencing and who we feel ourselves to be is good, valuable, and acceptable. When we are unable to validate ourselves we look to others to give us feedback on the reality and the value of our experiences. When we cannot validate ourselves and when we are also denied validation by others, we may begin to doubt our experience or feel shame about it.

Support is key to the maintenance and development of this identity over time. By definition, support comes to a person from outside of the self and consists of a communication that others are in favor of the direction we have undertaken. Support may take the form of physical assistance (providing resources, providing services) or emotional nurturance.

In addition, support may be provided by one person or by many people, by institutions (through programming and services), or by entire systems (of education or governance). Support provides bisexual women and men with energy, encouragement, and replenishment; it diminishes our isolation and enhances our perspective. Support frequently takes the form of sharing experience, strength, and hope with others on the same path. This sharing helps to offset difficulty and frequently makes the journey of self-discovery a more playful, confident one.

Community acceptance is basically a broadened experience of validation and support, wherein individuals sharing similar values and struggles experience a sense of belonging and caring concern from the larger social grouping within which they operate. Community support consists of the extension of goodwill and understanding. It need not be contingent upon all members of the community sharing the same sexual identity.

Very few of us have had the luxury of experiencing this kind of community acceptance, except perhaps in the smallest and most intimate senses of the term "community." I have felt fortunate to enjoy the consistent love and acceptance of small communities of friends and lovers, as well as a substantial measure of acceptance from members of my family. For the majority of us, our sense of community acceptance comes to us from that chosen family of friends and lovers whom we gather about us to share the joys and discouragements faced on our journey of self-definition.

In the society self-realized bisexual women and men help to shape, all of us will be guided to trust our feelings and experiences, recognized and validated in our individuality, and supported and accepted into communities consisting of people with sexual orientations of every possible hue and intensity. No longer bound by cultural expectations of sameness or duality, we may eventually transcend issues of definition entirely and become the whole and evolving sexual beings we were always meant to be.

Joe Rios

What do Indians think about?

I am always asked, "What do Indians think of..." this or that — from politics to psychology, from culture to ecology, from metaphysics to sexuality, and more. To the dismay of the questioners I have to say that there is No One Indian Opinion. I have to ask, What tribe are we talking about?

From the large population centers of the Incas, Aztecs, Mayas, and Mound Builders, to the small autonomous political units of California, the Arctic, deserts, and Amazonia, "Indian opinion" was based in each case on the customs of the tribe or clan. The entire Aztec and Incan empires were based on the clans, just as with the smaller tribal societies throughout the Americas.

Sexuality is also based on clan and tribal customs, and sometimes that tribal opinion has changed as a result of generations of governmentally approved and financed missionary activity. So what do Indians feel about homosexuality and bisexuality? Again, what tribe are we talking about?[1] Some tribes were as homophobic as fundamentalist Baptists. Others didn't think about it, since it was no big deal, while others revered homosexuals as gifted spiritually.

In ancient Mexico, among certain Nahuati groups, there was the priestess Xochiquetzal (Feathered Flowers), the Goddess of Love, who revered sexuality and sensuality as an art form and whose religious duty was to honor the creative life forces of Mother Earth. These people's art form and religious duty was not limited to one sex, one way or another, but rather open, inviting, and accepting.

History is nice, but a lot has changed after generations of zealous missionary activity. American Indians have been forced to grow up in a world of conflicts: tribal traditions vs. traditional Christian attitudes; ancient songs in new pickup trucks and traditional women fending off a television reality. In the middle of all this, the young Native American, female and male, has to fathom her or his own sexuality alone.

I grew up as a Native American, with tribal blood from both sides of the border, much like the Papagos, Pimas, Quechans, and other tribes. My family was like many other Indian families who either were relocated, or just moved to California looking for work. The area of California I grew up in was farm land, and my family worked in the fields. One of my first sexual contacts was with an eight-year-old Mexican boy, checking out what each other had. Later his older sister and I played doctor. As an eleven-year-old, I and another girl about my age would play together sexually when no one was at home. About the time I was twelve years old, a neighborhood boy and I would play with each other in the backyard playhouse. He has since come out of the closet and lives openly as a gay man. At the time it seemed natural and I had no problems playing sexually with my friends, although my partners made me promise not to tell anyone.

Except for making out and occasionally fondling a girl's breast, my only sexual experience at the age of sixteen was with an older man. At the time it was a strange mixture of scary experimental fun and knowing I'd been told that what I was doing was "bad." Entering the Marine Corps at eighteen, I was still a virgin in terms of sexual intercourse with women. My sexual initiation was guided by the Far Eastern ladies of the evening. They must have known I was a sexual novice, because my memories of them are dear in many ways; they took very good care of me.

Coming back to the "world" from Vietnam, I was still extremely naive in terms of social skills and how to interact with American women. I did not purposefully look for lesbian or bisexual women, but somehow, we seem to be naturally attracted to each other. I went back to school on the G.I. Bill and fell in love with an intelligent, attractive, loving, and simply wonderful woman named Katherine. We spent a lot of time with one another. We talked about classes and went to good bookstores. She would read me Sherlock Holmes stories from her collection of early editions. She was a lesbian, and I knew all of her lesbian friends. I was accepted as one of the regular gang. I used to love going to the lesbian bars, being all of one or two men in a packed place. After about two years of being friends I think she knew how deeply in love I was with her. She gave me a precious gift. The night we finally made love is one of the most cherished moments in my life.

I had a male lover in 1976, but most of my sexual experiences have been with women. I acknowledge my openness to express affection with someone I love. I will not prevent an honest friendship to manifest itself sexually, no matter what sex the person is. Although I don't go out of my way to meet gay or bisexual men, I have recently discovered the Bay Area Bisexual Network and to my delight found a bunch of wonderful and supportive people.

My openness to bisexuality is consistent with my tribal traditions. I cannot speak for the entire Indian world, and give "the Indian opinion," because each Native American develops his or her sexual orientation according to his or her tribal traditions and experience.

Note

1. For more about how Native American tribes feel about sexual diversity read Walter L. Williams, *The Spirit and the Flesh: Sexual Diversity in American Indian Culture,* Boston: Beacon Press, 1986.

Laura Johnson

Making my own way

I nearly died in 1984. I moved from Pennsylvania to Ithaca, New York, as a battered wife. The extremity of my situation forced me to re-evaluate all my prior experience and turn my consciousness around.

At that time, I was not a complete Total Woman.[1] I was in favor of equal pay for equal work, and I figured that husbands should help wash dishes from time to time. But I was not about to burn my bra; I don't even wear one. I was in favor of "people" and did not appreciate this divisiveness between men and women. I was thoroughly unconscious of the politics of my situation and that of women in general.

As I struggled to stay alive in this desperate situation, I began to see that the potentially lethal abuse I was experiencing was an exaggeration, a caricature of the structure of society in general.

So here I am, five years later at the age of forty-eight, coming out as a bisexual and feeling as if there has not been so much a radical change as a coming to awareness of things that had previously been unconscious. Like most of us, I was raised in the heterosexual world. Being properly white and middle class, I was expected to marry and be a stay-at-home housewife. To be an old maid was pitiful and unthinkable. In my Dick-and-Jane world, homosexuality did not exist. Sex was something I was supposed to do with men whether I liked it or not, and babies were supposed to result from it.

As a young adult, I found myself in a crazy-making double bind. I was supposed to be clean and virginal. At the same time that the pill had brought us "sexual liberation," I felt pressured to be a sex kitten. But to be a sex kitten was somehow wrong. I had learned from my mother that girls are "bad down there." The part of my anatomy contained in my pants was "not nice." To be virginal was to be prudish and old-fashioned. "What's the matter, Honey? Why are you so uptight?" boyfriends taunted. I couldn't win. I always felt unbalanced, off-center, inherently wrong.

As a young woman in the sixties I was man-oriented, believing that the right kind of heterosexual sex would somehow make things okay, even as I was being sexually humiliated and exploited. My life was not my own. I was an appendage and an asset to my husband. I felt a sickening emptiness inside, and I looked to all men with the question, "Can you fix it? Do you have the answer? Can you fill the empty hole? Can you make it right?"

I was oblivious to the fact that I had created the most exquisite and beautiful bonds with women. There was a barrier to seeing and acting on these bonds. We were the Ladies' Auxiliary. However close we might have been, the men were waiting at home for their dinners. The men validated us because we could not validate ourselves.

Since there was no genital sex with these women, I did not think in terms of lesbianism or bisexuality. In my heterosexual male pornographic world, genital sex was the only reality. Lesbians and bisexuals existed solely for the amusement of men. We invalidated ourselves and kept looking for the pot of gold at the end of the male rainbow.

Ithaca has a sizeable gay population. When I reached out for help to the Task Force for Battered Women, a large number of the women who were there to help were lesbians. In this environment, I am coming to expand my consciousness far beyond genital sex and straight romantic love and to feel the ways in which eroticism energizes and empowers my life. I am now validating my bonding with women, and as I love women more, I love men in a new and better way. I can love them as human beings rather than as superior beings from whom I am to derive my existence.

I distinguish between the 100-percent lesbian and the lesbian-among-other-things. As a bisexual I am a lesbian-among-other-things. I call myself bisexual because I am willing to respond to individual men who can relate to me in an honest way and are willing to deal with their sexism and homophobia. I used to say, "We're all people." Now I see that serious differences in power and consciousness exist. We cannot be "all people" as long as racism, sexism, homophobia, classism, and other such bigotries thrive. And yes, this means me, too. As a member of the white middle class I need to raise my own consciousness and confront my own ignorance about the realities of other people's lives. "We're all people" is my hope for the future, not a present reality.

My love for women grows together with self-love. The more I become my own woman, the more I love other self-determined women. I no longer look to men for my identity. I am an artist and a sculptor. I gain my satisfaction and identity from my own work. Getting away from *Playboy* bunny sex allows me to understand that sexuality is far, far more than genital sex. Instead I feel my own openness, power, joy, and wildness. Empowering myself, the barrier between women disappears and I feel, experience, see women with new eyes.

As a bisexual, I have to make my own way. I enjoy the support of a number of lesbians, and I participate in the gay world. I no longer identify as a heterosexual. My energy is turned toward the lesbian and gay world, where I occasionally run smack into some nasty biphobia. But I feel confident in my bisexuality. Although life would be easier if all women lived in a lesbian utopia and all men were villains, as a bisexual I perceive people as individuals rather than as members of a group. I will not reject a good man just because he is a man, and I will not tolerate mistreatment from a woman just because she is a woman.

Although I do not exclude men from my life, I do need to limit their access to my time and energy. I need to spend time in women-only space. I need room to create my own life. I give my business to women: doctor, lawyer, electrician, veterinarian, chimney sweep, karate sensei, bookstore owner. I want to see us empower ourselves and deal with the world from a position of strength.

I feel that I am constantly changing and growing. My consciousness continues to expand. As I honor the place I am in now, I can look back and validate those bonds with women that I was not able to recognize at the time. Bisexuals are accused of retreating into heterosexual privilege, but I disagree. Where lesbians and gays are forced into the closet, so are we. As bisexuals become visible in the community, I hope that we will retain our freedom from easy categorization and will not deteriorate into stereotypes. We're there in great numbers, and as we come out I hope we will have a liberating effect and bring freedom from confining roles.

Note

1. *The Total Woman* was a book by Marabel Morgan about how to please your husband.

Dave Matteson

Bisexual feminist man

I am a bisexual feminist man. I am also a psychologist, a father, a music lover, a traveler, and a social activist. But my calling myself bisexual and feminist, and still a man, seems to be hardest for others to understand. An incident a few years ago will illustrate: Two women faculty colleagues and I wrote a letter to the student newspaper questioning the appropriateness of the Alumni Association's fashion show; we signed the letter "faculty feminists." Shortly afterwards my graduate assistant overheard two male colleagues discussing the letter. They wondered aloud if I had a "gender identity problem!" Apparently they assumed that all feminists are women, and that "real men" are heterosexual.

Of course my use of the labels bisexual and feminist are attempts to convey in shorthand a variety of my experiences and decisions. As such, each label artificially categorizes certain aspects of my experience and leaves out others. Where I grew up in the tiny towns of western New York and northern Pennsylvania, people were first labeled boys or girls; there were only two categories. I was taught to think of myself as a boy and as a man, first.

However, there are other options to this bifurcated view of the universe. I will soon travel to India, where a third gender exists: a few persons who are biologically male but dress, and in some respects act, in ways Indian culture considers female. The custom says that one of these *hijras* should be present whenever a heterosexual couple marry, to ensure fertility. Categories of gender and sexual orientation are human inventions; they differ from culture to culture and through different periods of history. At best, categories are methods of summarizing our experiences. They profoundly influence our sense of identity.

Adolescent years

Part of being a man, I learned, was to get turned on by girls. I remember riding in the back of the car with Jane, a warm, outgoing girl, one evening when I was fourteen. My folks were in the front seat, and it was dark. My brother was in the back with us so we were snuggled close, and Jane kept laying her hand on my leg. I found myself aroused. I felt some guilt but I also was sure it was "normal." Thus I believed, throughout adolescence, that I had the same heterosexual responses other boys and men had.

Another memory is of one particular summer at my grandparents' farm in the Pennsylvania hills. Grandma ran a tourist home there. Chris, about a year older than I, was the son of a man who visited each year at hunting season. During those visits, Chris and I had enjoyed target practice and just being pals together, so, at our request, our families had arranged for us to spend some time together during that summer vacation. The bedrooms were all occupied by tourists, so Chris and I slept in a double roll-away couch on the sun porch. In this instance I was the aggressor, but Chris didn't resist. I knew this, like all sex, must be kept secret — but I don't remember feeling guilty about it. Somehow I got the idea that sex with girls before marriage was not quite right, but I'd never heard anything like that about sex with boys.

Unfortunately, once the vacation with Chris came to an end, homosexual sex, in the context of a deeply affectionate relationship, went dormant for me for about twenty years. I remember having sex again with another boy a bit later, but sex with him was in a category close to masturbation and had little to do with affection. He let me know that this kind of sex was only temporary, until we developed serious relationships with women. And since he was one of my school pals, he influenced my thinking more than Chris. By college I had a totally heterosexual perception of myself, but I do have detailed visual memories of my roommate's anatomy, which suggest that at some level the gay side of me was at least observing life.

One interesting difference between my high school dating experiences with girls and my sexual explorations with boys was that girls were always clothed and our touch was in the dark. With boys we always viewed each other naked and often in daylight. As an adult psychologist I began to wonder whether visual arousal or arousal through emotional and physical closeness (kinesthetic arousal) were separate and which ,if either, was primary according to our sex and our conditioning. And later I began to investigate how this related to bisexuality and sexual identity.[1]

Adult years

In college I thought of myself as heterosexual. I fell in love with a wonderful woman named Sandy. She shared many of my interests and values, including my love of classical music, and we were married. Sandy also appreciated the complexity of my inner life, which made it possible for me to continue to explore my fantasies and dreams, including those relating to my sexual identity.

Sandy and I were four years into our marriage, and both in counseling-related graduate programs, when I began to realize how competitive I was with other men. I decided, encouraged by two supervisors, that it was time I got into a training–counseling relationship.[2] My therapist was a moderately attractive man less than ten years older than me. I began having sexual dreams about him — what is often called "transference" in the language of psychology. I shared these dreams with Sandy. She was very accepting. However, when I dutifully reported them to my therapist, he quietly moved his chair back a few inches. My guess is that he had not faced his own homophobia. My therapy did not deal with either my bisexuality or the obvious sexist component of my anxiety — that I was socialized as a male to compete with other males to prove worth through performance rather than to get intimate with one another. But I dealt with both, outside of therapy.

The homosexual dreams did not seem a threat to our marriage relationship, partly because neither of us expected they required living out. But they were a part of my inner identity, and I continued to share that part of my inner life with Sandy, since my therapist seemed less comfortable with it.

At this stage other changes — new jobs, children, rethinking our husband and father, wife and mother roles — took much more energy than my emerging bisexuality. Sandy was at least as committed to her career goals as I was and had completed her graduate work ahead of me. We moved to the neighborhood of the first newly built total care community mental health center of the Kennedy era. Since I had the more flexible schedule I usually did the washing. I hung it outdoors to dry in our new neighborhood, prompting stares and occasional comments from our rigidly sex-role stereotyped neighbors. They knew Sandy worked full time at "that new crazy house," so it probably didn't surprise them that her husband was acting crazy too.

Since I came from a family of five siblings and remembered childhood with rose-colored glasses, I was much more determined to have children than Sandy. When we were unable to conceive we decided to adopt biracial children. Biracial children were hard to place at that time (1969–1970). Since I was the one pushing for parenthood I made a greater commitment to it than most fathers of that period. Child rearing forced me to face the ways I had not been trained to nurture. I insisted on being involved in all parental decisions and found living with and raising two children, a boy and a girl, the most incredible learning experience of my life.

Before our kids came, I taught courses in child development. After a few years as a father I was so humbled that I stopped teaching these courses. I felt that I simply didn't understand children enough to play expert. However, my investment in parenthood and the untraditional gender roles Sandy and I had carved out did help to prepare me for the growing feminist movement. Responding to public reaction to our interracial family also prepared us as a family to deal more with minority issues and prejudice of all sorts. I had become active in civil rights as a social cause during high school (1956), but our adoptions made equal rights a personal family cause.

During the seventies I became increasingly androgynous. Sandy and I had questioned traditional roles because they did not fit our own personal interests and needs. Sandy had strong career goals and I had a strong desire to parent. But gradually we began to meet women who were sensitized not just to the straightjacket of sex-role stereotypes but to the subtleties of male domination in our culture.

Up until then the challenging of stereotyped roles had met my own needs. But when a woman friend of ours whom we'd invited over for dinner pointed out how I subtly signaled Sandy to wait on me, I realized I had to face my own sexist patterns more personally. I tackled this academically at first. I began writing a book on sex roles and identity to use in Adolescent Psychology classes. Sandy and I helped convene a parenting support group which included some other fathers. The most helpful factor however was that Sandy's consciousness never outgrew her patience. I gradually learned more housekeeping and child-rearing skills, finally succeeding in caring for the kids several days in succession while Sandy was away at a conference. When I had accomplished this without her plans and lists, I knew I had "graduated."

Like all change, the process was slow. But the rewards were many. I felt more whole. Some feminine parts of myself I'd learned from my mother were now consciously accepted and integrated, as the ideal of "masculinity" was replaced by the hope of healthy androgyny. I no longer felt as protective of Sandy; she learned to care for herself better, instead of focusing her care on others.

As we became less dependent, less bonded out of complementary neediness, we were free to *choose* each other, not because we needed each other, but because we really wanted each other in our lives. As we found our unique identities, rather than our socially approved roles, our intimacy deepened.

My work on the book on sex roles and identity led us to spend a sabbatical year in Denmark, where I taught, and researched this less sexist society. Living in Copenhagen did nothing to help my continued suppression of gay desires. When we returned I was determined to explore what I then called "my gay side."

A number of factors, including the lack of racial diversity where we were living in Ohio, led us in 1975 to move to a larger city. I soon became a leader of men's groups — including groups for gay married men. A large gay organization decided to sponsor the groups I was leading, and began to consider more programming for bisexuals. Other volunteers in that gay organization came out as bisexual, and the professional staff tried hard to hear us as a legitimate sexual orientation. In the ensuing years I frequently have been asked to consult with training groups for the gay hotline volunteers, since many of the gay volunteers tend to disbelieve or discount callers who identify as bisexual.

I made a decision fairly early in my public coming out to frequently use the word gay when speaking to the mainstream heterosexual community. I did not want to have my bisexuality seen as minimizing the side of me that is gay. On the other hand, when doing work in the gay community I have stressed being bisexual, to help fight the prejudice there against bisexuals. A big piece of me still wants to just say "scrap the categories — I'm sexual." And even that is inadequate, as it makes it sound as if my primary interest in men friends, or in women friends, is sexual.

The integration of my gay and my straight life had two confusing factors. The first was geographic. Most of my activities involving gays or bisexuals — and most of my political activism — occurred in the city. However, in suburbia, where I lived and taught, I was seen as a straight, married man. It seemed as though I led two lives. Neither community knew me as bisexual, though I was open with my married life with all my gay friends, and I was open with Sandy about my gay life.

The second was sexual. I respond differently to men — more on a visual and less on an emotional level. The urban gay culture of the late 1970s that I came out into was a very visually oriented culture. In that pre-AIDS period it was, like Denmark, not caught up in puritan inhibitions — wonderfully sensual, and explicit about sexuality. On the negative side, the peer culture put such a high premium on being "beautiful people" that looks-consciousness reached obsessional levels. This was destructive to building relationships, or to allowing good personal relationships to develop into sexual intimacy if the immediate visual turn-on was not strong. I found it difficult, in that culture, to combine sex and love. I could develop sexual relationships, but they weren't really intimate, and we didn't share interests and values that much. I could develop friendships, but had difficulty integrating the two.

Through my gradual coming out to close friends, my children, and later my colleagues and extended family and through my work in men's groups, I finally could "own" that the oppression I had been fighting since high school was not just the oppression of others, but the oppression I'd felt fitting into male sexual and social roles that constrained and hurt me.

This oppression has two important aspects. The restrictiveness of gender roles encourages each sex to be only half a person. For men, the restrictions focus on looking tough (and denying the areas of vulnerability and the softer emotions), being "self-made" (denying the need for closeness and intimacy), and being "rational" and goal-oriented (failing to develop the sensitivity and skills to follow interpersonal process). The second aspect is our male socialization to dominate and exert power over others, even if it requires violence. This cruel side focuses on desecrating the feminine in oneself, in male peers, and in women. Advancement of oneself is thought to depend on controlling others, competing, and putting others down, leading, in the extreme, to the destruction of intimacy, to alienation.

Fortunately, the support I was receiving from my wife, from the leadership of the gay organization, and from my involvement in the feminist men's movement, allowed integration and intimacy, rather than alienation. It became clear to me that the civil rights work I had done earlier had emerged from my identification with blacks' oppression, and that feminism had helped me see the links between gender oppression, the oppression of sexual minorities, and racism — all of which stem from the hierarchical view of male power. Male domination was both my enemy, and a part of me.

The women's movement and the gay movement seemed to me to be one, and feminism seemed the clearest articulation of this unity. My acceptance of my sexual attraction to men, and my realization that I was both oppressor (as a man) and oppressed (as a bisexual man) forced me to move beyond "equal rights" to an analysis of the power issues in sexism and homophobia and biphobia.

During the eighties I came out completely, professionally, as a gay bisexual married psychologist and incorporated material on homophobia, sexism, and related issues into the courses I taught. I also succeeded in adding to our course offerings for counselors one in alternative lifestyles. And I've concentrated my research agenda on bisexuals and mixed orientation marriages for the last ten years.

Support for a bisexual feminist male identity
In graduate school I had recognized my anxiety and competition around men. Now, in leading groups for gay married men I was trying to nurture men, but needed nurturing myself. We as men need to get nurturing from each other, rather than always expect it from women — just as women need to seek empowerment from other women, rather than depending on men for their power. Fortunately, about that time the feminist men's movement was beginning to organize nationally, and I actively par-

ticipated. This consciously pro-feminist group grew out of a series of national "men and masculinity" conferences. At first it was called the National Organization for Men, parallel to NOW — the National Organization for Women. The name has now been changed to the National Organization for Men Against Sexism (NOMAS).[3]

The men's movement is small, compared to the women's movement, and even more divided politically. Some portions of the men's movement — including conferences and retreats influenced by the elder poet Robert Bly, who talks about reclaiming one's "wildman self," and men's centers such as the one in St. Paul/Minneapolis — focus primarily on how *men* have been hurt by sex-role stereotypes, especially by taboos against men expressing the softer emotions. Though helpful with healing wounded heterosexual men it is not often clear in these groups how the destructiveness of homophobia and biphobia relates, nor is there much focus on redressing the imbalance of power between the sexes.

Another wing of the men's movement focuses on legal and legislative changes, especially concerning paternity and custody rights. These groups possess a strong sexist, anti-feminist strand, and they have by far the largest constituency.

The pro-feminist segment of the men's movement, especially NOMAS and the "men and masculinity" conferences, is of special interest to bisexual men. The group includes a wide range of academicians, social activists, and personal-growth facilitators and seekers. Most of the men, like myself, have experimented with alternatives in their own marriages, couple relationships, and families, and most of the leadership has been involved with civil rights issues and other forms of social activism.

Here, finally, was a group of men who combined personal and political growth, theory and practice. And here, finally, was a place where the full range of sexual orientations worked together. I was welcomed into leadership positions as a bisexual, working with other bisexuals, gay men, straight men, and a few courageous women. The annual "men and masculinity" conferences of NOMAS, and the meetings of the council, provided places where I felt that all my values and longings were accepted as part of one whole person.

In the feminist men's movement I began to meet gay and bisexual men who, like myself, valued deep friendships, and commitment to social causes beyond our own selves. Being "beautiful people" was not the highest value. Some of these deep relationships also became sexual relationships — and some of these men became trusted brothers. At times, the integration of the personal, political, and social seemed so complete and full that I half expected angels' voices to resound in the choruses of the "Ode to Joy" from the end of Beethoven's Ninth Symphony.

But utopia has not yet arrived. There's still a lot of work to do, both my own personal work, and work to change our society. We folk who don't neatly fit the categories have a special role to play in the transitions yet to come.

Notes

1. Much of this discussion of kinesthetic and visual arousal has been previously published in two anthologies I contributed to: M. Scher, M. Stevens, G. Good, and G. A. Eichenfield, eds., *Handbook of Counseling and Psychotherapy with Men*, Sage Publications, 1987; and F. W. Bozett, ed., *Gay and Lesbian Parents*, Praeger Publishers, 1987.

2. Analytic psychotherapy requires that those training to be therapists undergo their own analysis. My doctoral program was eclectic, but a training and counseling experience was encouraged.

3. The National Organization for Men Against Sexism, 794 Pennsylvania Avenue, Pittsburgh, PA 15221, (412) 371-8007.

Laney Nelson

She kissed me!

In the ninth grade, I first realized that I was attracted to women as well as men. At first I believed that something was wrong with me and got really scared. I decided to ignore those feelings and if I was lucky, maybe they would go away. How did I know that feelings are the most difficult things to control?

In the tenth grade I met Sarah. In a matter of weeks we became best friends. We met every day in the public library to study. We talked on the phone for hours every night. One night while we were talking, I told Sarah that I loved her. What I needed to say was that I was in love with her. Not only did I care if something happened to her, I couldn't think about anything but her! I even looked forward to going to school; I had it bad!

One day while Sarah and I were studying, she asked me to go to the bathroom with her. As soon as the door closed, she kissed me. I was shocked, but got over that quickly. We never discussed what had happened that day. Later, we arranged to study at my house. We studied all of five minutes before Sarah began pulling the sheets back on my bed. We spent three wonderful hours exploring and making each other feel good. That was my first sexual experience with a woman. My relationship with her lasted for four months until she became pregnant by her ex-boyfriend and moved away.

Sarah was the only person I had confided in about my sexuality. When she left, I was terrified and very alone. I began to run from the person I knew I really was. I struggled for two years to face up to my sexuality. Until that time frustration was a constant part of my life. I wanted to tell somebody, anybody who would listen to my feelings, but I was afraid they wouldn't accept me and I would lose them. I was miserable. I felt like a fugitive — having to look over my shoulder, being careful of what I said and how I said it. When I moved away from home to go to college, all of that changed. I finally realized that I couldn't expect anyone to accept me if I couldn't accept myself as an African American bisexual woman.

During my freshman year I met a woman who was also bisexual. It was a prayer answered. At last, I had someone to talk to. Tracy and I became friends, and shortly thereafter lovers, along with her boyfriend Dale. This continued until I went home for the holidays. Tracy realized how she really felt about me. She cut things off with Dale and gave herself fully to me. We spent every possible minute together. After a couple of months, Tracy began thinking about what would happen when school ended. Would I stay or would I go? I told her I would be transferring schools the next semester, and we probably wouldn't be able to see each other again for a long time. She decided to stop seeing me because she didn't want to have to say goodbye.

I was back where I had been three years earlier with Sarah. Same confusion. Same doubt. Same pain. To make matters worse, I had to move back home with my mother for the summer. Once again I withdrew from life. I indulged in alcohol and was very promiscuous.

Since my mother is unaware of my sexuality, living with her was difficult. She was concerned about my silence, secretiveness, and defensiveness. It all seemed to tell her I was doing something wrong. One day we were listening to a minister on the radio describing the actions of a drug user. My mother turned up the radio unusually loud so she wouldn't miss anything. At the same time she was searching my face for a reaction. Little did she know that sometimes the secretive behavior of a drug user is similar to that of a closeted bisexual or gay person — or that we might resort to drugs because of the fear and loneliness.

I would like to tell my mom about my preference but, according to her, it is a sin against God to be attracted to and to make love with someone of the same sex. I'm a basketball player, and at one point she tried to talk me out of playing at a certain college because the coach was rumored to be a lesbian. I thought to myself, if she only knew about her baby girl.

I remained miserable that summer until I decided to call a gay and lesbian information hotline in New York, which gave me a referral to BiPOL, a local San Francisco Bay Area bisexual organization. Talking to BiPOL helped me see that I wasn't alone with my feelings. It also gave me someone to talk to when those feelings of despair and isolation crept back in my life.

As a college student about to graduate, I'm still struggling because I haven't met any fellow bisexual people, but I still have eight more months to go before summer, when I go back home to my mom's house.

C.J. Barragan III

More than a footnote

It has been difficult to address bisexuality within my life. When I was young, I always felt I was different from my peers. My sexual consciousness was very heightened. While I did not interact sexually with others till my late teens, I sought answers in libraries because school textbooks were vague when addressing sexuality, if it was mentioned at all.

Fascinated by the nude figure, I sought out a wide range of pictorials, from classic Old World statues to the airbrushed "perfection" of *Playboy* and the grainy shots from the corner newspaper rack with faces always hidden in deep squares of black. However, I totally ignored my own body, because of my strong Catholic heritage of ignorance of all that is sexual and the belief that while knowledge equaled power it could also equal sin, confusion, and challenges to who I was as a person.

Generally disinterested with most aspects of high school, I focused most of my social activity on a small circle of friends, a part-time job, and the school library. I explored the shelves and found no information on bisexuality in print. At that point in time, I thought that the androgyny label would apply to some aspects of my being, but I was frustrated that so little was available to help me deal with the feeling that perhaps I really was alone.

College was the key. The University of San Francisco provided a setting that allowed interaction with true peers, real intellectual discourse, and exposure to a far more diverse culture and community than Los Angeles could ever show me. Sexually active, I felt comfortable with the traditional rites, but there was something else, a promise yet to be fulfilled.

One key memory was the discovery of a friend's *Playgirl* magazine. I couldn't turn away from the centerfold. Even though it was put aside, it wouldn't stay aside. I had no physical interest in my male friends, but this male imagery stirred up feelings that can't be put into words, even now.

Hitting the libraries again, I sought answers to this dual attraction, addressing for the first time the possibility that I was a bisexual. I knew of the concept, but needed more to work with. The lack of hard information on bisexuality had not changed much. Most resources had the obligatory sections on homosexuality. Bisexuality rated a footnote.

My life is more than a footnote! The realization set in that since the media failed to provide answers, perhaps I should reach out to others for support. This took time, and eight years passed before I met Loon, the first person I heard call herself a bisexual. My heart really jumped; for the first time, I truly felt less alone.

Even though I was feeling more secure within myself, for the most part, I never discussed bisexuality with others. I let the heterosexual world assume that I was straight and entered the gay world with apparent ease. I was actually terrified of gay men. It was the sexual heyday of the late seventies and early eighties. Although the sex could be good, I never quite felt the connection I had with my old friends. It wasn't until I met Tede Matthews, my boyfriend and lover since 1984, that I felt comfortable enough to let others know about my orientation.

Up to that point, gay men seemed appropriate for sex only. I never developed much of a relationship with men outside the bedroom. Beyond the initial fright and inexperience, I found it hard to face the possibility of a well-rounded relationship with another man. Since Tede is a leader in the gay community, our relationship was impossible to hide, even if I had wanted to or he would have allowed it.

As my first male lover, he brought so much to my life, physically, intellectually, and emotionally. I came to grips with my own internal mechanisms of fear and denial. I learned to open up and relax and face up to the reality of loving another man, being public, and acknowledging the relationship.

Not that there weren't problems and obstacles. Tede is a wonderful, supportive man. But very early in the relationship, I'm certain he felt that I was "denying my homosexuality" and refusing to come out of the closet. When he realized that I was coming out as a bisexual, he accepted me for what I am. A friend wasn't so kind. When I came out, this person noted that being bisexual is "as bad as being a fag hag."

The most important thing is how I feel about myself. I am more in touch with who I am than ever before. I have come full circle in embracing the core of my being. I know that other bisexuals are out there. Our voices are being raised and heard.

As a fledgling community, we can do more to get the word out. Communication and the media are the tools to educate and enlighten the heterosexual and homosexual communities. The mass media must turn away from limiting the word bisexual to the personal ads, and the gay press must stop addressing bisexual concerns as only worthy of discussion as an "issue" within the context of a gay news event or feature. Considering the immense power of the media, the bisexual community would be better served if we work to ensure that the media educates society on the existence and well-being of another alternative.

Ellen Terris

My life as a lesbian-identified bisexual fag hag

What means this title? It means that it's all well and good to try to follow Plato's dictum, as well as that of many modern feminists, and get to honestly know yourself, BUT — what if the self you are thereby revealing steadfastly refuses to fit in any of the boxes society has created, even the supposedly most radical ones? I found myself in just that situation prior to discovering Boston's bisexual networks, and even after that point.

I did not have any early conscious knowledge of my sexual orientation. However, one thing I did know from childhood that modern nuclear-family heterosexual union was not for me. I spent too many years watching it destroy my parents, my mother especially. I think when Adrienne Rich wrote the line, "The woman I needed my mother to be died before I was born," she was reading my mind. Nor did the boy–girl games at high school thrill me. In fact, they hurt like hell. I was a fat girl with brains, rated as an asexual being, and thus not eligible to play. It took me years to figure out whether I wanted to play boy–girl for my own reasons and desires, or to show up those adolescent sexists.

If one is female, bright, and mouthy, one develops one's personality, wit, and humor. I am told I did a pretty good job. In fact, I got pretty outrageous by the time I hit college. And what I eventually discovered in the fair ivy halls was another oppressed group that, when confronted with its oppression, resorts to outrageous humor: gay men.

Suddenly I found myself up to my elbows in men of wit and poise, many of whom were physically beautiful, all of whom managed to look truly beautiful to my eyes, even beyond the physical stuff. Unlike the loutish straight jocks of my high school years, these guys radiated sensual grace. And man, did they throw the most stylish parties, and dish the wildest dirt!

Even better, I was accepted as one of the boys — one of the girls? — gender-fuck humor has such a delightful way of tweaking all those heavy distinctions. Nobody looked me up and down or rejected me from the group. Rather, I was celebrated for my wacky humor. I became the mascot, as it were, for a circle of gay men. I had made it as a fag hag.

There was one problem, though: no sexual fulfillment. I got some measure of vicarious, voyeuristic thrills in watching the guys cruise, and in dancing up a sweat with them in the clubs. But come 2 a.m., they went off in twos (or whatever), and I went home alone. Somehow I was once again not being allowed to play.

So I turned dyke and rode with the Amazons for a while. This was not totally out of the blue, as I had already become aware of my ability to be turned on by women. But the way Boston lesbian feminist politics were running in the early eighties, when all this was going down, you were looked at funny if you had male friends — even if they were *just* friends, even if they were gay. I remember having a couple of lesbians come to one of my household's big bashes — we were the only women in the joint. One of them said to me sympathetically, "Yeah, I used to hang out with a lot of gay men too when I was first coming out," implying that now she had her shit together as a lesbian and so she didn't have to hide among the faggots any more. The two of them left early. I did a slow burn the rest of the night. So I'd have to choose, would I? Dykes or faggots, one or the other, can't have both. Choose.

So I did: For a year I was a hard-core lesbian-separatist, and then tapered off to mellow lesbian-feminist. There were some wild thrills to that scene to be sure; it was even more counterculture revolutionary than fag-hagging. And oh, those women's music festivals! Thousands of women ran around in all states of dress, or undress, living out their dreams of the Amazon Tribal Nation in the sun and the rain and the mud and the mosquito bites — with me among them. I found a circle, my own little consciousness-raising group, and I became a fixture once again.

And once again there was a problem. The same problem. I wasn't getting any. And now I was running afoul of the political-correctitude types who were implying that I was still thinking patriarchal if I was hung up on getting any. Oh, I got laid, mind you, occasionally — and I navigated a major relationship. But the only politically correct lesbian sexuality seemed to be monogamy, or serial monogamy with a curious vacuum in the sweaty-passion department. No hot fucking, no "dirty" patriarchal stuff; no roles, no butch or femme; and *definitely* none of that stuff with the sinister acronyms like (gasp! horrors!) S&M! — apparently, no sense of humor either — allowed.

In the privacy of my own heart I knew that the way I really wanted to be was wild and free, happily nonmonogamous, or even kinky (if I felt like it), like the faggots seemed to do with such ease. Only Pat Califia seemed to be singing that song at the time; later would come Joanne Loulan, Susie Bright, Joan Nestle, and a host of other really liberated women. But those few who were standing up for such goings-on at the time were being viciously trashed in feminist newspapers everywhere. And still wanting to sleep with men — *nobody* was admitting to that!!!

Eventually I found myself leaving a two-years-plus monogamous relationship with a lesbian that had come down with a bad case of what Loulan has named "lesbian bed death." I met a new friend, a very sexy and kinky young gay man, and to my horror I discovered I was falling in lust with him.

I came to the Boston Bisexual Women's Network very confused and desperate. Would I ever get what I wanted? It didn't seem possible. The best I could describe my turmoil was that I felt like a faggot trapped in the body of a lesbian. Where was the support group for *that?*

I wanted to be wild and free, with both women and men, but the price seemed so damn high — ostracism from every community I had ever tried to make serve as home. And now, with AIDS floating around, even some parts of the gay male community seemed to be making sex-phobic noises. Was nothing sacred? And why were there separate women's and men's bisexual networks in Boston? Was I going to have more of the same old trips laid on me about choosing? I needed some integration of the fragments of my desires, not yet more turf wars!

I need not have worried. There are delightfully, frustratingly anarchic collectives of bi folks who are, just like me, sort of making it up as they go along. What seemed to have been the curse of past bisexual invisibility has turned out to have been a blessing in disguise. Since we supposedly didn't exist, nobody has made up any rules for us, and we can make our own. So, for instance, I was delighted to find that, while a few individuals still find the concepts scary, a greater tolerance seems to exist for things like open relationships, multiperson relationships, cross-dressing, group sex, kinkiness, and even for a mixed-up lesbian-identified fag hag who is finding that she was not mixed up at all, but the people who were laying trips on her were.

I'm still not where I want to be. This culture is not only heterosexist, homophobic, and biphobic, it is thunderously sex-phobic, and we women especially have borne the brunt of it. It seemed we could only choose between pristine purity — with attendant boredom — or infamy as sluts. Worse, if we showed any interest in sex at all, sexist men would take that as an invitation to walk all over us and abuse us. Even if we showed *no* interest, sexist males would take our mere femaleness as invitation. No wonder the radical-feminist line hardened around an anti-sex stance, and the whole realm of sex had become tainted by all that uninvited, often violent attention.

But, isn't it about time to reconquer the realm of sex for ourselves? Isn't it time for this woman to ask: "What do *I* want? What turns *me* on? *Who* turns me on if I'm not influenced by any attitudes whatsoever, neither from left nor right, neither from straight nor gay and lesbian? Isn't it time to finally drop *all* labels of sick or sinful or politically incorrect? Is this not the most revolutionary act that a woman could perform today?"

Oh, honey, you bet yer ass!

Chandini Goswami

My underself

I.

Where are the origins of my sexuality and where is my sexuality now? Are the origins the escapades with my brother when we would wake up in the middle of the night to read lusty stories about men going home with waitresses who wore garters and no underwear, when we would swim in our pool and my brother would touch or blow waves on my vagina, when we would shower and my brother would touch or lick my vagina and ask me to touch or lick his organs — all in adolescent curiosity? One must ask if I enjoyed these things, and the answer is yes. When my father would leave the pool, I would want my brother to come over and play with me. I would want him to come to my shower. And when he would wake me up in the middle of the night, I would be excited to gaze at his magazines. The women on the pages were so beautiful; I would stare and my pee machine would squeeze and stick out underneath me. And then I would read the stories, and my body would be happy all over. I would go to bed contently craving, and I would fall asleep with my hands running wildly all over my body.

Was I bisexual? What happened to my body when I looked at those pictures? Had I started to develop my breasts yet? Did I get my period yet? Did I masturbate? It would be a good thing, my brother insisted. Our showers progressed into his doing something with his fingers and tongue inside my forest. Whatever it was, I felt uneasy and disturbed. And then he would ask me to put his penis in my mouth. I didn't understand any of this, and it all made me very upset. I started refusing him. "But don't you want to look at the magazines?" he would ask. With my body curled up under my blankets, I would insistently whine my denial.

II.

All this was forgotten until about eight years later when I found myself in a conversation with my soul mate, Sung, who had recently become my lover. I understood Sung, and Sung understood me so thoroughly it made us giddy. I loved her more than I thought emotionally possible. We devoted ourselves to each other. The hardest and most pitiful agony was that I couldn't squeeze my arms tightly enough around her neck and be utterly devoured by her.

When we discovered orgasms, I didn't have them. When she and I were trying to understand why, I found myself, for the first time, telling the incident with my brother. My love mate became my sexual guru, and I entered a new stage of exploration to understand my sexuality.

The years that followed the incidents with my brother were a continuation of fibers that served to wind and twist and wrap over my sexual being, further repressing it, confusing it, blocking it. These fibers were the consequences of ordinary, white, United States society that refused me — a small, skinny, thickly eyeglassed Indian-American girl — any sexual appeal. So years passed with me trying to force away or hide my crushes, until today when I chant to a Gohonzon,[1] I always ask that I may understand my sexuality and let it exist naturally, and that my soul mate and I might someday fall totally in love with each other.

I return to my hometown for break, and I spend a day with Katherine. She stands outside with me in the sharp, cold rain pleading for me to rest all of my burdens on her while chiding herself for not being a magnet of my release. I stand quietly shaking because Sung has been teaching me the simple truth that one dependent plus one independent make a damaging relationship. My fist of tears slams on my skull, and Katherine bends down to kiss me on the forehead. My eyes timidly stare at her face because I feel forces pulling my lips upward toward hers — all the while knowing that I am not attracted to her.

Some nights later my companion Annah comes over for dinner. As it has been for a year, Annah and I exist separately with complication, simplicity, turmoil, or calm within ourselves; yet when we are together, our selves take on a simple, peaceful, ephemeral life. Later we smoke herb on a stack of mattresses under a small hayroof at the end of a long, colorful, dimly lit room. Annah lies with her head on my lap, and we talk about the way the wall seems to be the floor, and the ceiling the wall. Everything takes on curious perspectives to me and I comment on these to Annah's delight. I feel slightly like a man as her flattery esteems me. I wish to endlessly delight her, as well as endlessly impress her. I feel like a man too as my eyes gaze upon her long, graceful body. I carefully caress her hair as I rest back against the wall, think about the sadness underneath me.

I have a sadness because my burdens before I left school for break were very heavy. My shreds of independence were jumping up and down inside my skin while my soul mate devoted herself to me and wore herself thin to keep me above water. By the end I had worn her out. I feared that when we returned to school she would have no more love left for me. I have a sadness too because during those same burdensome weeks, I was having dreams about being with men, and during the day I would think about the men of my past who looked at me and touched me with strong desire, and who made me feel like a very sexy, sensuous woman. I was distressed because these things would never happen with Sung, my true soul mate, and me, not because she was a woman, but because of something I probably would never figure out.

Yet, at the same time I analyzed my sadness I lay there on the mattress with Annah's head upon my lap and my hand drawing circles in her hair, imagining a world of only Annah and me. Nothing needed to matter, whether I was straight or lesbian, masculine or feminine, butch or femme, because I was none of it. The point was to remain in that state of realizing that I was none of it and would never have to be.

Yet for some reason I cannot remain. My origins are in too many places.

III. Afterword

Society and events have controlled and corrupted my self-vision, my self-development, and my self-exploration. I have been controlled and corrupted from the way that I explore myself as a sexual being, to my orgasming, and to my sexual (non)preference. In my life, these things are all related to how my body, my self, wants to move in a certain manner. Factors corrupt me so much that I can't even guess who I am ... factors like my brother, or my desire for a perfect relationship with Sung, or society telling me that women are like this and men like that, or society telling me that there are only straight women and lesbian women. The intellectually easy resolution was to find definitions that fit me best and then force myself to conform. Of course, spiritually, that has been the most damaging resolution.

In the two years since I wrote the first part of this I have finally recognized that in many ways I transcend boundaries, and I have finally come to love this rather than to fight it. I don't have to make pre-facto rules for my desire the way that medical doctors have dictated women's pregnancies. When I feel something, it's just so wonderful to feel it. As I will always be devoted to women and to our liberation and empowerment, I must be devoted to my own sexual and emotional truth.

However, there is still a fight — many fights. There is the long list of false beliefs, or perhaps fears, that the lesbians I love have about bisexuals. My struggle to prove myself and to prove my devotion to women has not been so difficult. The toughest struggle of all has been fighting the damage wreaked in me by my brother. It is upon this fight that my strength and clarity about my sexuality, intimacy, and trust most depend. For now.

Note

1. In Nichiren Shoshu Buddhism, a physical place to focus your spiritual direction.

Nate Brown

A gift to myself

My childhood was one of isolation, mostly self-induced. For as far back as I can remember I could not participate in normal social interactions due to a severe stuttering problem. This resulted in a low self-esteem and fear of rejection that I'm still dealing with today. I had few friends, and those I did have were all male and mostly as introverted as I.

My first experience with feeling love and attraction for another person came in my last year of junior high school. I was infatuated with a boy in my class and knew somehow it was wrong. When he rejected my advances, I was shattered. For several years afterwards I buried my feelings for other boys, though my masturbation fantasies certainly belied my outward behavior.

I didn't want to be rejected again, so I avoided all contact with girls. I went through my high school years looking at the naked boys in the gym and wishing I could be more like them. In my early twenties, while at college, I had a crush on a fourteen-year-old high school boy, and later in the military I worried that my strong erotic feelings for a fellow soldier would be discovered. I became even more isolated when, at twenty-eight, I moved with my parents to the country.

In 1967 I was approaching thirty and thus far my only sexual experience had been with myself. I was still living with my parents, and felt an increasing anxiety that unless I did something soon I would never have a satisfying relationship with anyone outside my family. I knew my feelings for men were not sanctioned by society, and I'd be punished if I ever acted on them.

After moving away from home at thirty-five, I made attempts to socialize with women. I eventually met an older, experienced woman, and had my first sexual experience at thirty-six. I married her three years later. I wanted to put my erotic feelings for men to rest and be accepted by society as "normal." But they wouldn't go away. In fact, unbeknownst to my wife, I made them part of our lovemaking. I thought even less of myself because I needed these fantasies, often to complete the sex act with her. My marriage turned into one of hidden desires for my own gender, masked by what I perceived as approval by the outside world.

After a few years of marriage, I happened across a classified ad for a rap group at the Bisexual Center in San Francisco. Bisexual? My vocabulary had never included that word. Not knowing what bisexual was, I put the ad aside for several months. When I happened to notice the ad again, something told me to check it out. My life was changed forever — I finally found a description for those old feelings deep down inside me. Perhaps if I had had a gay experience earlier in life I would have gone in a different direction, but I'll never know. I do know that after I began discovering others who felt loving and erotic feelings for *people* rather than a specific gender, I could never go back.

I became actively involved with the Bisexual Center. I had my first sexual encounter with a man, ended my marriage, and finally accepted myself for the feelings I now knew were normal. I could love whomever I wished without feelings of guilt or fear of recrimination. In succeeding years, through additional work in socialization and self-awareness, I have been able to love myself unconditionally for the first time, and allow love from others to enter my life.

At present my interpersonal relationships include both men and women as friends and lovers, emotionally and sexually. My sexual orientation is defined at last, so much so that it need not necessarily be labeled. But my gift to myself and to the community is to acknowledge that I physically and emotionally desire to be with whomever I wish, and I call myself a bisexual to define this quality of my life, and to acknowledge that we do exist as a separate but coexistent entity within the straight and gay world.

C.K. Ferrier

Points of reference

It is Saturday afternoon, Pride Day in Rhode Island. It's also the day that my brother, sister-in-law, and six-month-old nephew have come for their monthly visit. I don't have to stay home with them. I could go to the march and lend moral support — maybe even participate and show that there is such a person as a working-class bisexual feminist who's proud of her identity. I want to be there; I want to declare myself but, as in all other years, I am scared shitless of letting my secret become known. I have not come out to my family or to most of my friends. I don't feel that I can tell them — yet. My ambivalence with my identity angers me. When will I finally be able to make a stand? "When Dad is dead and buried and you're living far away from here," I think, as I make my choice and stay home again.

Is it my bisexuality I am having difficulty with? Is it the realization that I am living in several conflicting worlds — academia, factories, heterosexual communities, bi and gay communities — and trying to reconcile all of them? Is it fear, anger, disgust at both what I am and what I couldn't be? Or is it what society might think of me if I told the truth about myself? My fears and worries have silenced me for quite a while.

The only way to make some sense out of my bisexuality is to write about it. The awareness of who and what I actually am hit me with the force of a Mack truck when I found myself seriously attracted to a female classmate. Susan and I spent hours each day discovering our similarities in social class, family problems, hopes, dreams, and worries. I understood very quickly that I was about to fall in love with a woman. I didn't know what to call this feeling, as I didn't even know anything about lesbianism. But I sensed danger and difficulties ahead if I allowed it to continue with the same intensity, especially since I felt that Susan probably wasn't attracted to me in the same way.

Before I could do anything, the relationship, such as it was, disintegrated a few weeks later. I felt a vague sense of relief that the danger had passed, but knew that I had somehow changed.

I didn't know there was such a thing as bisexuality, so I decided to learn what I could about lesbianism, reading books and subscribing to newspapers that I thought would give me some insight. However, I felt alienated from the gay community because I insisted on my right to have male friends and relationships. It wasn't until 1985 that I finally realized that the word for what I am is bisexual.

I have tried to inhabit this world but have had little success. Most bisexual women in my home state of Rhode Island are in it only for the swinging times it can offer. The few bi women I know who are more like me are either unable to or uninterested in forming a community of support for one another.

My points of reference are limited, as are my opportunities. So I wait, biding my time and occasionally trying my wings through personal ads. I try to reconcile my "deviant" desires with the values and opinions I learned from being raised in the working-class community where I remain today. These have marked my soul indelibly. I am easily offended by assumptions that mill workers are ignorant and stupid, unable to read "literature" or comprehend vital issues — they can, but they don't necessarily choose to. I resent activists seeking to remold workers and poor people into their own image, trying to impose dogma about class struggle when the need is for better wages and police protection, at least in the short term. The theory can wait. I am protective of "my people" and I understand their needs.

At the same time, I am frustrated by those I've grown up around, because their parochialism limits me. Communication with the people who live in my neighborhood, one of the poorest in Pawtucket, Rhode Island, is often impossible. There is a large influx of immigrants and elderly subsisting on low incomes. The educational level averages, at best, tenth grade. Reading is often limited to *The Evening Times,* or some romance novel. Conversation concentrates on safe issues — the neighbors, "the crooks in the State House and City Hall," or television. There is a feeling of being threatened by things that aren't "normal," and a fear of the unknown. Patriotism, morality, sexuality, religious beliefs are all what the majority thinks they should be. God save you if you think otherwise. Don't let the neighbors see you with someone you shouldn't be with — guilt by association, after all!

I have grown up with these feelings, and they have inhibited me. I live at home while doing graduate work in history. Home is a tenement, situated in the midst of other closely built tenements. Although I don't know everyone who lives around me, I am aware of them, what they do, and most of their activities. What I don't know, my father tells me.

My father prides himself on being very tolerant of deviance, and at times seems more "New Age" than most New Agers I know. He is quite proud of his gay nephew, who designs store windows and has his own business. He is unfazed by the sight of same-sex couples. Yet, should a child of his declare his or her homo- or bisexuality, moral outrage would set in: "Homosexuality is a sin against God." His defenses against deviance are words he wouldn't utter to strangers or distant relatives but feels free to use to attack his child's choices. My brother would never allow his newborn son near a "queer" — no matter who it was. I have been taught, in spite of books and articles to the contrary, that being gay or bisexual is immoral, sinful, and something that must be hidden. My fear of being separated from the few family members I have left is stronger than the need to seek community with those like me. My hatred of censure and fear of disgrace, my need for a job, and the worry of bringing shame to my father, who practically raised me during my late mother's alcoholism and long struggle against cancer, overwhelm me.

So I hide, wishing my sexuality would go away. Over the hum of machines around me, I hear my co-workers use every epithet in the book to attack those with whom I have chosen to align myself. I hurt for myself and for others who also hide but don't have access to books, periodicals, and like-minded people to help them feel "normal." And I try to laugh at those who would define "normal" as being heterosexual, but the chasm grows wider and deeper.

It is also painful to hear those with whom I thought I could find solidarity attack the world I've come from for its insularity. I am well aware that ignorance exists in all classes and modes of sexuality. I find it much easier to excuse and forgive the people I live among for their inability to see the trees for the forest. In spite of everything, I am still one of them and one with them. That will never leave me, although I might leave them behind, when I find the courage to swallow my fears and enter, openly and proudly, the gay and bisexual community I've denied for too long. And, when I look back at my old community, perhaps I might just see them wishing me well, glad that I'm happy even if they disagree. I can dream, can't I?

Wayne Bryant

Love,
friendship,
and sex

My coming out as a bisexual began at age sixteen and is an ongoing process that will probably never stop. As long as we continue to examine who and what we are, we will always learn more about ourselves, how we relate to other people, and, hopefully, become more comfortable with being who we are in the world.

I have a decided preference for women, especially in long-term relationships. But I'm definitely bisexual. What else would you call a person who is attracted to both women and men? A lot of people think they must not be bisexual, because they have a preference for one gender over the other. They have been told that if they can just work through this phase they're going through they will be okay as heterosexuals or as homosexuals. I have never understood why people think that mono-sexuality is a more natural condition than bisexuality.

I think most bisexual people have a preference, or are attracted to the different sexes in different ways. That doesn't make them any less bisexual than those I know who are equally attracted to both men and women.

In my early years I experimented and learned about sex with several people my own age, both male and female. It was exciting and naughty and quite a lot of fun. Later I learned that boys who have sex with other boys become the object of ridicule — and worse. So my friends and I never talked about our experimentation with anyone. By the time I was fourteen, I was convinced that this had just been typical adolescent behavior and I was well on my way to becoming a "normal," if somewhat overly shy, heterosexual adult.

In the summer of my sixteenth year I attended a boarding school for the gifted. I am still not clear whether they meant intellectually gifted or just financially. I was on a scholarship, but a lot of the people I encountered were much more gifted in the latter way than in the former. There I first encountered peers who were obviously gay, even though they were not very "out" at school. Only much later did I find out that I had teachers in my high school back home who were gay also. I already knew of several straight teachers who were sleeping with students, but somehow people accept that more readily than a teacher who is homosexual.

One sunny afternoon that summer I spent some time meditating on sexuality. I knew I didn't have any gay role models, certainly no bisexual ones. I thought about the people I met at this school, what their lives must be like now, and why they made the choices they did. And I remembered my early experimenting. Eventually I came to the conclusion that, since nearly all sex is recreational, as opposed to procreational, it really makes no difference whether you engage in sex with people of your own gender or of the opposite one. The only requirement is that you both enjoy it.

When I was twenty-one, I had a very close friendship with an ex-co-worker who was much younger. During the course of our friendship a bisexual woman helped him to realize that he was gay. For her efforts, she was ostracized by her homophobic classmates, including one who eventually became a lesbian feminist. He told me that I was the object of his love. I was certainly tempted to make love with him. I was also terrified of being found out, particularly since he was not what one would call discreet. So I decided against it. Many years later we did consummate our relationship during a summer party. He is now in a long-term happy relationship with another gay man, and we are still friends.

Unfortunately, another six years passed before I was able to overcome the fear and denial and actually have an ongoing, intimate sexual relationship with another man. My first male lover was another former co-worker, older than me, slight of build, very gentle, and well read. I will always be grateful to him for seducing me, willing, but still frightened, though I was.

All this time I was attracted to many kinds of men and women. But mainly the ones who really made my head turn the minute they walked into the room were lesbians. I confessed this once to a gay male friend who said that I desired them because they were "forbidden fruit." Forbidden or not, I was attracted to women who love women. As I met more and more bisexual women, I realized that these were the kind of women that really turned me on. On the other hand, I have never had a fascination, as some gay men do, for straight men. In most cases I find them anything but desirable — although there have been notable exceptions — and I feel very sorry for straight women.

In the summer of 1986, I met another out bisexual man. I knew lots of bisexual women, but no men. I had no one with whom I could share thoughts, debate ideas, or discuss experiences on being a bisexual man. That summer I attended a retreat sponsored by the East Coast Bisexual Network (ECBN), at Another Place in New Hampshire. The retreat was the beginning of my involvement with the Boston Bisexual Men's Network (BBMN) and, later, ECBN. I have given a lot of time and energy to both. In turn, each has rewarded me with new friends, lovers, and an understanding of myself and the people I relate to in a way that I would certainly not have been able to achieve in isolation.

My lover of over sixteen years has been very supportive in my coming-out quest. She was convinced of my bisexuality long before I was. Through her I first came to understand what bisexuality was all about. Her friends were the first bisexual women I came to know.

Our relationship, though deeply committed, is mutually nonmonogamous, which has allowed both of us to grow and learn about other people without, for the most part, becoming resentful of each other.

My partner and I both travel a lot and so the times that we are home together are always special. Our relationship is hardly typical. But then, one would be hard-pressed to say that a typical model for bisexual relationships exists. One bisexual friend practices serial monogamy. When she has a lover, of either gender, she will not have sex with anyone else. When she is involved with a woman, she has been told, "That must make you lesbian, since you have sex with a woman and not with a man." Her response is that she is still attracted to both men and women. She just happens to be monogamous with a woman for now. If this relationship ends, the next one could as easily be with another woman, or with a man.

Another friend is celibate by choice. People challenge that she couldn't possibly be bisexual because she doesn't have sex with men or women. But bisexuality is not a matter of whom you sleep with, but who turns you on. A bisexual man who is living in a monogamous relationship with a straight woman or a gay man is still bisexual. He just chooses not to have sex with others to whom he may be attracted.

Other friends satisfy their bisexual needs in a group relationship. That may take the form of a communal threesome or foursome, or some sort of formal exchange of partners within a group of people who have separate living arrangements. Members of those groups may or may not also have other relationships outside the group.

Over the years, I have been involved in a number of relationships, most of which are ongoing today. This, along with discussions with other people and various workshops at bisexual conferences and retreats, has given me some insight into what makes relationships work or not work and what is the role of love, friendship, and sex in those relationships.

Biotypes

by B. Weise and C. Smelser

IF NEGOTIATING SAFE SEX IN A DISPASSIONATE, NON-EROTIC ENVIRONMENT SEEMS COLD, UNSPONTANEOUS, AND ALSO REALLY EMBARRASSING, CONSIDER THE ALTERNATIVES.

We should have had this discussion two hours ago

I didn't know we'd BE here two hours ago

NOTE: THIS CARTOON IS CERTIFIED **BI-CORRECT** IN THAT IT CONTAINS NO GENDER-SPECIFIC REFERENCES.

Reprinted with permission from *North Bi Northwest,* newsletter of the Seattle Bi Women's Network.

Two of the biggest killers of relationships are jealousy and lies. Jealousy is particularly difficult because it relates to some sort of survival mechanism in this animal we call human. On the other hand, we seem to be inherently nonmonogamous, or only monogamous for a season (serial monogamy), as in various other species. Even strong societal and religious taboos have not changed that fact.

My solutions to this conflict have been to carefully negotiate a set of ground rules which take into account the jealousy factor and the guilt factor and to tell no lies and have no misleading expectations between those concerned. I have not always scrupulously followed these two rules. They developed over time, and sometimes the short-term gain of bending them has just been too tempting. In the end, however, I have always paid the price.

I try to apply these rules to all my relationships. A screwed-up nonprimary relationship can easily destroy your primary one as well. Lack of clarity invites trouble. It is important to be explicit about expectations before one enters into any kind of long-term relationship. It is not good practice to assume that one's understanding of the rules is the same as one's partner's. People come from vastly different cultural backgrounds, even within the same ethnic group, religious heritage, and economic class. In general, one has no way of knowing what effect one's partner's upbringing and past relationships have had on their ability to cope with the current situation.

Another big problem with relationships is that people often confuse love, friendship, and sex. These are three independent types of interactions, none of which should automatically imply the others. Having sex with someone does not automatically mean she or he is one's friend, or that one loves him or her, or that sex will happen again in the future. Also, there is no reason why sex should ruin a friendship. Or why one's lover cannot also be one's best friend, as mine is.

Love without sex is a perfectly normal condition. Think of how one feels about one's parents or one's siblings. Many couples who are very much in love don't have sex with each other. Sex without love is equally normal, whether or not one's partner is also one's friend. The term "fuck buddies" is sometimes used to describe people who have sex together just for the enjoyment of it and understand that there is not necessarily anything more to the relationship.

It is very nice when friends can sleep together without the pressure of sex and the commitment of love. Much can be said for curling up next to a close friend and spending the night cuddling and caressing, with no other expectations. I am lucky enough to have a few friends like that. It shows a great deal of trust in the friend and in the friendship.

A person can be one's friend, one's sex partner, or one's life partner. Or they can be any combination of the three. They are entirely different concepts, with entirely different responsibilities and benefits. Only when people confuse them and think that one implies another or excludes another, do misunderstandings and rifts follow.

In my few years in the bisexual community, I have made a lot of new friends, learned a lot, and have seen the community grow from a few small scattered groups to an international network of organizations. I have bi friends from as far away as Japan and Denmark now. I am happy to be one of the people who is helping to change the way the world thinks about bisexual people. The momentum is building.

Lisa Yost

Bisexual tendencies

I am a lesbian with bisexual tendencies. I find myself admitting that I am a bisexual, and then quickly saying, "But I'm involved with a woman." My brief experiences identifying as a single, available, bisexual were thrilling, but difficult. During that time I dated a lesbian who decided to stop seeing me partly because she was put off by "that bisexual thing." Similarly, I don't think that the man I saw soon after believed that I wouldn't end up leaving him for a woman. Both of these people also thought that being bisexual means being nonmonogamous.

Not for me. One lover is all I can handle. People have told me they assumed bisexuals were usually involved with a man and a woman, otherwise we'd feel as if something was missing. I don't experience it that way. You get something from each person that cannot be found with anyone else. While I have been plagued at times by the longing for some undefined other relationship that would be more perfect than the one I am in, this has not necessarily meant someone of the other gender.

In my late teens and early twenties I was often in a group of men, one of whom was my lover, arguing about feminism. I loved the fun and camaraderie of being "one of the boys." But when I walked away, when I tried to get a job or into graduate school, I just didn't have the same privilege. Though my lover did everything he could to equalize power in our relationship, I didn't feel as if we could ever be equal because of our experience in the world. I felt like growing up a girl and being a woman in the world separated me from men in a way that understanding could not bridge. Sex with men was never the problem, nor was a self-acknowledged attraction to women. I wanted a partnership of equals, and I just never felt that I could be equal with a man in the eyes of the world.

I began to identify as a lesbian in the late seventies in Ann Arbor. I wanted to be surrounded by women who had the same stake in feminism and leftist politics as I did. Coming out was like dropping backwards into a pillow. Falling into homosexuality was scary, but the life was soft. I felt giddy. The first couple of years were sort of like an extended slumber party, with gossip and dancing and romance. And politics. I marched for women's studies, for gay and lesbian rights, to take back the night, and to protest U.S. interference in El Salvador and Nicaragua. After several years and a number of relationships with women, I began to admit that I wasn't just interested in feminism or politics, but that I had — and have — strong sexual feelings for women.

During my first few years as a lesbian, I had only the most superficial interactions with men. I spent some time in an all-woman world, which gave and continues to give me a sense of my wholeness as a woman and helped me begin to feel that I am enough. It also helped me to have healthier relationships with men. When I did begin to have men in my life again, mostly at work, I was able for the first time to really be friends with no possibility of a sexual relationship. That was a big step. At one point, when I left my job, I cried because I had left behind my only male friends.

Eventually I admitted that I was still attracted to men and had several flirtations. When I did begin to go out with a man again after eight years of love relationships with women, I encountered some surprises. I appreciated the level of understanding of feminist issues I now found in some men.

However, walking down the street with a man was a different trip. With my women lovers, I had been called a lezzie and a dyke, and once someone was so creative as to call my friend and I dyke-osauruses. I had forgotten what looks you get when you walk down the street with a man. I had imagined I might feel safe and accepted. Wrong. I felt measured, as if the women were checking out their interest in the guy I was with and their ability to obtain him. Similarly, the men were gauging their attraction to me and competence to beat my boyfriend in a drag race or some other primitive competition.

Then there were my friends' reactions. One said that it was fine if I wanted to see the guy I was dating, but that she didn't ever want to hang out with us together. This is all too familiar to me, having faced the pain of not having my relationships with women accepted, much less welcomed and celebrated, by my family or co-workers. Most of my lesbian friends were supportive, although some appeared concerned. Others revealed that they too had been attracted to men and seemed to take a vicarious pleasure in watching my progress.

At least two otherwise pleasant dinner parties were spoiled by my casual mention of my bisexual tendencies. I brought them up innocent of the inferno of reactions the *bi* word produces. One lesbian attorney argued quite convincingly that I had no right to call myself a lesbian if I ever have sex with men. At a safe distance, I'm not so sure. I think "lesbian with bisexual tendencies" is fairly descriptive. I told a straight friend at work that I was exploring my heterosexual tendencies and although she was accepting, I felt as if I lost some credibility. Maybe she no longer knew what to expect from me. I had opened the door to all sexual possibilities.

Sex, after all, is something to be contained. Sex unties all of the nice packages we use to keep ourselves — and to try to keep one another — from slipping off the edge of the cosmos. Our sexual identities tell us how to live. But I need to remember that I can define my own sexual identity. I take courage from some of the bisexual activists I see around me. As a feminist, I want to see more viable alternatives for women. When I acknowledged my attraction to women *and* men, the world became exponentially larger. It's a big, big world, full of interesting and attractive people.

Rifka Reichler

A question
of invisibility

I am a 23-year-old married Jewish woman. I have never slept with a woman, nor do I expect to. Yet, I am a bisexual.

To the world at large, I may appear "straight." Certainly many of my actions seem to imply this. But I am a bisexual and participate in the bisexual community. The newspapers and newsletters I read, the conversations I have with friends, the buttons I hang in my study, and the organizations I join affirm my bisexuality. The term *bisexual* affirms the part of me that loves women, now and in the future, regardless of with whom I am sleeping. For me it implies choices, because a person's gender is not a prerequisite for loving them.

I have mild athetoid cerebral palsy. I don't use a wheelchair, braces, crutches, or hearing aid. I don't sign or read lips. I have involuntary, usually minor, muscle spasms and muscle movement that I can't control. It's almost an invisible disability. You have to be medically knowledgeable to realize I have a speech defect and am not just hard to understand. "Please speak clearer," asks the airline reservation person. "I *can't!*" You have to know about my disability to understand why it took me an extra few seconds to get off the bus at the University of Minnesota campus. And only if you ask will you know how many contact lenses and earrings I have lost or ripped because my hands couldn't quite achieve the fine motor coordination necessary.

So what does all this have to do with my Jewish bisexual self? Being differently abled, bisexual, and Jewish in a world that is mostly not these things gives me an element of invisibility that can be very frustrating. Even if being Jewish and differently abled are legitimate in our society, they are not always viewed in a positive way. On the other hand, bisexuality is not seen as an authentic way of being in almost every community. I hear people say that sexual preference should not be anyone's business. However, as long as heterosexuality is the "norm," and anything else, if not wrong, is less than heterosexuality, we non-heterosexuals must be willing to speak out and say we are here. I am out to my parents, family, and friends. I want people to know all of me. I am a proud married woman who is differently abled, bisexual, and Jewish, and who loves women.

Double quest

On a fall morning in 1985, the phone rings in my suburban Chicago home. My daughter, a sophomore at the University of Wisconsin, Madison, invites me to meet her halfway, late in the morning on Sunday. I agree. We set a time and place, and hang up. I wonder what this can be about; obviously, it is not a matter for telephone chatter. What is my nineteen-year-old daughter wanting to share? This middle child, and only daughter, has been sensitive, bright, loving, and open. Our relationship has been unique. We've been close, while allowing one another individuality and respect for our viewpoints and actions.

A few days later, I dress in snug jeans, warm sweater with diagonal stripes in various shades of blue, and my hiking shoes. I gather together the picnic lunch we'll share and head for the highway. Even my Holly Near tapes don't drown out my growing concern about our meeting. I play with a variety of dialogues as I speed along the road, but they're dead ends. I arrive just as her bus does and am excited to see her. She looks so attractive with monochromatic colors and interesting textures draped on her tall, slender frame. Her earrings hang close to her long neck, and her hair is very short. She smiles warmly at me. We soon find a park with a table and benches.

After our meal we talk. She begins to ask me how I feel about bisexuality. She's been thinking seriously about this. Her male lover is absolutely behind it. It's important, in her process, to know how I feel. She knows she can trust my honesty.

I try hard to walk the balance between staying in touch with my feelings and retaining some degree of distance and objectivity. I know this day is important to both of us, and to our relationship. I tell her that it's imperative to be true to oneself, which might mean experimenting and satisfying curiosities. I feel some anger toward her lover, who may be an instigator. I express the fear that she might choose to be a lesbian once she crosses the sexual boundaries. All of this is now out in the open; I have read her my version of the "riot act" as we walk in this vast park where leaves have fallen on the ground. We crush them with our shoes. I remind her that I will always love her, regardless of her sexual choices.

She asks me if there's ever been a time in my life when I've considered a choice other than heterosexuality. I tell her that just before I was forty, just after I came out of my marriage, I considered it and rejected it because my motivation was based on anger, disappointment, and bitterness. She appreciates my sharing this and indicates the difference in her own attraction to women.

We continue to explore the park and find a quiet brook, where we sit for a while and play with twigs. We talk about her brothers, my new lover, my practice, her classes. It's soon time for her bus back to Madison, so we collect our belongings and drive to the station.

My head whirls as I drive back to Chicago. She's never hinted at this, certainly never put it into words. She's a strong feminist, but so am I, and that has nothing to do with it, anyway. She dated in high school, had love affairs in college. These thoughts spin around as my wheels move home. I don't play Holly Near this time; I need to listen to myself.

When this girlchild was born, bisexuality wasn't even a concept in my sophisticated mental make-up. It was not the dream I had for my baby. How dare she? She dares because she was raised to dare — to look, to listen, to touch, to be aware of her heart. She was raised to be curious, to explore, to be an adventurer, and an independent thinker.

Her next two years are a struggle. She defines herself as a lesbian and comes out to her father, her friends, and later to her brothers. She tests herself, and those she loves. She explores possibilities to attend the University of California and chooses Santa Cruz. When her arrangements are made, she gets involved with a woman she loves, and they maintain a long-distance relationship.

In this same period of time, I've accepted a teaching position, sold my home, and moved to California to be closer to my lover, who had moved the year before. My daughter's lover visits for Thanksgiving, and I invite them to dinner and to spend the night. My tension is evident. In actuality, the time is pleasant, but it is emotionally difficult to see them sharing a bed and showing physical affection. I get through it. Being able to share it with my lover comforts me. As a parent, he understands she will do whatever she needs to do, anyway. After a year in the community in which she has lived, I hear her using the term *bisexual* again.

At just about this time, my lover and I begin fantasizing about a threesome for my next birthday — my fiftieth — with another woman. It is titillating to me; it is also frightening. I question my femaleness. I have concerns that he will view me enjoying sex more with a woman than with him. Some of the fears I'd expressed for my daughter are also the ones I have for myself. My lover and I talk them through, and our intimacy deepens.

We begin to imagine how we will make it happen. We think aloud of people we know and ultimately reject this avenue in favor of answering ads. Within a month, we *are* responding to ads, but find few single women advertisers. We run our own ad; two women and three couples respond. We meet them all and arrange an evening with one of the women.

It had all seemed incredible at first. Once the ad was in print and people who were strong possibilities responded, I felt extremely high and powerful in that I had the courage to follow my fantasies. But my usual confidence subtly alters. Perhaps I am more tightly gripped by homophobia than I knew. I am certainly nervous and awkward with the newness. I also fear that I might want to choose a lesbian lifestyle. I talk about my fears beforehand, making it less foreboding, less ominous.

The night of our exploration I experience moments of self-consciousness, but no disgust. Although I had a moment of fear and disbelief when I felt her hand on my breast, it passed. I felt turned on when she made love to me. I felt no impulse to be active with her, nor did she encourage me. I began to feel pleased with my chutzpah and daring to risk for this pleasure. It was a one-time event with her. Two months later I responded to an ad in the *Bay Guardian* by a woman looking for a friend, companion, lover. She called me and said she planned to invite the seven women who'd responded to a party. Not being my style, I declined.

My lover was dumbstruck that I was considering this leap, and we shared a long period of dissension over the implications to each of us, and to our relationship. He plunged into deep thought over sexual events with men, and we subsequently pursued an evening with a man, a counterpart of sorts to our exploration with the woman.

A year later, I feel freer about my mind, my body, my possibilities. As fluid as I felt with my bisexual encounter, I feel clearer about the choices I might make in time. I don't feel closed off, and I'm able to be appreciative of my ability to enjoy gazing at a woman, as well as a man. A year later, I am still digesting the array of possibilities that bisexuality has to offer. By exploring it the way my lover and I chose to, we gave ourselves the opportunity to open up our other sides, facing the myths and fears.

It's fall again. I've come a far distance since 1985. I had a great deal to learn that crisp autumn day when my daughter shared her hopes and dreams with me. I've allowed the doors to open in my new environment, as well as within myself. I lay ambivalence aside and grow bolder each day, confronting my own "mixed" desires. By my sixtieth birthday, I just might be a wiser and experienced woman, for I am open to possibilities. I will have gotten there primarily through careful listening to my daughter, who activated an area of openness and sensitivity in me. I will have gotten there, too, through a relationship with a man who is in touch with his own bisexual interest and capacity to explore with me. I wouldn't doubt that the two of them were a trigger for my own quest, which continues to move forward, inch by inch.

Victoria Woodard

Insights at 3:30 a.m.

I am a bisexual woman who recognized my identity through feminism. For many years I saw myself as essentially bisexual, but my actions were those of a heterosexual who slept with women — sort of the inverse of a lesbian who sleeps with men. Sexual encounters with women friends in ménages à trois with men punctuated, or added spice, to my otherwise heterosexual life. I wasn't necessarily satisfied with the superficiality of this, but none of my women friends were interested in making our sexual relationship more serious. I made two attempts to start lesbian relationships with friends; both told me they wanted to be just friends.

As my feminist consciousness developed, I began to wish I were lesbian. It would be so much tidier politically! However, I didn't feel honest coming out as a lesbian because I was attracted to both genders, and because our heterosexual society hadn't given me enough of a chance to compare my attractions to women and men. I didn't know how to get more experience being sexual with women because as a feminist I didn't want to "use" a lesbian that way.

The question of my sexual orientation began to really agitate me when I worked on femininity, masculinity, and androgyny themes in my M.A. thesis. At the time I didn't recognize my psychic disturbance as coming out. I thought I was just extraordinarily creative when my sleep began to be disturbed and my perceptions altered.

Visions of sentences forming on my computer screen started waking me up at 3:30 a.m. The sentences criticized the concepts of femininity, masculinity, and androgyny. Captive in the dark, I lay awake till dawn fleshing out in my mind the insight which had awakened me, then got up and entered it on my computer. This happened night after night for about two weeks. Normally someone who works at a measured pace, I was driven to type for hours at a time. My thinking felt crystal clear for one of the few times in my life, and I *had* to record it. I knew I was a little manic, but I enjoyed my heightened mental state.

I determinedly refused any social invitations so that I could passionately focus on my work. When I finished the thesis, I suddenly had more time on my hands and nowhere to focus my passion. At that crucial moment I miraculously walked into a sexual affair with one of my lesbian friends. She likes bisexual women, heterosexual women, *all* women. She especially likes "bringing out" women, being a woman's sexual partner while she comes out. I didn't worry about "using" her. I never imagined such a woman existed, but I see now that whatever your situation, someone will be attracted to exactly that situation.

The focus of my psychic disturbance shifted to my lesbian relationship. I continued waking up in the middle of the night, these times thinking about her and theorizing about gender identity issues. In talking with her I began to remember how I felt at age four, before being made to wear skirts to school. I found a picture of me at four in pants and boots, no skirt. From my new perspective I was a baby dyke! I was thrilled. I began re-editing my personal childhood myth.

As a child growing up on a ranch, I always thought I should have been born a boy. Outwardly I imitated Mom, but inside I knew I didn't share her interest in raising a family. The myth I spun about this when I became a feminist was that my childhood wish to be a boy, and my young adult preference for male friends, was male identification. I critiqued my male identification as internalized patriarchal oppression and sought to replace it with sisterhood.

Getting in touch with my four-year-old self reminded me of my simple adoration for my father. At age four my love for him was so complete that I wanted to *be* him. I wanted to be strong, gentle, independent, and have people look up to me, just as they did to him. Later, as I grew older, this changed to wanting to *have* Dad. An older me thought I could never marry because the only possible partner for me was Dad, but marrying him was out of the question.

In rewriting my childhood myth, I realized that the part of me attracted to women is identified with my father, just as the part of me attracted to men is identified with my mother. I began to reclaim what I had previously rejected as male identification, even renaming it "butch identification" — more acceptable from a feminist perspective — and fantasizing about getting a short haircut like my brother's.

Meanwhile, my attraction to my male lover paled in contrast to my vivid coming-out experience with my woman friend. I decided that I didn't want to be sexual with him any longer. This choice was apparently mine, because both of my lovers were encouraging me to continue seeing the other, each for their own reasons. I couldn't stand the internal tension of being heterosexual and lesbian at the same time. I decided that my attraction to women was strong enough that, coupled with my feminist politics, I could honestly come out as a lesbian, so I did.

My boyfriend was very upset by my unilateral decision to change the nature of our relationship. We argued, and I left our house feeling scared of him and very shaky. This separation intensified the psychic disturbance I was already experiencing. I became paranoid and felt as if I were falling apart. You could say coming out gave me a nervous breakdown.

While I stayed with a friend for the next three weeks, I started to fear that coming out would be too much for me. I was very unnerved to feel the "me" I had known for thirty-six years disintegrate around me. I was still awakened every night at 3:30 a.m., now by disturbing realizations about myself. My eyes were never so wide open as then, stripped of most of my assumptions and social conventions: the easy, familiar hetero plan for my life. I felt physically wrenched by this unfamiliar strong attraction to a woman, after so many years of sexual relations with men. I was a mess at work, able to manage only the most menial tasks. I was emotionally volatile and completely exhausted from sleep deprivation. But I was able to hang on because through all the uproar an essential part of me was excited and exhilarated about the change.

One day as I walked between appointments, musing about how my woman lover seemed to be out to get me by putting me in double binds, I suddenly remembered concluding just a couple of weeks earlier that my male lover was out to get me. I realized it was unlikely they were *both* out to get me, objectively speaking. Obviously I was paranoid! This thought made me even more paranoid, because suddenly I couldn't trust myself.

I swung into action to counter this feeling of falling apart. I know exactly what to do when my survival is threatened: eat! I quickly made a ninety-degree turn into the nearest restaurant, not caring that it was a fast-food chain, and patched myself together again while I ate three rounds of fried chicken and corn-on-the-cob.

As I sat there, I realized I had been denying the lesbian part of myself for over twenty years. My heterosexual veneer was what was falling apart. This thought comforted me. I realized that my heterosexual self was cracking because my lesbian self, unacknowledged for so long inside, insisted on being part of my conscious identity. I knew that coming apart was my way of coming out. I sensed that time and looking inward would bring an end to my upset. I longed for a quiet winter to consolidate, and I got it.

The affair with my lesbian friend ended that winter, and I went through a period of mourning for the loss of both my lovers in such a short time. I lived in a household of very accepting bisexual lesbians, who believed that any sexual attraction is sacred. At first I was determined to find a new lover right away. But when spring arrived, I found myself savoring my new sexual feelings. I didn't want to share them with anyone! I spent several weeks in a joyous, expansive mood, in love with life itself.

This was followed by a period of nagging doubts, which I brought up every week in my coming-out support group: I didn't think I was really a lesbian. Then over the summer my friendship with my boyfriend became sexual again, which forced me to accept that I'm not a lesbian; I am bisexual.

I had to come out again as bi. While I didn't experience the psychic upset that accompanied coming out as a lesbian, I found coming out to my friends as bi much harder. I was embarrassed about it, because I live within a radical, alternative subculture where being a lesbian feminist is greatly respected and being bi not understood. At first many friends, both women and men, gay and straight, were disappointed with the new bi version of my sexual orientation. I was disappointed too. My identity was no longer tidy. It felt neither hetero nor gay, but in limbo.

Then I attended a bisexual support group at the West Coast Women's Music Festival. I saw for the first time the possibility of bisexuality as a legitimate orientation, a third option, not just the non-orientation of someone who can't make up her mind. The power of that group of like-minded others was amazing. After that experience, I searched for and found an ongoing feminist bisexual women's support group which continues to help me consolidate my identity as a bisexual woman. From my new, stronger position I began to realize that my friends who were most clear about their own sexual orientation were, in fact, supportive.

But now, sometimes I'm scared to tell people I'm bisexual. This is new for me; before I came out I didn't feel self-conscious saying I was bisexual. I think that when I was a heterosexual sleeping with women I was safe in my heterosexuality. From that hetero perspective I had a liberal, tolerant attitude toward my own bisexuality. I reasoned that most people are bisexual to some degree. I assumed that lack of opportunity kept most people from sleeping with others of the same sex. In these ways I assured myself that I was normal.

With my new bisexual identity I no longer have that safe, liberal, heterosexual perspective. I feel vulnerable, in part because as a bisexual I'm only one year old, but also because as a bisexual I'm a sort of stepchild. Both the lesbian community and the larger heterosexual culture are reluctant to include us. We have to create our own community; and fight for inclusion in the gay and lesbian world and for recognition and rights in the heterosexual world.

I see myself in an historical context. I'm able to come out as a bisexual now because a bisexual movement is afoot. Just as feminism allowed me to acknowledge the importance of my feelings toward women, the gay liberation movement gave me the courage to act on them. I like to trace my lineage; it gives me strength to know who went before me. I see the bisexual movement as a logical outcome of the success of feminism and gay liberation.

Ronda Slater

What I need is

In contemplation of bisexuality

What I need is
an angular man
with muscles and bones
built for thrusting
or maybe

what I need is
a satin-skinned woman
with fingers that dance
on my body
or maybe

what I need is
a Trojan Horse lover
who is really a woman
named Helen, in hiding,
or maybe

what I need is
a magical man
who grows gardens of herbs
and heals with the laying
on of his hands
or maybe

what I need is
a lyrical lady
with hair down to here
who writes poems and songs
about *me* for a change,
or maybe

what I need is
a sensual socialist
androgynous feminist
who doesn't smoke cigarettes
or maybe

love is like water
and when you find out
you need it, who cares
where it comes from,
or maybe

everyone is a well
just waiting for me
to send my ladle down.

II.

Spirituality:
Healing the splits

Overview

> To understand Gay people ... the entire society will need to
> literally transcend, rise above, envelop the system of perceiving
> everything as "either/or" ... The ability to simultaneously see
> "both/and," inner and outer, male and female, black and white,
> the individual and the community, strong and tender ... suggests
> ... the wholistic stance toward which I believe we modern people
> are moving.   — Judy Grahn, Another Mother Tongue[1]

In ancient times our minds and bodies, spirits and nature were not
split. There was no opposition, no dichotomy. Even last century, in
Hawai'i for instance, a chant to Pele, the goddess of volcanoes —

> 'O Pele ko'u akua
> He ali'i no la'a uli,
> No la'a kea[2]

— praised the chieftess of both the sacred darkness and the sacred light.
Neither was considered better nor more holy, neither was over the other.
Women and men, light and dark, spirit and body, man and nature were
not always so separate or split. In fact, in many cultures, to embody the
opposite, or both, sexes used to be considered holy, not something to
be scorned or pitied.[3]

Today we hardly know what is natural or how to heal the body-
hating, homophobic, sex-negative culture we have inherited. Yet there
is a time our bodies remember (consciously or not) when we were new
and had that trusting, awe-filled spark. We arrive on this earthly plain
with a natural curiosity to explore our bodies and our surroundings.
Gradually that curiosity was numbed out — by religion; by the institution
of parenting where patterns of ignorance, silence, secrets, and abuse are
handed down from generation to generation; by the media that bombards
us with alienating messages; by schools; by you name it... Our curiosity
and desire, the sacred spark, is thwarted at every turn. But the inner light,
the inner truth stubbornly persists. We survive with some glimmering
memory intact. We push ourselves through the accrued fear, the shame,
the doubt to rediscover and reclaim the curiosity and passion, the sacred

spark of life expressed through, but transcendent and separate from, gender and genitalia.

A long time ago when western culture and religion became alienated from sexuality and nature, our awareness was made dichotomous, split asunder. At this same time, men were establishing their control over women. To justify their domination, men rationalized that their sex was closer to God, and that women were closer to nature. Thus women were seen as more lowly, more irrational, more in need of being protected and tamed. At the same time men were establishing their control over women, stronger men were establishing their control over weaker men through the transition from small nature-centered communities to large city-states. Over the centuries, as this trend progressed, it became increasingly important to propound the belief that the desires of the flesh and the desires of the spirit were opposed, just as the male mind and female body were seen as separate. Again, it was no coincidence that it was the women, the racial minorities, the gays who were most equated with the flesh, with irrational emotions, with the dark side of the psyche, while the dominate rulers always appropriated the rule of spirit, of the light, of rationality, of mind over body, of white equals right for themselves.

Within the false safety of these rigid dichotomies, the awareness that change is a constant got lost. Fear of change and of other (or of becoming like the other) took control. Even if you were queer (as opposed to "normal") you at least knew your place in the greater scheme of things. What is ignored however is that all life is a process of growth and change, much of it uncharted fluid movement. The ambiguous middle ground is as important as the beginning and end result of change.

We have come to a place in our evolution where the reality of our survival on this earth depends on our recognition that destructive, dichotomous power dynamics alienate us from ourselves, each other, and nature. Reconnecting to the earth during this twentieth anniversary year of Earth Day, comes at a time when even industrial-polluting capitalists realize a bit of the damage caused by this alienation and exploitation and the global healing process that is imperative.

Recognizing bisexuality is part of this healing process.

The writers in this section speak to peace-making and integration of all parts of the self, of a healing vision for repair of the world — *tikkun olam,* as the ancient Hebrews called it. We reclaim our roots. We repair our world, slowly, bit by bit. Part of this is telling our stories, as we do in this anthology. Storytelling has always been a part of people's spiritual practice.

Today there is a renewed sense that sex is spiritual without con-tradiction; that sex can be a sacred art, a spiritual discipline. Sex desperately needs to be re-envisioned as such so we may reclaim our bodies from the degraded, trivialized way they and their responses have been represented. Reclaiming our bodies also means reclaiming Mother Earth, her body, too.

We challenge good and evil dualities, we dare to question the dichotomy between sacred and profane and claim all of life as sacred. We call the old tribal polymorphous ways back into being and assert that they are necessary to heal the alienated spirit within us.

Both modern spirituality and modern sexual identities are in flux. The old contradictions are exposed as never before, old rules are being challenged across the globe. We are changing. We have never stopped changing. This cycle of death and rebirth is familiar. The passage to the other side is an arduous one. We are growing, pushing, stretching, yearning to be free. As midwives from time immemorial have counseled, the best thing, and the only thing to do, is to let go, relax, and breathe deep. We must concentrate on what the moment-to-moment reality requires, how best to honor this brief life now pulsing within and between us.

The biggest changes are yet to come. We ain't seen nothing yet!

Notes

1. Judy Grahn, "Gay is Good and Gay is Also Baed," *Another Mother Tongue: Gay Words, Gay Worlds,* Boston: Beacon Press. 1984.

2. Mary Kawena Pukui, E.W. Haertig, M.D., and Catherine A. Lee, "Holiness and Healing," *Nana I Ke Kumu [Look to the Source],* vol. 2, published by Hui Hanai — An auxiliary of the Queen Lili'uokalani Children's Center Publication, 1979, pp. 122–123.

3. See, for instance, the numerous examples of holy transvestism in Evelyn Blackwood, ed., *The Many Faces of Homosexuality: Anthropological Approaches to Homosexual Behavior,* Harrington Park Press, 1986.

Closing ritual, First National Bisexual Conference,
Mission High School Auditorium, San Francisco, June 1990.

my foundations
are in the universe
my spirit is universal
despite all pressures against me
to choose sides
black or white
man or woman
gay or straight
I am still a child
and an old woman
my blood is red
my choice is not to choose
I cannot choose
I am the exception to the rule of choice
I am one and all without exception
I defy the rules
I am me.

—Dajenya

Karen Hurley

Coming out
in spirit and in flesh

Dominating my earliest memories of going to church on Sunday mornings at St. Paul's is the enormous cross that hung over the altar, with Jesus larger than life and very dead. He was also unclothed except for a loincloth, the only statue that showed any flesh. The figures of Mary, Joseph, and all the angels were entombed in voluminous robes that covered their bodies completely. By contrast, his flesh was shocking; it was meat. He was mortally passive. His pose, with his body curved, one leg slightly raised, his feet touching, in a twisted sort of way looked erotic.

My early perceptions of my body and my sexuality, before I knew what that was, were all filtered through that image of pried-open vulnerability and humiliation. Flesh was dangerous; it reeked of betrayal. It was dirty, out of control, with its smells, burps, giggles, tears, and hungers that would burst forth out of nowhere just, it seemed, to embarrass me. My shame cowered from the hushed purity of the other statues, and I wanted to float above my body like an angel, eternal and safe. As the apostle Paul taught, I "set my mind on things that are above, not on things that are on earth."

Thus, body and spirit, sex and religion were split apart, hidden from each other, taught to hate each other. For the two to come together again, each element would first have to emerge from hiding. Therefore, I have not one coming-out story to tell, but two, one of sexual identity and one of spiritual identity. Given that what eventually emerged from the closet — or split-level house, if you will — was me being bisexual and a feminist witch, the time spent in hiding was as protective as it was restrictive. These two aspects of myself began coming out around the same time, in my early twenties, because they were manifestations of a single impulse to reknit body and spirit, but when they first began making themselves known, I merely thought that I was becoming weird in every possible way.

Let's start with sex. Despite my Catholic guilt, I did manage to have relationships with men and even to enjoy sex. I got married immediately upon graduating from college. However, I gradually became aware that I had always had feelings for women that I had refused to acknowledge. I was aware of having crushes, but could not name them. These feelings emerged from nowhere and hung in silence, like ghosts, too dangerous to be real.

In the meantime, marriage was what I had expected. I was in love with the man I married, but not with the role I felt pushed into playing. The pressure was not coming from him — on the contrary, I think he was feeling it himself — but from our parents, our relatives, people at work. After the wedding we were no longer seen as two individuals who loved each other, but as people who had functions to fill, chiefly to have children and to "make a nice home," i.e., acquire things to match the silver and china wedding gifts we had received. If one of us went somewhere without the other, the inevitable question was "Where's your spouse?" I finally realized that I loved him for who he was as a person, his interests, his intelligence, his beautiful eyes, and not for how well he fulfilled the role of spouse or male. I noticed that the things that made him special had little to do with gender. By those standards, wouldn't I be equally likely to choose a woman as a lover? I asked myself. Bless their resilience, all those nameless little feelings popped up and said "yes."

At the same time, after not going to Mass for years, I started drifting back to religion. I did not miss in the slightest the process of scraping my soul for sins to confess, nor the gory stories of tortured saints. However, I missed the atmosphere of magic, where light was transformed by stained glass into dark jewels and water turned to wine. I got involved with the Unitarian church, a liberal, nondogmatic branch of Protestantism that shared my political values. In the interest of finding a career that would allow me to teach, write, and counsel, I even decided to become a minister.

Before graduate school I took a course on feminism and theology. I was fascinated with the work of Mary Daly, Rosemary Radford Ruether, Carol Christ, and others who described how Christianity, as a patriarchal religion, propped up male domination in social and political spheres. But what captured my imagination were essays about women who were forming groups and celebrating ancient holidays of the changing seasons with rituals that used images of the goddess and symbols from nature. It was a revelation to me to discover that the aspects of Christmas that I had loved the most — the smell of pine, the carols, the candles, the special foods — were, in fact, taken from the winter solstice celebrations of an older, goddess-worshipping religion hypothesized to have existed in Europe before being wiped out during the witch-hunts of the Middle Ages.[1]

The night of the last class I took down a phone number and joined a coven of four other women. Many times since then we have stood in a circle, chanting the names of goddesses, feeling our strength, our power to heal ourselves and each other. The beauty of the ritual candles and incense that I had once associated with alienation and fear now touches the deepest parts of me. The unearthly harmonies of our chanting transport me on inward journeys to places of power beyond the night sky. I found myself repeating our ritual blessing when making love with a woman: "Bless your lips to speak of Her; bless your breasts, formed in strength and beauty..."

I might easily have ended the story here and sailed off into a lavender sunset, except for two things. One was that I was still in love with the man I married. Secondly, I had a strong reaction against what I felt was implied in Mary Daly's work, that women were a race of noble beings kept apart by evil men. That the Goddess would be immanent in all of nature except for human males or to assume that all men are equally determined to oppose the tides of elemental energy that she represents didn't make sense. In the midst of my struggle here, a group of women in my city called an organizational meeting for "Women Loving," a network for bisexual women. In that room of seventy women sharing their stories of loving women and men, I again felt I had found my home.

At this point I felt more secure identifying as bisexual, but in de-emphasizing the importance of gender in forming relationships, I found myself confused by the blurring of friendship and sexuality that resulted. I felt acutely embarrassed by the realization that every person was potentially a lover. Rebecca Shuster notes in her essay "Sexuality as a Continuum"[2] that bisexuals "can become closer to any person along a fluid line from acquaintance to intimacy, deciding whether sex will be part of the relationship or not." I was afraid, though, to live without rules — if I let go I would run completely amok.

I found in Starhawk's book, *Dreaming the Dark*,[3] that I am not alone in being afraid of sexual attraction: "A fear runs like a thread through Western culture — from the church fathers to Freud — that sexuality, if unleashed from the control of the internalized authority, the self-hater, would run wild and destroy civilization. But sexuality has its own regulatory principle, its own rhythm of expression and containment, arousal and satiety." Our coven rituals, like those of many witches, contain cyclical symbols: the turning of the seasons, the waxing and waning of the moon, the rise and fall of breath. These are all symbols of nature's ability to regulate itself and our ability to regulate ourselves.

When we trust our bodily rhythms, we can perceive and appreciate desires and feelings without automatically acting them out. As I learned during my coming-out process, once I was dealing with an actual feeling rather than the fear of having the feeling, I had a more realistic picture of how strong the feeling was, and how it was best expressed.

My joy now in loving women and men convinces me, in a way that no intellectual argument can, that bisexuality is neither sinful nor politically incorrect. I do not need to rely on an authority to tell me what is right or what I want — my knowledge is as solid as my bones. But when shame, guilt, or fear blocks desire as an emissary of knowledge, then authority must originate outside of the self. Dogma usurps the knowledge that exists in the body and substitutes functionalism for desire. In the Catholic teaching, regardless of the desires that spring up, sex can only occur at certain times (after marriage), in certain ways (not by yourself), with one person of the opposite sex for the purposes of reproduction. With desire so muted, people must then be told by church authorities to "be fruitful"; otherwise, they might not have sex at all.

Evicting desire from the center of the self freezes the heartbeat, the natural push for growth. Desire is caught, like a butterfly, fixed into a noun such as homosexual or married person, and is no longer a living process. Even to say I am bisexual, as opposed to heterosexual or lesbian, is just one more noun. To understand something in the dogmatic sense is to stop the flow of continuous revelation, of growth, and of openness to new experience.

In Wicca, the Goddess becomes a metaphor for the verb Being. She has not one name but many, and she grows and changes as all living things grow and change. We celebrate her in process, throughout the life cycle from maiden to mother to crone, just as we live our lives in process, not stopping at any one age. She could even be He; there are covens who celebrate the Horned God, the Hunter, the Seed. Even the Christian image of God as father is not in itself bad; only the rigid insistence that he be the only image is destructive. As the Dischordians, a pagan group who celebrate chaos, say, "To stop at any one metaphor and establish it as dogma is to put the mind in chains." To stop at any point in one's life and say, "Regardless of my (homosexual) (heterosexual) experiences and fantasies, I am (heterosexual) (homosexual)," is to put one's history and future in chains.

At a time in which AIDS is seen by some as God's punishment for sexual wickedness, I draw strength from my religion in which "all acts of love and pleasure are Her rituals."[4] The symbols, metaphors, rituals, and myths of Wicca relate my "inner" experiences of spiritual union with my "outer" experience of relating to others as bisexual. The mutability of metaphor links the changing face of immanent power, of the goddess, with the mutability of expressing intimacy with others, be they men or women, and be it through sex, hugging, talking, working together, doing ritual, or healing. Understanding Being as a verb, as cyclical movement, and celebrating this movement in seasonal holidays, affirms my life as a process that evolves. To celebrate the sacredness of physical experience means that my body is no longer pinned to a cross of shame, is no longer a betrayer, but is my source of authority. I no longer wish that I could float above my body; I want to join in the dance of the universe and work up a good sweat.

Notes

1. In our Christian culture, the name "witch" has negative connotations. There is a reason for this. Millions of people, many of them female, bisexual, and/or gay, were killed during the Middle Ages during the Inquisition. They were healers, herbalists, and midwives who challenged the Church's claim that healing could only be accomplished through the prayers of a priest. The Craft, or Wicca, as practiced in feminist, neo-pagan communities today, has nothing to do with Satanism, which is merely the underside of Christianity.

2. The Boston Lesbian Psychologies Collective, eds., *Lesbian Psychologies*, University of Illinois Press, 1988.

3. Starhawk, *Dreaming The Dark: Magic, Sex, and Politics,* Boston: Beacon Press, 1989.

4. Starhawk, *The Spiral Dance,* Boston: Beacon Press, 1979, p. 77.

David Lourea

Just another lingering flu

The other day, a friend of mine, Jason G., came running up to me with tears pouring out of his eyes. When he calmed down enough to talk, he screamed out in anger, "It's not fair! It's just not fair! I did what you said. And it's just not fair." Jason G. is three years old. The other adults and I at his day care center have been encouraging him to stand up for himself and not to let the other children bully him. "It's his fault, " he continued. "He started it first. He hit me back!"

Jason had done exactly what he thought he was supposed to do and was still in pain. He felt betrayed and enraged, and I knew how he felt.

Helping children deal with life's inequities and unfairness is easy at the day care center. Someone is always there to pick you up and wipe away the tears when life's hurts become overwhelming. You learn that falling down is part of growing up, that pain is just another part of life, and life is about learning how to deal with not getting what you want. Life is also accepting what you do get.

At the day care center your friends don't get lingering flus or come down with rare opportunistic infections. They aren't diagnosed with AIDS or die agonizing deaths on what feels like a weekly basis.

I have been desperately trying to figure out how to handle accepting that which I find totally unacceptable. Like Jason G. I feel betrayed and enraged. Sexual liberation, gay liberation, bi liberation, human liberation were *tikkun olam* (the repair of the world[1]). We were doing what we were supposed to do — standing up for ourselves, fighting back, and not letting others bully us or cage us with their own narrow limitations. We were building a better world. Today "the repair of the world" is about helping friends, loved ones, members of our communities, and ourselves learn how to die ahead of our time or to manage devastating amounts of grief.

I'm angry. I'm angry that there are so many lingering flus that are much more than just "lingering flus." I'm angry that as of June 1990 more than 83,000 are dead of AIDS in this country — we are still counting. I'm angry that there is so much pain and suffering, that there are so many absent friends, and that grief is my constant companion.

I am angry at the lesbian and gay communities that still find the word bisexual sticking in their throats. I am angry that they are more willing to risk lives than to acknowledge a great many dykes and faggots are having "breeder sex," because it might be politically incorrect to talk about such things. And I'm angry too at the heterosexual community that is just as willing to risk lives than acknowledge queer sex. What could be more politically incorrect than dying of AIDS ahead of our time? I'm angry at the organizers of national and international health conferences who refuse to hear the need for bi representation and must be convinced that bi people's concerns are *not* addressed in workshops designed for gay mens' issues by tacking the word bisexual on to the presentation or seminar title.

I'm angry at the greater percentage of bis who stay comfortably hidden in their closets, giving substance to the myths and stereotypes that a handful of us are so earnestly trying to dispel. I am angry at those so trapped in the cages of their own homophobia that they can't see the need to identify and work for change from within the gay, lesbian, and heterosexual communities as out-of-the-closet bisexuals.

Most of all, I'm angry that after ten years into this epidemic there is still no national policy governing AIDS. I'm angry at the critics of the past and current presidents' commission on AIDS who don't want to accept the need for eight billion dollars more in funding and the need to declare a state of emergency over AIDS to avoid embarrassing the present administration by pointing out that they have been, at best, grossly, criminally, and purposely negligent. Thousands more will die because of a lack of adequate handling of the AIDS epidemic, but we can't embarrass the past or present administration. To hell with the past and the present administration!

For a long time now I've been in a great deal of spiritual trouble, regarding what seems today like a sophomoric journey with which some of you may be familiar. You know how it goes. How can G_d allow this to be happening? Why? Why now? Why this one or that one? Why so much pain and so little compassion? Why the false hopes? Why so many lingering flus? Why no relief in sight? What kind of G_d does not intervene? Why can't I have what I want? Do I have more compassion than G_d? Does G_d even exist?

AIDS does not have the corner on tragedy. There is Nicaragua and El Salvador. There are the Palestinians. There are the homeless. Apartheid still exists in South Africa. Thousands of women die of breast cancer every year. And there was the Holocaust. I thought that if I could get a glimpse of how people managed to exist through the worst horror I could imagine, I might gain some perspective on how to continue today.

So I borrowed a copy of Rabbi Allen Bennett's *Out of the Whirlwind*,[2] a reader of Holocaust literature, and went off to the Russian River to decide whether G_d existed or not, over a Memorial Day weekend. Cynthia, a close friend, companion, mentor, student, occasional lover, playmate, and member of my adopted family for the past fourteen years, had just been told that her "lingering flu" was diagnosed, as we all feared, as pneumocystis. She was in the hospital, and it didn't look good for G_d. The painful accounts I read assaulted my senses. Even though they were not anything I hadn't heard before, they reaffirmed the importance of bearing witness to the realities of the horrors I experience today; they inflamed the intensity of my Jewish identity — but they did not give answers. Instead they only seemed to ask more questions. One chapter in particular was especially disturbing: "The Concept of G_d after Auschwitz" by Hans Jonas. In it he asks whether, after Auschwitz, there can be a G_d who is all powerful, all just, and at the same time, comprehensible. Well, that one's easy, I thought. I'd been letting G_d slide by for years with the rationale that any entity that could be responsible for quantum physics and an ever-expanding universe (not to mention all those black holes out there) was far beyond my ability to comprehend, and it was the height of arrogance for me to imagine I could. But Jonas points out that the idea of an incomprehensible G_d is not compatible to the concept of Judaism. I knew that it wasn't G_d I was letting off the hook, but myself. I didn't want to have to contemplate the distressing possibilities — to challenge the comfort of my complacency concerning the judgment of the Almighty. I didn't want to have to renegotiate my concept of the Creator.

Harold Kushner suggests in *When Bad Things Happen to Good People*[3] that G_d might not be all powerful, that there is chaos in the world over which G_d has no control. Great! So does that mean if Judaism represents the victory of time over space, we have the possibility of spending infinity with a kindly, just, but somewhat bumbling deity? Could AIDS, the Holocaust, or worse, exist in an eternity over which the Supreme Being has no control? No, I need a higher power more powerful than that.

So I returned home from the Russian River with no questions answered and to more bad news. Jerry was in the hospital with pneumocystis, and Mark was in a coma and would die two days later. I still had not responded to Wesley's beautiful and touching letter letting me know of his diagnosis. Enough! Hasn't G_d ever heard of a safe word?[4]

Then I realized one of the problems of being raised as a Jewish prince is that you develop the notion that all you have to do to get what you want is want it bad enough. And what if the Almighty did eliminate the AIDS virus? Shouldn't a heavenly being also do something about the atrocities happening every day in South America; get rid of breast cancer, lung cancer — all cancer, all diseases — house the homeless; remove hate and bigotry, anti-Semitism and racism, homophobia and sexism from our hearts?

The absurdity of the idea began to dawn on me. Like the children in the day care center there would be no end to the list of corrections G_d needed to make. I too must learn to deal with not getting everything I want and how to accept what I do receive. Life outside the day care center is not that different. And as for prayer and wanting, Kushner suggests that the purpose of prayer is not to get G_d to alter the laws of the universe in order to grant our personal wish list but rather to gain the strength to handle whatever life has in store for us.

So I took a walk to clear my head and noticed that the sun felt warm and good on my hands and face. The trees were green, the sky was blue and, whether by an act of divine creation or accident of evolution, it felt good to be alive. Yes, even in the age of AIDS. And it seems to me that there really is a lot to be grateful for. While it doesn't mean I have to deny my anger at all the things that are wrong with this world, it is important for me to acknowledge my gratitude. Even if my friends or I do not survive, even if bisexuals are never recognized, even if the whole human race fails, the universe is a pretty amazing place.

Jerry died six weeks ago. Cynthia's been gone for more than eight months. Wesley can no longer manage to beat the statistics. Billy's flu won't go away. I would like to believe that my rapidly diminishing T cells count and persistent fungus infections do not indicate what I know they do. I still haven't cast my vote as to the existence or nonexistence of a supreme being, but I am sure, if there is a G_d, that it is just fine that Jason G. and I are angry today.

Notes

1. *Tikkun olam* is a Hebrew term meaning repair of the world. This piece was originally given as a sermon at Ahavat Shalom, a lesbian/gay/bisexual synagogue in San Francisco.

2. Albert Friedlander, ed., *Out of the Whirlwind,* Schocken, 1989.

3. Harold Kushner, *When Bad Things Happen to Good People,* G.K. Hall, 1988.

4. *Safe word,* a term from the S/M scene, means an already–agreed upon code word between people that signals "enough," that a limit has been reached which cannot and should not be crossed.

Annie Sprinkle

Beyond bisexual

Debbie Moore

I started out as a regular heterosexual woman. Then I became bisexual. Now I am beyond bisexual — meaning I am sexual with more than just human beings. I literally make love with things like waterfalls, winds, rivers, trees, plants, mud, buildings, sidewalks, invisible things, spirits, beings from other planets, the earth, and yes, even animals.

I started out monogamous. Then I ended up with two lovers. At present I have many lovers. There are four main ones. One is a woman I have deeply adored for three years. Another is a female-to-male transsexual/hermaphrodite — the perfect playmate for bi-sex! Number three is a "gay man." Then there is my beautiful lover, the sky.

The sky and I have a very special relationship, and we love each other very much. Sex with her is divine. Mostly we make love through my eleventh-floor Manhattan window. She calls to me when she is feeling tired, haggard, smoggy, lonely, or sometimes when she is feeling great and powerful and wants to celebrate. Or, I call to her when I need and want her, and she is always there for me. I breathe her air deeply into my lungs. She envelopes me, giving me lots of her sexual energy. It thrills me, turns me on, and overwhelms me. I give her all my love and lust. I have an orgasm — sometimes several. Maybe she has an orgasm too. Perhaps her rain is her arousal fluid and her thunder her orgasm. Often I cry because our sex together is so beautiful and nourishing. Our love is real. I feel it strongly.

Obviously, my concept of sex is "more expanded" than most people's. To me, sex is not about sticking a penis into a vagina (unless it's sex for procreation). Sex is about tapping into, building, sharing, and utilizing sexual *energy*. The genitals are simply an exquisitely perfect generator for that sexual energy. Whether the genitals are male or female, or whether there are no genitals at all, does not matter to me. It's about the energy. Since I have learned this I'm reaching whole new levels of sexual intensity, adventure, enjoyment, and satisfaction and have come to use sex for more than recreation and satisfying physical needs. I use sex as a healing tool, as a meditation, a way of life, and as a path to enlightenment.

Ever since I lost my virginity seventeen years ago, I have passionately and obsessively explored and researched my own sexuality, plus the sexualities of a wide variety of people and the ways of sex in our society in general. I read some books, but mostly I learned from vast amounts of firsthand experience. I had sex with thousands of people of all races, religions, colors, sexual persuasions, tried most every kink and fetish imaginable, worked in pornography and prostitution, took wholistic sex workshops, and even tried monogamy and celibacy. Many people won't consider these very respectable credentials, as we are taught most of these things are wrong. But I have learned a great deal and want to share my findings.

I have to confess. For a few years, my sex life was in a slump. I had become jaded, unsatisfied, I lost some interest. Then AIDS hit, and my whole erotic existence seemed threatened. I thought my sex life was virtually over. But lately, my sex life is better than ever. Whole new erotic worlds are opening up. I'm excited by what's been happening and very optimistic about the future. I'd like to share with you how I healed my sex life. Perhaps others can benefit from my story. I have organized my thoughts into:

The Annie Sprinkle sex guidelines for the '90s: You can heal your sex life — A 13-step program

1. Honor your sexuality and realize its incredible value.
Sex can cure a headache, relieve stress and tension, help digestion, strengthen the heart, relieve menstrual cramps, help you sleep, wake you up, clear the mind, open you up to feelings, improve concentration, create life, burn unwanted calories, and cure depression. Research shows that just thinking about sex will strengthen your immune system. Sex can create intimacy with another human being, be an expression of love, bond people together, relieve loneliness, not to mention it can feel really good and be a hell of a lot of fun.

When our sexuality is repressed, violence results. We develop disease and disorder, tension, frustration, anxiety, drug and alcohol addiction, and a whole host of other destructive forces. This repression can come from outside of us through the pressures of society, or from within ourselves.

I'm not advocating that everyone run out and have lots of promiscuous sex. Simply allow your sexual energy to flow freely, pleasurably, guiltlessly through your body. You can be celibate and still honor and express your sexuality. Just lying in the sun or swimming, eating a meal, or walking down the street can be sexual.

2. *Do not judge yourself or others.*

We are *all* at the right place at the right time in our sexual evolutions. Our sex lives, like all the parts of our lives, go through many phases. We learn from all of our experiences, including our mistakes. Allow others their own paths. Allow yourself your own path. Whenever you find yourself being judgmental toward yourself or others' sexualities, replace the judgment with compassion.

3. *Get rid of any last vestiges of sexual guilt and feelings that you don't deserve pleasure.*

We are sexual beings. Enjoying sex is our birthright.

4. *Abstinence can be dangerous to your health.*

The surgeon general tells us that abstinence is one form of safe sex, but it can really be outright dangerous. Using your own creative sexual energy celibately, for yourself, is one thing. You are honoring that energy and working with it for yourself. But abstinence — pushing your sexual feelings down and suppressing them because you think you shouldn't have them — can cause incredible anxiety, frustration, depression, disease, etc. If you like sex then don't give it up. It's too precious.

5. *Accept the fact that you are living in the AIDS era.*

Stop complaining that sex isn't the way it used to be and that you hate condoms. Yes, you may need to mourn for the way it was, but then get over it and accept reality. Total acceptance of the AIDS era will release fear and frustration and bring awareness and compassion. Educate yourself on safe sex practices. Learn to love latex. Use condoms, so we can stop the spread of the AIDS virus and other sexually transmitted diseases. Let your sexual energy flow. Open those floodgates. Realize that AIDS is not caused by your sexuality. There are a million, billion ways to be wonderfully sexual without risking any exposure to AIDS or exposing anyone else. Know that you *can* trust yourself and control yourself to have sex that is not risky.

6. *Redefine your concept of sex.*

Find new ways to make love, to be intimate, to enjoy and express our sexual feelings. Let go of old ideas of what sex is "supposed to be like." Open your mind and heart and explore new territory. Be willing to be creative and experimental.

7. *Learn to focus on energy, not the way your bodies touch.*

You can have an incredible, delirious sexual experience with someone without even touching, if you focus on the energy between you. It's like learning a new language. At first feeling energy will be subtle, but before long you will feel where the energy exists in your body, you will be able to move it around with the power of your thoughts and will. You can focus this energy to heal something in your body, send it to a sick friend for their healing, use the energy to pray, mediate, do magic, etc. Focusing on energy will greatly intensify any touching. You will seldom lose energy during sex, because you will know how to keep building it.

8. Know that you can choose how you want to express your sexuality — self-lovingly or self-destructively.
Many people are shutting down their sexuality because they have come to realize that they had a lot of self-destructive and addictive behavior revolving around sex. But you have a choice, just as you do with what you eat. The way I see it, there is junk sex, health sex, and gourmet sex. Junk sex is fast, very genitally focused, and not always very nourishing. It can even be harmful to your physical and emotional well-being. Health sex is healing and nourishing. Gourmet sex takes a lot of time to prepare and savor, as well as a certain amount of skill and knowledge. Try to make self-loving choices as to what kind of sex you have, but if you don't, then don't beat yourself up for it.

9. Learn about your breath.
Sexual and orgasmic energy travel on the breath. Conscious breathing can make sex much more powerful and satisfying. In fact, orgasm is possible from breathing alone, without any touching. (Is this the safe sex of the future?) Believe me, rhythmic deep breathing is the best thing since the invention of the vibrator! Learning that breath was an important key to sex came as a big surprise to me and is perhaps the single most important key I've learned.

10. Take care of your body.
Eat well. Exercise. Pamper your body with long, hot baths with obscenely expensive toiletries.

11. Visualize a safe and satisfying future for your sex life and the sex lives of people of future generations.
Our society is just in kindergarten when it comes to sex. There is so much more to learn, so much more potential. Past cultures, such as the ancient Taoists and Tantrics, some Native American tribes, some geisha, and the Sacred Prostitutes from ancient cultures like Sumeria and Mesopotamia, were far, far more developed.

12. Make time for enjoying sex.
If you like sex, give yourself and others the gift of loving sensual and sexual pleasure. It's well worth the time. Throw away your TV if you have to.

13. Make love to the earth and sky and all things and they will make love to you.

Open yourself up to the great web of energy that connects all things, become a channel for some of that ecstasy that's available just for the asking. Breathe it in, and you will be guaranteed many benefits. For one thing, you will find that perfect, ideal lover that you have been searching for for so long. That lover is yourself.

Neil MacLean

Let me doctor your love

To really uncover the basis of hope,
to really come to my own rebirth
in the midst of actual tangible love;
my friends and I, Charlie and Sara,
three points on a triangle
with two long dicks pointing inward,
and one slightly scared vagina wondering,
all of us staring down at our genitals, arms around our necks...

Those long penises, mine and Charlie's, looking out at some kind of love, and Sara, my twin lover, who skipped school several times a week to lie with me in the fields or beside the tracks. I used to hide in the bushes until I'd see that cream-colored Volkswagen with her mom and dad drive away to work, and then rush over to be inside her.

And there was Charlie, who sheltered me when I judged my guardians unfit, who hid me in the shed and brought me food without telling anyone.

There in my parents' living room holding each other and pointing to the possibilities and searching for that feeling of being love.

And then, too, the first time I really put my own finger up my own ass,
above the lake in the hillside park,
just beneath the capital dome,
and felt the fullness of self-powered round ruminations
until the peak-out pang of evermore
crept up onto the holy return of the incarnate virgin
and I myself became enough.

What is coming out?

In our medical religion, babies don't feel.
Birth, that most inspirational of out-comings,
is not an experience.
According to the ego-religion of our daily life
we never had the experience of our own birth.
But there are two sides to every threshold,
I remember my birth, and before it too.
Any experience can be wiped from memory
or magnified to proportions exploitable in microscopic detail.
It depends on the interests of those involved.
And between the interests of soul and market our birth
constructs a rope swing that our life experience is a whirling ride
between.

We generally think we got our genes from our gender parent. The
truth is that we got equally from them, and chose gender on the basis of
sexual feelings we wanted to have in the future. Who is it that does not
want to know the experience of this choice?

If I love you, if you were to let me rub you and rub against you, if
you let me come so close that the festoons of defenses are shattered by
the waves of affirmations, does the gender of your genital decide?

I like pectoral beams, above the breast, holding much of the energy
of the arms' possibilities. In my mind, a women's is often more luscious,
but a man's more determined.

I want to know about how you chose your genitals. Let me see them.
Tell me, will you, was it so you could surround and contain, or probe and
explore? Or did you choose those genitals so you could feel as a container
with genitals that probe, or feel as a probe with genitals that surround? The
inversion of the physical often creates space for a mental being.

I came out loving both sexes:
    because there is this mystique about a woman,
    and about my mother,
    that is illuminated by my sexual experience as receiver,
    because I want to be my father,
    confident and self-absorbed,
    because I want to be able to match the energies they put into me
    and so take charge over my birth initiation,
    because I want to be myself,

because I want to observe love between them, real, full, me in the middle of, confident of, knowing about,

because the field of power it establishes is the calling of matter to spirit, is the right action of political relevance in the earth-world,

because there the exploding source of light and the wafting nocturnal vibration issue as charmed, strayed, delinquents, mating in the hallway of infinity.

My freedoms are the decisions I make to be in this great chamber. To go in and out of its doors, and to writhe in the psychotic tapestry of its throw rug.

Here I spring life from the hopeless jail of rigid identification schemes with their packaged goods, like our media minds, produced by corporate giants, to be consumed by micro-orgasmic envy.

Because of this tapestry I want to love you, in the deepest way possible and with the biggest opening to your special skills.

Because if you don't believe sex is love then I am asking you to let me doctor your love until sex is well in you.

And because I am still coming out, and I don't really believe in identities,

because I am both inside myself and surrounding this

and because I am the same as myself

and because I love that too.

And I don't even know if it was sex when I stood nude on the bed flapping my prick in your male and female faces and chanting chords of desolate content in the tremendous proximity to orgasm that lifts hope from the soul up to the mouth of life.

Karla Rossi

Sacred rituals

Warm, wet mouths suddenly become ravenous as each of my lovers' tongues eagerly explore my sensual abundance. As I am being caressed, as my sexuality is being celebrated, my consciousness melts into vague memories of holy sexual union. I slip back into a time when I embraced, when we all embraced the feeling that *She,* the goddess, was everywhere: in the vaginal roses carved in the temple stone walls; in the rays of hot sunlight that illuminated the altar; in the soft tongue that now brushes my face and slowly finds its way to my yearning mouth. I consecrate my sexuality as the source of my creative power. *So when did the sacred rituals transgress into unholy prostitution? And how in the hell did I become the evil Eve, responsible for Original Sin?*

My lovers' fingers are now brushing, pinching, clawing, pointing out my deepest fear ... to feel love and to need love. My lovers' fingers are rubbing, sliding, fucking, pointing out my greatest desire ... to feel love and to need love. *Tell me, Aphrodite, when did my deepest desire become my deepest fear?*

Tonight, my lovers and I are one in orgiastic celebration. The smell and taste of them intoxicate my psyche. Mystical healing tongues lick my juices. The smell and taste of me on my lovers' lips remind me of my struggle to love myself. *Why was I taught to love god the father instead?*

As I partake in this sacred, sensuous dance, I am in touch with my joyous, erotic nature and with the power of the goddess within me. As I partake in this spiritual, sexual rite, I know that I, a woman, am entitled to express my sexual self in *any* way that pleases me.

Tonight, I got religion, and it was in bed!

Loraine Hutchins

Letting go

An interview with John Horne*

When did you first know you were bisexual?*
For a long time I lived vicariously, alternately, in two cultures. But I was also very rebellious. When I finally recognized that I might not have to choose, I stood in the middle and surveyed both sides. I saw the way I was homosexual and the way I was straight.

Why didn't you chose one or the other?
I suddenly knew that neither of the exclusive choices was acceptable to me.

How old were you?
I'm thirty-two now. This acceptance of my bisexuality started about four years ago when I was twenty-eight.

You've been married ten years. Were you straight when you were married?
Well, no. I mean that four years ago I really started to *act* on the transformation of feeling bi. When I married I knew there was a part of

---

* *Interviewer's note:* I met John at the 1987 East Coast Bisexual Network Conference in New York. At first I didn't realize he was a person with AIDS. What I realized was an incredible, bright beam of love energy coming off him. He invited me to take his healing workshop the next day. I went to that workshop confused and shaky, and emerged feeling calmer and safer. Five months later, at the October 1987 March on Washington for Gay and Lesbian Rights, he dressed in a black leather vest, magenta-and-black tiger-skinned tights, and cowboy boots and walked the whole march route, pushing another PWA in a wheelchair in front of him. This interview was conducted shortly after that event.

me that enjoyed being with women and a part with men. Really, my inclination was more toward men. Madie just happened to be female.

Eventually I began to realize that I needed a man in my life. I needed a man so that I could somehow take some of the faltering moments in the heterosexual part of me and deal with that on a man-to-man level. But I knew that that was not going to work unless, or until, I could somehow bring those two elements together, like fire and water.

You mean, creating a balance?
Yes... I had to trust myself, let myself be me. I learned I could travel, leave Madie, have other experiences. Now, when I come back to Madie, I love her so much more. That's what most relationships don't have and won't allow, because people don't want to trust their own feelings, to believe they can have what they want, that it's good.

I've always been a very spontaneous individual, even before I had AIDS. And I think that's what makes Madie love me so much, because she's not. And I love her because she allows me to do that. She allows me to be me, in order for her to be her. It's the experiences in life that we let happen, that, to me, are the underlying philosophy of being bisexual. It transcends sexuality, it gets to the heart of life, period. It's spiritual.

So how did you bring your two lives together, your gay and straight ones?
We tried triads, two different times, opening up our marriage each time to a man we both liked and trusted. I don't regret either one, even though they didn't last long. Bill, the second man, brought a lot to both Madie and me, even though he was only twenty-two. He complemented both of us. There was a transformation in Madie's and my relationship. Seeing his youth, we both reflected back on our own. And then there were certain stages of his life that we couldn't wait for to be over, and we would have to ride them through with him. One of those stages was his leaving us. I've dealt with men leaving so many other times in my life, I was a little bit jaded, but Madie wasn't as prepared. She had believed it was forever and took it harder.

Madie was reacting to the loss of a partner?
Right. She *loved* him. She had never had sex with him, but the love they achieved was one of great quality, of caring and sharing, nurturing — so rich. It transcended sexuality and gayness.

But you were the center?
I wasn't the center. Only sexually was I the center. Part of the ground rules that were set up when we first came together as a triad were that we all needed to expect certain things in the relationship in order to stay together. One of those things was that, if the expectations we had,

whatever they were, if these separate visions were not met, the relationship itself would not survive. The expectations were that intimacy — between Bill and me, between Madie and me — had to be established and respected. And both of these relationships, as well as Madie's relationship with Bill, were each very different.

The first time we'd tried being in a triad, with Barry, we weren't very experienced. For instance, I slept one week with Barry and one week with Madie, and I forgot about me. I forgot about taking any time for me. When Bill came along we renegotiated the rules. Yeah, I needed more time for me, because that's really important. I perceive that one of the reasons that I have AIDS is because for so long I neglected John.

Why?
Well, because I felt that something had to give, and since I was the one bringing it together, it might as well be me.

What you do mean?
Well, I'm the bisexual in the relationship. Madie, for the most part, is heterosexual, and Bill's been homosexual.

Do you think that bisexuals have a different role to play in sexuality issues?
We have a lot to teach. I can only talk about my own personal experiences, but I feel that, in general, bisexuality isn't something that all of a sudden one just turns around and says, "Okay, I'm turned on to both sexes." In fact, I don't think I've ever met a bisexual who told me that's the way it happened. Their bisexual development has always been due to an acute awareness of the unfolding of life around them and within them. It tends to go with spirituality.

For me, being bisexual is spiritual. It's knowing that I love the world, which is what the world needs so badly right now ... people to love one another.

But that's what the world's afraid of, too.
I'm not talking just about genital love. I'm talking about emotional, spiritual, intellectual, as well as genital, love. There are lots of people, men and women, whom I run across that I just am not turned on to on a sexual level, but I just am totally turned on to intellectually. Or an emotional bond happens, something clicks in my head. Believing nothing happens by accident, I have to listen to these people I'm attracted to on an emotional level. It may just be a glance. It may be a complete stranger in the airport. It may be the shoeshine lady, it may be the bus driver. It may be the student who stopped and asked me directions some place. I think of it as more bi-*sensual;* the sensuality comes from the heart, not from the genitals.

Many people accept bisexuality in themselves. They understand it, on probably a gut level, when they think about it in terms of, "Well, I'm married, and I might cheat on my wife tonight and get a blow job from the guy in the bookstore." Or the wife might go out with her best friend to watch erotic male dancers and get real horny, and, in a moment of passion, they let themselves go with each other. But these incidents are probably not without some guilt. And they're still one-on-one. Society has a problem with going beyond the one-on-one, to having three-way love relationships, or four-way relationships, or five-way. Maybe it's a process of overload that really makes people fearful, as to whether they may be able to measure up, whether they're adding more pressures or burdens to their life than they really want, and that's legitimate.

But what's not legitimate is putting down the people who can or want to go that extra mile and take that extra chance to experience something different, something new, something precious — *love* — you know, the love of experience. That's what's difficult for our society to envision. When I talk about our society, obviously I'm talking about the westernized cultures. Less so in Europe, but definitely so in the United States, we're just not ready to let ourselves totally bare our souls. Probably 95 percent of us come from dysfunctional families.

You mean people in general, or bis?
Ninety-five percent of the living human beings on the planet. But I don't look at dysfunctional as "bad." I look at dysfunctional as not living up to our fullest potential. And I see bisexuality as a step toward fulfilling the potential that we all have as human beings to experience a lot more than we're experiencing ... *a lot more.*

When I leave this earth plane, whether it be from AIDS or something else, I want to make sure that the experiences I have are the ones I'm directed to have to fulfill myself. I don't know where I'll go when I leave here, but I don't want to come back this way again. I look forward to something new. I want to dance my way out of this life.

A lot of AIDS support groups seem to focus too much on "Why me?" I would like to see them focus more on acceptance. Buying into the notion that you're a victim doesn't help anything, unless you exchange it for feeling powerful and taking responsibility about changing yourself and others while you live. You have to speed up time. You don't have the luxury of going gracefully from one stage to another, or of sitting on your deathbed when you're ninety and looking back at the memories and feeling tired and ready to go. It's very different lying in that same position at twenty-nine or thirty years old. Your body feels decrepit, but your mind is still young. I've accepted the fact that if I die tomorrow, I still have had a good time. I have no problem with death, it's what surrounds it — the dignity or lack of it.

Do you talk about your illness with your parents?
I've told them, yes. But they never talk about what it means to them —
never. They really don't believe that's what I have. I think that, on a
conscious level, they believe that what I have is serious, but on a much,
much deeper level, they don't believe that it's going to happen. They just
won't believe it, and that's fine. I don't believe it either! So big deal, why
should I get down on them for not believing? I've finally become prepared
for whatever happens. The AIDS thing just opened the Pandora's box,
and let me peer in much earlier in my life than it would have been opened
without it. And so I feel myself much more prepared than the average
person, which has allowed me to do other things that I wouldn't ordinarily
do, like get through the grief, get through the pain, get through the anger,
get on with my life.

You wouldn't ordinarily?
I wouldn't have the perception that I have now. I would have hung on
to the anger, hung on to the guilt, hung on to the pain that is inflicted
and cast upon every single human being as soon as they take a breath
on this earth. Whether you're bisexual or not, whatever color you are,
it's intrinsic to life. And I'm letting it go.

On January 2, 1989, John took his life, leaving a note saying he was ready
to go, that the pain had become too great. His body was found with his
dog and cat curled up by his side.

Leonard Tirado

Reclaiming heart and mind

Thrown into the world

Martin Heidegger, the German existentialist, uses "being thrown" as a metaphor for how we come into this world. For me it was being thrown against a barrio wall and shattering into disordered pieces along Lower East Side and Brooklyn sidewalks, then picking myself up in adolescence and, by half-guesses, building myself from scrap.

Half my life I spent either ducking or running ... from others and myself. Until I realized I was acting somebody else's script. Once I stopped ducking and running, the constrictive identity pulling me in a dozen directions gradually fell away.

Running in circles. The time came when I realized I might be better off standing still a moment in the center of one of those circles. When I did, I watched a whole assortment of confused and self-battling mes fall away. The chaos then became a pattern, a beautifully changing pattern I'm only *now* realizing is me.

Always there, but I never noticed it. From childhood I'd always been looking at my feet as they hurriedly, anxiously crossed the ground. Or else I looked long and hard at the sky overhead. Feelings swept through me from the Earth. Images from the sky flowed down to meet them.

But their meeting was like a backhand's hard brutal slap against chafed, reddened skin. Feelings were jarring, and the images colliding with them confusing, fearful. I didn't know patriarchy caused this then, that there was an artificially created image of white, heterosexual, preferably Christian, upper-middle-class men controlling everyone's reality. This false master is carried around in each of us, deep in our hearts, far back in our minds. Sometimes he's that nagging unease which suddenly arises when we've "crossed the line" of what's permissible or acceptable to those uncountable "others" who wield power over our lives. Other times he's that slide rule by which we measure the most intimate, most vulnerable, most hurt parts of ourselves. He's the Western dominator, more lethal than any virus within us because his consumption will stop at nothing, not even consuming himself after all human life on Earth is gone. Yet his massive pathological craving for control is born of his innermost suspected inadequacies before nature. The self-hating rage we oppressively project onto each other because we're talked into believing somehow we're not right, not up to par, below standard, flawed, beneath his mark of being human. Years ago, he and the culture which evolved him as the standard mesmerized us with that malignant message. And we've all complied through self-hypnosis too.

Marital rape and me

The *mandala* that is me still hears the shouting, raging, swearing of my *Puertoriqqueno* father, sees the marital rape of my mother that both my younger sister and I witnessed as kids, feels the blows upon my mother, and experiences being dragged across the supper table when all the fear and frustration imploded in him and exploded onto us.

That fear ruled my father's life. He was always scared of the *policia*. He was terrified of staying too long in the sun because he "knew" it would bring out the black in his complexion. A frightened, small brown man always conscious of his *ingles,* when near death from kidney failure, lying in a hospital in his own feces, my father nearly cried for fear that nurses were laughing at how he talked.

Only with age and gradual insight have I come to understand him and have some forgiveness. The male model ate at my father constantly, consuming him with a craving to be *all right,* to become that ideal which every day spat and shat on him, telling him that he could never be all right.

The white male ideal worked on my mother. Consuming *mi popi,* it devoured her as his abuse drove her into madness. She had always valued her Jewish "intellectualness" and her vital immigrant working-class consciousness, had gloried in her Yiddish earthiness, too. Insults and blows beat all that out of her. She cried to her family for escape; they admonished her to endure being a wife. That killed all the Jewishness in her; so, in her isolation, she deserted *Yahweh* just as he had deserted her. Grief broadened into madness. She ran to Jesus, sought salvation alternately in His promised love and His Father's imminent destruction of the horrible world she found herself in.

But she didn't measure up there either. My father's Catholicism sneered its Augustinian loathing of femaleness every time he fucked her, rose immediately, and hurried from bed to shower, as if to wash off her femaleness, rid himself of her — of which my sisters and I overheard her accuse him outright.

I have been their death-ground — and rebirthplace — the gaping wound their hemorrhaging lives flowed into. Their bloody fragments became my torn facets: male and female, white and black, mind and body, spirit and soul, man and Nature — all at odds. The world became an immense process of rape ... fucker taking fuckee, fuck or be fucked. Yes, rape seemed the perfect metaphor for what I saw everywhere both within and without.

But every so often, unexpectedly, when chasing my selves so wearied me I could drop, I'd glimpse the sky in its expanse of harmonious clarity and corresponding cloudiness. Behind my confusion was an inkling, a dim suspicion the sky I often looked to for momentary refuge was connected to that bloody ground from which I rose, was its slaving twin.

But I didn't break from my running. My family half-ran, half-pursued from one "better" neighborhood to the next, so caught up were they in their fearful blue-collar denial. I half-ran, half-pursued, too, until I realized that I was one of the "them" that all the Euro-Americans were fleeing.

Rock radio showed me

Sky and ground finally met in the late sixties and early seventies for me. I more than dabbled in my fair share of chemicals from acid to coke, but my idea of transcendence was *not* dancing to the Dead, mushroomed-out for hours on end. My identification was steadfastly urban, blue-collar, Afro-Latino influenced. Soul and Salsa were my musical mainstays. When I danced for hours, it was to the Wicked Pickett and Willie Colon. I had my Anglo tastes: the White Do Wop survivors like Dion and the Belmonts, anguished Rockabillies like Roy Orbison and Del Shannon, and all the permutation of Phil Spector's "Wall of Sound."

Rock radio remains the signifier of sky and ground's conjoining (to this day maintaining an irresistible hold) and music the equation of sex. But a disturbing wrinkle fouled me. Bubbling to the surface were perhaps the greatest doubts of all for a young male in heterosexist, patriarchal America: doubts about my maleness and my sexual orientation.

I had a delicious secret pleasure: listening and singing, quietly to myself, songs sung by either sex, and identifying with each plaint about the other. What I took to be innocent enjoyment was really signifying what I held secret from myself and others. My sexuality in adolescence was "stalled" and lacked direction. The "delay" agitated me, yet was also palliative. It relieved me of having to choose. So well layered were my reinforcing levels of denial that I easily managed not to notice even this through the posture of progressive intellectualism.

Amidst all the violence and tears between my parents there had arose something even stronger, and strangely surer — my first stirrings of sexuality. Earliest memories of my mother were as a "terrible" two-year-old running around her bedside as she dressed in the sheerness of panties and hosiery. I still feel the excitement and awe, the crazy, out-of-control joy, and fear of mischievously slapping her loins. Mysterious, the simultaneous attraction toward *and* identification with her. While I had more obvious reasons to fear him, the same sense of the forbidden, excitement, and attraction filled me whenever I saw him naked. I was simultaneously spellbound and desirously scared each time we showered together at a vacation resort. Only in adulthood did I realize I'd been denying my equal identification with him, projecting it instead by both being and fighting him as an admirer and supporter of the radical Young Lords gang.

Denying it to myself, I was yet a budding faggot, a *maricón,* with hots for sundry females, schoolteacher, and fellow student alike, fighting for attention with avoiding glances at other guys' baskets. But up on the latest liberal psychology, I told myself my strong homosexual feelings were "only" fleeting impulses, natural for any true-blue hetero, Lenny Bruce–tolerant, Hugh Heffner–type sympathetic toward fags and dykes.

I knew I was simultaneously hot for Ronnie Spector and longing for the guy she and the rest of the Ronnettes were asking to "Be My Baby." "Admiring" Mick Jagger and Ray Davies, just as I had done with Jackie Wilson and James Brown, my head was able to deny what my body and soul were screaming. Those singers drew me with more than just their stage grace and envied male masterfulness. But I didn't dare admit the desire.

Medication for my hurt

Eros one way or another is never denied. And my denials were swept away by external, society-wide chaos greater than my own. The psychedelic, New Left years provided my chance to jump ship. Blindly — or so I thought — I careened into the mad mix of what I didn't quite know. But anything was better than the hell at home. High school graduation and I was gone. I had already been blocking out large chunks of childhood memory. The promise of drugs, sex, and rock 'n' roll meant I could block out a lot more a lot quicker.

It didn't matter with what or whom. After all, it was all going to end ... either in lysergic nirvana or apocalyptic flames. My expectations as to which seesawed manically; the apocalypse usually won. My two strongest images from the time are that photo of the Vietnamese peasant clutching her napalmed infant, shouting in pain and rage at the American bombers in the sky; and, much closer to home, the memory of my darker, older sister tricking and chasing the White Ghost of the barrio, she who died alone, disease-riddled in some tenement before I knew.

At first, I used fucking like any other drug: to forget and escape. Waking up in a roomful of naked people, wine bottles, rolling papers, and reefer strewn across the floor wasn't utopia for me. It was medication for both my hurt and my hatred of self even as I felt inferior to straight white males and riled at their external political mechanizations. I was not questioning or reflecting, just reacting. Twelve-Step programs[1] talk about "bottoming out." It happened to me through the excesses of drugs, sex, rock 'n' roll, and revolution-for-the-hell-of-it. Deeper and deeper grew the rut of revolving conflict, pushing out past and future for the sake of a feeling-numbing present. I needed a discourse understandable to the warring sides of me: Anglo and *Puertoriqqueno,* male and female, intellect and feeling, homosexual and heterosexual. Around and around I revolved in hermaphroditic self-rape: father brutalizing my mother, me taking on both roles and the consequent wounds, elliptic repetitions of trauma.

Virginity twice lost

But my bisexuality was sending out word, stronger each time I had sex, even as I strove to bury myself in the big "O" and momentary release. The message was there when I lost my virginity *twice*— heterosexually and homosexually.

I had "straight" sex for the first time with an older divorcée. The flash and imagery that swept by with the arousal and satiation of desire startled me. As we fucked, a man's form appeared in my mind's eye, then faded. As I thrust deeper into her in response to her tightening thighs wrapped around me, the awareness of being male inside a female momentarily receded, leaving me as the woman she, as the man, was fucking.

I went down on another man, another older person, a carpenter, working class like me, for the first time soon after. I was overwhelmed by the same wash of changing sensations and images when I first felt his cock snaking in and out of the round oval of my wet, sucking lips, tasted the bitter thick cum upon my tongue, and swallowed hard. I had the same strange, scary feeling of something more going on than just getting off — boundaries being crossed, thresholds being stepped over, never to be recrossed again. A vague realization began to dawn, that everything the patriarchy had been whispering in our ears was untrue.

I realize now that my psyche was setting its own course toward reclamation of my heart and mind. What I felt as sexual confusion was actually soul-healing. The gay liberation and feminist movements, and my own growing understanding of psychology and spirituality finally helped me understand. I became a psychotherapist and a Buddhist. All these things helped me see my bisexuality as expressive of my whole. Being cannot be split into male or female, gay or straight, self and other, active and passive, subject and object. Life is not neat, distinct, manipulatable, controllable categories.

Psyche's tongue endless interwoven

For many, sex is terrifying because it can flood all boundaries, all categories, unless one can somehow dam it up or push it back down. Sex *is* a language of the soul, but it makes too intimate a connection with everything in the cosmos. Unsuppressed, unlabeled, unexploited, unmanipulated, Eros cuts through the societal lies and mass denial and rationalizations we assume are "reality."

Eros as Psyche's tongue, as intercourse with the world on all levels. "Making" the soul is making the world. Sucking and fucking, rubbing and frigging, licking and lapping refuse reduction and labeling. Sex quivers, flushs, throbs, and hardens; shakes and shudders, groans, cries, gushes, and softens with its strength and tenderness. There is no one else's standard to follow. You becomes we becomes life.

Fucking is separation's end. Sex in its imaginativeness can play out all categories and distinctions to the maximum, twist and reverse them, mix and match them until their actual relativity and mutually dependent character is revealed.

Bisexuality can be soul-healing at its deepest. Through it we can tap into a commonality, an empathy, a state of communion that shares with others all of life's fullness. Each of us is far broader and vaster than sexism and its overseers can stand. Our psyches are limitless. "Thrown into the world" I "splattered," but at that very instant, "threads" had unwoven, which have been years cohering into a *mandala* both new and ancient, unique yet primal, making me anew.

If healing is the integration of what had been disharmonious, salvation is achievable by the realization of inseparability, and struggles are won by mutuality and unity. The design becomes clearer each day.

I came into a social world whose constructs and dictums had already fast begun to crumble, only no one was ready to notice, let alone admit it, so remarkable is our human penchant for denial. Inherited fragments I'd thought myself hopelessly afflicted with, I realize now were really also the beginnings of recoherence.

Sex is the lifeblood of this new cohesiveness. When young, I thought it was just another conflict, the roughest of all. Yet the psyche spoke of wholeness, gradually inspiring me to remake myself, wholecloth it seemed, from fragments of a dying empire and its pathogenic "norms."

Rather than another conflict or confusion, my bisexuality is the living of a truer *Selfhood* not confined to or constricted by conditioning imposed from outside, which arises from a matrix of shared existence and mutuality increasing.

Threesomes touch me

Touching a reality beyond words, the bloody ground has become a sweet, sad bedsheet of reconciliation. Three bodies are conjoined, I in a woman, a man in me. Am I still clinging to my mother while trying to win my father's withheld love? Is my life a revised replay of the primal scene I witnessed as a child, I possessing both my mother and father? If true, then my bisexuality can play with even these neuroses and make them life-affirming.

I recall what Buddha taught: Our suffering is also the source of our awakening. In mid-fuck I look up at the sky and see its azure clarity through the open ruin roof of a dying empire. And there, sitting on an immense opal pearl upon the surface of which flow the events of my life, right leg extended languidly before the crocked left, is Avalokitesvara, Buddhism's Indo-Tibetan embodiment of compassion. He is dressed in white, cloud-colored silken robes, necklaced in gold, with a thin circlet crown, sun-bright, from which cascade thick ringlets of black hair. As orgasm approaches I stare at his roseate, rouged cheeks, the long limpid lashes of his kohl-rimmed eyes, and his slightly parted, pink lips. Life simultaneously rushes in upon me and resonates out from me. Avalokitevara's countenance changes ... becomes that of Kuan Yin, his Chinese female counterpart, Maiden of Mercy, yet Mother of Us All, almond-eyed, turquoise-jewelled, the same black hair piled high above a silver tiara and crowned by a gossamer veil. Quivering cherry lips smile from a sparkling moon-ivory face.

Back and forth that visage shifts, like the ebb and flow of gently audible waves upon a shoreline, with the grace of breeze-kissed clouds across an ever-extending sunset horizon. And as it does, the rocking and rhythm of making love becomes the mantra, *Om mani padme hum ... om mani padme hum ... om mani padme hum ...*

And I know I'm coming closer to being like "He Who Clasps Both the Lotus and the Gem..."

Note

1. Alcoholics Anonymous (AA), etc.

THE BI·MONTHLY

Newsletter of the Bisexual Center

Volume 7 Number 4

BiPOL
EDUCATE ▼ ADVOCATE ▼ AGITATE

July–August 1983
Bisexuals
Washingto

North Bi Northwe

BiWays

Hasbia

Action
Bi Women

The Newsletter of the
Seattle Bisexual Women's Networ

BI-LINES

Bay Area Bisexual
Network Newsletter

Building the Bisexual Community

News, Views, and Networking
sexuality
The North American Journ

BOTH SIDES NOW

SIDE BY SIDE

PHOENIX

rising

Bi
Women

The
Asian/Pacifica
Sisters
Newsletter

The Newsletter of the Boston Bisexual Women's Network

III.

The bisexual community: "Are we visible yet?"

Room for you*

But they say there's room for one kind in a heart that's true
But I'm finding more and more I've got room for you

Now some say man and woman are the only lasting bond
Others love their own kind, while others call them wrong
Well the love I've shared with women's been the center of my song
And the hand stretched to my brothers
Has been burned but still is strong

And some of you don't like it
I can see it in your face
You say pick one or the other
Rest your heart in just one place

But the tides are always shifting, the land is never still
You cannot tame a river and bend it to your will
Boundaries I believed in are melting into sand
Now it's me and my own footsteps starting over once again
But they say there's room for one kind...

---

* From the third verse of "Room for You."

Overview[1]

Without community, there is no liberation, only the most vulnerable and temporary armistice between an individual and her [his] oppression. But community must not mean shedding of our differences, nor the pathetic pretense that these differences do not exist ... It is learning how to stand alone, unpopular and sometimes reviled, and how to make common cause with those others identified as outside the structures, in order to define and seek a world in which we can all flourish. It is learning how to take our differences and make them strengths.

— Audre Lorde, *This Bridge Called My Back*[2]

What is community?

Culture. Stories. Poetry. Dance. Song. Rituals. History. Friends. Family. Laughter. Shared meals, the way we build our homes, and live our lives. All races, cultures, classes, ages, abilities. Bisexual community.

What is bisexual community? What is our history? Who are we? What are the stories that make up our lives?

Bisexual behavior has existed throughout time. However, since it has been trivialized as a phase or stage to heterosexuality or homosexuality, our historical sense of bisexual community identity is vague, hidden, nonexistent.

As bisexuals, our situation is similar to any population who have been made invisible by the dominant culture. In the flush of the early women's movement the recovery of the massive erasure of matriarchal culture was an exciting process that built pride and gave women a sense of our place in "herstory." As women we sifted through photographs, paintings, poetry, songs, stories, history lessons with new eyes and ears. We reclaimed those labeled "God" who had round bodies, breasts, and vulvas and reclaimed the works of women who had to use their husband's or father's names so they could produce the paintings, music, and art that was the passion of their souls. People of color, lesbians, and gay men have been and are also recovering a sense of their history and are tapping into their roots with a growing sense of pride.

Bisexuals must begin this work. We have to learn to look and listen carefully at what information is given and draw our own conclusions.

We too must identify the obvious, reclaim our writers, poets, painters, and activists. We must reclaim those who danced, sang, cooked, cleaned, lead everyday lives or lead political revolutions. By doing this, we will gain a sense of pride in ourselves which will strengthen our understanding of what we mean by bisexual community.

Who are we? What are the stories?

There have been rare "out" bisexual communities that we know of: The Bloomsbury group is one. It flourished in Great Britain at the turn of this century and included famous writers Virginia Woolf and Vita Sackville-West. Because Bloomsbury members were writers themselves and have been subsequently studied by Western literary scholars, documentation of their bisexuality is readily accessible. They were white, upper-class, well-educated. Their privileged status granted them the freedom to be public and vocal about who they were, what they were doing, and why they were doing it. Bisexual people lacking such privilege could not be so public about their lives.

Because of social prejudice and outright discrimination, it's terribly difficult to compile a list of historical figures who've had significant love relationships with both genders throughout their lives. We do know, though, for example, that Anaïs Nin, Edna St. Vincent Millay, Alice Moore Dunbar-Nelson, Colette, Frida Kahlo, Angelina Weld Grimke, and Lorraine Hansberry are all women who wrote about or were known to have had both kinds of love relationships. Walt Whitman, D.H. Lawrence, Oscar Wilde, James Baldwin, Ram Dass, John Maynard Keynes, Langston Hughes, W. Somerset Maugham, and Gore Vidal[3] are a few of the many men who have loved both men and women.

Many popular artists have had the leeway or took the power to express their sexuality not usually allowed "ordinary" people in a sexist homophobic society — Janis Joplin, Elton John, David Bowie, Tallulah Bankhead, Madonna, Sandra Bernhard, James Dean, Errol Flynn, Boy George, and Patti LaBelle and many other artists and show-biz people have expressed the importance of not limiting the relationships in their lives.

A recent film, *Looking For Langston,* strongly suggests that black poet Langston Hughes was homosexual. The gay filmmakers who made this beautifully erotic meditation on his life are now fighting with Hughes's angry family over the showing of the film. Several Hughes biographies document his heterosexual experience. As so often occurs, both the homosexual and heterosexual sides are engaged in a do-or-die battle to claim Hughes as one of their own, when quite likely, he was bisexual.

Like Hughes, blues singer Ma Rainey was also part of the Harlem Renaissance — that flowering of black artistic culture centered in Harlem, New York City. In a recent study of Rainey, Sandra Lieb concludes, "There is strong evidence to indicate that Ma Rainey ... was bisexual."[4] She also alleges that Bessie Smith, who wrote and sang wonderfully heterosexual lyrics, was Rainey's lover; thus Smith was bisexual, as well.

Before the Harlem Renaissance there flourished in Europe a literary circle of exiled Americans that included Gertrude Stein, Alice B. Toklas, Djuna Barnes, and Natalie Barney, all widely known as lesbians. But, at least one in the circle, Djuna Barnes, had heterosexual relationships as well. Charles Henri Ford, author of the first gay novel, and part of the literary circle, asserted recently that the clear distinctions we presently experience between gay and straight worlds did not exist back then. Many people moved casually between the gay and straight worlds and felt they belonged in both. They did not feel they had to choose or declare undying loyalty for one or the other group. In fact, some of these artists now claimed as gay, such as Djuna Barnes, refused that label for themselves and were more comfortable with no label, or, if with any label at all, bisexual. As Ford says, "They're always referring to Djuna now as a lesbian, but ... she had many lovers, male and female."[5]

Within all populations, bisexuals have lived, loved, and felt at home. The history of our community has been recorded quite accurately at times, but the monosexual orientation misses the obvious bisexual experience. As we see the world with new eyes and ears, we will begin to feel our growing community.

Building community
Nowhere do we know of a bisexual community emerging in reaction to the polarization of heterosexual and homosexual people as is happening today. There are political circumstantial reasons for this, the key escalator being AIDS, which has exposed the false assumptions supporting this charade. Building bisexual community is crucial. Community gives a shared sense of pride and acceptance of the whole. It breaks down the isolation and fear, giving strength to those who come out. As people identify with each other, a sense of caring and sharing emerges. The only way to fight AIDS and discrimination is with people who feel a responsibility and pride for their community, and who share a sense of history, belonging, and trust.

However, we have to carefully and consciously acknowledge and respect all our various lesbian, gay, and heterosexual experiences, as well as the racial, class, and cultural differences in this emerging community.

Are we visible yet?
So, why does the attitude exist that there is no bisexual community, and why has it been used against us so effectively? Why have we "accepted" invisibility, and why haven't we, up until this point, projected a more visible presence, creating a prominent community that even the most

virulent biphobes would have to recognize? The answer, of course, is that this is the way oppression operates, in this case bisexual oppression. On some level bisexual people believe (have internalized) the lie that what is shared isn't community, isn't a commitment of any significance, isn't comparable to those communities we are in (lesbian, gay, hetero-sexual, etc.). The fear is that, if we come out, we will "lose" these other communities. We will be isolated, targeted for attack — simply put, rejected.

Anyone who has ever been closeted for any reason knows the fear of exposure and alienation. We live in a society that is based and thrives on opposition, on the reassurances and "balanced" polarities of dichotomy. The decision to come out as a bisexual makes the issues surrounding personal behavior and labels confusing because

we are challenging
the fundamental
belief system
that posits
everything
into
either/or
left/right
light/dark
male/female
masculine/feminine
hetero/homo
white/of color
upper class/working class
middle class/homeless
young/old
able-bodied/differently abled

No room
for all points
in b e t w e e n

No room
for the perfect
Kinsey 2,3,4,5

and

absolutely
no room

for both/and
    middle ground
    dawn/dusk
    transsexual
    transvestite
    bisexual
    mixed race/culture/class
    middle age
    temporarily abled/hidden disabilities

By trusting ourselves and our experience enough to come out, we are saying that differences are to be celebrated and appreciated, not denied or downplayed. When we bisexuals tell our stories openly and honestly it exposes the complexity of truth and moves us closer to an inclusive community. And, as the people in this section show, the possibilities are endless. This is no doubt a confusing and disturbing thought to those heterosexual and homosexual people invested in the image of a fence that neatly separates one from the other, maintaining a static level of security.

The liberation of bisexual people is intimately tied to that of lesbians, gay men, women, people of color, and the working class. We cannot back down in the face of discrimination. We must come to terms with our personal sexualities and identities as bisexual people, of whatever race, class, or gender. As we understand the links between oppressions we learn to challenge them together as a community. The issues of sexual orientation are at once intimately personal, and also deeply political. The fact that there is a closet at all is a testament to oppression.

Come out, come out wherever you are!

We need a Bisexual Community more than ever. I don't think we should turn our backs on the lesbian and gay communities; certainly, many of us are grateful for the support and role models we found even in the most biphobic communities, but I do think it's time we stopped bothering the nice dykes and faggots with our timid pleas for validation. We need to create a bifriendly place here, and the best way to do that is to be Bisexual and proud, Bisexual and brave, Bisexual and honorable. For that, we need to find each other. Besides, some of us are out here already and we're waiting for you!   — Elise Krueger[6]

Coming out is not an easy task. It takes courage and practice. We want to make it clear that we do not mean to apply undue pressure, nor are we discrediting those in the closet. We recognize those of you who live in places where coming out is more difficult or impossible to do. The personal stories presented here demonstrate that each of us comes out in our own way, at our own pace. It is still very important to practice coming out, so that when the opportunity arises you will be ready.

We are serious about practicing. Come out to your cat, for instance, or your dog, or just get in front of a mirror, look yourself squarely in the eye, and say, "I'm a bisexual." Do this a few times, and have a good laugh, or maybe a cry. Coming out is an act of courage. Don't be hard on yourself. It isn't easy, but the reward is worth it. Look yourself in the eye, it starts there.

As bisexuals we have to create a safe supportive atmosphere in our lives. We have to sometimes ask for it from people we don't know, and yes, demand it from people who love and respect us. How can we feel secure or have self-respect if we are closeted from our friends and allies? How else do we change the stereotypes and the media image? How else do we get the respect we deserve if we are hiding from it? What does our community look like? We are the ones who must define it.

It is obvious how important visibility and validation are to us as a community. AIDS is a crisis of deadly epidemic proportions. Bisexuals are constantly listed in disease statistics. How many bisexuals are closeted for fear of losing the "supportive" community they belong to? Is selling ourselves short worth this awful price? We are seeing the tip of the iceberg where AIDS is concerned. Double lives are exploding in the cities, suburbs, and rural areas of America. We have to take ourselves seriously and replace negativity with positive images which build pride. The power of pride can never be underestimated. The truth is we are fighting for our lives.

We know the phrase "we are everywhere" gets trite. However, within the context of our emerging bisexual community, it is not. Realizing we're everywhere fills us with joy and pride, at once ending our isolation and presenting us with a variety of people who share a common experience. Yet it is crucial at this point to look at our differences and find where there are connections. We know only too well, from past organizing experience, that the best way to slow a wave of collective pride from developing is for fear to take control, so that different factions, affinities, and tendencies are pitted against each other. Building coalitions begins at home, begins with us. There is no one right way to be a bisexual; there are many.

The goal is to be able to look anyone in the eye, and with a sense of our history, acknowledge the truth of who we are. Yes, some of us are swingers, and some of us are married and monogamous; some of us are proud dykes and faggots, sex radicals and sexworkers, and parents and grandparents; some are prudes and some are celibates. Some of us are transvestites and transsexuals. Many of us are courageous people living with AIDS and HIV infections. We are all ages, colors, abilities, ethnicities, classes. Our identity as bisexual people and our desire for recognition unites us. The diverse voices in this section arc but a slice of the emerging bisexual community. They speak to the trials, tribulations, and joys of being bisexual and of the right to love whomever we choose.

Notes

1. Parts of this overview appeared in other forms in: Lani Kaahumanu, "The Bisexual Community: Are We Visible Yet?," *Civil Disobedience Handbook for the National March for Lesbian and Gay Rights,* October 1987; Lani Kaahumanu, "Are We Visible Yet?," *Coming Up!,* San Francisco, June 1987; and Lani Kaahumanu, Keynote Address, Fifth Annual East Coast Bisexual Network Conference, Harvard University, Cambridge, Mass., May 13–14, 1989.

2. Audre Lorde, "The Master's Tools Will Never Dismantle the Master's House," in *This Bridge Called My Back: Writings by Radical Women of Color* (pp. 98–101), ed. Cherrie Moraga and Gloria Azundula, Kitchen Table Press, 1983.

3. Dell Richards has compiled the names of many of these women in *Lesbian Lists,* Boston: Alyson Publications, 1990. Dr. Fritz Klein's soon-to-be-reprinted *Bisexual Option* (New York: Berkeley Books, 1980) lists some of these same people and more in the chapter "The Bisexual in History and the Arts."

4. Sandra R. Lieb, *Mother Of The Blues: A Study of Ma Rainey,* University of Massachusetts Press, 1983.

5. Gabriel Rotello, "Present at the Creation: C.H. Ford, Author of the First Gay Novel, Talks about The Village in the '20s, Paris in the '30s, and Coming Out 40 Years before Stonewall," *Outweek,* December 17, 1989.

6. Elise Krueger, letter to Lani and Loraine, 1988.

Elizabeth Reba Weise

Bisexuality, *The Rocky Horror Picture Show*, and me

The sun falling through high windows onto the strong lines of a classmate's shoulders, highlighting her silhouette. The clear, happy features of a man dancing to the Talking Heads, his whole body caught up in the music. A smile, the line of an arm, the timbre of a voice. Connections and making gingerbread. Life is not always about strictures, cultural or countercultural, and sexuality is not always about gender, but feeling. Some men, some women catch my heart, make me take a deep breath before I go on.

I have sat at a table in a bar silent with shock and been unable to move for want of the dark-eyed man talking earnestly to me. I have stood in seeming indecision as pumpkin soup was heated up for my dinner, wondering how my arms could leave my sides and slide around the narrow waist of the graceful woman before me. These feelings come first. What happens with them afterwards, the realities of introducing a man or a woman to this or that circle of friends, comes later. That is the realm of politics. I live in both worlds, but I make my choices from my heart, and let the rest fall into place. My heart and body are not up for discussion.

I came of age in that odd non-time, the 1970s, the decade that felt like a long afternoon nap after the rush and activity of the sixties. So let me begin by explaining how I *didn't* become a bisexual. It wasn't because I couldn't make up my mind, it wasn't because I have an overactive libido, and it wasn't because it was a hip thing to do in the glitter rock seventies. It did have to do with everything else in the universe, or perhaps nothing.

When I was thirteen I made a list of all the things I wanted to do in my life. Two of the top items were someday having a girlfriend and someday having a boyfriend. I wrote romantic stories about meeting serious young women over the recorder music files at the library and then falling in love on rainy walks after folk dances. And even in those stories, when the other woman would declare herself to be a lesbian, I'd say, "And I'm bisexual."

I have always considered myself a feminist. I remember reading about the ERA marches downtown, and finding *Sappho Was a Right-On Woman* at the library, and being overwhelmed by the ideas. The political basis for the essays escaped me, but the ideas struck home. I knew that out there somewhere were women who cared about things that were important, who didn't play silly games with silly boys about who got to touch what when. Somewhere there were people who met on another, more honest level.

I worked part-time at the library, where the (doubtlessly) lesbian librarian took me aside and gave me *Rubyfruit Jungle* to read "to see if it would be appropriate for the Young Adult Section" and went out of her way to get ahold of a pamphlet about "Being Gay in High School" put together by some really radical high school students in Ann Arbor.

In some ways the seventies were a magic time to grow up with an alternate sexuality. In our sophomore year of high school my class discovered *The Rocky Horror Picture Show*. We'd talk someone into driving us to the Friday midnight showing and sit in the dark and watch five hundred rowdy teenagers sing along to lyrics about the joys of gay sex. I watched Magenta and Columbia fall into bed together and imagined the feel of soft skin under my hands. I'd read about lesbians, but here were two women actually touching each other, and the kids around me weren't disgusted. They were straight, as far as I knew, but I felt a little safer as on stage people my age danced out the parts, boys wearing fishnet tights and high heels, girls running their hands seductively down one another's bodies. In the movie, everyone was bisexual, and it wasn't dark or dreary, but playful. The guys at school who made fag jokes still sang out in the call-and-response ritual of the movie. When Brad discovers he's been in bed with Dr. Frankenfurter instead of his girlfriend and moans, "I thought it was the real thing," all the would-be macho studs yelled out, "It is, Brad, it is."

Having read about those wonderful lesbians who were out there somewhere, but not at my high school, I went looking for them. In the tenth grade I signed up for the Northwest Women's Action Conference. Riding the bus out to the university, I tried to imagine what I would find there, what I would dare do. After walking past the door a few times to get up my courage, I finally managed to go into the lesbianism workshop. I think I expected someone to plunk themselves down next to me and take me under their wing. Of course no one talked to the scared-looking fifteen-year-old sitting at the side of the room. The discussions meant nothing to me. I left still no closer to finding that elusive lover who would at the same time be my best friend.

I did fall in love of course, with my best friend. And a few others along the way. I knew that talking about it wasn't going to get me anywhere. I told a family friend that I liked women and men, and his response was "I hope you get together with men first." I asked why. He said, "Because if you end up with a woman first you'll never bother with men." I came out to myself, but as *what?*

That was the problem. It was easy to be a lesbian. There were *evil forces* working against lesbians, and being one put you automatically on the side of all that was good and right. But I knew that I was as interested in men as I was in women. So when I met an intellectual, English-speaking socialist from Sweden at a science fiction convention, I was only momentarily saddened that he was male. Being seventeen and in love was enough for the time being. After living two years in Lund, Sweden, I began to rethink the whole thing. I'd joined the local women's center and spent many cold afternoons poring over its library, looking for love stories between women. They all seemed to be in Danish, which meant I spent lots of time at the local library with dictionaries trying to figure out the plot lines. I got crushes on women I met, none of whom had the slightest lesbian tendencies.

So I went home to Seattle, bound and determined to finally *be a lesbian.* I almost managed it. I hung out at the younger women's night at the Lesbian Resource Center. I went to a women's coffeehouse where another young woman took a fancy to me. One day, as I was frantically studying for finals, she showed up on my doorstep demanding a back rub.

I remember kneading the soft flesh of her back, wondering dazedly if my straight roommates would come back before I'd decided to either ask her to leave or take her into my room. It was a long back rub, because I was trying to decide if making love with a woman was worth making love with someone I wasn't particularly attracted to. In the end I did the honorable thing, and told her to go home because I needed to study.

And before my big chance came again, I fell in love — with a man. We met at a party where the lines of sexual preference were tenuous at best. To the pounding of The Clash, swarms of politically active types danced court around each other. He sent his lesbian housemate over to check me out while he danced with a woman she had her eye on. In that atmosphere your interest and not your persuasion mattered. I remember thinking, "But he was supposed to be a woman." However, he *was* clear-thinking and deep-minded and appreciated good science fiction. In the following years he introduced me to *The Hitchhiker's Guide to the Galaxy,* Bob Dylan, and Miss Manners. I decided what sex he was didn't matter.

That went on for many years. At times we lived together, at times we lived apart. During one of those times I went to the lesbian support group at the university the night they talked about bisexuality, and kept going back. One evening a born-again baby dyke, all het up about her newly won status as Oppressed Person, shouted at me, "You oppress us by sleeping with men! You steal our woman energy!" I stopped going to the support group.

I learned not to allow myself to be attracted to straight women after spending a long winter mooning over a voluptuous woman from my Danish class. She would invite me over to her house to study etymology. I would spend long hours lying on the floor of her room, listening to her talk about how all of her friends from high school were now lesbians, and how she wondered when her turn would come. Then she'd ask me to brush her long auburn hair. Finally, when I thought I couldn't possibly be mistaken, I put it to her that perhaps her chance had now come. I felt her neck stiffen under my hands. "Oh, no ... I mean ... I'm not that way. I mean, that's not what I want." It was years before I could even look at women with long hair.

Then, finally, I found a girlfriend. I was working at the women's commission on campus and pulled in a young woman who was cautiously reading the bulletin boards outside our office. We ended up in a feminist discussion together and one evening at a potluck she mentioned she was gay. I hadn't seen it before, but suddenly I couldn't see anything else.

It was a wonderful thing to be young, in love, and a dyke. It was vindication. Walking down the street hand-in-hand just daring anyone to say anything, I suddenly felt as if everything in my life had fallen into place. I was attracted to a women. I was in love with a woman. I was a lesbian.

But reality broke through soon enough. There was the fact that I wasn't a "real" dyke, defined by Kate Clinton as "penis-pure and proud." Again, after the honeymoon of acceptance, everyone was waiting for me to renounce my feelings for men. I wasn't part of the family.

My girlfriend and I broke up. I got back together with my boyfriend. I began an existence as a closeted bisexual in the lesbian community. My hair got shorter and shorter. One day I realized I felt uncomfortable walking down the street hand-in-hand with my lover for fear someone would see us and my cover would be blown.

I moved out again. A friend and I rented a huge old blue farmhouse in the middle of Seattle and by default started a bisexual women's household. The women who answered our ads for "nonhomophobic, nonheterophobic" housemates had an amazing tendency to blurt out at some point in their interview, "Well, I've been out as a lesbian for a long time, but last year I somehow got together with this man..."

A bisexual women's group had just begun in town, and it started meeting in our house. We were a feminist bisexual nexus. We held support groups, potlucks, slumber parties, dance parties, and political screaming arguments. It was everything I'd always wanted from the lesbian community, without the fear of getting thrown out. Being a part of the Seattle Bisexual Women's Network gave me the support to stop worrying about what other people thought about my sexuality and get on with life. We helped each other relearn that it's what you do and not who you sleep with that matters.

The baseline fact is that I, and many of my friends, am drawn to both women and men. For some, the gender is immaterial. In my case it is not. The differences are too great, in culture, in understanding, in pheromones. I think many of us who take the label bisexual waver back and forth a great deal, wondering if indeed we are bisexual enough, just as lesbians worry if they are lesbian enough. Certainly heterosexuals spend a great deal of time posturing to prove that they are straight enough.

What are the differences? In comparing one person to another, there can be no absolutes. I do not always respond to women in "this" way, always respond to men in "that" way. There are ebbs and flows. At some deeper level I find that I am more immediately attracted to men. The gut level desire, the chemical attraction, comes most often with them. Is this two decades of training by our sexist culture? Is this a basic fact of biology, that I am destined to always lean in the direction of those Y chromosomes? Does it matter?

I believe it does not. Note that I said the desire is "most often" for men. I remember a warm summer day when a red-haired woman strode into the deli where I worked, and I couldn't speak for the sheer lust she brought forth in me. I didn't know her, didn't know about her, but her physical presence left me tongue-tied and panting. Is this a chemical component to attraction that (for me) occurs more frequently in the opposite sex, but which is also found in women? Is this a slight break in the oppressive compulsory heterosexuality of the culture I grew up in? Again, does it matter? The feelings are there. We don't stop to ask where the impulse comes from when we kiss.

There is no question in my mind that I like women better than I like men. Ninety percent of my friends are women. The person who has been closest to me for the last fifteen years, my best friend, is a woman. The people I fill my life with, spend my time with, choose to be with, are women. Perhaps this is the cultural component. As children, girls gravitate toward other little girls. As an adult I find the pattern hasn't changed. I do have male friends, men I care for very much. But they are few and far between, and the level of intimacy I know with them seldom approaches what goes on between my women friends and I.

The reality I have slowly come to recognize in myself is that while I am generally more attracted to men, there are women who fan those same fires within me. And while I like and care for men, I choose to spend most of my time with women. This is the crucial intersection — the men whom I like and am attracted to and the women whom I am attracted to and like. These are the people with whom I become involved. As I look for a mate to settle down with, I cannot imagine what gender this person will be. As I near thirty, the whys seem less important, while the hows become more interesting.

Michael Brewer

Two-way closet

Growing up on Fire Island, New York, in the 1970s allowed plenty of opportunity for me to explore my crushes on both boys and girls. I felt uninhibited in doing so. I understood that men could choose to be with men, women with women, and men with women. These role models were all around me. Yet never did I find a role model for what I was feeling. I failed to understand why a man couldn't choose to be with men and women or why a woman couldn't choose a similar life. I only knew I was different and kept my secret to myself.

I quickly learned how to function in both worlds with smooth efficiency. No one in the gay bar would ever guess I had a girlfriend, and the same went for my straight friends. Why did I keep my two worlds apart? For safety. In gay circles, it was a major *faux pas* to sleep with a "fish," while in the hetero world in which I was raised, to be a fag was an unpardonable offense. This lifestyle bred self-deception and self-contempt. I knew I had to find another way.

I moved to California in 1976. It was the height of the sexual revolution. I still ran up against the stereotypes and prejudices I had grown up with, but on the West Coast it was possible to meet more open-minded people. I began to meet other bisexual men and women who were also tired of deceit. I found that the gay society disliked us for our ability to "hide" in straight society. Most of the bisexuals I met hardly dared to tell their straight family and friends about their secret lives on Gay Street. So we formed "rap groups" or found cliques where we felt safe. One bisexual friend who was able to accept both sides of my sexuality was worth an army of gays or straights.

Many of my bisexual friends could not stand the pressure. Being bisexual often meant disrespect and discrimination from both the gay and straight worlds. Some of my bi friends felt forced into making a choice. My first bi girlfriend ran off and married a "dyke on a bike." It was years before she could face her true bi feelings. To my straight friends, my homosexual feelings were closeted, so to them I was heterosexual. Some of my bi boyfriends got married to straight women. They didn't always tell their new wives and sometimes they didn't give up their bisexuality; they only stifled it. Sadly, all too often, the bushes of San Francisco and highway rest stops now contain their tales of quiet desperation.

I find it hard to blame these friends. I, too, yearned for a lifelong relationship and family. I have always felt that I would never find one person able to satisfy all my needs. Some of my friends settled for the next best thing — many of them suppressing their "other half" in the process. For me, this is the great challenge and often the great tragedy of bisexuality. Satisfying my need for a life partner with just one person is difficult. The nature of my being calls for relationships with both sexes. This is not to say it is impossible to have a monogamous relationship; I know bisexuals who are quite happy and satisfied in monogamous relationships. But, in my experience, I have found it difficult to do.

In order to rectify what I perceived to be an imbalance in my life, I began to integrate my social life. I was still in the closet to many friends and business associates, but found myself spending most of my quality time with those people with whom I felt comfortable. I began to seek what I yearned for: a way of living in peace with my sexuality. I was in college then and in love with a schoolmate. At this point I learned that being bisexual doesn't mean the same thing to everyone. It seems to me that a bisexual doesn't necessarily have to desire women to the same degree that he or she desires men. I feel that this can be more accurately described in percentages such as a 20-percent preference for women and an 80-percent preference for men. The boy I was in love with at school had a 90-percent preference for women and a 10-percent preference for men. Too bad for me, I needed more than 10 percent. Several semesters passed in a less than satisfactory manner. A new woman enrolled one fall and fell in love with me. She was 70-percent straight and 30-percent gay. Eventually we all lived together in a stormy passionate triangle and most of our needs were met. It was short-lived, but it showed me that it was possible to live an openly bisexual lifestyle.

Not long after I was finished with school, I began a spiritual exploration. I began to see my sexuality as less important, and that relationships are based on much deeper foundations than sexual pref- erences. I put my quest for my life partner on the back burner while I pursued inner peace. During this time, I found my life partner. In 1984 I met a European woman in California on her own spiritual quest. We formed a strong, instant, and lasting bond. I told her about my sexuality;

it seemed insignificant in comparison to all that we were feeling and experiencing together. She was not bisexual and had very little experience in this area. She taught me that relationships are based on much larger things. We planned to live together in California, and we married to ease the immigration problems. For a while the sexuality issue slept.

Later when it awoke, I began to dream. I felt restless and realized I had done what so many of my friends had done: choosing one side while suppressing the other. It scared me into action.

Although my wife had talked about my sexuality before our relationship, and had met my gay and bisexual friends, she had yet to deal with the reality of my sexual feelings. I realized that bisexuality meant nonmonogamy to me. At first I had anonymous encounters or dishonest short-term ones. They left me with feelings of self-loathing and revulsion. The pressure built until I had to pour all my pent-up feelings to my wife. She was shocked that I could be going through so much inner turmoil without sharing it with her or showing it to her. She didn't know what a consummate actor I could be.

I found the Pacific Center in Berkeley, where they have a weekly support group for married gay and bi men. With her encouragement I began to attend. Most of the men in this group were older and divorced or in the process of divorcing. However, I did meet a man my age who was married and trying to make it work. A relationship developed between us and a friendship grew between our wives. It was not easy for any of us. My wife and I went through many traumas and sleepless nights coming to terms with my bisexuality. I experienced feelings of guilt and other emotional issues. Together we all learned that although a relationship is built on a deep and spiritual foundation, sex is still an issue and can be filled with strong emotions. It proved too much for my boyfriend and his wife; their marriage ended. He wanted me to end mine and go away with him. I couldn't. I knew that the woman I was with was my life partner.

Since then we bought a home and moved outside of the city. I have developed close platonic friendships with several men in similar situations. For a long time I was unfulfilled in my bisexuality. One day I decided to change all that. I contacted the local gay and lesbian newsletter, and with their encouragement, wrote an article about my bisexuality. I received over sixty supportive, affirming letters and phone calls. As a result we now have a bisexual support group and a bisexual social club here. I also write a regular feature entitled "Bi the Way." These activities have opened a world of friendship, support, and satisfaction for me. I feel enriched and empowered. I only wonder why I didn't stand up for my bisexuality earlier.

Today I live a very full life. My wife and I are happy to be raising our baby girl. I have a relationship with a bisexual man who is supportive of my chosen lifestyle. He and my wife are friends. I feel freed of my own bondage, and this has freed me creatively. I am writing more and more, and with greater clarity. I can happily say that I know of dozens of bisexual men and women — most of them live in my own neighborhood.

It seems to me that bisexuals are one of the most closeted groups. I also believe that if we were to stand up and be counted, we would astound the world with our numbers. I now wear my bisexuality as a badge of honor and no longer carry it as a liability.

I am proud of my gay brothers and lesbian sisters. They have made great strides for personal freedom and have done much of the ground-work that has made it possible for me to stand up, affirm my bisexuality, and feel safe in doing so. I believe that it is time to become more visible, to have a group identity and pride.

The palmist knew

I grew up in a small town in the South. When I graduated from high school, I moved sixty miles away to another small town to attend a small college. During my senior year there was a spring carnival and at this carnival a palm reader.

I believe in powers that some may define as occult, so I approached the booth and waited for my turn to ask the questions that would tell the future. What other questions would I ask but "Will I be married?" and "Will I have children?" These are the questions any well-socialized and -trained female would find important. As she held my hand, she said in a very calm, self-confident voice, "Yes, you will be married but when the time comes for you to make that decision there will be two people interested in you. Both these people will want to marry you, and it will be up to you to choose which one you will be with."

Here I sit six years later, twenty-seven years old, and everything she said has come true. There was just one small detail she forgot to add — that I would have to choose between a man and a woman!

I knew at a very young age that I had feelings for women; it was also clear that I was attracted to men. I did not experience any positive lesbian, gay, or bisexual role models growing up in the South, although I do remember two lesbians in my high school. We were in the same gym class. I used to watch them together. I would sit and stare, thinking how gentle and special it was for them to be so close, while other people screamed verbal slurs. I got the message loud and clear that any feelings that I was having about women were wrong, and I dare not tell anyone. I kept them locked away for many years. Being accepted as a black woman was a struggle, there was no way I would ever be accepted if I was a lesbian.

College was the first exposure I had to gay and lesbian people who were out in any public manner. Needless to say this brought up all sorts of feelings for me, mostly complete terror. Of course it was very easy for me to get close to gay men and hang out with them, but get me within ten feet of a lesbian and I would lose it.

I attended a forum at school that supported lesbian and gay rights on campus. There was a panel of lesbian and gay men who basically told their coming-out stories and answered questions. I talked during the discussion about how I was able to be close to gay men but not to lesbians. After the group broke up, one of the professors, a lesbian, came over to me and said, "You know the reason you are so afraid of being close to lesbians is because of your fear of your personal sexual orientation." That was enough to send me flying out the door more terrified than ever before. I remember spending most of my time in college confused because even though I still wanted to be with men, I had all these feelings for women. I did not know how to resolve my feelings, so I continued to stuff them deep inside where they would be safe.

I came out to myself about eighteen months after I graduated from college. After careful research and lots of lesbian friends in my life, I began a relationship with a woman. She had identified as a lesbian all her life. It was crucial to her that I identify as a lesbian, and that I would not be with a man again. I was stuck in another box, having to hide part of myself. There was no room to have feelings for men. I put those thoughts away in that safe place and didn't tell her, or she would leave. The catalyst for me to end that relationship was the process of feeling trapped again. I couldn't honor all of who I was and was being forced to hide half of my feelings. I bought the lies and misinformation about who bisexual people were. It meant I would be invisible; that I wanted to have my cake and eat it too; I would not have a community, and above all else it was "a betrayal of the lesbian community."

I was fortunate to fall in love with one of my best friends who is a bisexual man. In this relationship I learned what it was like to be in a loving relationship where I was allowed all of my feelings about being with men and being with women. I got to be an out bisexual, telling people that I am not straight and I am not a lesbian, this is who I am. What a difference to be supported as a bisexual, to have a place to go and people who can relate to the trails and tribulations of being bisexual in a world that only recognizes heterosexuals, excludes gays and lesbians, and ignores those that fall center point on the spectrum. That relationship ended for many reasons, one of which was my desire to be with a woman again. I learned to love, honor, and respect myself in that relationship and that who I love is who I love. It was then that I had to choose between my best friend, a bisexual man, or exploring my feelings for a woman to whom I had grown close.

So in this chapter of my life I am out as a bisexual. I am also in a wonderful and supportive relationship with a lesbian. Some of us are born on one end of the continuum, while others are on the exact opposite end. Just as much as anyone heterosexual or gay would not want to be forced into denying their sexual orientation, neither do I. It is the heterosexism and the internalized heterosexism that forces me to be on the outside of both communities. I believe true sexual liberation can only come with the acknowledgement of the diversity of orientation that exists within the heterosexual and the gay and lesbian communities.

As the palmist had foretold I would have to make a choice, that choice was between a man and a woman, the choice was about choosing to love myself as a bisexual. After all, love is love is love, isn't it?

Hap Stewart

A healing journey

High in the east the golden eagle sheds a feather on the winds of dawn. Something that was rigid and frozen breaks apart. It is the root. As the sun feather drifts across the sky, the root takes hold. The name of the root is Spring.[1]

I love this description of the East, one of the four directions on the Medicine Wheel. The images speak clearly to my heart and the journey of my soul. Let me say, right from the beginning, that this journey has been and continues to be difficult, inconsistent, mired with resistance from a conditioned mind and addictive behavior. Let me not imply that I'm healed, the journey complete, for there is much work still to do, cautious steps into the unknown and more opening of the heart toward self-love and compassion for others.

You may sense that I'm a contrary person, quietly rebellious to the core. So on that summer day in 1982, when the cardiologist stopped the treadmill test and later intoned, "You have arteriosclerotic heart disease and you may require bypass surgery," it was almost natural for me to question this pronouncement and begin wondering about other possibilities for healing. In a concerned voice he added, "You shouldn't ever get far away from medical care." Amid the confusion and fears I felt, I didn't realize that this was the beginning point for new adventure, difficult lessons, and more questions than answers. At first, these questions focused primarily on the possibilities for short-term survival, yet, gradually, they shifted toward dimensions of mystery — who am I, what is my life purpose, what is the nature of creation, what is the nature of death, what is the nature of healing?

Three years later in the summer of 1985, a counselor at the San Rafael public health clinic explained to me what I already intuitively knew, "You are HIV positive; the tests show antibodies to the virus." There was little shock. Rather, I remember a feeling of deep sadness about the perceived loss of sexuality and the potential loss of life.

There was immediate recognition that my life was irrevocably altered.

Perhaps it's time for some personal biography, facts, that sort of thing. What to say?

I'm a 56-year-old, white, middle-class, bisexual man, father of three mid-twenties children, grandfather of three young children. I was born and went to public schools in suburban New York. I received my college degree and served in the U.S. Army in the 1950s. I lived in New York City thirteen years, came to San Francisco in 1974, then on to Marin County in 1982. I've been through two marriages, two divorces. I've been a social worker, professional photographer, taxi driver, massage practitioner. I am a volunteer AIDS counselor, spiritual explorer, and person with HIV infection.

Did I say bisexual? Yes, I did. Let me say it again. I'm a bisexual man! It feels good to acknowledge that in print. I'm not going to kid you, however. Bisexuality has been and, sometimes still is, a source of personal pain, confusion, guilt, and secrets. Only slowly has it evolved into a source of pride and replenishment and joy. Sometimes it's seemed that not only do heterosexuals and homosexuals misunderstand and not quite trust me, but I neither understand nor quite trust myself. The path toward self-celebration has been long and arduous. Now, while honoring my bisexuality, I need to add that, for me, I find this definition somehow constraining and incomplete. Perhaps, I just see myself as a sexual human being.

So there I was with heart disease which I considered in remission, if not healed, through three years of regular acupuncture and, now, a diagnosis of HIV infection. In the 1970s through 1985 I had acquired ulcers, hepatitis, herpes, venereal disease, shingles, and heart disease. Paradoxically, since I'd never been a hospital inpatient in my adult life, I thought of myself as healthy. While there were elements of self-deception influencing this assessment, I think now there were also elements of truth.

In any case, in the middle of 1985 not much was known about the epidemiology of HIV infection. Treatments such as AZT, fluconazole, and aerosol pentamadine were not yet developed. In general, the medical profession and news media voiced a portrait of worsening health and inevitable death for everyone HIV infected.

This same attitude existed in agencies responsible for administering care. Volunteers were taught how to be present for a client's dying process but not how to support a client in the difficult challenge of living creatively with the virus. Many, if not most, HIV-infected persons also bought into this situation a mindset of inevitable deterioration, which then became self-fulfilling.

There were some individuals who took a different point of view about wellness, but it was not until 1989 that a conceptual shift occurred and HIV infection began to be described as a "chronic manageable disease."

Shrouded by this background of passive doom I made some decisions. These decisions were not made all at once and they are still being recreated today. I call them my Twelve-Steps Program. I decided:

1. that I am capable of staying physically well while exploring the nature of healing.
2. to acknowledge my confusion, anger, and fear of both HIV and death.
3. to learn as much as possible about HIV infection, and there followed almost monthly workshops and seminars for the next three years.
4. to take responsibility for my infection and its healing with the support of a Western-trained M.D., an Eastern-trained doctor of oriental medicine, and other resources.
5. to create my own program of wellness that includes Western medicine, acupuncture, Chinese herbs, vitamin supplements (particularly vitamin C and garlic), meditation, visualization, prayer, and service.
6. not to take pharmaceutical drugs unless absolutely necessary. The only time I've done so was in 1989 (flagyl, to eliminate intestinal parasites).
7. to share information about both the HIV infection and its context, as a bisexual man in the 1970s, with my children, friends, co-workers, and others. This was a gradual and still ongoing process. In 1989 I began to speak before public groups.
8. to create more fun and joy in my life. I bought a motorcycle and took a winter trip alone to Acapulco. Often I was far from medical care.
9. to participate in HIV support groups at Marin AIDS Support Network (MASN) and the Center for Attitudinal Healing. I became a MASN client and requested the emotional support person who has assisted me so much these past three years.
10. to serve others with HIV infection. I have been a volunteer for over four years at MASN. I serve on the Marin County Aids Advisory Commission and pledge money regularly to the Ministry of Light, which spiritually supports our lesbian, gay, and bisexual community.
11. to connect with nature at a deeper level.
12. to explore the dimensions of limitless mystery that lead toward union with self and mother-father-Spirit God.

Now, it's early February 1990. Bay Area activists prepare to participate or boycott this summer's International AIDS Conference in San Francisco while, here in Marin County, we are attempting to create an HIV clinic offering quality medical care for the indigent (there *are* poor people in wealthy Marin) and all persons with HIV infection. It is not clear at this writing whether the Board of Supervisors will respond and appropriate the money. New experimental drugs are being tested. Compound Q and other drugs provide increased hope. HIV persons are living longer lives, yet more people are dying, too. AIDS has become a global epidemic; there are AIDS babies in Romania and PWAs in China, although the governments have tried to conceal their existence. AIDS continues to multiply among people of color, intravenous drug users and, to a lesser extent, the heterosexual population. I work on my own healing and ask my creator for guidance and courage and an open heart. And when I am angry at the heterosexual community of Marin for its indifference to AIDS or the homosexual community for its secretive lifestyle which contributes to that indifference, I ask for the wisdom to express that anger with love.

During the last months of his presidency, President Reagan declared October National AIDS Awareness Month. After eight years of executive silence, this was announced through a White House press release on October 28, 1988. Recently, Reagan's former Surgeon General C. Everett Koop told a House of Representatives subcommittee that a Federal AIDS policy is "almost 10 years overdue!" In January 1990, former President Reagan said that people with AIDS need our understanding. At the time of this writing there are 117,781 cases of AIDS in the United States and more than 70,000 Americans have died. I acquired the HIV virus sometime in the years before 1980 and remain symptom-free.

> *Never yield a minute to despair, sloth, fantasy.*
> *I say to you, you will face pain in your life.*
> *You may lose your limbs, bleed to death,*
> *shriek for hours on into weeks in*
> *unimaginable agony.*
> *It is not aimed at anyone*
> *but it will come your way.*
> *The wind sweeps over everyone ...*
> *Come on everybody! Love your neighbor*
> *love your mother, love your lover,*
> *love the man who just stands there staring.*
> *But first, that's alright, go ahead and cry,*
> *cry, cry, cry your heart out.*
> *It's love, It's your only path.*[2]

Notes

1. Steven Foster and Meredith Little, *The Book of the Vision Quest*, Prentice Hall, 1987.

2. Ted Rosenthal and George Braziller, *How Could I Not Be among You*, Nilgiri Press, 1973.

I like loving. I like mostly all the ways any one can have of having loving feeling in them. Slowly it has come to be in me that any way of being a loving one is interesting and not unpleasant to me.
— Gertrude Stein

J ust because
I made that
wonderful
glorious
leap
to love women,

does not mean
I have lost
the capacity
to love men,

does not mean
I want to deny
my past.

And
just because
I may still
love men

does not mean
it is any easier

to live in
this uncomfortably
(often destructively)
heterosexual
world,

does not mean
I would ever stop
choosing to be with,
to love exclusively,
the woman
who I would want
to be my partner,
should I ever
find her again,

does not mean
I can be
without the support of
a women-loving-women
community.

But both worlds
seem to
find comfort
in their labels,
are threatened by,
and have little
space for
the complexities of
the likes of me.

How silly,
inhuman,
painful,
and outrageous
are the judgments.

I would choose
to suffer isolation
rather than
live a lie,
rather than
betray

this special
part of me
that loves
and can be loved.

Instead,
let us build
a world
where we
rejoice in,
rather than
condemn,
all forms of
positive
non-power-based
loving.

Gray-haired and above suspicion

T he outdoor construction season was slack that 1975 Maine winter.
Our longtime friends, B and C, arranged for their carpenter daughter,
Pat, to survive it by coming west to help me with the major remodeling
I had started in our home. Pat and I hadn't spent a lot of time together,
but we knew and liked each other, were both feminists, and were both
excited by the new women's music. As we measured, sawed, sang, and
nailed, we began to talk about our lives. And after about a week, Pat
started talking to me about her lesbianism, her lover, and her work as
an organizer among Maine lesbians.

Initially, my college Freudian and Jungian training flooded back with
notions of homosexuality as "sick" and "deviant." But soon I began to
think again: Pat had always seemed a healthy-minded person. Her
parents were close friends of ours. Her brothers all seemed okay. I had
even met and liked her partner. Could a mere label change all of that? I
decided my training must be wrong and my observations right. I could
at least listen and learn.

After Pat went back to Maine, I thought more about women as
partners. I had many opportunities to observe women's relationships in
the local feminist community. I worked and played with a variety of
women, lesbian and straight. (No one ever identified herself to me as bi
at that time.) There wasn't a particular moment when I saw the light;
instead, there were gradual changes in my thinking as I observed the
interactions of many of the women I already knew. In retrospect, I think
I was beginning to consider their alternatives for myself.

Through Pat, I had met a very attractive younger woman who was
involved in many of our local feminist activities. I knew she was separated

from her husband and had been romantically involved with several women. Later that year, after months of working and playing together, I realized I was falling in love with her. She was clearly pursuing me. Love bloomed. Finally, I told her I wanted to make love with her.

For my body, the experience was like I had "come home." Making love with a woman was equally wonderful and quite different from making love with a man. I loved both. When I heard the word "bisexual," I knew that must describe me.

Telling my husband was not terribly difficult. Strangely enough, I wasn't as worried about his thinking me "queer" as I was about the "alienation of affections." I knew his younger brother was gay and somehow assumed that would make my same-sex experience all right. But I was terribly confused about loving two people simultaneously. It didn't fit in with the one-and-only American dream I had always accepted. How was he going to deal with sharing me with another person?

He accepted my disclosures with his usual equanimity and curiosity — the disinterested and ever-inquisitive scientist. Here I was, making a shocking revelation, and what did I get but complete acceptance. To him, it was just another way in which I was me, the me he loved.

With considerable fear, I wrote about my new discovery to my dearest friend, Helen. How could I not tell her? But how would I survive if she rejected me after so many years of closeness? She must have realized how scared I was. She called me long distance and reassured me that my discovery was fine and didn't change the love between us.

Back home, I came out to the children, both of whom accepted my preference and my lover. My daughter was delighted to have a label for her sexual preference. She was bisexual too!

By Christmastime I had ended my relationship with that first lover and was nursing a wounded heart. I was devastated to find that not all women could be trusted in love relationships, and that I had to be as careful in my choice of women as in my choice of men.

To help me through that tough time, I went to Maine to visit Helen. She heard my story and tried to console me. She even seemed to understand my particularly bitter disappointment in being treated badly by another woman.

Naturally, since I was nearby, I traveled a little further north to visit Pat's parents. In the evening, when we were alone, I told Betty I was bisexual. I described my wonderful sexual coming out and my enormous disappointment in how the affair had ended. Although I was still in a lot of pain about that particular relationship, I was delighted with my discovery of bisexuality. She listened sympathetically and allowed my tears to flow.

In the morning, after her husband left for work, I went to their bedroom and crawled in under the covers for a comforting snuggle. In

January, sleeping alone in a Maine farmhouse is not the warmest of pastimes.

I was pretty sure I would get the nurturing I wanted because I had joyous and comforting memories of several wonderful weekends Betty and I had spent with a third close woman friend back in the Midwest. The three of us had shared the trials of our lives, laughing, crying, hugging, and snuggling together. And that was long before any of us discovered bisexuality. Imagine my surprise, after a few minutes, to discover Betty was making explicit sexual advances! And the rest, as they say, is "herstory."

We were hours late for our cross-country ski date with Pat. When she finally recognized her mother's passionate glances for what they were, Pat laughed with joy, delighted for her mother and reassured that both Betty and I could now understand more about the joys of Pat's lesbian life.

After that, Betty and I had periodic rendezvous on the East Coast, which included some pretty wild sexual encounters and a couple of weekends which we still consider "herstoric." To my surprise, however, Betty never identified herself as bi.

In the fall of 1976, I began a long-term relationship with A. She was a wonderful woman — witty, intellectual, musical, and bisexual. She had a marvelous way with words and delighted as much as I did in playing both with ideas and language. Together over ten years, we truly blended minds and bodies. Our lovemaking was a celebration of the growth of our relationship. In some ways, the celebrations with A were similar to what I had developed with my husband as we worked on our partnership through many years of marriage. And much of our lovemaking had been delicious indeed. But there was a different quality to celebrating with another woman's body and the sense of unity with someone like me.

Helen was still my best friend and confidante. I still traveled to Maine every year to visit her, and I always spent time with Betty. But as my love for A grew stronger, I wasn't interested in a sexual relationship with any other woman.

After A and I had shared our bi relationship with some of our friends, several of them talked with us about it and later disclosed they were now beginning to think of themselves as bi too! Was it contagious? I don't think so. I think our self-disclosure presented them with a new option — one they hadn't known about before and which described their actual experiences better than straight or gay.

By 1979, there were inexplicable changes in my relationship with my husband. We tried talking, negotiating, and marriage counseling, but got nowhere. Finally, I decided to give up trying to "fix" our relationship. I discussed divorce with our children and notified friends and relations of my intentions. After twenty-three years, I filed for divorce in May 1980.

A few weeks later, he was dead of a brain tumor that had been slowly killing him for five to ten years and that went undetected until the day before he died.

Nothing could have prepared me for the pain of that loss. I was glad for the process of divorce. At least I had done some of my distancing and grieving already. A sang with me at the memorial service, and part of a letter from Betty was one of the readings.

My husband had accepted my relationship with A and the time we spent together. With him gone, she and I grew even closer. But a few years later, she took a job in another state to further her career. I felt abandoned again until we began to make plans for me to move there after my younger child completed high school, and I finished my professional training program.

As planned, after two years, hundreds of phone calls, and many visits, I moved to be near A. With regret, we began to recognize how much we had changed in those years apart. I was more "out" about my bisexuality. She had become a very busy executive, and she had mounting fears her bisexuality would be discovered. She insisted I keep my bisexuality a secret from all of my new friends and avoid meetings of sexual minorities. We eventually split up.

I quit my job and decided to move near the ocean for a period of rest and recuperation. Wanting easy access to beaches and woods, I chose Portland — a choice very much supported by my friends, who lived not far away and by my still closest friend, Helen, who had moved across the border to Canada. So, in the fall of 1986, I moved to Maine.

At first, I mostly grieved. But after about eight months and a thousand miles of beach walks, I began to feel a lot better. Betty and I planned a spring trip to Cape Cod. And one morning, in our motel room, I realized I wanted to make love with her again.

Since then, we have built both romance and friendship. As "older women," we consider ourselves above suspicion when we are demonstrative in public. Gray hair carries a certain immunity we intend to enjoy. Besides, how many cops would want the glory of arresting two grandmothers for public indecency? Better they should look the other way or pretend we're acting normal. And when we get totally carried away, we are usually on the Provincetown beach, where anything goes, or deep in the Maine woods.

Betty has joined me in the Maine Bi People's Network which provides us with companionship and support for our relationship. We have attended two East Coast Bisexual Network conferences together, gathering (and spreading) ideas about alternative lifestyles and receiving support for our partnership. We even met some other bis who were over fifty-five. One was eighty!

For me, our relationship is sometimes difficult. I would like more time together and more spontaneity, but her marriage definitely limits when and where we are together — usually our mutual weekday off and occasional weekends. Still, I think the relationship is worth struggling for. We have been friends for twenty-five years and, in that time, have become very special to each other. Besides, we like the challenge of being among the bisexual pioneers. We believe this lifestyle can work.

I feel particularly lucky about my children's reactions to my coming out because both of them seem totally supportive of my choice. They are comfortable with my coming out, but they don't tell anyone without checking with me first. For the most part, they have had very friendly relationships with my lovers. Sometimes, they tell me why a particular person doesn't seem to be a very good match for me but always with respect for my choice. And they have remained nonpartisan enough so they have continued their own relationships with my exes when they have wanted.

My daughter has been out to all of her friends and lovers. She says, "it is part of who I am." Apparently, she never considered any other preference! We have enjoyed sharing about our bisexuality and even attended some bi events together. Although I suppose our bisexuality has made our mother-daughter talks about sex a little different from the usual, it has all seemed perfectly normal to us.

What of the future? I'm interested in bi-activism. I'm already involved in the struggle for bi recognition within the Unitarian Universalist Association. With considerable trepidation, I hope to plan a bi week at one of the annual summer conferences. Another target is my professional field of social work. A friend and I have already given a presentation on therapeutic work with sexual minorities and hope to do more.

When I think of relationships, I think of myself as primarily monogamous. I like building and living in an intense and committed primary relationship while enjoying the comfort and support of an extended network of friends. Right now, my ideal is to find a primary partner. Given the statistics, my primary relationships will probably be with women although I have a strong desire to try a relationship with a man again, too. I can't think of a better way to spend my retirement than living and loving bisexually.

Billy & Peaches Jones

Growing up
with a bisexual dad*

Billy: Every parent who's gay has a concern about what effect their own lifestyle, sexual orientation, behavior will have upon their children. Will the fact that I live a certain lifestyle have a negative impact on my kids? I think the way that I've compensated is to really want my children to have an openness and tolerance about others' lifestyles and to understand, also, why I need to be honest about my own. And whereas, at this particular point in my life I'm in a committed relationship with a man, I still define myself as a bisexual. In fact I often jokingly refer to myself as a "recovering heterosexual prone to relapse but doing fine in recovery right now," and explain that my kids are examples of my "relapse."

What I mean is that I have hetero-affectionate feelings for women and I've been sexual with women and have been in multiple relationships from time to time with a man and with a woman.

---

* *Editors' note:* This interview was conducted by Betsy Ringel and Ann Lewis at the National AIDS Network office in Washington, D.C., where Billy Jones worked as Minority Affairs staff person. Billy, age forty-eight, and his daughter Peaches, age twenty, discuss their relationship and how his coming out and his identity have affected them both. Billy is an outspoken advocate for what he calls the marginal populations or fringes of our community. As a recovering addict, ex-hustler, and ex-con, he has pioneered street health educational efforts to at-risk populations in the nation's capital and nationally. In the seventies, he helped found Gay Married Men of Washington, D.C., and the National Coalition of Black Lesbians and Gays. He was an organizer of the 1979 National March on Washington for Gay and Lesbian Rights, and he organized the first black gay delegation to meet with President Carter's White House staff that same year. Peaches is his middle child, a junior at Howard University in Washington, D.C., and a math major.

As a kid I learned that I was not 100-percent heterosexual. I was attracted to both men and women and adventuresome enough to explore that. When I was with men I certainly explored my attraction to them, but sometimes I fantasized about women. Or with women, I would explore the encounter with them, but would fantasize about men. Where I've been on that continuum from het to homo has varied. The person that I'm with is a great stimulus and affects how I show my affection.

I was one of those kids always getting caught in sexual encounters. I got caught in the living room by my mother. I got caught in the garage by my father. But I didn't feel that my family was reprimanding me for what I was doing sexually or for whom I was with sexually. I always felt comfortable and natural, but inside I knew I should not talk about my experiences with the same gender. But I also didn't talk much about my experiences with women. My peers would brag about their sexual encounters with girls. I never did that. I began to explore more seriously when I went into the Marine Corps. In that situation, where I was around men, I explored a lot . But it was understood you weren't supposed to talk about it.

I remember coming home on leave once and deciding that I really needed to talk about this with my dad. I was having lots of fun, but somehow I felt that I was doing something wrong or taboo. I was trying to explain that I thought I was queer, a sissy. I didn't use the word gay. When you're black, the terms are "you're a punk" or a "sissy." I don't remember the term faggot. I think I knew the term homosexual, although I probably said homo. My dad just sat there with this blank stare, saying, "What's the problem?" And I mean, I'd been *telling* him, and his response was, "What's the problem?" (Laughs) Finally he says to me, "Look, all men play with other men, and so do I." It was like a coming out between us, us coming out to each other and my dad saying, "You know, that's fine." His talk to me was around being discreet, being careful, which included a health lecture about sexually transmitted diseases. Then he said you'll meet a nice lady and get married and have kids. He was a model for that, because he had a boyfriend and was discreet. I kind of knew that was going on.

After my father died, I remember this same conversation came up with my mother. Her response was, "Honey, if you had a husband as horny as your dad was, you'd be grateful for all the help you could get!" She said, "He was a great husband, a great father, and if he got a little on the side, that was great."

So I followed my father's example. I met a really nice woman, got married, and had kids. I loved her very much. I still do. Our divorce and separation had nothing to do with whether we loved each other or not. It had to do with it being very complicated to live an alternative lifestyle and give equitable time, quality time in a multiple relationship. I found that even though I tried to give everyone equal time, it was really difficult. So I decided I wanted to try living in a relationship with a man and give that some quality attention. She wanted to go on with her life and have a relationship where she could have a partner too, so that meant having to separate. We remain very close friends.

What was life like for you when you were first married?
B: When I first got married, for about seven years, starting in 1967, I wasn't open and honest about the fact that I was attracted to men. But gradually I began to explore relationships with men outside of my marriage — just sexual encounters, getting off. I still had no consciousness of the gay movement.

Then I became aware of a movement — not a bisexual movement, but a gay movement. What happened was, after seven years of marriage, I actually began to feel a stronger bonding with men and became aware that emotional affection for men was more than just the sex part. I also still had a very strong bonding with my wife and my kids. It became very difficult. I was getting something very different from each. I was sexual with both a man and a woman, and torn between the two.

Did you think of yourself as bisexual at the time?
B: Kind of, but when I used that word, I'd be put down for it. Most people in the gay community would say, "There's no such thing as a bisexual." Only my heterosexual friends wanted me to say I was "bisexual not gay," as if I hadn't "gone all the way yet," so I decided to go all the way.

When I first fell in love with another man, I attempted to do an alternative lifestyle — setting up two households, maintaining my relationship with my wife and with the man. This was in Minneapolis.

When did you tell your wife?
B: I didn't. At that time we'd had a brief separation due to an employment change. She was finishing her old job and I'd gone ahead to purchase the new house in Minneapolis. That gave me time to explore a whole social world that I'd never been exposed to before, and I fell in love with this man. When my wife and kids came, he couldn't deal with me as a married man. He ran away to Key West, and I tried to follow him.

In the heat of all this passion, my wife said, "Are you in love with Tom?" I decided to tell the truth. We were very calm and rational. It's not that we've never argued. We've just always both been very civil, probably because we both came from families where there was a lot of bickering and arguing, and I think we both decided we weren't going to have that kind of relationship.

So seven years after my coming out, we attempted to have an open relationship in which we both tried to relate to other persons, but respected each others' emotions and feelings. By 1981, we recognized that we needed to part, that neither of us was totally satisfied with the relationship we had in terms of a traditional marriage.

What's happened since then?
B: For a while she dated several persons and eventually fell in love with the man to whom she's married. I dated both men and women, but made a commitment to the person I'm still in a relationship with, Christopher. We've been together eleven years. So the kids have seen both their mother and I in stable relationships. She and I have also maintained a stable relationship. In good times and bad times, we have still been there for each other.

Peaches, when did you first realize your dad wasn't straight?
Peaches: I was in elementary school, third or fourth grade. My father had an office in the basement. They called the three of us downstairs into the basement. We thought we were getting in trouble for something. My mom tried to explain that Dad had something to say to us. She tried to spit it out, but she couldn't understand it herself. My father goes with his open-minded self and says, "I'm gay." Well, the three of us look at each other, and I just assume that Dad's *happy* about something. I really was too young to understand, until my father started bringing us to Washington to visit with him, and we saw him and Christopher together. I thought it was strange — why is Daddy sleeping with a man?

Dad, remember the time when we were spending a week or two, and you and Christopher were in the bedroom, and I knocked and opened the door? I was shocked and didn't know what to say. When you and Christopher came out, you told me that you and Christopher were just playing. I think that was the day that it really sunk in, that this is what "gay" means. Well, my father always dragged the three of us to these Gay Pride Days and the Coalition of Black Gay Men; weird functions. The three of us hated it, not because of what it was, but just because it was so boring to us.

We never really lived anywhere any longer than two years. After we moved to New Jersey, I didn't see my father as often. I was more upset over the move (than the separation). And really his gayness did not have an effect on my life, honestly, I don't believe, until I was actually in college. By high school I knew my father was gay, but I wouldn't dare tell anybody. I think I was more embarrassed because I knew my friends wouldn't understand. I didn't think there was anything wrong with it, but my friends had families that were just father and mother, or father and girlfriend. I had something different. I had Father and Christopher-father, and Mother and stepfather. I couldn't really say, "Well you know my father's gay." I don't think they would have understood that, so I kind of kept it hush-hush.

When I went to college I took on a new attitude. A great deal of my friends now know. I kind of took the attitude — to hell with it, this is my father and I love him. He's still a father, he's no different. He still reprimands me like he's my father, he still teaches me like he's my father. And because of my father's openness, I feel we're closer. I always tell my dad, you are my closest friend. I tell my father everything, partly because I feel he's told me everything. Well, almost everything...

When my friends at college ask "What does your father do?" I tell them he works as a national AIDS activist, a trainer, and health educator. He made an appearance on BET (Black Entertainment Television), and I was telling all my friends, "My dad's going to be on television."

I told my friends I was more afraid that your clothes weren't going to match. But actually I was also still hoping that he would not slip up and let people know that he was gay. That's when I was home. But when I'm here that's when I finally realized, I can't keep hiding it, I mean, there actually is nothing to hide.

I feel that I know more than a lot of people my age because of my dad. I know more, I've experienced a little bit more, I feel like my mind is a heck of a lot more open because of him.

What effect do you think Billy's coming out to you has had on your own sexual identity?
P: I don't really think it's affected me at all. For a long time, I wondered if it was hereditary. Am I going to wake up and start having feelings for women that I can't explain? And then it just dawned on me another day that being gay is not hereditary. Just because my father's gay does not necessarily mean that I am, and at this point in my life I've chosen not to be.

Dad, I know I ignore your and Christopher's relationship. When I'm with the two of you together I don't think of it the same way I think of Mom and my stepfather. I mean, I know, Mom got remarried and Daddy is quote-unquote remarried, recommitted, or whatever. But it's so hard because I'm so used to seeing a man and a woman and then to have to see a man and a man. I accept it, but I don't truly understand it, probably because I can't picture myself that way.

B: Yes. I've noticed that if I'm dating a woman, my kids' responses are almost joyful, like, "Ah, maybe he's going to get his act together, maybe he really *is* heterosexual and this was just a phase he was going through."

I think my kids are still working out their comfort level with my relationship, my bonding with men. They themselves are going through a coming-out process. And with Peaches here with me in D.C. now, at Howard, I've seen more of an acceptance of the relationship.

P: I love Christopher. And I love my father. But I don't necessarily love Christopher and my father together. I think they have a wonderful friendship. Christopher puts up with a lot of my dad's shit. Christopher is in the shoes that my mother was in when she was with my father. So that's why I can sympathize with Christopher.

B: My kids have had difficulty in seeing me for so many years with a male lover. They probably would rather have me relating equally to women and men, but I believe that has a lot to do with the oppression that is imposed upon them by society as a whole, peer pressure. The same discomfort I have to work through in my relationship with a man, in terms of when it's okay to be affectionate and not affectionate, and when it's okay to be open and out with this man I'm in a relationship with are the same issues that my kids also have to go through.

P: I think you're doing a pretty good job of it.

Why have you politically identified as gay up until now?
B: Even though I do see myself as bisexual, I decided to go to the other side of the spectrum because I feel that the oppression is really coming from there. It's really easy for people to ignore that side of me. So in order for that not to happen I have chosen to define myself as a gay activist, even though in reality I know that there is always another part of me.

Also, because of the political issues of homophobia and hetero-phobia, from a gay community perspective, it's been easier to be gay. From a straight community perspective, it's also easier to be gay, because it gets them to focus on homosexuality. Whenever I've come out as bi, particularly in the black community, people just discount my identity and my reasons for it. So I've often just gone for the politics that was most easily articulated and taken seriously, which has been gay politics. With friends I tend to keep reminding them I'm bi, but publicly I feel I have to make political statements that force the issue of homosexuality, particularly in minority communities where bi-ness is often used as a term to "pass," to deny, or to cop out.

I have multiple identities that all relate and influence each other. For instance it's very different to identify as a gay black man or as a black gay man, and I think carefully about how I use these labels in each case.

Why have you decided to come out more publicly now as a bisexual?
B: My politics and my thinking on bisexuality is much like the other complicated parts of me — it's always changing and evolving. Like racial politics — politically, ideally, I'd like to be lovers with a black man, but I love a white man and that's important to me to stick with too. I think it's similar about relations with women for me. Bisexuality is my ideal,

just like a multicultural, multiracial society is. But it's one thing to be bisexual and quite another to live as a bisexual person, to make that space in the world for yourself every day, to consciously work to blend those feelings and relationships. It's a real charge, a turn-on, when I can do it.

I don't think you can talk about bisexuality without talking about the possibility of open relationships. Chris and I have an open relationship. To say that everyone has to have a closed, monogamous relationship is oppressive. I get very upset with safe sex literature that says you must be in a monogamous relationship. That's not the point at all. We've also opened our relationship to a lesbian couple. They've had two kids with our help (through alternative fertilization).

P: It hurts sometimes when I look at my friends and don't want them to know I have a gay father. But lots of things hurt. You get used to it.

B: I would hope at some point that my openness isn't painful to her, isn't an embarrassment. I think that as Peaches gets more comfortable with herself and her friends, she'll come to see that it's somebody else's problem if they are uncomfortable with it, and that what counts is how we interact with each other. I think also that she knows that Christopher and I are going to be there for her, and that her mother and her stepfather are also going to be there for her, so she does have an incredible extended family.

P: My friend said to me this weekend, "Peaches, what's going to happen in about five years at your wedding? You're going to have your father and your stepfather and Christopher sitting out there in the audience. Are you going to have your father give you away first and then bring you back down the aisle and have your stepfather bring you up there, while Christopher sits there waiting for his turn, too?" I don't want my dad to feel funny about bringing Christopher to my wedding. I want Christopher at my wedding. But on my wedding day, Dad, I want you to give me away.

It seems that the hardest part about owning one's bisexuality is resisting the pressure to choose one label over the other. Everyone wants you to do that. There's a very strong pull to choose one and say that it's better and that the "other one" is an aberration.
B: That's true. And my whole belief system is that bisexual is probably far more the reality than a pure het or homo. Especially if you accept the fact that bisexuality is not only a physical interaction but also an emotional connection also. We do have affections for both men and women. We may choose to act with this specific person or this specific gender, but that doesn't imply that we're not capable of physically interacting with the opposite sex. That's another myth that's not true.

My kids may or may not be comfortable with who I am, but I think they have a great deal of sensitivity for other people who define themselves as bisexual or gay or cross-dressers or whatever and recognize that there's no one way. You cannot just say, "Well, this is what a gay person's like, or what a bisexual person is like." They know that we're all very different, and that the world needs to just be open to that. I think that is really beautiful.

Chris Girard

A few brave
and gifted people

About ten years ago, I was heading back to Mexico to buy local crafts from mountain villages and towns for import to the United States. I was married to Zenaida. We were open to one another to a fault, and after seven years of a very intense though closed relationship, she declared that she was ready to open it up. I was in shock. I'd gotten somewhat used to monogamy, and in the process, perhaps, we had worn each other out. We needed to bring a fresh outlook and new experience into our relationship. I had forgotten how.

After a couple of days in Mexico, Zenaida called to tell me she had met an Ethiopian fellow at the Library of Congress, where she was doing research. Outside his professorial demeanor, he was apparently quite a lover and quite "safe," which in those days meant he wanted to remain unattached. She said she was having a wonderful new experience. "Go do your thing," she urged. "You've talked about exploring men again. Go do it. I'd feel better if it was a man rather than a woman. I won't feel competitive!" We were very concerned about one another's feelings and what we felt we could or could not cope with.

In Mexico I was working with several of my ex-students and staying with my in-laws — not exactly a setting for adventure. One evening on my way out of a theatre, as I approached the corner, a striking, curly-haired man nodded and smiled. I naturally returned the gesture and walked on a few feet when I decided to take a second look and turned around. He had also turned around. He was beautiful. After a couple more double takes, we had a drink and spent the night talking at his house. During the night we decided to leave the next day for a long weekend in Morelia. I returned home at four in the morning and jumped over the fence and through my bedroom window in order not to awaken anyone.

I was impatient for the long weekend to begin. When it did, it was eventful. But in our eagerness to be together, we had failed to realize that this weekend was a national holiday. All the hotels in town were full, and we spent hours looking for a place to stay. I was so happy just being with a guy who would talk about his sexuality that I wasn't too concerned with finding a place to stay. We could have slept in the car. But Malec was clearly desperate and annoyed, so after checking over forty hotels, I suggested we try the cathedral. As a kid I had stayed at a monastery and knew that a Catholic church will never turn away a traveller in distress.

We rang a bell at the bishop's residence and were received first by a page and finally by the bishop, who warmly heard us out, offered us hot chocolate, and had a page take us to our quarters — a series of cubicles next to one of the great steeples. We spent the night hugging, quietly whispering, falling asleep, and being awakened as the church bells struck the hour. I felt good hugging a guy in church. We were both rather impressed at the sanctity of the place, and even as we lay there, we fantasized about possible reprisals.

Our conversations were intense, much like those I'd had when I'd met Zenaida. I very much wanted to know everything: why, where, when, how? How had a guy three years younger than I already had more sexual partners than I may ever have in a lifetime? Malec was exciting. A doctor, no less, he specialized in child psychology, and he could talk about feelings or even, as was sometimes the case, admit not being able to feel.

Two days later we found a hotel with a shower and a bed. By this time we were both very hot for each other, although our idea of what to do with this heat differed. He quickly realized I was essentially a virgin and broke me into anal sex first by offering himself and then taking me in return. He assured me that if anything went wrong, being a doctor, he'd fix it! My very first time penetrating a man was a bit strange. He was very tight and young and perhaps in this respect a near virgin himself. I couldn't imagine what he must be feeling. I couldn't discern if he felt pleasure. Despite this, his beauty was over-whelming to me and if for no other reason than being stimulated in a very special way that I'd never been before, I came exuberantly. A bit later when I was penetrated, I almost died. I was overcome with waves of physical and emotional feelings never experienced before. Initial thoughts of being violated slowly gave way to deeper feelings of being multidimensional. Parts of my body which I had totally ignored began to make themselves known in beautiful ways during this intercourse. It was in a special way perhaps like the pain and pleasure of giving birth or what it must feel like to go from liquid to gas or gas to fire.

During our five weeks together, one adventure seemed to follow another. I sensed I had stepped onto new ground and would not turn back. Through it all Malec was very concerned about how I was going to deal with my return to Zenaida. I assured him that I didn't feel there was any conflict. I actually felt more strongly about her. I didn't discern the conflict this was creating in him. I thought that based on what we shared in Mexico, everything would work itself out. I don't know why I had so much confidence.

Unfortunately, I didn't have them both for long. Malec broke down and persistently called me on the day of my arrival. I wanted to be with Zenaida. Malec interpreted my aloofness as rejection and refused to speak to me for several years. Zenaida continued her exploration. I wasn't totally disillusioned by this initial implosion in my love of both sexes, but I was deterred from pursuing them simultaneously for a while.

Winding my way through a labyrinth of experiences over the years, I met my life partner Billy. We joined two lesbians as co-parents of two wonderful kids.

I feel that it is important to find others who are creatively capable of diffusing prejudices by honestly living out feelings and integrating those experiences emotionally, intellectually, physically, and spiritually. Like most things in life, it takes a mixture of disposition and discipline to make it work. And like happiness, it is at times elusive.

The hardest aspect of being bisexual is that there is little known precedence. But in the free flow of feelings there are times when one would like to be the wife of a wife or the husband of a husband. The lack of precedence provides tremendous freedom and flexibility on the one hand, but also from time to time creates a tremendous vacuum. I think that the onset of AIDS has been particularly difficult. I feel that all the love and caring of the ill for the ill and the well for the ill compensates for the tremendous loss of humanity, but I also hope that out of the experience we learn to be more fully sexual, rather than to recoil in fear of sex.

As far as my children are concerned, I'm glad their lesbian mothers are rather square and unadventurous. If we were all adventurous, the kids would have less of a comparative view of things. They might be reactionary. As it is, they are both exposed to and can enjoy different lifestyles. My daughter, like many kids her age, vacillates between marrying boys and girls when she grows up. My son is still too young to verbalize his fantasies about these things.

I find that a lot of energy is required to maintain my eleven-year relationship with Billy. We are both intense outside of our relationship and find a lot of peace in being together. We are each there for the other when we come home. I have had several other very close ongoing relationships with longtime women and men friends. The sexual aspects over the longer term tend to change because one either desires more or less than the other can give. Or at times, coming together is so intense that one is really fulfilled for a long time.

Will bisexuality be more accepted in my lifetime? I don't know. It may well take our kids growing up in an atmosphere where there is less pressure to be one thing or another, or to learn to enjoy being both to the extent that it is in their nature. From my heart I can deeply love several people, each in unique ways. Practically, though, this love requires very special types of energy, and very deep honesty. I am learning how to share and overcome jealousy, how to overcome my socialization, and how to define my role models. All this will take time and a few brave and gifted people.

Richard Susan Bassein

A day in the life*

It is 7:30 a.m. on a spring Friday morning. Emma, who is four, is up, naked, cold, and hungry. I reluctantly leave Judith asleep in our bed, pull on sweat pants, and go to help Emma dress. Her older sister, Anna, must be awakened and prodded to make her lunch. Despite her baby-smooth skin and lovely innocence, Emma says that she only feels pretty when she's wearing a pretty dress. Her preschool teacher reports that she likes the attention that dresses bring. It must be a phase; at ten, Anna prefers an oversized t-shirt and stretch pants for school, although she does love dressing up for play and parties.

"What's for breakfast?" turns out to be Daddy's Best-in-the-West scrambled eggs. After an exhausting sequence of tooth brushing, nagging, and bag packing, we are out the door to drive Anna to school and Emma to preschool. I will not see them until next Wednesday, for this weekend they will be at the house of their mother, from whose ten-year shackles of normalcy I have been free for two years — two years! two years of growth, discomfort, and emerging happiness! I will miss the kids these five days, but enjoy the freedom their absence grants me. Although they know about the dualities of my life, I still hesitate to involve them too much, as I worry about the reactions of their friends and their friends' parents and the possibility of a renewal of their mother's attempts to take the children from me. I introduced her to all my sexual interests before we married or had children; indeed, we even

---

* Richard Susan's day as described here is representative, though not typical, and true in all but the details, which have been altered only to make the story more cohesive.

had sex together with another man! But during the divorce, she took advantage of my honesty by attempting, albeit unsuccessfully, to deny me custody of the children by reporting all those interests to our Family Court Services mediator.

Back home awaits Judith, sweet Judith, to whom the normal world is as bewildering as it is to me. Her jeans and shirt complementing her blonde buzz-cut hair, she's the only butch member of our household. I shave my face and legs, shower, dry and brush my hair, now long enough to curl gracefully around my neck. "What are you going to wear today, Susan?" turns out, under her caring eye, to be a white blouse, a navy jacket, a mid-calf-length tan skirt, black flats. I add a scarf, which does not meet her approval. She thinks my neck is beautiful, I think it's hideous, thick and stubbled, and must be covered. Perhaps that is my phase. Judith is off to work for the morning; I am home today, running errands and preparing lectures for the mathematics classes I will be teaching next week. This is a critical year: I have been a tenured associate professor at the college for five years and will be reviewed for a promotion to full professor next year.

Gail and Bert, in their seventies, live next door. They are watchful, but sociable and tolerant: the perfect neighbors. We wave as I drive off to go shopping, though Bert is noticeably uncomfortable. Perhaps it's just Berkeley, but the people I meet about town are friendly. The checker at the bookstore compliments my purse, the one at the supermarket admires my necklace, and the salesman at the plumbing supply store is simply helpful. Most people don't seem to notice (or care) about my gender mixing, some clearly enjoy it, and others find it hilarious. They and I smile and laugh about it, and the exchange of good feeling warms us all. Nevertheless, some of the anxiety I cultivated for so many years in the closet, though diminishing the more I come out, still haunts me each time I am on my way out the front door.

I have lunch waiting for Judith's return home. After lunch, we head out to shop for clothes at bargain outlets and secondhand stores, one of the pleasures we have shared during the seven months since our first date. Heading down Solano Avenue, we arouse curiosity of three teenage boys. One of them runs ahead of us, faces us, and charges us with being two women together, holding hands, no less! He doesn't believe my smiling denial and then announces to the world that we are lesbians. The world doesn't noticeably care, and we walk on, barely able to control our laughter.

Atypically, Judith and I are enjoying ourselves separately this evening. She is visiting a man who is an old friend and lover for dinner, a video, and sex. I am at an S/M party for gay, bi, and straight men and women with a former male lover of hers. I have found that I need some male sexual affection to be able to participate fully and happily in a heterosexual relationship. On other occasions, Judith has gone to an all-women sex party or together we have invited a man home. We do not bring others into our home separately, however; a genuine concern for and appreciation of each other's needs is blended with a touch of jealousy. But as our relationship ages and survives other attractions, the fears of abandonment subside. After our adventures we meet again, late at night, secure in our bed in the home we share.

Never, never boring...

I'll always remember how, in the heat of an argument, my husband would say, "You're turning into a lesbian!" For him the remark was a convenient way to quickly disarm me. I worked with many dykes and it was "obvious" to him they were filling my head with ideas and were, therefore, the reason for many of "our problems."

His verbal attacks confused me. Did my attempts to assert myself mean I was a lesbian? Where was the truth? While I knew in my heart of hearts I was surely finding my voice and standing up for myself, I was also confused because I was having a lot of sexual fantasies about women. Whenever my husband brought home a porno movie, I hoped that there would be women "doing it" with one another. I wanted to see women with each other because I definitely got turned on by what I saw. I worried about what this said about me until I started reading sex books. They informed me that fantasies about women were normal and healthy. It certainly didn't mean I would act them out. What a relief. The thought of being a lesbian was terrifying, because it seemed as if I would have to cut out whole aspects of myself in order to fit the lesbian mold. Not surprisingly, I never told a soul about these fantasies. They were my secret.

For the next two years I struggled with this issue. Then one Thanksgiving morning, when my loyalty and guilt were no longer strong enough for me to accept the pain inside, I saw what I had to do. Divorce was the only option, and with this realization I never once steered from my course. Within two months I was in my new apartment, living alone for the first time in my life. The break was exhilarating; I felt alive! I could hardly contain myself. I would come home from work and just dance and laugh in my living room. I felt like a child; the world took on a new color. Oh, boy, my life was really going to start now!

Six months later I stopped by my brother's for dinner before going to a dance. He was having some friends over, one of whom I knew. I had always liked Jeremy, been intrigued by him. He was in an open relationship, and I thought that was as exotic as hell. So I flirted, had a wonderful time, and went to the dance. Two days later, I heard that Jeremy asked about me. Holy stars, someone had noticed me! Upon hearing this news, I immediately called him. "Sure," he said, "I'd love to come over and share a bottle of wine."

Later that night as we lay in my bed with the moonlight streaming into the room, he whispered sweetly in my ear, "Tell me, Mattie, what are your fantasies?" I'm not sure what made me say it. Perhaps it was the delicious love we had just made, so different from what I'd ever known. Perhaps it was the knowledge that he had a sophisticated love life, or perhaps it was just the bottle of wine we had shared. At any rate, my heart opened, "Women. I fantasize about women." He held me tighter and told me it was beautiful. I couldn't believe it! Here was a man who thought my fantasies were precious. That was all I needed to hear. Just one validation, and I found peace within myself. We talked some more and quickly realized the mystery was solved. I liked men and women. I had finally come home. Who would have imagined I was bisexual? I revelled in the thought.

But where was I going to meet a woman? It was torture to be aware of what I wanted but not know how to go about finding it. At least now I was aware of why I rarely looked at men, but women, oh, the lovely women. Unashamed, I watched constantly the curves of their bodies, their walk, laugh, clothes, hair, everything. Women were never, never boring.

Six months later when vacationing with Jeremy, I was talking a lot about my good friend Greta. Greta this, Greta that. Finally he looked at me and said, "You have a crush on her!" When I got home I was ready, but at the airport she immediately told me she had just had a painful miscarriage. To make matters worse, the fellow involved had made himself scarce. I felt so guilty. Not only had I not been there for her, but I had designs on her as well. Because of this, I never told her what really happened while I was away. I enjoyed the relationship as it was.

This went on for several months, until during one of our frequent discussions of sex, men, and horniness, she told me that a fellow was coming over, and she was going to tell him she didn't want to see him any more. I jokingly told her that after she kicked him out the night would still be young, and she would still be horny.

Later that same night the phone rang, it was Greta, could she come over? "Of course," I replied. When she arrived I let her in, and as usual she was gorgeous. Greta confirmed the events of her evening and settled into my couch. Accustomed to our relationship as it was, I didn't even realize what she had in mind until I sat next to her and found her looking into my eyes. The air was charged as I comprehended what I had waited for so long. Slowly we kissed, not as friends, but as lovers. She spoke of the time she first noticed me, found ways to be near me, realized she loved me. But in our timidity we had misread all the signs given to one another, until this night.

While I don't remember all the details of that night, I will never forget the feelings and sensations: finally able to touch all of her and express my love without boundaries, finally to have her caress me and murmur her passions in my ear, and to fall asleep curled up with her breasts against my back. My life was never the same.

Selena Julie Whang

T hough I was born in Detroit, Michigan, my family moved to Seoul, Korea, when I was five years old. We lived there for two years. Detroit and Seoul both have cold winters with snow and hot humid summers; the seasons existed as extremes, like me. I remember eating warm yams in the fall with my girlfriend after school. I thought she was very exotic and beautiful because she was only half-Korean and had big eyes. Yes, I was attracted to her. She was similar to me in some ways. We were Americans, had Korean blood, spoke English fluently, and were learning the Korean language at a rapid rate. We spoke Korean in the classrooms of the American school in Seoul as an act of defiance. And yet she was different from me which made spending time with her exciting and exploratory. Her mother had long black hair, and my mother didn't like her, thought her a wanton woman. I never met her father, but there was a picture of him in his military uniform.

We moved to a suburb of Los Angeles when I was eight or nine years old. It was warm and smoggy. When I reached high school, I wanted a best girlfriend and a boyfriend. A boyfriend to kiss and a girlfriend to tell secrets to was the ideal situation. I wanted a static situation that would be wonderful and last forever, or at least a long time.

For many years I felt my lower half was locked up. My stomach hurt, and I didn't know why. Sexuality was limited to impossible illusions, half-baked fears, and something not integrated in my life, a true mystery. But I was happy enough before sex. I was really into my schoolwork, my friends, and my appreciation of others' art and music. At the time most people were discovering their sexuality, I was content hiding behind makeup, dark dresses, and binding tights. A post-punk Korean American teenage girl-woman, a virgin.

I am more fluid now.

When I had my first sexual experience the day after my twenty-first birthday, my roommate symbolically threw a pine cone into the fire. I had asked a friend to have sex with me as a favor, because I knew he wouldn't trip on it. The next day he gave me a box of apples he had picked. I was touched.

The first woman I slept with four months later was a little out of control, a little out of reach, and a woman of color. We were about the same socioeconomically. She had come from Chicago. She had dropped out of U.C. Berkeley and wanted to be a writer. I had my B.A. when I was twenty years old and was taking a break. I didn't know what I wanted to do when I grew up.

Neither of these first experiences developed into "relationships," the kind of romantic emotional entanglements that last a while. I suppose I would rather identify as bisexual because I cannot identify with being heterosexual, and I cannot be a lesbian because I am attracted to men. To me, being heterosexual conjures up images of these cool and sophisticated people role-playing, the kind you see in the movies like *9½ Weeks:* cocktail dresses, sexual intrigue, and glamour. I used to put lesbianism on a pedestal until I realized, with real-eyes, that any relationship could be as fucked up and immature as the next, and that lesbians weren't better people by virtue of being lesbians.

I have gone out with more men than women, but I don't know if that is because I am attracted to men more than women, or that men are always around and available and women are not. The issue of race complicates matters exponentially. What races are more politically correct to sleep with, what races I am more attracted to? I have been with more white men than men or women of color or white women. But again, is it just a matter of so many white men making themselves available to a young attractive Korean American woman?

I don't know, but this is how I've seemed to function in regards to sexuality and sexual choices. I cannot feel lust just like that. I have to make a lot of choices before my lust for someone or something can really manifest itself. The politics definitely figure in and so does personal taste. And then there are the incongruities between the two, and the resulting tension.

When I told my parents about being bisexual, my mother said nothing surprised her about me any more.

Shu Wei Chen — Andy

A man, a woman, attention

I first met Christina in the summer of 1988 . We were sitting side by side at a bus stop on a foggy night in San Francisco. She wore her hair in a blunt cut down to her shoulders, while her painted almond-shaped eyes and large loop earrings screamed for attention. Except for her Adam's apple, it was hard to tell Christina was really a young male from the Philippines. She was rather tall for a Filipina, but her slenderness and smooth, soft complexion helped her pass as a young woman.

Christina's personality was a mix between a spoiled teenager and an adult going through tough times. She spoke about how happy she was working at the nearby fast-food place like a teen getting her first pay and then seriously spoke of how difficult it was to be evicted from her apartment.

I began telling her how difficult it was to be an Asian bisexual, and how disappointed I was not being accepted by gays and straights when I crossed from male to female. At this point she realized I knew. The knowledge drew us closer and made us trust each other more. We understood our double minority status and how our cross-gender lifestyle was not taken seriously.

I was disheartened to hear Christina describe how her stern father went into her room on the previous night and had thrown away all her cosmetics and had beaten her to change her ways. She was teary-eyed when she mentioned his ultimatum of either becoming a boy or getting out of the family house. Deep inside, though, I didn't feel sympathetic to her street hustling while she was living at home, even though her parents didn't know.

She kept nagging me to room with her and split the rent. I moved into the apartment she had found for a few weeks. My days were spent as a man and my nights as a woman. Some people cross-dress because they are into the clothing, but Christina and I wanted the attention we got from others after our transformation. Our high was to be able to create the illusion of being a woman and to emotionally cross this gender line. We were in our early twenties, living for each day, and having fun at night when we went to straight clubs undetected.

Later that year in Los Angeles, Christina introduced me to Breezy. Breezy had a certain coolness in the way she sat cross-legged, collected and composed. There was something serene about her. She projected an inner astuteness. Before I uttered one word to her, she focused those gorgeous almond-shaped eyes that were so open and understanding on me. Because of her Filipina–Italiana heritage, she had a beautifully defined bone structure that extended from her high cheekbones, her sexy chiseled chin, down to her long tanned legs. She had started taking hormones when she was in her teens, which enabled her to develop soft and high breasts and proportionally wide hips, while keeping her maleness intact. Seldom did she ever have to wear a lot of makeup, because her facial complexion was so soft and feminine.

There was a mutual attraction when we first met, and we gradually fell in love. During our physical lovemaking, Breezy was able to express her female and male energies at the same time. Gentle versus fast, soft versus hard, and give versus take were all in constant change. What I will always remember is the affection and caring we gave to each other during our lovemaking, and the openness to telling each other what we wanted — from gentle caressing and stroking through my first oral experience. We experimented with role reversals: I became a woman and she a man, or both of us were women. I will forever remember the laughter that ensued when the ink from her painted moustache covered the tub while we were bathing each other, or the difficulty we had putting on each other's condoms.

I was sad that our affair lasted only four days. Breezy had gotten into a serious argument with a girl who physically threatened her. She decided to go to Sacramento for a while. The image is ingrained in my mind of that long drive to the bus depot on Vine and Sunset — of the sadness that we were parting, the high hopes that we would meet again in San Francisco, and all those traffic lights and bright streetlights that stretched along the boulevards. She called me later while I was in San Francisco. She was going to move to a new place in Sacramento and would give me her number when she got a phone. Sadly, that was the last time I heard from her.

Janet Bohac

Don't call me

You shall call me poet
I shall point to the novel
In progress at the typewriter
Shaking my head.

No, I am not a poet.

You shall call me a novelist then
A manipulator of words
I shall point to the screen
Where only the light hits
Where there are no words.

No, I am not a novelist.

You shall call me a prostitute
Of cinema, and of stage
I shall point to the fruit trees
And the stings of insects
Upon my arms

And smile.

No, I am not a prostitute to anyone
Or anything
Except, maybe, my love of life,
Maybe the Muse.

No existentialist am I
The thought of things to come intrigues me
No capitalist am I
No socialist
Only the personal is political

You call me a woman
Until I touch my own sex
You call me a Lesbian
Unless he is here

But if I had my way
You'd call me nothing but my name,
Given and born into
And nothing else
For it is the only way
To define me.

Paul Haut

Bisexual movies

I've just made up a new favorite expression: "bisexual movies." One may ask, what does this mean? Well, I'll tell you. *Doctor Zhivago* was my first "bisexual movie," a movie in which I was attracted to both a man and a woman in the same film.

As a matter of fact, it was quite an experience for me back in 1965. There I was, fifteen and horny, on a school field trip to see the hot new flick *Doctor Zhivago*. And there they were, Omar Sharif and Julie Christie, pulling me back and forth in a kind of adolescent turned-on tug of war.

I was reminded of Omar and Julie the other day when I saw *Bull Durham,* another "bisexual movie." Okay, so now it's a middle-aged tug of war, but it's the same idea, just twenty-three years later. I could have died for Susan Sarandon and Tim Robbins (alas, not Kevin Costner). The big difference is that my new tugs of war are delicious things, feasts of plenty; as opposed to my old tugs, which were guilt-ridden, making me feel like the freak I felt I was.

You may wonder what has happened to me in the ensuing two decades–plus that has transformed me? Mainly I've learned from bitter experience that I had been twisting myself into pretzel shapes trying to live by other people's definitions of what my sexuality was, is, or should be.

From the dawn of my sexual feelings, certainly before I was married, I was attracted to men, so I thought surely I must be gay. I so much wanted to feel "normal," I resisted my gay feelings like crazy. Then, when I had gained *some* measure of self-acceptance about my gay feelings, I would become confused as hell when I'd be attracted to a woman. I felt as if I were somehow betraying being gay. I was always, *always* trying to make myself be one way or the other. My psyche couldn't handle the concept of wanting or needing both men *and* women in my life in a sexual and/or emotional way. And I *certainly* didn't recognize any sort of bisexual option that seemed remotely viable or acceptable.

When I was married, I vowed to myself that I wouldn't be with men. I had told my wife beforehand that I was attracted to men, and the silent assumption during the three-year marriage was that I would be monogamous. We *never* talked about it again. The issue was buried, and so was any real chance for the relationship.

After my divorce, when I hung out with gay friends, I felt pressured or embarrassed. I wouldn't talk about women or being with them. But I missed women because I was denying the wholeness of my sexuality and self. Always this either/or, it was craziness having to choose.

Now at age thirty-nine, I'm really just beginning to shed this craziness. For too long I allowed society, people, and institutions to take away big chunks of my life and happiness. Who the hell are these people anyway?

The truth is, I have a multitude of choices. I have my likes and dislikes, loves and turn-ons, hatreds and heart-throbs. I will never be pressured into giving up my heart and my lust and my unique self again. I'm back in my life and sharing my love. Anybody want to go to a "bisexual movie" with me?

Kei Uwano

Bi-loveable
Japanese feminist

I am Japanese. I have lived here for ten years. When I was growing up in Japan there was no concept, no word for sexuality. When we say heterosexual, it translates to heterosex-love. The word for gay or lesbian is homosex-love. Bisexual is only referred to in slang and translates as "one who uses both souls." Yes, we distinguish, but historically there is no strict concept for human sexuality or consciousness of sexuality. We don't talk about it. We do it. Sex is just a natural part of life. The idea of sexuality is now being imported into Japan from the West.

I identify myself based on the structure of love. Technically, I am bi-loveable and monogamous. My soul is androgynous, which means I am fully human. Should I call myself a human loveable? A whole sexual? How do I say this? In the process of giving birth to the words from my soul, I wonder how I can name the dawn and the sunset contained in the day and night.

When I was five years old, my mother asked me, "Which do you like — climbing a tree or playing with dolls?" I answered, "I want to be close to the sun. I love climbing the tree with the dolls on my shoulders!" Then when I was seven my father asked, "Won't you be a bride someday?" And I said, "Since I love my mother, I will never leave her. But I also love you. You gave me lots of colorful condensers and showed me how to build a television. So maybe it is a good idea to become your bride." The word "bride" was too new for me to question, but I thought it was something women do with men and they lived together. Even at a young age I did not identify with the sex roles.

One spring evening, with the light of the sunset filtering through the student union windows at the girls' high school I attended, a group of us were talking about the drama of the universe — the "big bang," the meaning of life, the joy and agonies. We also discussed the origins and reasons behind the politics of life.

I remember Yukie. We had been so passionately involved in a theater production. Silk-screening the fliers, writing the scenes, preparing the sound effects, and even painting the backdrop for the scenes together. We called that our "season in lime green." After the performance, there was much laughter, tears, and excitement with the other students. Yukie and I went to the union room, happily joking and exchanging the leftovers of our lunch. Then all of a sudden, in the clear full lights, we looked into each other's eyes and kissed. For both of us it was a first. After several months and lots of kisses, we smiled at each other and said, at the same time, "Let's get married!" It was sundown, and I remember it fondly when the sun sets.

The afternoon sunlight is also filled with memories. The soul woven with romance blossomed in December of my twenty-second year. When two of us stopped time, I asked, "Are you tired?" and Marie answered in Japanese with an American accent, "People will never be tired in heaven." We shared eight years of warmth in words, smiles, body, feminism, lesbianism, Japanese and American culture, and our sense of humor. Once, wearing a Japanese wisteria kimono, I gave an angry speech on a Tokyo public train addressing how inconsiderate, sexist, and racist a Japanese man was to Marie. To tell you the truth, I cried in her arms after we went back home. I felt so sorry for her. My black eyes and her blue eyes were constantly reflected in each other's spirits. In the yard where I am looking now, there is a garden full of forget-me-nots. It makes me feel sentimental.

Months, a few years went by, and then one autumn the time rested its wings in black eyes. The passion led us to look into each other's eyes with the desire to see the color of our souls. A pure desire to follow our hearts. Oh, Buddha! whether you can believe it or not, I heard a rude noise coming from his lower half. "Oh, I am sorry!" he apologized in English with a Japanese accent. In the next moment we both burst out laughing. Surely that fart brought us the gentleness of living and laughing, and reminded me of being a child.

I loved Yukie, Marie, and Taro, two women and a man. The passion of my life is the desire to share another soul with the wisdom, the passion, and the strong will called "love." For me it is beyond sex, gender, racial differences, and class. I am a total human. To those who say "not feminine enough," *no*. I am more than a fragile flower. To those who say "not masculine enough," *no*. I am more than muscle. Yes I am totally feminine and totally masculine in my humanistic ways, which means loving and respecting people just how they are. "What is the nature of sex and sex roles?" I don't know because nobody asked me to give them my input when they defined it.

Even though I don't have time to talk about the agony of those dark days and sleepless nights that brought me to this point, I am very clear about the core of my soul. Without thinking about why, I just am. I never conformed to the Japanese role of woman, I have always been direct. When I was in my animal dissection class wearing my long flower-printed skirt, I was adding the "accent" in the boring, 90 percent–male student atmosphere. When I showed up for tea ceremony with my handmade tie, I added a modern reality.

Spring has come, and I am sitting under a cherry blossom tree, the petals dancing in the wind. At thirty-six, I now say that the "last" kiss of my life belongs to the person who has developed both the feminine and masculine sides as one and who wants to actualize her or his love beyond and contained in the dualities.

Marcy Sheiner

The most natural thing

An interview with Arlene Krantz

W*hat was your process coming out as a bisexual?*
I was probably about nine years old when I first realized I had an attraction to women — I thought about what it would be like to be with a woman, but I was raised in the fifties, so things like that weren't options. Nothing was ever said about it, but it was there in my mind.

I got married in 1959 and had two children, and I'd never acted on those feelings. I wouldn't have known where to begin. But it was in my subconscious, waiting for the right moment to come out. My husband was a typical straight male in the sense that he had fantasies of being with two women. From the time we got married, we looked for other women for a threesome. We started swinging in the late sixties when it became popular. We connected with some kind of swingers publication — that mentioned a party — and we went. The party turned out to be sort of a convention, with a dinner — a place to meet people. We met this couple and got together with them in two separate rooms. He didn't want to see his wife do anything, which I thought was stupid.

Then the second or third time we connected with a couple, the woman was beautiful. She and I started getting it on — I touched another woman's body for the first time and it was the most natural thing that had ever happened to me. We just melted into each other. I remember touching her breast and thinking I would just die from ecstasy. I should have been doing it all my life.

But I had other experiences with swinging that were not as pleasant. I would get together with another woman, and I was always the assertive one. The women would lay back and say, "Oh, I just love being with women," and they wouldn't do anything. I had a lot of resentment about that.

Finally we got out of swinging, but my husband was still pimping me to go out and find other women. That's what it felt like to me. There were instances where it was enjoyable for me, but I had issues about it. We'd go to swing parties, and I wondered why it wasn't okay for him to get involved with a man while it was okay for me to be with women. Also, I was a feminist, and I always felt like men had the edge in those situations.

After our swinging days, we left the country for four years, came back, and moved to San Francisco in 1974. My husband discovered an ad in the paper for a bisexual center and informed me about it. I called and spoke to a woman who invited me to go with them to a women's bar. I was a total nervous wreck. I was afraid because I figured lesbians were these women who looked like men, and I was attracted to women who looked feminine. I sat there and watched all these women connecting with each other, and I just thought I would love to have that happen to me.

Later, after I had separated from my husband, I went by bus to visit my daughter at college. On the way back I started talking to this guy who later called and invited me to a party. It turned out to be a fundraiser for the bi center — total coincidence. I walked in there and I said to myself, this is where I want to be. Here I can be myself. I can get turned on to women, I can get turned on to men. I became extremely active — I was on the board, I was the social director, I started the women's rap group, I helped with paperwork. It was a big turning point in my life — it was important for me to find out who I was, and what I was all about. Who was Arlene Krantz who had played housewife and mother all those years and went from living with my parents to having a family. Finally I got to be by myself.

So you never went through a stage of being confused, wondering if you were straight or lesbian?
No, never. Even now, I have a lover who's a woman, and when I'm with her I feel this is the most natural thing in the world. And I felt just as natural being with a man. I think women are wonderful, and I'm learning more about myself as a woman. Sometimes people say to me, you're having a relationship with a woman so you must be a lesbian, and I say, no, I'm not a lesbian. I've been out to my family for about ten years as a bisexual.

How did you come out to your family?
When I separated and lived on my own and got involved in the Bi Center, I didn't want to have to hide the newsletter or things about bisexuality. That's not what my life is about — I'm not in the closet by any means.

So when my kids came over one time, I said, okay, sit down, we need to talk.

How old were they?
Around sixteen and eighteen. They were sitting there crocheting or doing needlepoint, both on my bed, and I said, "This is what my life is about — I like men and I like women." I told them if they had any questions, I wouldn't hide anything. They never even looked up. You read a lot about the problems parents have over their kids being bisexual, but with me it was the opposite. My kids were having a hard time with their mother being bisexual.

It's interesting, because I have a son and a daughter and my son is fine about it, but my daughter is not.
Well, one of my daughters is really wonderful about it. I told her, "You don't have to like it. I'm not asking for your approval. I just want you to know who I am. I'm your mother, and this has nothing to do with my being your mother." The bottom line is that children look to you as a mother, and regardless of what you do or how much they can accept, a mother should not be a bisexual. Mother is a woman who has no feelings, takes all the abuse, keeps the family together.

My daughter and I had a big fight once. I told her, "Don't put me on a pedestal. That is not what I want. I hurt, I cry, I have feelings, I love, the same as you." What is mother? Mother is a goddess. Well, shit, I'm not *that* kind of a goddess! It's hard for her to see me as anything other than mother.

What about your parents and your sisters?
I told my sisters, and they've been extremely accepting. When I was back east, I wanted to go to a women's bar, and I asked one of them to come with me. She said, "But what will I do if a woman asks me to dance?" I said, "You do the same thing you do in a straight bar. You say I'm sorry, I don't want to dance."

About five years ago my father and I were having a conversation on the phone, and he said something about how we should take all these bisexuals and round them up or something. I saw stars. I said, "Dad, I'm a bisexual, and I'm still the same person." And he said, "No, you're not." I felt like he'd stuck a knife in my heart. But what could I do, I just said, "That's the way it is."

Then I went back east, and I brought all these articles and magazines to show my mother. There was a picture of me in the *Oakland Tribune*. I'd already been there four days before I got the courage to tell her. We were about to play cards and I said, "Ma, before we play, I have to tell you something." I was choking, I had tears in my eyes, I was falling apart. I took out the picture and said, "Ma, I want to show you what my life is about these days." I showed her the articles. I said, "I'm a feminist," and she said, "Oh, like Gloria Steinem." I said, "Well, you might say that." She's looking at the headlines, and I said, "Ma, did you see where it says bisexual?" She said, "Yeah. That's the part I don't like. Does that mean you have sex with women?" I said, "Yes." We never talked about it again.

Were you a feminist before you got involved in bisexual activism?
I've probably always been a feminist. I can remember early on sitting at home with my kids, yet always wanting to be involved in business. Whenever I told my husband, he ignored me. I always had a lot of resentment about that. I always questioned why it's okay for men and not for women.

How would you say feminism affects your bisexuality and vice versa?
I came out as a feminist before I came out as a bisexual. When I was job hunting in San Francisco, I hadn't worked in fifteen years other than raising my family. The only skills I had were that I could type, and I had graduated from high school. I went on a job interview, I was thirty-five years old, and they asked me for my junior high school grades. I went to the Age Discrimination Committee, and that was the beginning of my being a vocal feminist. I eventually became co-chair of the Age Discrimination Committee of Women Organized for Employment. Being involved in the bisexual movement complemented my feminism.

Are you still politically active around bisexuality?
Always. I got involved in a gay synagogue in San Francisco about six years ago. David Lourea, his wife Lee, and Maggi Rubenstein and I went on the High Holy Days and sat in the back row. All of a sudden the guy giving the sermon says, "Gay, lesbian, and bisexual." I thought the four of us were going to pass out. Nobody had ever said that before. I decided this was the synagogue for me. We all became very involved in it. When they had their board meeting, they talked about changing the name to include bisexuals, but they said, "How can we do that? Where are the bisexuals?" And one guy said, "I'm bisexual." See, when I come out as bisexual, then other people come out too.

Do you think bisexuality is part of a certain personality — are there other things about you that kind of fit in? Like being ambivalent, not in a negative sense, but being open to different possibilities?
I've always been open to new things. I've been involved in so many different things in my life. The past ten years has been a big turnaround. I don't even want to go back to who I was before. That's why I like having my own business where I can be who I am.

What do you think of the bisexual community today, and what direction would you like to see it take?

I'd like to see it more organized. There isn't a bisexual movement like there's a gay movement. We're lacking strength because we're missing numbers, and that's what hurts us the most. We know statistically that there are a lot of bisexuals out there, but we're not together as a unit. Right now I'm not involved in a group, but individually I always talk about being bisexual. If I'm walking down the street with a gay guy and he's eyeing somebody, I'll eye them too and say, see, when you're bi you can look at both men and women. I keep putting it out there all the time. It's important to say these things to make it more accepted.

I just wish people could be more relaxed about their sexuality. Somewhere along the way this country became very uptight. I'm very happy, I'm successful, I'm a good person, yet I have to make concessions around my bisexuality, and I just don't want to. I want people to know what bisexuality is, to say, oh yeah, I have some friends who are bisexual. I want to be acknowledged as a bisexual woman.

Christopher Alexander

Affirmation:
Bisexual Mormon

Many times in my life I've wavered between labeling myself "bisexual" or "gay." Although I've always known that my orientation was bisexual, I've identified my sexual attractions depending upon the situations. Getting comfortable with myself as a bisexual has been a lifelong process.

I "came out" as a nonheterosexual when I was sixteen years old. I had had a few minor sexual explorations with both boys and girls up until that time, but I started "getting sexual" at that time. I had full awareness of my deep attraction to boys, but I also had an intense awareness of my attraction toward girls. I experienced little conflict about these dual feelings. Although brought up Mormon, I managed to avoid some of the highly significant anti-homosexual messages that many in the Mormon Church, as well as in other churches, transmit. I was aware that society perceived homosexuality as wrong or bad, but this public perception posed no threat to my feelings and experiences.

High school presented me with some of my most significant challenges regarding life. A great deal of this, naturally, had to do with sexuality. I lost my virginity to Michelle on my sixteenth birthday. This event opened the way to sexual experimentation with members of both sexes. We considered ourselves bisexual. By the time I finished tenth grade, I was quite comfortable with my mutual attraction to both males and females, and I found that I had little need to put a label on it.

I got involved with a crowd too wild for me, and after breaking up with a girlfriend, I became severely depressed. My girlfriend and I got back together, and for a while things settled down. I began acknowledging that there was a homosexual part of me. I wrote a lengthy letter to my gay uncle confiding in him. During the years that followed, I often referred to myself as gay. Saying "bisexual" has often resulted in lengthy explanations and justifications, and since I had relationships with men for the next few years, I continued to identify myself as gay. But I was still attracted to women. I often found myself attracted to lesbians (never openly expressing this to others), and I still found women that I saw on the street very attractive. However I was involved monogamously with a man during my senior year in high school, and 'most everyone knew I was gay-identified by that point.

My parents confronted me shortly after I moved away to college, asking if I was gay. My mom told me that it was all right with her, but expressed the feeling that "we're on this planet to procreate." She said, "The important thing is that I wouldn't want you to enter into a relationship with a woman just to find out later that you really are gay, thus leaving her with a broken heart."

I continued to write about being attracted to both men and women. A great deal of my time was spent with a straight woman, three years older than myself. Together with friends, we saw *The Rocky Horror Picture Show;* took short day trips together; went to concerts, camping, or dancing. In time we developed a sexual relationship that was a natural outgrowth of our mutual affections.

Still in college then, I was amongst people who knew me as a gay man. The relationship with Teresa really surprised them. Some people expressed relief, feeling that I had finally "gone straight," but many of my gay friends felt betrayed, not believing that the person who had often served as their gay role model was now dating — and having sex with! — a woman. Other friends took it in stride; they are the ones who have remained close to us to this day.

Teresa knew about my sexual identity and history. I felt good having someone in my life with whom I could share so much. Teresa knew that I wasn't particularly promiscuous or sexually active with many different men, but unlike her, I was nonmonogamous. We agreed that I could be sexual with others as long as I did it with respect for our relationship.

The next summer, Teresa and I broke away from our shell of isolation. We started going out more and found an apartment with another woman who lived in the dormitory. Teresa and I attended the Lesbian and Gay Freedom Day Parade in San Francisco and met with one particular contingent called "Affirmation: Gay and Lesbian Mormons." I subscribed to their newsletter and found that a few of the members lived in our area.

Over the next several months I attended weekly Sunday meetings and developed a new network of friends. I was quite candid with them from the onset. I told them about being involved with a woman and was met with a variety of responses. I got involved in the leadership of the local chapter and began traveling to different conferences around the country. On one of these trips, I met Tom. We really took to each other and had a nice time sexually, socially, and emotionally. Unfortunately, the feelings didn't end when the conference did. We both went away feeling very strongly about one another.

Tom and I wrote and talked regularly, and he spoke of taking a job in the Bay Area. A mutual friend of ours called me after the conference with a strong warning to be honest with Tom about my relationship with Teresa since he sensed Tom's strong emotions for me and didn't want Tom hurt. I explained to him that I had told Tom about my relationship with Teresa. What followed, however, became a theme not just unique to Tom, but to many other gay men I have met: an inability to understand the seriousness of my relationship with Teresa. I still question what role I had in not being clearer with Tom about Teresa. Yet I've also come to learn about the problems other bisexuals in my circumstances confront not having their opposite-sex relationship taken seriously, especially when the partners aren't married.

I struggled with my feelings about Tom, but I was clear that I wanted to maintain the relationship with Teresa, that I didn't want it to end to pursue something further with Tom. It wasn't until he came to visit that he was able to understand my relationship with Teresa. Tom and I tried to clarify our roles with one another for quite some time. Tom was angered by the visit and told me that he felt I wasn't being very honest with myself.

By this time AIDS was a more pronounced part of our society. I realized that I was at risk based on my prior sexual practices. Teresa and I were very concerned about HIV infection. I assured her that I would use condoms when having anal intercourse and adhere to other aspects of safe sex guidelines. The HIV test was developed shortly thereafter, and I tested negative.

In late 1985, Teresa and I began looking at longer-term goals. I was getting ready to apply to a doctoral program, and we were deciding whether we'd stay in the Bay Area. A late-night discussion turned into an agreement to get married the following summer.

Getting married frightened me. I feared I would lose what "gay" identity I had. I was afraid that my being married would cause me to be rejected by many gays. I spent a great deal of time over the next several days talking to gay men about their feelings on marriage. Some had been married while others were longing for a life where they could be. But overall my friends' expressions of support were positive. This made the prospect easier for me. We did get married and had a large reception with half the people being gay and lesbian and the other half being family members.

Some of our friends accepted us after the marriage, but others didn't. Teresa and I remained involved with Affirmation. Three months later I attended an Affirmation meeting in Chicago where I was nominated to be the next general coordinator. At that point a representative of another chapter said that they had reservations about my assuming the role and wanted to ask some questions. They were concerned about public image, especially the perception by the Mormon Church of a "gay and lesbian" organization being run by a married bisexual male. This caused quite a stir. The San Francisco chapter finally defended me and my capabilities. I served as general coordinator for one year, with no conflicts, other than some members' difficulty with my being bisexual.

In 1986 I started working at a local AIDS service organization that was staffed primarily by gays and lesbians. Word about my being bisexual quickly spread. Many co-workers were superb about accepting my bisexuality. Others however didn't share such acceptance, and I experienced some difficulties. One colleague commented to me, "Why are you bisexual? How can you stand to be sexually involved with a woman?" Others expressed a concern that our department didn't have any gay white men. When it was explained to them that I had an extensive history of being involved with the gay and lesbian community, they responded, "He doesn't count, he's bisexual."

At one point I was selected to give part of a presentation on AIDS because of my knowledge of how it was affecting the bisexual community. Some people in the agency were angered, believing that other nonbisexual staff persons might be able to communicate the issues better. However, by this time I was much more secure with my identity as a bisexual. I was doing presentations on bisexuals with AIDS and had started leading a support group (which I still lead) for heterosexual and bisexual men with HIV, AIDS, or ARC.

In 1987 I attended the International AIDS Conference in Washington, D.C. I met a man to whom I was very attracted. In the course of our conversation, he disclosed he had AIDS. Noting the mutual attraction Martin and I had for one another, I had to ask myself if I would have sex with someone I knew had AIDS. I answered "yes" after some thought, trusting that I wouldn't do anything differently if I didn't know he had AIDS. We had a beautiful, romantic, and exciting week in Washington. At one point I remarked to Martin, "My life is such that there's no way our relationship can continue once we return to the Bay Area." He said, "Good. My life is set up so that I can't either; I'm getting ready to die."

Martin and I continued to see each other fairly regularly since I was preparing a presentation for a conference he was coordinating. We recognized the intense emotions we had for one another were still with us and were both concerned about Teresa. She knew of him, but they had never met.

A little less than a month later, at the Lesbian and Gay Freedom Day Parade, Martin and Teresa met. The three of us made plans to go out to dinner. When Teresa and I arrived, he was looking great. This was the first person with AIDS that Teresa had met in any substantive way. At one point while I was in the restroom, Martin commented to her, "I want you to make sure you take care of Chris when I die." Later, Teresa cried. She liked Martin a great deal.

Over the next several months Martin and I grew closer, as did he and Teresa. They each found in the other something neither had with me. Eventually, Martin spent weekends over at our place, and I would occasionally stay over at his place. Martin and Teresa traveled to Lake Tahoe at one point and later made a one-week trip to Europe. The three of us would cook, lie on the fold-out bed, and watch TV. We even went to an Affirmation conference in Salt Lake City together. Our friends liked Martin a great deal, and his friends seemed to like Teresa and I, but all were at a loss to comprehend our relationship.

This relationship certainly wasn't without its problems though. Both Teresa and Martin would want more private time with me, and occasionally they each got annoyed by the other. On top of that, Martin's health was in flux, and he required extra care and attention at times. People at work knew of my relationship with Martin. It certainly caused some dissonance among my colleagues. Martin liked the "confusion" of it all and welcomed the opportunity to attend work-related social functions with Teresa and me.

Sometimes Martin attended workshops with me when I spoke about bisexuality. Once he and Teresa even spoke on a panel together. We continued for a little more than a year until Martin died. In the eight months since Martin's death, Teresa and I have been going through our individual grieving processes, sorting out our feelings about Martin's life and death and the impact he had on our lives and relationship.

I'm currently doing research on bisexuals with AIDS and have submitted a few articles on this subject to some publications. I will finish school in less than two years. I attend a weekly group for married and formerly married gay and bisexual men, and I'm able to give and get a lot of support. I believe more people could make bisexuality work in their lives if they didn't restrict their views of themselves into one sexual category. I hope my story may help others by encouraging them to explore all sides of their sexuality.

Suzanne

I have always been one

When I was seventeen, an impatient lesbian said accusingly to me, "Why do you spend so much time with gay people if you're not a lesbian?"

I was dumbfounded. I had never been sexual with anyone — male or female. The gathering was a wrap-up to a gay rights demonstration in which I had participated. I was a freshman in college and had never dissected my reasons for supporting gay liberation (not yet known as lesbian and gay rights). For me this was just another way of protecting individual and civil rights. I did not yet consciously know that these rights were as much personally mine to fight for as those of women or blacks.

The next year, when leaving another gathering, a lesbian friend said "goodbye" by kissing me on the lips. I was shocked. Her kiss was warm and tingly. To my surprise, it did not feel "weird" as I would have guessed. It felt natural and I liked it! I glided down the street squealing, "Ahhhh, a woman kissed me!"

Back at the dorm I grabbed a close friend to tell her the details. Mind you, pre-party I, too, identified as straight. She flipped. No wonder I was still a virgin, I had been watching the wrong sex! We fiddled with the idea that I was a lesbian. In our young minds, it seemed plausible that an acceptance of a kiss from another woman, plus an inability to lose my virginity, equaled lesbianism. She offered to scope out pretty girls for me.

Between the boys after me to sleep with them and the recurring vision of that first kiss, I felt compelled to further explore relationships with women. On the strength of that alone, my next move was to come out to my friends as a bisexual. I thought I would explain that I liked boys just fine at arm's length, but the tender, unhurried embrace of another woman was worth checking out.

As it was, my great coming-out statement — "I think I am bisexual" — was delivered to a room full of partying dorm friends who probably did not remember what I had said moments later. In response, I got a resounding "We know." Since I was still a virgin, I could not figure out how they knew I was bisexual. I believe the internal struggles I faced about my sexuality were simply more obvious than I realized at the time. At any rate, I was glad that my young friends were being so casual and supportive.

One year later, I came out as a bisexual to the gay rights group for which I worked. I no longer wanted to be considered a "straight supporter." I was given much encouragement and was readily embraced by all, except for that same impatient lesbian who'd stirred such unpleasant feelings two years before. She leaned over to someone and rudely sniped, "I bet next year she finally admits she is a lesbian."

By the time I became president of that gay rights group, four years after the impatient lesbian's initial remark, I had lost my virginity twice, broken my engagement to a bewildered young man for the less-than-true love of a woman, and was positive that I was a bisexual. Not gay. Not straight. Bisexual.

And, still, the impatient lesbian said, "You just haven't met the right woman." I was sick of arguing "political correctness," and I very much resented the smugness of the lesbians who were sure my evolution was incomplete. They sounded just like the chauvinist pigs who said all I needed was a good fuck and I would never make love to a woman again. Although I understand sexual politics, I could no sooner change my sexual orientation, nor would I want to, any more than a lesbian could. And no, I do not feel enslaved by men simply because I occasionally sleep with one.

I have been out of college and working in both the heterosexual and lesbian communities as a writer for a number of years. I have been able to decipher the mysteries of my sexuality's origins while experiencing lesbian relationships. All the subconscious trappings from my childhood started pouring into my conscious mind as if a floodgate had opened.

Sometime in high school my socialization to pursue relationships with boys kicked into high gear. My earliest, innocent explorations were buried in the whirlwind of trying to attract boys — even ones I did not want.

I quite suddenly began to remember the crushes on girlfriends, and more serious experiences. I remembered exploring the bodies of at least three girlfriends between the ages of seven and twelve. While curiosity in children is normal, I now realize that my friendships with these girls, and our activities, were more intense and sensual than routine childhood attachments. These new memories clearly knocked aside the "usual" ones of boyfriends and spin-the-bottle kisses. Oddly enough the memories of kissing and fondling other girls were not as shocking to me as the fact that I had had to repress them.

I was elated to have my earliest memories back. They served to complete a picture of me. The fact is my first same-sex kiss happened long before college. I did not wake up at eighteen to "become" a bisexual. I have always been one. And, although my sexual orientation is bisexual, I am politically and emotionally a lesbian. I do not deny that I am woman-identified. I do resist any faction of this society, straight or gay, telling me how to act, think, or make love.

As a bisexual I feel I have the best of both worlds. Why narrow my attentions? I find a political awareness in the lesbian community that is unmatched, and I enjoy socializing with my lesbian sisters, but it is just as easy for me to fall in love with a feminist man as a feminist woman. And I would not want that to change.

As an "out" bisexual, I will always proudly be active in furthering lesbian and gay civil rights. Recently, I became a plaintiff in a lawsuit that hopes to strike down my state's sodomy and gross indecency laws. These are the laws most often used to justify arrest and harassment of lesbians, gays, and bisexuals.

It is important to me that bisexuals and gays decompartmentalize. Bisexuals are not the pesky younger siblings or unfinished counterparts of homosexuals. Rather than judge or separate from one another, we must get on with the common struggle against the oppression of certain types of sexual expression. If bisexuals, for fear of ridicule, remain closeted from gay brothers and sisters, how can we stand united and strong against society's sexual phobias that oppress us all?

Obie Leyva

¿*Que es un* bisexual?

As for most people, coming out is a daily process for me. I began two years ago during my sophomore year at the University of California at Berkeley. First, I came out to my close friends, then to my family, with the exception of my father. I received negative responses from both my straight and gay friends, and my family was confused because they did not know what a bisexual was. This was because in the Chicano and Latino culture, bisexuality, although practiced, is not discussed openly, nor is there a word for it in the language.

The incredible amount of biphobia that both my gay and straight friends possess has made it hard for them to accept my bisexuality. They seemed to share the same criteria: "How many men and how many women have you slept with?" as if being sexual with a certain number of men and a certain number of women makes me a "true" bisexual. My straight friends saw my sexual identity as "trendy" and that I was really straight. To my gay friends, my sexual identity was my fear of identifying as gay.

Around this time, many of my male friends were coming out as gay. I noticed that they were getting support and validation from me and one another, but during my coming-out process I received biphobic comments. I began to confront my friends with the fact that my bisexuality is not a phase, and that I, too, need support and acceptance for who I am.

When I came out to my family, I faced a different problem all together. They lacked the understanding of what bisexuality is. "¿*Que es un* bisexual?" my mother asked when I came out to her. I told her that I am attracted to members of both sexes and have the ability to fall in love with both.

She reminded me of the Chicano and Latino community's view toward gay men. They are referred to as *jotos,* sick and evil men who will go to hell for engaging in such activity. A *joto* plays the role of the "bottom" and is considered gay. The man who is "on top" retains his "machismo" and is considered to still be heterosexual. In the Chicano and Latino community, when a man engages in sexual activity with another man, as long as he is the "top" and expresses no romantic feelings, he is considered to be using the *joto* as one would use a woman, and his behavior is regarded as acceptable. This ideology creates a polarized view of male sexuality with the belief that a man is either macho or *joto,* leaving no room for bisexuality (sound familiar?).

For me, being out also means educating others on bisexuality, whether it is to dispel the myths or to make people more aware. At the University of California, I am a co-founder of a support group called La Familia. We are a group of Chicano and Latino gays, lesbians, and bisexuals offering each other support and friendship. I am also involved in a support group called BLOOD (Bound by Love of Our Diversity) which was formed for bisexuals, gays, and lesbians of color. Both groups have weekly meetings and serve as social networks and educational forums. I educate people on bisexuality within my peer group, in my academic community, and in my cultural community. It just never stops. Now when people ask, "*¿Que es un* bisexual?" I smile and proudly answer, "*Yo soy!*"

Marcy Sheiner

The foundations of the bisexual community in San Francisco

An interview with Dr. Maggi Rubenstein*

How *did you come to know you were bisexual?*
I didn't really think of myself as sexual. I had an abusive childhood —
which attacks your self-esteem — so I didn't feel that good about myself.
I knew I had crushes on both boys and girls. Seeing girls made me very
nervous and anxious, so I avoided the girls' locker room like the plague.
And I couldn't get into the boys' locker room!

When my first marriage ended, I dated straight men and made very
bad choices. I still wasn't feeling good about myself. Then I started
hanging out with gay men, and through them I met my first woman
lover. She led a very glamorous life in Hollywood. She was a screen-
writer and had a whole community of lesbian women. She tried to talk
me into being lesbian too, saying I couldn't possibly like men. All her
friends treated me like the new kid on the block, and I got a lot of
attention. But the strongest message was that it wasn't okay to not be
lesbian. And this was before the feminist movement had come out with
the idea that "feminism is the theory and lesbianism is the practice." So

---

* *Editors' note:* Dr. Rubenstein has been a bisexual activist for almost twenty years
in San Francisco. Currently she is dean of students at the Institute for the
Advanced Study of Human Sexuality and maintains a private therapy practice. In
1972 she helped found San Francisco Sex Information and the University of
California Program in Sex Counseling, and in 1976 she co-founded the Bisexual
Center. Her community activism includes working with the Women's AIDS
Network, the AIDS Health Project, and the Committee to Preserve Our Sexual
and Civil Liberties, which she co-chaired in 1985. She was a founding member of
Mobilization against AIDS and served as co-chair in 1985–1986.

it was a separatist time for me. I had gotten burned enough by men that I wanted to stay away from them. And I was in love with this particular woman. After our relationship ended, I dated several other women and men.

Then I married an artist. He was a communist, great on workers' rights, but terrible on women's or lesbian or bi rights. We had a six-year marriage, and my two children came from that. We divorced when I was in my early thirties, and I decided I didn't want to be coupled again.

I began to grow up. I began to affirm my bisexuality and to come out about it. I was working at the Center for Special Problems, a mental health clinic, and I remember sitting at a meeting and coming out to the staff. I was absolutely terrified. I had come out to friends and partners, but not to my peers, to my colleagues. I've made hundreds of speeches since then but that was the most exciting and scary one.

You must have been the only bisexual you knew at that time?
I was.

So when you were going through the transition of not knowing what bisexuality was and being told you should be lesbian, were you in a lot of conflict?
I knew I was bi. I knew I had an attraction to women and an attraction to men. I knew I wasn't monogamous, though many bisexual people are. I didn't want to be coupled, I wanted to have quality time with a number of people. I was sexually active, and I was politically active.

Later I did my Master's thesis on bisexuality and androgyny and my doctorate at the Institute for the Advanced Study of Human Sexuality on bisexuality and self-esteem. My research showed that the longer someone is bisexual and the more support they get, the better they feel about themselves, the higher their self-esteem.

Which came first for you, bisexuality or feminism?
They coincided. Getting into feminism and my power as a woman gave me the courage to come out as a bisexual.

What is the essence of bisexuality for you? Do you think it's a personality construct? Do you find yourself ambiguous in other areas?
I hate the word *ambiguous*. But yes, I do think it's a personality type as well as a true orientation. I like to look at the whole picture. In regard to the Kinsey scale, I'm more at the straight bisexual end sexually. I've had more men partners than women partners. In terms of friendship, I have more women friends. In terms of politics, I'm way over at the lesbian and gay end. You can be all over the place on the Kinsey scale. When I look at the major relationships in my life, my great loves, half of those have been men and half women.

When did you start organizing politically around bisexuality?
When I left my job at the mental health clinic, I helped several others
organize a community switchboard called San Francisco Sex Information.
I also started running workshops at the National Sex Forum and always
insisted that there be a bisexual component to our training. Once I
asserted that bisexuality exists and is normal, other people started coming
out too. It gave them permission.

In 1976 the Institute for the Advanced Study of Human Sexuality
was established so that people could get academic training. And at the
same time Harriet Levy, the woman I was involved with, and I called
people together from the switchboard community to start the Bisexual
Center. We put a little notice in the paper and in a national magazine,
and we got hundreds of phone calls. It was very gratifying. Some people
were out and some weren't and it was okay. I came out publicly on
television. Somebody had to do it, and I felt it was my responsibility.
I wanted to.

**Why did the original Bisexual Center fade? Was it because of the
advent of AIDS?**
That was one factor. Some people went back into the closet. Others
moved on to other organizations. But the center had served its purpose.
There wasn't the energy to revitalize it. Eventually a second wave of
bisexual people came along. There's new leadership now, and other
bisexual community organizations have formed. I've been able to help
with that.

The bisexual community in its second generation is more diverse.
Some people are sexual radicals, and some are not. There are some
people who are even uncomfortable with sexuality. I certainly think that
being bisexual isn't just about your sexuality with yourself and others,
but to leave it out, to talk about other aspects of bisexuality and not talk
about the sexual aspects, is a huge omission.

**Do you think this omission is out of fear of perpetuating the myth
that bisexuals are promiscuous?**
Well some of us *are* nonmonogamous. And some of us aren't. But we
need to spell it out. Some bisexual people are monogamous, some aren't,
some lead very kinky lives, and everything in between. We want to honor
them all.

I've been the first one to say that being bisexual is not about who
you get it on with, it's about how you feel about yourself. But to deny
the fact that biphobia exists because of our sexuality, to deny the fact
that because of our love for men and women we sometimes act on it,
sometimes in outrageous ways even, is begging the question. I do safe
sex education workshops and I know that the more someone is out, the
more responsible they're going to be about safe sex.

For instance, I worked with Mobilization Against AIDS, starting in 1984, as well as the Committee to Preserve Our Sexual Liberties. The committee fought to keep the bathhouses open and to use them as centers of education. When they were closed down, it meant that the most sexually active community didn't have that same direct opportunity to get safe sex education.

AIDS has killed a lot of sexual energy. It's put many people back into the closet. It's been dreadful. But I personally have not changed my feelings, nor do I think anyone should change their feelings about being bisexual because of this terrible disease. Sex isn't bad, bisexuality isn't bad; it's the virus that we have to protect ourselves against. It's important to be out to our partners about our sexual health, as well as being bisexual.

Would you call yourself a sex radical?
Well, I'm politically radical. I'm very much to the left on most issues. And I'm also sexually radical. I support all people's rights, all lifestyles that are consensual and not coercive. I have many friends in the S & M community and in the transsexual and transvestite communities. I support people in the sex industry — I'm a prostitutes' rights advocate. I myself haven't done sex for money, but you never know. I'm only sixty.

Do you see a need for a separate bisexual community?
I don't like separatism. I'm interested in bringing the gay, lesbian, and bisexual communities together, but just as there are lesbians involved in the gay male community who also meet separately, just as there are men's groups who meet to get a sense of their own personal power as men, the bisexual community has a right to get a sense of its own power.

I don't like gay and lesbian people's ignorance about bisexuals. It's rare to find a politically savvy bisexual person who isn't involved in the gay and lesbian community, but many gays and lesbians have no knowledge of bisexual people. We're still laughed at, trivialized, seen as purveyors of disease, seen as riding on the coattails of the gay rights movement, as if we weren't there all along.

To me, these attitudes toward us come from ignorance and self-hatred. If somebody feels really good about who they are, they don't feel threatened by what other people are. We are a stronger movement now than we were a few years ago. Many people in the gay and lesbian community are now acknowledging bisexuals.

Hearing and saying "gay, lesbian, and bisexual" is music to my ears. Because the more unity we achieve, the more we put aside petty differences, the more strength we have.

Matthew LeGrant

The "b" word

My earliest recollection of my bisexuality was in the third grade. I had two crushes: one on the most handsome boy, and the other on the most beautiful girl in the school. I did not know anything about sex; I just remember being attracted and imagining being close to either of them. I was a very shy person, so I didn't even talk to either of my interests. I just dreamed — a lot!

This type of fantasizing was about all I did regarding romance. By the time I became aware of my sexual feelings in adolescence, I had been indoctrinated by society's attitude that any attraction to the same gender was wrong and bad. So I just ignored my feelings toward men and led a "proper" straight life. For the next fifteen years, I struggled with my feelings for men, direly wishing they would go away. I did not act on them and controlled my behavior scrupulously so as not to "let on." I never told a soul, and it wasn't too surprising I didn't have a happy love life.

The first time I read the word *bisexual,* I knew instantly that that's what I was. I didn't go so far as to acknowledge my feelings, or do anything about it, because of my deep fear that I might really be gay.

When I was twenty-seven, I moved from southern California to attend graduate school at the University of California at Berkeley. Somewhere in the back of my mind I knew San Francisco's gay community was also a reason to move there. But it was the beginning of the AIDS epidemic, so I had another "reason" not to explore my gay side. After many years of thinking about it — usually staring at the ceiling at 1 a.m. — I had to begrudgingly accept that at least on an intellectual level I was bisexual. I had a lot of problems dealing with my feelings. There was no one to talk with about it. I didn't know of any bisexual groups and had a hard time finding any books. I even looked in the card catalogue at the University of California's main library under the "b" word and found nothing! This library is reputably the fourth largest in the country!

A couple of years later, as I neared graduation, I had my first real relationship with a woman, or with anyone for that matter. At first, I did not tell her about my bisexuality for fear of being rejected. After four months, we were very much in love. I decided to come out to her. I had learned her sister was a lesbian and hoped for the best.

She was shocked at first, then supported me in dealing with my feelings, but told me that a long-term relationship was out of the question. I felt so guilty for not telling her from the beginning that I felt it was all right for her to reject me, but I hoped we would not break up. Being a counselor herself, she encouraged me to seek counseling. The fact I had never talked about "it" was what upset her the most.

After a few false starts, I found a therapist and began talking about my bisexual feelings for the first time. In a little counseling office my therapist gently prodded me toward self-acceptance. Finally it all came pouring out: the lies to myself, the fears, the stifled desires, and many tears. The relationship with my girlfriend lasted two more rocky years.

By then I was going to a bisexual support group at the Pacific Center in Berkeley. I started going to gay bars, which was both exciting and terrifying. Finally, I met a man in the White Horse bar. We made a date. We met for dinner, went home, and I had my first gay experience. It was incredibly exciting to be able to express my full sexuality. Afterwards when I told him it was my first time with a man, he didn't believe it.

One by one I came out to my close friends. They were all straight and were all supportive. My fear of being ostracized started to diminish. Each time it was easier. One of my friends was more surprised (or bothered) with my seeing a therapist, than with my bisexuality!

In June 1987, I went to East Bay Gay Day and saw a booth about the March on Washington for Lesbian and Gay (and Bisexual) Rights set for October of that year. The march was in protest of the then recent Supreme Court decision on the Hardwick case, which upheld state laws against sodomy, even in the privacy of your own home. By the time I had walked passed that booth for the second time, I felt a deep chord strike within me saying *go!* I went to a meeting and learned there was going to be a bisexual contingent. For me, going to the march was not only to demonstrate for our rights, but was also the last major step in my own personal coming out process.

I flew to Washington, D.C., feeling that the march was going to be bigger than most people expected. I showed up at the ellipse on the morning of October 11. Over 600,000 men and women gathered to demand our civil rights as full human and sexual beings! I marched proudly with the National Bisexual Network contingent.

As each contingent joined the ever-growing crowd assembled on the Mall, we listened to Holly Near. We all joined hands and sang, "We are a gentle angry people, and we are fighting for our lives..." I was both moved and soothed by the sight and sounds of hundreds of thousands of people singing and swaying in unison. At that moment I accepted the person I am — and felt at peace with myself.

A month later, although very apprehensive, I came out to my parents. I was lucky to have their unqualified support. They told me they loved me for who I was. More tears helped wash away the pain of the many years of denial.

Since then I have become very active in the Bay Area Bisexual Network (BABN). Formed in May of 1987, BABN provides an umbrella group of resources, social activities, a speaker's bureau, and information for people in the San Francisco Bay Area. I was recently elected co-chair.

The best part of being in this new community is talking, socializing, and just hanging out with men and women who support bisexuality as a valid and healthy lifestyle. We are not going back into the closet, nor will we endure the ignorance of not knowing our personal and collective experiences. I feel we are building a new community of bisexuals drawing on the strides and prides made by the civil rights and women's movement, and the gay and lesbian struggles that went before us.

Robyn Ochs

From the closet
to the stage

I was a self-avowed heterosexual for the first eighteen years of my life. Then in November of 1976, during my first year at the State University of New York, one of my roommates broke up with her boyfriend and began seeing a woman. I was surprised, intrigued, fascinated. The implications were staggering to me. If beautiful Ellen could be attracted to a woman, what about me? This possibility had never before entered my consciousness. I had always had boyfriends and had not felt dissatisfied with these relationships. I enjoyed making love with men, or at least with some men. Over the next months, I watched Ellen and her new sweetheart carefully. I developed a full-blown crush on Ellen, and a smaller one on her sweetheart and on most of the women-loving women who had become Ellen's new social circle. I bravely wrote in my journal that I was bisexual. I read *Rubyfruit Jungle* and *Patience and Sarah* in my women's studies class. One of my professors was an out lesbian. All in all, I had a very auspicious start for my budding bisexuality.

Then I got stuck. I was terrified. I was afraid I would lose all of my friends. I felt that I couldn't talk to anyone, not even to Ellen or the three gay men who had become my constant companions. I kept my silence for the rest of that year. And again the next.

In my second year at college I was involved for several months with a male theater student. That relationship ended, and the following fall I fell for Daniel, a campus activist who was the object of many crushes. I pursued him relentlessly. We were involved for two and a half years and lived together for about half of that time. I loved him but felt very confused about who I was and what I wanted. He seemed much more certain of who I really was than I myself was. I held back, and he pursued me. Finally he grew tired of the pursuit and began to leave. I was twenty-one, sad, and relieved.

In the meantime, Ellen came back into my life. I had watched her from a distance since freshman year and followed her activities. I watched how the lesbian clique on campus had teased her for being pink and fluffy, for not following the unwritten rules of the community. She had always held her own and was in fact quite popular despite her "shortcomings." My crush on her had ebbed and flowed over the years, but was still intact.

I invited Ellen to stay with me in my apartment near the campus for a few weeks while she finished writing her thesis. She accepted the invitation and moved in. We were on completely different schedules. I would work evenings and then come home and go to sleep, while she was up all night writing. She was sleeping on a cot in my room. After a few days I invited her to share my bed, explaining that we were hardly ever asleep at the same time. We curled up next to each other, and she went to sleep. I don't think I slept for a single minute that night. I was so excited to feel Ellen next to me that I could hardly breathe. By early morning I had worked up enough courage to put my arm around her and finally I fell asleep. This went on for days.

About a week later we watched a Bette Davis movie and drank an excess quantity of White Russians. At some point Ellen kissed me. I was so terrified — of responding, of not responding, of doing the wrong thing, of doing the right thing, of not knowing what to do at all — that I froze. After a couple of tries she gave up and never tried again. We never talked about it. Ellen moved back to her parents' home, and we remained friends.

I was starting to come out as bisexual to a few select friends. I had a lightweight relationship with a man all the next year. Then, on Valentine's Day of my twenty-fourth year, I met Chris, a new co-worker. Something had changed inside me, and I acted quickly and decisively for the first time. I was ready. I flirted and initiated conversation. After her second night at work, I asked her out on a date. Within a week we had become lovers. She moved to my town, just a few blocks from my apartment.

While I was very comfortable while I was alone with Chris, I was still terrified of how the rest of the world would react. When leaving my house to go over to her apartment, I'd close my bedroom door in the hope that my roommate would think I was home in my own bed. I'd rush home in the morning in order to be in my own bed when my roommate woke up. During my seven-month relationship with Chris, despite the fact that we saw each other daily, I did not once tell my roommate that she and I were lovers. I found out after we had broken up that my roommate had known about us all along, and that she and Chris had discussed our relationship in great detail!

While Chris was very kind and thoughtful to me at home, she could be rather abrasive to people at work and on the street. She was one of those women who fit mainstream society's stereotype of a lesbian, and she had encountered a lot of homophobia and harassment. As a result, she had adopted an "I don't really give a damn" attitude toward those who were not close to her. This was very hard for me, as I most certainly did care what other people thought. Walking with Chris around our small Connecticut city was to me like walking around with a billboard stating that we were lesbians. I was nowhere near ready to do this. I also felt not completely welcomed by the local lesbian social circle. I suspect that some of their reaction had to do with the fact that I was just coming out and was very unsure of myself, and part had to do with the fact that I identified as bisexual.

During my time with Chris, I began to *really* apply academic learning about lesbianism and feminism to my own life. Why was I so afraid of coming out? What was I afraid of? I began to understand the systematic oppression of gay people. I began to question my own assumptions. I had always accepted that I would eventually find a male partner and have at least one child. What if I didn't? Why would that be so upsetting to people? What if Mr. Right were a woman? Why were so many people threatened by Chris's being butch?

Monogamy and commitment were major and recurring themes in my relationship with Chris. We were most definitely in a monogamous relationship, which suited me just fine as I have always been most comfortable with monogamy. Chris also preferred this situation. The problem was that Chris was convinced that I would leave her as soon as a man came along. She mentioned this repeatedly, and I repeatedly said that I wouldn't. My bisexuality was very threatening to her, as she felt I could and would choose men at any point. At other times she would take the opposite approach, discounting my bisexuality by telling me that I was really a lesbian who just hadn't finished coming out yet.

I did end up leaving Chris, but not for a man. I left her for a new city and a new life. On Labor Day of 1982, I moved to the Boston area. During my second week in town, I went to a discussion on bisexuality at the Women's Center in Cambridge. There were about twenty women in the room identifying as bisexual, and I was ecstatic. So many bisexuals in Cambridge! At the end of this meeting, a woman stood up and invited those interested to form a support group. I was one of eight women who joined.

Our group, which we named the BiVocals, consisted of eight very different women. We held conflicting opinions on almost every issue — sadomasochism, the raging debate over the proposed anti-pornography ordinance, monogamy. A couple of us were involved with men, a couple with women, a couple were celibate, and a couple were single and dating various people. We were secretaries, graduate students, social workers, writers, musicians, administrators, real estate developers, and various combinations of the aforementioned. One member was married and gave birth to two children during the seven-year life of our group. We argued, cried, and talked about our lives.

During its first year of existence, members of the BiVocals assisted in the formation of two more support groups. In June, we decided to hold a social event for bisexual women. We expected that twenty women, the total number of women in the three support groups, would attend. Instead twice that number showed up. We realized that there must be a lot more of us hidden out there. In September 1983, we held the first official meeting of the Boston Bisexual Women's Network. We expected about thirty women. Instead, over eighty women attended. We filled the largest meeting room in the Women's Center and overflowed into the street and into the hallway and even up the staircase. The general mood was ecstatic. So many bisexual women! It was a powerful contradiction to the isolation which most if not all of us had been feeling. I grinned so continuously all evening that my cheeks ached. The Boston Bisexual Women's Network was born.

In my personal life I've grown and moved in new directions. I've become quite comfortable with my bisexuality and am completely out of the closet — at work, at home, and sometimes even in print, on stages, and on television. I've been in a series of monogamous relationships since I moved to Boston, about half with women. At one point during this time, I went through a period of feeling that I must really be heterosexual and wondered why I bothered to identify as bisexual. That was just before I fell in love with a woman. A couple of years later I went through a period of feeling that I must really be lesbian, so why was I bothering to call myself bisexual? Not too long afterward I got involved with a man. I then resolved to accept my bisexuality fully, with all of its myriad twists and turns. At present I'm single and learning for the first time how to date (the time spent between meeting someone and getting "married"). I'm still not sure whether "Person Right" will be a Ms. or a Mr., though I kind of hope that the person I fall in love with will be a Ms. I'm quite happy to be me, and very fortunate to be a bisexual woman.

BI-PHOBIA SHIELD

BISEXUAL PRIDE!

RBWN

BISEXUAL AND PROUD TO BE LESBIAN

ASSUME NOTHING

BISEXUAL AND PROUD TO BE GAY

Happy Bi Nature

Bi

Bi the way, don't assume I'm gay

BI-PHOBIA SHIELD

UNITY IS OUR BI WORD
BI-POL 1984

SAFE SEX Bi ALL MEANS

Fairies for FERRARO
BI-POL 1984

Blatantly Bisexual

BI-PHOBIA SHIELD

IV.

Politics:
A queer among queers

Overview

Hey queer! Hey you are queer aren't you? What kind of queer
are you? QUEER — you know what it means — odd, unusual,
not straight, gay. I am queer, not straight. And ... I am odd.
Odd in the fact that I have been an active open out-of-the-closet
Bisexual *in the lesbian and gay world for the last seven years. I*
am not alone. There are many of us in your community. And
many who feel compelled to stay closeted due to discrimination
... But we are kin — the struggle for gay rights is our struggle.
We have been part of this movement since Stonewall ...
Acknowledgement and acceptance of Bisexuals is crucial to the
growth of the gay rights movement. By supporting us, by helping
us reach out to closeted Bisexuals and those who identify as
straight, our numbers will increase ... We must unite to fight
common enemies; we must not squabble among ourselves over
who is more queer or more politically correct. Our real enemies
gain when we fight each other.   — Autumn Courtney[1]

Bisexuality was one of the most denied issues of the eighties.
Nobody, except "out" bisexuals and those involved with AIDS work,
wanted to talk about it rationally or give it recognition beyond the
usual scapegoating. The public–private behavior–identity doublespeak
of the lesbian, gay, and heterosexual communities was amazing, yet
in keeping with the Reagan administration's uncanny ability to say
one thing and do another. At the same time, the entertainment industry was blossoming with more bisexual, gay, and androgynous
images, while people were bending over backwards to avoid the "b"
word at all costs. This created an absurd and endless parade of
obfuscating terms: gay married men, lesbians who sleep with men,
heterodyke, heterosexually married gay men, queer hetero-sex, heterosexual women who swing with women, lesbians with "boy toys,"
lesbians and gay men who sports-fuck with the opposite sex, even
heterosexually identified men who have sex with men, or simply "men
who have sex with men," as the Centers for Disease Control now puts
it. Our idea of what sexuality is is obviously in a state of flux. Language is searching for new meaning. But terms, once coined, move

into common usage and acquire the power to control, define, and divide us.

As people whose experiences have been denied within the rigid monosexual framework, and who have been scapegoated in the AIDS epidemic, we must question the current practice of separating sexual identity from behavior. Isn't it ironic that they are (supposedly) so unrelated to each other? We must ask what role internalized biphobia, homophobia, and heterophobia play in any or all of these identities and behaviors. What if the bisexual community was a thriving, recognized part of the lesbian, gay, and heterosexual communities? What if the bisexual movement was already an established and respected force within the many liberation movements? How would labels, assumptions, identities, and behaviors change then?

When the entire continuum of sexual behavior is validated, it liberates everyone from the tyranny of being forced to "choose sides." The recognition of bisexual orientation is the next logical step in the sexual (r)evolutionary process. When this step is taken, it will move toward recognizing the strict categories themselves as false.

During the last twenty years, bisexual accomplishments, struggles, and victories, even our contributions on the frontlines of the AIDS epidemic, have been rendered virtually invisible and unnewsworthy in the women's, straight, and gay media. There are many unsung heros and heroines. Because of this the stereotypes remain in place, and many bisexual people remain closeted or censored in fear. Bisexuals have been queer among queers, queer among straights, and just plain queer.

Though many of us may have once collaborated in our own invisibility, we can no longer afford it. The tragedy of AIDS has forced us to make the connections between self and other. Coming out encourages us to trust our experience and be our own role models. When we communicate our bisexual pride, it heals us and builds a strong community that gives our movement its juice.

As a young movement caught up in our initial rush of pride, we cannot forget what other liberation struggles have to teach. Building a bisexual movement without a multicultural, feminist perspective is disastrous. Bisexual liberation necessitates the recognition of not only all the sexual dynamics among us but all the race and class dynamics that impact and affect one's sexual identity as well. It requires a willingness to do the work of consciously dismantling them, so we don't repeat old, confining, or oppressive patterns. We have to ask ourselves hard questions and prioritize the issues the answers demand. Those who have traditionally spoken out must listen more carefully. Those who have been silenced must risk speaking up. Only then will we arrive at an authentic understanding of the spectrum of sexuality among all peoples. Only then will we grasp the rich variety of life itself.

As we affirm our identities we must nurture all the leadership potential of our community. In turn, these leaders will influence and inform the many communities to which we belong.

Gay and feminist roots: We were there!

Although easy to forget, now, in the 1990s, the current women's movement and gay liberation movement developed separately in the late sixties and the early seventies. Many women identified as gay or lesbian before they identified as feminists. Many men knew they were gay before they came to understand how their own sexual liberation related to women's condition. Some once-straight men came to their love of men only through studying feminism and then wondering about the relations between the sexes and how they could then love men more fully. And some once-straight women, of course, came to their love of other women through the open door of feminism.

Lesbians separated from the gay liberation movement when gay men's sexism drove them to seek common cause with other women. The lesbian and the mainstream feminist movement diverged too as lesbians found they could not work with straight women who denigrated and invalidated them. During this same period in history (the seventies), people of color confronted middle-class white activists about organizing against racism and class oppression in their own white communities instead of doing "civil rights organizing" and "anti-poverty work" in working-class and nonwhite communities. Many people of color had come to the gay and women's liberation movement with a determination to integrate the liberation of their own ethnic or racial group into gay or feminist analysis. However, they often left, and still leave, or don't join these white-dominated groups due to the unexamined racism, sexism, homophobia, and/or classism they encounter to create their own groups.

As lesbians began to identify with women's issues, and specifically lesbian issues, a dialogue between straight and gay women about the relation of sexuality to women's rights occurred. Simultaneously the mass (white male–dominated) media was getting wind of a revolution brewing in the land as citywide women's strikes, demonstrations, and the first gay pride parades began. Lesbian-baiting was used as a tactic to intimidate and divide all women in the movement and to nip the dialogue in the bud.

Into this discord walked bisexual writer and sculptor Kate Millett, who had just published her ground-breaking theoretical work *Sexual Politics*. Kate was invited to speak at a New York City college forum on sexual liberation. A *Time* magazine reporter was in attendance. As Kate spoke, a young black woman in the audience asked her, "Why don't you say you're a Lesbian here openly? ... Are you or aren't you?" Millett had already stated that she was a bisexual and repeated that.[2] Wendy

Wonderful jumped to the microphone. "I am bisexual, but I've realized something. I can tell my friends I'm bisexual, and they say how groovy, as long as I'm having a relationship with a man. If I say the same thing and introduce them to a woman I'm having a relationship with, they are very cool about it. I'm bisexual, but it is for my homosexuality that I'm oppressed. Therefore I say I'm a Lesbian as a political statement."

Meanwhile *Time* magazine came out with a December 8, 1970, piece, "Women's Lib: A Second Look," attacking Millett on the basis of her declared bisexuality. That same week, Wendy went to a Women's Strike Coalition meeting to lobby them to support Kate. They marched wearing lavender armbands and handing out flyers that stated *Time* magazine was trying to discredit the women's movement by

> publicly attacking Kate Millett for her courageous statement that she is bisexual. It is not one woman's sexual preference that is under attack — it is the freedom of all women to openly state values that fundamentally challenge the basic structure of patriarchy. If they succeed in scaring us with words like "dyke" or "Lesbian" or "bisexual" they'll have won. AGAIN. They'll have divided us, AGAIN.

While women were writing freely about exploring the parameters and possibilities of their own sexuality, the men of the early seventies found themselves infected with this fervor of new possibilities too. Underground newspapers such as Oakland California's *Brother* newspaper, New York's *double f journal: for "effeminist faggots,"* edited by Kenneth Pitchford (Robin Morgan's bisexual husband), and a men's consciousness-raising anthology, *Unbecoming Men,* emerged as local grassroots publications for national conversation. They discussed men's sexism toward women and the way sexism had conditioned men to distrust other men and themselves. They called for a new men's movement inspired by and taking direction from feminism and visualized a new world where men could explore loving each other, women, and themselves. There was a permission to experiment, to explore, to be bisexual or gay.

Women of color, gays of color, and differently abled people also began organizing. As each of these groups split off for separate agenda-setting in the seventies and early eighties, labels and identity definitions all became more polarized. Bisexuals identified with and were active within many of these movements, developing a sense of our agendas and ourselves.

By the end of the eighties, there had been years of debate, divisiveness, learning, and separation. The realizations we feminists have had to face were sometimes difficult:

♦ Yes, sisterhood is powerful, but not all women are our sisters, and it's not men but their socialization that is the enemy.

♦ Yes, anti-sexist feminist brotherhood is emotionally nurturing and powerful, and as a movement has been an ally in abused women's services, and abortion rights, but very few men face the reality of how they too have been damaged by patriarchy, nor do they give up rational control and trust and explore their feelings with other men.

♦ Yes, racism and classism are connected to sexism, but we are not free of it by just recognizing that it is alive and woven into the fabric of our lives.

♦ No, not all lesbians (or women for that matter) are feminists or even want to be.

♦ Though the potential is there, all gay men are not yet our allies.

♦ Heterosexual people have been, can be, and are radical feminists.

♦ Some of us who identified publicly and privately as lesbians and gay men now identify as bisexual people.

Media images and stereotypes:
Drag queens, bulldykes, and swingers

For bisexuals, the eighties was a decade of activism, birthing a national bisexual pride movement and many visible communities within the lesbian, gay, and heterosexual communities in the larger cities and in some smaller college towns. The eighties were also a time of frustration and devastation, watching our friends, lovers, husbands, wives, mothers, children, and leaders die of AIDS, while we struggled with invisibility and invalidation on the one hand and scapegoating and trashing on the other.

Coming out, which took an act of courage, was often a very painful, isolating experience. The nature of internalized oppression is such that we ourselves take on the dominant culture's stereotypes. So, just as gay men and lesbians have had to deal with the homophobic misogynist drag queen faggot and the man-hating bulldyke images, bisexual people face the apolitical sexually insatiable swinger stereotype. Although there is an element of truth in each one of these stereotypes (i.e., some gay men are drag queens, some lesbians are bulldykes, some bisexuals are swingers) the media's narrow focus sensationalizes and perpetuates the stereotypes, dehumanizing the real people behind and beyond each stereotype.

Fortunately, those of us who once identified as lesbian and gay, and who came up through the ranks of the gay liberation, feminist, and people-of-color movements, understood the importance of visibility and breaking down stereotypes, understood that the most valuable tool we possessed as a people to change attitudes was to tell the truth of our experience and risk coming out. We understood the power of pride and trusting ourselves. As bisexuals we have come to understand that swingers are indeed the drag queens and bulldykes of our movement and, like the drag queens and bulldykes, are to be claimed with pride to break the cycle and reclaim the truth of all our lives.

Bisexuals braved the scorn of our families, our communities, and our heterosexual, lesbian, and gay friends. We also became the "confessors" of those closeted in the fear of losing their family, friends, and community status. (Status means the chauvinistic sense of "community" that is exclusive rather than inclusive, that relies on identity, not necessarily one's behavior, as the necessary criteria for belonging.) Declaring our bisexual pride disrupted and confused the communities in which we belonged. If not overwhelmed with biphobia, bisexual pride forced an examination of identity, behavior, and the monosexual framework of these communities.

Many lesbians and gay men had come out in the post-Stonewall rush of the seventies when women-loving women and men-loving men birthed lesbian and gay pride. They found themselves painfully disowned by homophobic family and friends. The strong sense of creating and belonging to the gay liberation and the women's movement partially replaced this loss. When people within the ranks of this family of friends and community realized that they were bisexual and began to come out, their bisexuality was unsettling to this fairly new and fragile foundation. There was a renewed sense of loss, accompanied by anger and the fear of betrayal. The fear was not only based in unresolved feelings for the opposite sex (heterophobia) but in the concrete power imbalance of heterosexism. Even with a clear understanding of why things are the way they are, being bisexual is still not easy in the lesbian, gay, or heterosexual community.

Building a movement

The idea of purity is a pervasive one in the lesbian and gay community ... an insidious one. The notion is that, because we're all queer, we must be essentially the same at heart with no fundamental differences, no real diversity or vagueness of definition. This conformist ideal makes our politics and controversy particularly divisive and vicious ... If we feel that there's only one right way to be queer, then seeing someone who does it differently forces us to either condemn them as a traitor or perceive of ourselves as failures ... How can we demand of the straight world, "We will love whom we choose and in the way we choose, you must accept us as we are," and then turn around and tell others (bisexuals) in our own community, "The way you love is misguided and wrong; we will not accept you because you are not exactly like us." Craziness.

— Greta Christina, *On Our Backs*[3]

With the lesbian and gay communities still so vulnerable to attack, anything we say here can be lifted and used out of context. However, to silently ignore behavior that is damaging and hurtful is also wrong.

The main focus of the bisexual movement has been and continues to be the visibility and liberation of all bisexual people. Currently and most urgently this is in our struggle against AIDS. The intense homophobic oppression that we share with the lesbian and gay communities, and to a much less degree the heterophobia of the lesbian and gay communities, have also been issues we have addressed. Acting as natural bridges, bisexuals who organize in the bisexual community educate the more heterosexually identified people about heterosexism, homophobia, and the struggle for lesbian and gay rights and how this directly relates to bisexual liberation. It is equally important to name the heterophobia within the lesbian and gay communities when we experience it. We are just becoming visible to ourselves, coming out as a bisexual pride movement, recognizing that we have a history, a culture, a community. As the voices in this section will attest, everyone's sexual liberation lies ahead.

Notes

1. Autumn Courtney, co-chair of the 1986 San Francisco Lesbian/Gay Freedom Day Parade, speaking as BiPOL representative at the June 1988 San Francisco Parade Celebration.

2. Sidney Love and Barbara Love, eds., *Sappho Was a Right-On Woman: A Liberated View of Lesbianism,* Stein & Day, 1972, pp. 120–122.

3. "Drawing the Line," *On Our Backs,* May–June 1990.

Lisa Orlando

Loving whom we choose

The struggles of "sexual minorities" within the lesbian and gay and feminist movements have revived interest in issues of sexual freedom. Within our movements such interests seemed, over the years since Stonewall, to have become increasingly confined to our radical margins. Now, however, S/M, man–boy love, butch and femme role-playing, sex workers, cross-dressing, and other sexual behavior are widely discussed in our publications and community meetings, with the result that a renaissance of our early "sex radicalism" seems to be occurring. However, in the midst of all this talk of sex, one sexual practice — bisexuality — is rarely discussed. If we really want a sexually liberating renaissance, we must discuss and rethink bisexuality in the same way that we have other forms of gay "deviance."

In the early days of our movement, many gay liberationists agreed that both homosexual and heterosexual potentials existed in all human beings. They believed that heterosexual culture so vigorously oppresses those who insist on expressing homosexual desire because, as Martha Shelley, one of the first post-Stonewall theorists, wrote, we are heterosexuals' "own worst fears made flesh."[1] Even later separatist lesbian-feminists like the Furies collective affirmed the inherent bisexuality of human nature.[2] If the feminist and gay liberation movements succeeded, they thought, the gay and straight dichotomy would disappear. Although, as Dennis Altman pointed out, many people would still not *practice* bisexuality, we would nevertheless achieve the "end of the homosexual" as a meaningful category.[3]

Belief in bisexuality as a utopian potential has not always coincided, as it has for Altman, with support for and acceptance of bisexuals.

Nevertheless, bisexuals who were active in the earliest days of the gay liberation movement seem to have had little trouble being accepted as gay. But times change. Few gay activists now claim to be striving for a bisexual paradise or to regard bisexuality as a repressed human potential. And while many nonbisexual gays have, as individuals, supported us and encouraged our attempts to organize, the lesbian and gay community abounds with negative images of bisexuals as fence-sitters, traitors, cop-outs, closet cases, people whose primary goal in life is to retain "heterosexual privilege," power-hungry seducers who use and discard their same-sex lovers like so many Kleenex (see cartoon below).

These stereotypes result from the ambiguous position of bisexuals, poised as we are between what currently appear as two mutually exclusive sexual cultures, one with the power to exercise violent

BISEXUALITY INSURANCE

Gay Community News, the "gay community's newspaper of record," published this cartoon in its 1983 April Fool's Day issue. One staff person complained that such stereotyping was oppressive but was overruled by the rest of the staff, many of whom made additional disparaging remarks about bisexuals. The letter opposite was sent in response to the cartoon. (Reprinted with permission from *Gay Community News.)*

repression against the other. Others grow out of the popular assumption, contrary to that of early gay liberation, that homosexual and heterosexual *desires* exclude each other. Still others result from lesbian-feminism,[4] which argues that lesbianism is a political choice having little to do with sexual desire *per se*. From this point of view, a bisexual woman "still define[s] herself in terms of male needs"[5] rather than, as she herself might argue, in terms of her own desires. Since lesbian-feminism equates meeting male needs with supporting male supremacy, it considers bisexual women traitors by definition.

Other factors may have played a role in shifting attitudes toward bisexuals in the lesbian and gay community: the growth of lesbian and gay "lifestyles" and ghettoes, the boundaries produced by constructing gay people as a "minority," the development of sexual identity as a

---

gay-identified bisexuals

Dear *GCN*:

We are a group of radical gay-identified bisexual women who have been meeting together for almost a year. At the risk of seeming humorless, we would like to point out some problems with the "bisexuality insurance" cartoon which appeared in the April Fool's issue of *GCN*.

1) The joke seems to be directed not to but against bisexuals: most bisexuals would not find it particularly funny and most of us have found it hurtful. When we add to this our past experiences with similar incidents and the almost total lack of attention given to bisexuals in *GCN*, we can only conclude that one subtext of the cartoon is that bisexuals are not considered part of the gay community.

The fact that we too experience homophobic discrimination and violence in our lives isn't enough for some people. Lesbians have sometimes told us that this is because bisexuals won't commit themselves to a lesbian lifestyle or to lesbian feminist politics. We challenge the right of anyone to set these requirements. In fact, some of us *are* active and committed members of the "women's community." Others find the so-called lesbian lifestyle (is there really just one?) unattractive or disagree with lesbian feminism. So do many lesbians.

We insist that all people who are sexually attracted to others of the same sex are gay. All other characteristics are secondary. And if "gay" is used to refer only to those who have consciously chosen a "gay identity" many bisexuals are gay and many homosexuals are not.

2) The cartoon perpetuates two stereotypes of bisexuals which we find particularly painful. The first is that we are really "experimenting" heterosexuals. In face, everyone in our group *strongly* identifies as bisexual — even though we range from being primarily attracted to women to being primarily attracted to men — and most of us have done so for years. For many of us it is as much "all women," as the cartoon puts it, as it is for any lesbian. Obviously the real problem which some lesbians have with us is not that we don't love women but that we haven't rejected men.

The second stereotype is that we are more lack-ing in compassion when we end relationships than lesbians are. This is bullshit. Sometimes bisexuals *do* leave women for men. We also leave men for women, women for women, and men for men. But we don't leave our lovers any more cruelly or frequently than any other group. All too often we get left ourselves. Some of us are incredibly monogamous and tenacious, others promiscuous and restless. And sometimes we *are* assholes, just like some lesbians.

3) The cartoon is not only directed at bisexuals. It also exemplifies an attitude towards women in the process of coming out which is all too common: if you don't know exactly what you feel and want, if you're at all ambivalent, if you're not prepared to commit yourself totally to a lesbian identity, you should stay in the closet rather than "experiment." This attitude keeps some women in the closet their whole lives. We think the lesbian community should *encourage* any woman who thinks she might be gay to explore those feelings. *We* certainly do. This doesn't mean that we don't fear rejection — everyone does. Nor do we necessarily feel less than lesbians the particular pain which accompanies being left for a man. But we recognize that this pain comes from our oppression. We owe it to women who are trying to come out not to blame them for it.

All the members of our group identify as bisexuals not because we are clinging to "heterosexual privilege" but because we are proud to affirm the full range of our desires. Bisexuals do exist. The message we get from both the lesbian/gay community and the straight world is that either we don't exist or we shouldn't. We refuse to accept this any longer. We refuse to deny ourselves or to be silent and invisible.

We understand that years of pain and anger on both sides of the barriers which separate us from homosexuals cannot be wiped out with a few words. We also realize that humor might be a necessary outlet but we doubt that jokes about "bisexuality insurance" will help to dismantle those barriers. And they must be dismantled. Bisexuals are not the enemy: the enemy is institutionalized heterosexuality. And we must unite against it if our movement is to grow stronger.

The BiVocals (Doris, Joanna, Linda, Lucinda, Lisa, Marcia, Megan, Robyn)
Cambridge, MA

political concept; and even, as Cindy Patton has argued, the brief heyday of media-created "bisexual chic" was a factor that trivialized bisexuality as just another fashion.[6]

But these stereotypes also resonate with some people's personal experience and with the gay subculture lore developed out of collective experience. Most stereotypes reflect some small aspects of reality which they then serve to reinforce. Some bisexuals do act in stereotypical ways, often because we have internalized our social image. And because nonbisexuals view this behavior through the lens of the stereotype, they perceive it as evidence of the truth of the stereotype rather than as an individual action. As more bisexuals refuse to hide our sexuality, as we organize within the gay community, we can better challenge these negative images and demonstrate that they are, like other stereotypes, essentially false. Other gay people will be forced to recognize that as a group bisexuals are no more "promiscuous" or incapable of commitment than anyone else (like many stereotypes of bisexuals, this also runs rampant in the straight world). "Heterosexual privilege" doesn't prevent us from being queerbashed on our way home from the bars or having our children taken away when we come out. We look just like other queers; i.e., we range from blatant to indistinguishable from straights. And many of us not only involve ourselves in lesbian and gay struggles but also identify ourselves primarily with the gay community.

As we challenge people on their more easily disproved beliefs, they may also begin to question whether they perceive their personal experiences with bisexuals in a distorted way. For example, I think we might better explain at least some of the stories about bisexuals who leave their same-sex lovers for heterosexual relationships in the same ways we explain being left, period, rather than as some special form of desertion and betrayal. And if gay people examine the problems we have had with bisexual lovers whose primary relationships are heterosexual, they resemble quite closely the problems we have had in similar "secondary" relationships with homosexuals.

Since most bisexuals are acutely aware of the differences between heterosexual and homosexual relationships, some probably do "settle" for heterosexual relationships, at whatever emotional cost, and for all the reasons one might imagine. I find it as difficult to condemn them as to condemn homosexuals who seek therapy to "become" heterosexual — oppression is ugly and we all want out, whether we seek individual or collective solutions. Other gay people rarely notice, however, that most bisexuals continue to have homosexual relationships *despite* the weight of heterosexist[7] oppression. This can only testify to the fact that heterosexual relationships generate their own problems — and that the power of desire often overcomes that of oppression. Many homosexuals resent the fact that the thoughtless pleasures of a heterosexual relationship always exist as an option for bisexuals and fear that, as homophobia intensifies, more bisexuals will take that option. But "option" seems a strange expression to describe repressing an entire aspect of one's sexuality, and the closet exists as an "option" for *all* queers.

We all suffer oppression when we choose to express homosexual desire. We may suffer even more when we force ourselves to repress it. And although the experiences differ, we suffer whether, as with bisexuals, our desire might take other paths or whether, as with homosexuals, the only path is total repression. In each of these cases, our suffering results from the power of a homophobic society. We *all* share an interest in assuring that bisexuals make their choices, conscious or not, on the basis of desire rather than oppression. And gay liberation offers the only guarantee that this will happen.

Those who view bisexuals as untrustworthy because of our "options" at least acknowledge that we exist. Others insist that we are closet cases temporarily stuck in a transitional stage in the coming-out process. I hope that as bisexuals begin to speak for ourselves, we will weaken this notion since many of us have identified as such for years — and lifetimes. I wonder, however, if the power of this belief might not resist such evidence. While I would argue that gay identity is essentially political — something we construct to promote solidarity and oppose our oppression — for many people, gay identity seems to imply that we all naturally possess a *sexual* identity and that this identity just as naturally fits into one of two categories.

Why do so many people who oppose the other forms of madness created and perpetuated by the psychiatric and medical establishment so wholeheartedly embrace the notion of a strict division between hetero-sexuality and homosexuality, a notion which originated alongside that of homosexuality as disease? As much gay historical research has shown, "homosexuality" as we understand it in the West didn't exist until, with the advent of capitalism, religious ideology began to lose ground and medical ideology took its place. What Christianity saw as a sinful potential in everyone, psychiatry reconceptualized as a sickness which permeated one's being, displacing heterosexual desire.[8] But if we reject the psychiatric definition of homosexuality, why do we cling to the notion of homosexual desire as exclusive? That we do testifies, I think, to the incredible power of our need to fit things into neat dichotomies.

Human beings tend to use dual classification when we think about our world — pairs such as up and down and hot and cold as well as pairs such as human and animal and man and woman, where more value is placed on one term — possibly because such oppositions structure the human mind itself. Many anthropologists believe that when some aspect of a culture gains particular prominence or importance people feel an even stronger need to fit it into such a scheme and will become uneasy in the face of ambiguities. The "disorder" resulting from central features of our lives which we cannot fit into dichotomies with sharp boundaries disturbs us deeply.[9] I suspect that the homosexual and heterosexual dichotomy gained acceptance as both sexuality and "personal identity" became central to our culture. Whether or not this is true, most of us feel threatened when the categories we believe in are challenged, especially if they shape our sense of who we are. Not only do bisexuals contradict a primary set of cultural categories — our culture calls us "decadent" because we refuse to play by the rules, thereby undermining the social "order" —but we challenge many people's personal sense of what constitutes sexual identity. Whether we threaten by introducing a third category or by undermining the notion of categories altogether, we cause enough discomfort that many people deny our existence.

If we wish to develop liberating politics, we must ask, as early gay liberation did, whether our need to classify simultaneously violates the truths of at least some people's desires and plays into heterosexism. Obviously we will never stop classifying; we couldn't speak or even think if we did. But we must be wary of both our obsession with order, with getting rid of "dirt,"[10] and our tendency to see the categories we use as natural or simply given rather than as the social and political constructions they are. This is particularly true with those categories which bear the most political weight. But the historically specific categories we adopt in order to think about our world, including our selves, do more than merely describe, or violate the truths of, our desires. They also shape and even create them. We must question as well the whole notion of an essential sexual truth which somehow resides in each of us.

I don't think anyone knows what desire is, where it comes from, or why it takes the general and specific forms it does. I'm inclined to believe that some kind of interaction between a more or less shapeless biological "drive" and a combination of individual experiences and larger social forces creates each of our unique sexualities. But the way we as "modern" people experience them, the mere fact that we experience something we call "sexual identity," is peculiar to our particular culture and historical period. Much current historical research argues that all our talk about "identity crisis" and "finding ourselves," even our very notion of sexuality, would mean nothing to people from another time and place.[11] If both the way we view our selves and the categories into which we fit them are modern social constructions, not timeless truths, I can't view my own sense, however subjectively powerful, that I am "really" *anything* with less than suspicion. The human mind too easily interprets — and reinterprets — anything and everything to fit its current beliefs.

But we still have no better way of describing our experience than by saying that we have discovered what we "really" are. In using the term "really," we acknowledge the experience many people have either of having "always known" or of coming to a place where they finally feel at home. I, too, believe, seventeen years after "discovering" my bisexuality and ten years after relinquishing my lesbian identity, that I am "really" bisexual.

Bisexuality: A stage

Many exclusive homosexuals *do* experience bisexuality as a stage (as indeed do some heterosexuals). This obviously bolsters the belief that "real" bisexuality doesn't exist. People who have had this experience tend to look back at their old selves with condescension and embarrassment. I suspect that the word "bisexual" triggers unpleasant feelings in many of them which they project on anyone claiming a bisexual identity.

While most self-defined homosexuals and heterosexuals may be correct in seeing their own bisexuality as just a stage, inevitably some people who see themselves as exclusively homosexual or heterosexual will have repressed rather than "grown out of" bisexuality. As some lesbians in the fifties who were neither butch nor femme felt forced to choose,[12] so do some bisexuals. Both sides often exert so much pressure to "make up your mind" and direct so much contempt at people who are unwilling to do so — and most of us are so unaware of bisexuality as a legitimate possibility — that a simple need for acceptance and community often forces people (particularly, and often most painfully, young people) to repress one aspect of their desire. Just as closet queers (also perhaps bisexual) often lead the pack in homophobic attacks, so may closet bisexuals be the most intensely biphobic. I think this is particularly true among women who came out via lesbian-feminism.

Many women, in fact, who now identify as bisexual, experienced *lesbianism* as a stage. I identified as bisexual before the women's movement, but as happened with many women, consciousness-raising and traumatic experiences fueled an acute anger and disgust with men that led me to lesbianism. Some women became lesbians because "feminism is the theory and lesbianism is the practice."[13] Or they may simply have succumbed to peer pressure (even some heterosexual women "became" lesbians for these reasons). Over the years, many of us, often because of working in political coalitions, have reconnected with the world outside the "women's community" and have discovered our heterosexual desires. We are now attacked for having "gone back into the closet," as traitors, and as self-deceiving fools.

The theoretical and emotional need to keep alive both the notion that all true feminists are lesbians and the belief that no rapprochement with men is possible fuels lesbian-feminist hatred of bisexuals. Many lesbians who oppose other forms of separatism, who work with men politically and have male friends, still see *sexual* separatism as an eternal given. But as political separatism falls into disrepute, sexual separatism also loses its rationale. As many lesbians recognize that class, race, age, etc. may be as powerful sources of oppression as gender and sexual orientation, they also recognize the futility of separatism as more than a stage. Few people — and fewer sexual radicals — really want a movement which forbids us to relate sexually to people whose race, sex, class, physical abilities, age, looks, etc. aren't exactly the same as ours. And many of us also refuse to have our desires and sexual practices dictated by anyone else's idea of "political correctness."

Many bisexuals, like many homosexuals, have never identified with gay politics. But some of us, including many women who have rejected lesbian-feminism, *have* committed ourselves to gay liberation. We see gay identity and solidarity as crucial, since heterosexism oppresses all gay people, whether homosexual or bisexual, and we can only struggle against it as a self-conscious group. The ambiguous nature of our sexuality needn't imply any ambiguity in our politics. By choosing gay identity we acknowledge that sexuality dominates our identity in a heterosexist world while recognizing that in a non-oppressive society no one would care who we wanted or who our sexual partners were, and sexuality would no longer be so central to our sense of who we are.

Unfortunately, political movements and embattled subcultures have particular difficulty acknowledging ambiguities of any kind.[14] Add to this the current plethora of "ex-lesbians" and we can see what haunts the political unconscious of the lesbian and gay movement. Clearly, the rest of the gay community ignores or ostracizes us at its peril; embattled as we all are, we need all the forces we can muster. Bisexuals often encounter unusual opportunities to confront and contradict homophobia and, if we have been encouraged to develop a gay consciousness, we will act powerfully and efficiently in such situations.

But if it rejects us, the gay movement loses more than numbers and strategic force. It also loses another opportunity, similar to that offered by other "sexual minorities," to re-examine its commitment to sexual freedom rather than to mere interest-group politics. What would it mean for the gay movement to acknowledge that some people experience their sexuality as a lifelong constant, others as a series of stages, some as a choice, and many as a constant flux? It would certainly mean a drastic reworking of the standard categories which have grounded gay politics over the last decade. And it might mean a renewed commitment to the revolutionary impulse of gay liberation, which, believing that homosexual desire is a potential in everyone, insisted that "gay" is a potentially universal class, since sexual freedom for all people is the ultimate goal of our struggle.

Notes

1. Quoted in Dennis Altman, *Homosexual: Oppression and Liberation,* Avon Books, 1971, p. 69.

2. Loretta Ulmschneider for the Furies, "Bisexuality," in *Lesbianism in the Women's Movement,* ed. Nancy Myron and Charlotte Bunch, Diana Press, 1975, p. 88.

3. Altman, *Homosexual,* especially chapter 7, "The End of the Homosexual?"

4. Throughout this article I use "lesbian-feminism" to refer to the ideology explicated in the text. It does not refer here to the belief that women's and gay liberation requires each other (a belief to which I subscribe) nor to the belief that lesbian and gay oppression is merely a by-product of women's oppression (lesbian-feminists share this belief with many feminists and gay activists who otherwise disagree with them). Nor am I using the term simply to designate all women who are both lesbians and feminists. One of the earliest and most comprehensive explications of lesbian-feminist doctrine can be found in Myron and Bunch, eds., *Lesbianism in the Women's Movement.*

5. Ulmschneider, p. 86.

6. Quoted in Arthur Kroeber, "Bisexuality: Towards a New Understanding of Men, Women, and Their Feelings," *Boston Globe,* October 10, 1983, p. 53.

7. "Heterosexism" designates the ideology that posits heterosexuality as the "natural," "normal," and "superior" sexual orientation and condemns deviations from this norm. As with other oppressive ideologies, heterosexism is supported by law and custom and reinforced by socially condoned violence.

8. For historical writings on the "homosexual" as a modern construction, see Michel Foucault, *The History of Sexuality,* Vol. 1, *An Introduction,* trans. Robert Hurley, Pantheon, 1978; Jeffrey Weeks, *Coming Out: Homosexual Politics in Britain,* Quartet Books, 1977; John d'Emilio, "Capitalism and Gay Identity," in *Powers of Desire: The Politics of Sexuality,* ed. Ann Snitow, Christine Stansell, and Sharon Thompson, Monthly Review Press, 1983, pp. 100–113; and Robert Padgug, "Sexual Matters: On Conceptualizing Sexuality in History," *Radical History Review* 20 (1979): 3–23. See also Mary MacIntosh, "The Homosexual Role," *Social Problems* 16 (1968): 182–192.

9. The above argument draws primarily on Barry Schwartz, *Vertical Classification: A Study in Structuralism and the Sociology of Knowledge,* University of Chicago Press, 1981. See also Mary Douglas, *Purity and Danger: An Analysis of the Concepts of Pollution and Taboo,* Routledge & Kegan Paul, 1966.

10. Douglas, ibid., defines "dirt" as a "residual category rejected from our normal scheme of classification" (p. 36). In retrospect, I think the point I am making here would have been stronger if, rather than drawing on the notion of "vertical classification" in the above passage, I had discussed Douglas's arguments about boundaries and margins, ambiguities and anomalies. The point that bisexuals transgress boundaries which, in our culture, are intimately related to notions of pollution and contagion hardly needs to be belabored, especially considering the

current hysteria over Acquired Immune Deficiency Syndrome (AIDS). Nevertheless, it seemed a more difficult argument to make from the perspective of the margins themselves.

11. Foucault, Weeks, d'Emilio, Padgug, op. cit. Here I refer particularly to the work of Michel Foucault on the "technologies of the self," especially his comparison of the ancient Greek notion of the self as an aesthetic creation to our notion of the self as something "discovered." See, for example, Paul Rabinow and Hubert L. Dreyfus, "How We Behave: An Interview with Michel Foucault," *Vanity Fair*, November 1983, pp. 60–69.

12. For a discussion of the pressures in lesbian subcultures in the 1950s, see Elly Bulkin, "An Old Dyke's Tale: An Interview with Doris Lundin," *Conditions* 6 (1980): 36–48. The degree of pressure that existed in the 1950s is a topic of debate in the contemporary lesbian community. For other viewpoints, see Joan Nestle, "Butch-Femme Relationships: Sexual Courage in the 1950s," *Heresies* 12: 22; and Merrill Mushroom, "Confessions of a Butch Dyke," *Common Lives/Lesbian Lives* 9 (1983): 40.

13. The slogan originated with a heterosexual feminist, Ti-Grace Atkinson, who first used it in a speech before the New York chapter of the Daughters of Bilitis, an early homophile organization, in late June 1970. Toby Marotta, *The Politics of Homosexuality*, Houghton Mifflin, 1981, p. 258.

14. Douglas, op. cit., p. 124.

Cliff Arnesen

Coming out
to Congress

In 1958, at ten years of age, I was living at the Wiltwyck School for emotionally disadvantaged boys in Esopus, New York. I had been placed there on the recommendations of the New York City Department of Welfare and state court to protect me from a physically abusive and alcoholic father. Most of the boys came from broken homes in Harlem or state juvenile centers and courts.

At Wiltwyck I realized that I was physically attracted to those of my own gender. A group of boys were undressing to swim, and I realized I was staring at a beautiful blond-haired, blue-eyed boy as his towel slipped from his hips. He had a smooth, lean body and the most gorgeous buns I had ever laid eyes on. My heart raced, pulse quickened, and a feeling of excitement which I had never known possessed me. At that moment I knew I was "different."

I was elated and scared simultaneously as I looked out of the corner of my eye to see if any of the other boys had observed my reactions. I knew then that I had a secret that I would have to hide and carry within my heart and soul the rest of my life. So I thought!

During my four years there, I met and became friends with the late First Lady, Eleanor Roosevelt, who was on the board of directors. Every summer she would invite all one hundred of us to a picnic at her house in Hyde Park, New York. We had a wonderful time as she read tales of Winnie the Pooh to us in her high-pitched voice and fed us candy and hot dogs. I loved exploring the small pond near her home, which contained many fish, turtles, frogs, eels, and snakes. During my second visit, I asked Mrs. Roosevelt, "Do you remember me?" and she replied, "Of course, how could I forget you?" I shall always remember her words, realizing how important it is to an eleven-year-old, or anyone else, not to be forgotten.

In 1962, at the age of thirteen, I was transferred from Wiltwyck to the Floyd Patterson Halfway House in Manhattan, New York. During my three years there, I went to high school in Harlem. I began drinking cheap wine, smoking, and joined a street gang. I also began to notice girls and eventually got to kiss a few. I started to get very confused as I was having sex with boys at night while I was kissing girls during the day. I thought perhaps I was in a stage that would pass. But what would it be, boys or girls?

Upon turning sixteen, I was too old to stay at Patterson House. I was sent to my mother's house in Brooklyn, where she lived with another alcoholic man. We moved three or four times to escape from my natural father, who was constantly drunk and threatening our safety.

During this time, I lost my heterosexual virginity to an older woman of about twenty-five. Her husband was in the Marines, and she was alone. She stopped to ask if I could fix something in her house. I was nervous as I was supposed to return home after running an errand. She put her hand on my thigh and slid it up my waist, then down into my pants. I got excited and helped her pull my clothes off. It was pleasurable but impersonal, and I wished I had more time. I never saw the woman again.

We moved back to Brooklyn. My mother left my foster father, and we went on welfare. I had had enough! I needed to find some security and identification, so I asked my mother to sign papers for me to join the Army, which she did.

I was nervous about leaving home. I also knew that the armed forces has a policy against homosexuals that stated, "It is the official policy of the United States Armed Forces that homosexuality is incompatible with military service." Furthermore, the department requires the discharge of any service member who, prior to or during military service, has stated he or she is a homosexual or bisexual, "unless there is a finding that the individual is not a homosexual or bisexual."

I never really wanted to join the Army, but like so many other seventeen-year-olds and minorities, I had to escape from a harsh home environment where love was scarce. I loved my mother deeply, but she was trapped as well; like many women of that time she was unskilled and existed at the financial and physical mercy of men — drunken men at that. I thought maybe I could send money home to ease the burden. So I dropped out of high school in the tenth grade and enlisted. I finished basic training at Fort Dix, New Jersey, and went AWOL to Greenwich Village, because I hated the discipline and could not suppress my attraction toward the other soldiers.

I got a job as a waiter at a cafe on Christopher Street where the Andy Warhol crowd hung out. I had an infatuation with a 23-year-old woman who dismissed me as too young. Also I started to notice that I liked girls with short hair who looked like pretty boys and vice versa.

It was becoming much too confusing. I began seeing both boys and girls. Some nights I would go to a gay bar to watch the boys strip, and other nights I would be making love with a girl. I was excited by having so much to choose from. I couldn't figure out, however, which side my bread was buttered on. I considered myself gay, and it never dawned on me that I might be bisexual. Though I had a pleasant and diverse sex life, I was slipping into the grip of drugs and alcohol. I was living with a chemist from Brazil and a prince from India. The chemist made his own LSD and I took my first "trip."

After a month of nonstop sex and drugs, I was burned out and decided to turn myself in to the military police at Times Square. They handcuffed me and drove me to Fort Dix, where I was put under house arrest. While there I told them I was gay. I was interrogated by the intelligence division, sent to a psychiatrist, and placed in the stockade for four months. I served my time in segregated confinement, as some of the other soldiers had threatened to rape and kill me. One day I was marched several miles through the base on my way to the courthouse, while a young soldier held a fully loaded .45 caliber pistol to my back in an attempt to humiliate me. He remarked that he didn't believe I was gay, and that I was using it as an excuse to get out of going to Vietnam. I informed him that had that been the case, I would have shot myself in the foot! That was the end of that conversation.

After receiving an "undesirable" discharge, which I burned at the exit gate, I returned to Brooklyn and the life I had left. I made excuses to all my friends as to why I got out, but my mother knew and continued to love me. Five months later she died of breast cancer. I was now eighteen, and there was nothing left for me in Brooklyn, as my father had disowned me.

I moved to West 110th Street in Manhattan with a straight friend. For the next four years, I maintained sexual and emotional relationships with both men and women while living in a straight environment. I found I liked girls physically, but emotionally something was lacking. They played too many girl games: flirting, flicking eyelashes, gossiping, being coy, and I couldn't stand the makeup. But didn't the boys in the gay bars do all these things as well? I was really confused.

I was drinking and taking drugs again, and my straight friend asked me to move. I lived in rooming houses for the next several years, hustling in bars to pay the rent and survive. I moved in with a woman who was a heroin dealer and became hooked for a year and a half. All my friends turned away from me. I knew I needed help! I called my gay friend and former teacher from Wiltwyck who loved me as a boy, and I moved to upstate New York. I went through withdrawal there for four or five days because the hospital would not treat me. I stayed and worked for my former teacher and mentor until I earned enough money to start a new life in Albany, New York. I was then twenty-two years old.

In Albany, I met and deeply fell in love with a seventeen-year-old boy named Donnie. I had never felt this way before with a boy or girl. We got an apartment together. At Christmas we had dinner at his parents' house, and I told them I was in love with their son. To my surprise, they took it as best they could and treated me decently and sincerely.

For the next one and a half years we had an on-again, off-again relationship because of my drinking. I got arrested for public intoxication and disturbing the peace. I was also arrested three times for drunken driving and marijuana possession. He left me on a number of occasions; each time I begged him to take me back, promising that I would stop drinking. He did, but finally he left for good.

I left Albany broke and depressed and returned to my gay mentor's house. I called Donnie again, and he came up for part of the summer. I saved some money and moved to Boston. Donnie met me there but stayed only a week because I was still drinking. I went to a therapist, but it didn't help.

In 1973, when Donnie left Boston, I took a room in Cambridge. I continued to drink even more because I was depressed and guilt-ridden, having lost the only person I had ever loved besides my mother. I bounced from boyfriend to boyfriend, rooming house to rooming house. While drunk I fell through a plate glass window and severely cut my arm, and I almost died in two separate fires that resulted in burns requiring skin grafts. During the next five years, I lived my life in an exclusively gay atmosphere. I needed help and was getting tired of life and running.

In 1977, I petitioned the Army and was granted an upgrade from an undesirable to a general discharge under honorable conditions. I was attempting to put my life in order but was still drinking. In 1978 I met a wonderful lady named Ellie, who was twelve years my senior. We began a friendship and relationship that has lasted eleven years. The first five years, however, were a disaster.

For the first year I lived across the hall from Ellie. I stayed with the building superintendent, Lowell, who was gay and in love with me. Lowell provided me with shelter and vodka while Ellie was at work, and at night I would go over to see her. It was a twilight existence. They both saved me from certain destitution, and Lowell and I remain the best of friends today.

Then, however, I was drunk continually, lost jobs, apartments, and friends, and got arrested for disorderly conduct. In 1983 I was drinking a quart of vodka a day and began to have brain seizures.

I was terrified of the seizures and afraid of losing this courageous woman who had been so loving and kind to me. Both fears drove me to seek help. I dried out and went to therapy and AA sessions for a year to get my footing and control. It was very difficult at first, but I feared for my life because of the brain seizures, and I could not bear hurting Ellie or losing her friendship and love.

Keenly aware of my lack of education, I decided to enroll in an evening course at Boston's Bunker Hill Community College. No one in my family had ever gone beyond high school. I talked with Ellie and other friends, and they urged me to go for it. I was still living in a rooming house with a bunch of drunks and drug addicts when I began school, but Ellie let me study in the quiet and comfort of her house. I owe her so much because she believed in me and provided me with the security and foundation I needed to advance myself.

I liked school and I passed my first course with an A. This boosted my self-esteem, and I decided to take additional classes. With Ellie's support I decided to go for a degree. For three and a half years I attended summer school, night school, and also held one or two jobs; I knew recovering alcoholics need to utilize their time so as not to get in trouble.

Finally, June 4, 1988, my dream came true. I graduated with high honors and received my degree in human services, as well as a one-year certificate for mental health workers. As I was handed my degree, I thought of how proud my mother would have been. I also thought of Ellie, who had stood by me with her love, support, and friendship in those darkest moments. I was proud of myself for having beaten so many odds along the way. I could hardly believe I had really done it. I could hold my head up high! I have been sober now for six years.

There were still other conflicts to deal with. For many years I had an inner confusion about being gay, and now, with Ellie, bisexual. I knew it would hurt her for me to see other men because she is straight. So I did it quietly, but always felt guilty and told her. I am still trying to work this out between us. Today Ellie and I are best friends and sometimes lovers. I still see other men, but always engage in safe sexual behavior.

Political activism
In late 1988 I took a job as president of the New England Gay and Lesbian Veterans (NEGLV) in Boston. That decision altered my life. The NEGLV is a Boston grassroots, nonprofit veterans organization founded in 1985. It provides advocacy, networking, and referrals to other organizations. The issues dealt with are overlapping and are not exclusive to veterans. They include AIDS education, alcohol and drug abuse, homelessness, post-traumatic stress disorder, Agent Orange, homophobia, biphobia, prejudice, discrimination, violence, and the upgrading of "less than honorable" homosexual-related discharges.

Having spent four months in the stockade and being harassed there for the "crime" of being gay and loving men, I decided this was an opportunity to sublimate my enmity and resentment toward the military into a constructive and positive outlet; it would allow me to expose and combat centuries of discrimination, hypocrisy, and subhuman treatment of gay, lesbian, and bisexual people in the military.

In May 1989, NEGLV was invited by the William Joiner Center for the Study of War and Social Consequences (University of Massachusetts, Boston) to participate and present a workshop on the health care concerns of gay and lesbian veterans of Vietnam in Washington, D.C. We were part of a group of minority veterans that included African American, Hispanic, women, and Native American veterans. During the Eighth Annual Speaker Conference, we met with Congressman Barney Frank and Congressman Gerry Studds. Also attending were Senator Edward Kennedy, Congressman Joe Kennedy II, Congresswoman Nancy Pelosi, and Speaker of the House Jim Wright. They all knew we had come to Washington as gay, lesbian, and bisexual veterans.

Representative Barney Frank and Congresswoman Nancy Pelosi acknowledged our presence, but no one used the "bi" word, as it was quite a lot for some to digest. For the most part we were received warmly by all the minority veterans as well as the members of Congress. It was a great experience to be on the cutting edge of creating an awareness of veterans who happen to be gay, lesbian, or bisexual.

That same month I was also invited by Congressman Lane Evans to testify before a Subcommittee on Oversight and Investigation on the health care concerns of gay Vietnam veterans. This was the first time in history that gay, lesbian, and bisexual veterans were formally represented during congressional testimony.

However, I had just come out to some of my friends as a bisexual. I found myself pressured by NEGLV's vice president and others to refrain from using the word bisexual at the conference and in testimony; they maintained that it was "politically incorrect" and would "confuse people." I was angry! Here I was fighting to secure equal rights for all gay and lesbian veterans, yet I was not supposed to fight for mine as a bisexual? Bullshit! I would not capitulate to anyone who would dare to rob me of my hard-won dignity, self-esteem, and identity. I explained to the vice president of NEGLV that I was not in the business of politics, and anyway, people were already confused.

So, on May 3, I testified openly as a bisexual veteran before the Veterans Affairs Subcommittee on Oversight and Investigation. Upon my return to Boston, I asked for and received the resignation of NEGLV's vice president. That was my first confrontation with biphobia, and undoubtedly not my last.

My second official coming out as a bisexual occurred two weeks later on Mother's Day of 1989. I was invited by Woody Glenn of the Boston Bisexual Men's Network to deliver the closing presentation at the Fifth Annual East Coast Bisexual Network Conference, held that year at Harvard University. I told the 200-plus bisexual brothers and sisters of our recent trip to Washington, D.C., and updated them on the current status of "witch-hunts" being conducted in the armed forces against women accused of lesbianism.[1] I also shared with the audience some of my personal experiences and the origins of my own bisexual identification.

I left the conference on cloud nine. Very rarely have I ever felt so comfortable with such a diverse group of people. My bisexual brothers and sisters filled me with a feeling of empowerment and affirmation by their acceptance, love, and visibility. I was intoxicated with relief and gratitude that we were indeed not alone. We hugged and kissed, exchanged phone numbers and addresses, and promised to meet again soon.

Upon my return I asked for and received a vote of confidence from the Executive Board to rename our organization the New England Gay, Lesbian, and Bisexual Veterans. Our treasurer, Joe Harper; vice president, Rick Buchanan; and co-founder, Bob Derry, all gave me the green light. I was grateful for their courage, vision, and acceptance, as this change turned a corner on a segment of the bisexual movement. We were the first gay and lesbian veterans organization to do so. Others are now beginning to follow suit.

Whenever I feel oppression, hatred, or fear, I am constantly reminded of the eloquent words of my friend Eleanor Roosevelt, who said, "No one can make you feel inferior without your consent." These words have helped me through my journey in life, and with the process of coming out as a bisexual person. We all deserve dignity and respect and should never, ever let anyone try to make us feel inferior.

Bisexuality is not a counterfeit behavior, lifestyle, or sexual orientation for the millions of people in this country who have either a sexual attraction to or engage in sexual activity with both sexes. It is a welcome relief and a flexible alternative to the rigid and culturally defined norms of both heterosexuality and homosexuality. As bisexuals, I believe we all have accepted the premise that there should be no universal map of how one can love or be loved in return.

Note

1. Each year more than two thousand women and men are discharged on grounds of lesbianism or homosexuality.

ONE...

1. ONE

Well
the straights talk of
heterosexual thrusting as if it were the only real form of
sexual fulfillment and
the straights tense if I touch them and
the gays make jokes about "breeders" and
fall silent if I mention my (male) lover
I look for books on bisexuality but
they are all about married men or
have titles like "two lives to lead" —
Well I am NOT a man and will never
lead two lives   I am one woman

ONE ONE ONE

I thought Gay Rights meant being able
to love who I love

2. You see
    I am white Chinese
    I am bisexual Lesbian

3. My father
   is Polish and Irish and German
   long blended in America
   My mother is the child of
   two brave Chinese   who survived
   in an alien and hating land
   to raise bright and beautiful
   middle-class
   daughters
   who no longer speak Chinese
   who work to succeed
   to pass
   White racism against my yellow
   family and self is a crime   The criminals
   are of my own white
   family, my own pale skin color

4. We loved
   Though she and I separated   I
   vowed never to forget nor
   deny the fires she ignited in my body & soul
   I chose at 17 to
   claim
   the word Dyke   to commit my fate
   to that of the lesbians
   when the witch hunters came they would have to come for me too

   even if by that time I had married him

   None of the coming-out stories
   or other writings I devoured
   Seventeen alone and bisexual   never once
   validated my reality   never once offered a story
   of a relationship
   neither abusive nor boring
   with a male lover
   My new & fragile lesbian world was
   as important to me as my own bones   But
   in the women's journals were
   quiet signs of
   You Are Not Welcome   everywhere

I looked at myself and realized
I was holding a man's hand
I was tainted
Sometimes I
dropped his hand
like it was poison I
attacked and humiliated him
who was my friend and brother I
made him to be dirt   because
he had no woman's body   with which
to grace his soul

5. I am a man-hating dyke

    I talked with women friends and felt our pain,
    abused and negated for being female
    heard even my "nice"est "pro-equality" male friends
    justify rape, heard them blame women
    saw the books on mutilation
    felt the horrifying silent absence of heroines
    or women's perspectives in my schoolbooks
    experienced the nightmare of watching TV
    seeing women slandered   victimized   raped
    (my family looked calmly on, munching chips)
    and the cruelty of date rape
    he who loved me carried the one-eyed demon in him too

    I learned distrust

6. Distrust

    of feminist theory written by heterosexual women
    Distrust of feminist books written by white women
    The exceptions are precious, but rare —
    People who can identify with the oppressor
    will write things that hurt me
    I learned distrust
    of people like me.

7. If there is anyone
   I am committed to the struggle for peace
   There is no camp in which I feel wholly welcome
   I am looking and looking for a home
   I do not find it
   Maybe I will have to build it

   My neck is locked in tension
   One side of my head is always pitted against the other side
   of my own head

   If there is anyone who
   looks like a likely traitor of our cause
   it is me

   If there is anyone who knows that oppression kills
   it is me.

Naomi Tucker

What's in a name?

From the day we are born we are given a set of labels, set up as dichotomies, by which to define our identity: race and class, which cast us as either the oppressor or the oppressed; a nationality or ethnicity, which gives us a specific language and paints us with stereotypes before we even know who we are; and gender, which affects every aspect of our socialization. By the time we are old enough to have a sense of our sexual identity, we are far too well socialized to kick the label habit.

Labels are always limiting because they conjure up different feelings to individuals based on their own experiences. If we identify ourselves with standard definitions, we shortchange ourselves, painting an incomplete picture of who we really are.

When I was nineteen, I underwent a process of "coming out" to myself. But my coming out did not include choosing a label or a new limitation; rather, it involved expanding the horizons of my sexuality to include women. I had never once considered that I had to lessen the validity of any past, present, or potential intimacies with men. My first sexual attraction to a woman grew out of a loving bond with my close friend Lisa, with whom I discovered the fine line between intimate friendship, sensuality, and sexual attraction.

Although Lisa and I did not have sex, which meant that this label-happy society did not consider us lovers, we always knew we were much more than "just friends." So we floated through college together as emotional lovers, and gradually became involved in the lesbian-feminist community. However, when we mustered the courage to attend a support group for lesbian and bisexual women, it quickly became apparent that our welcome was contingent on an unspoken promise that we would only discuss our "lesbian half." It was an ongoing struggle to fit into a community that seemed to demand a list of female bed partners or "real" relationships with women as a prerequisite for acceptance.

In retrospect I am not sorry that the lesbian community excluded me, because I learned to stand on my own as an individual and make my own personal, political, and sexual choices. The "lesbian" label precludes — and therefore invalidates — any attractions to men. Bisexuality, on the other hand, breaks down the label dichotomies and challenges assumptions by including all possibilities of same — and opposite — sex attractions.

In the absence of a ready-made label, I must continually explain, in depth, my various intimate connections, friendships, and romances. Politically, I believe in "coming out" to others as a positive educational force which may radically change people's feelings about varying sexualities. Socially, I believe in the "coming-out" process as a means for breaking through the cold walls of isolation that separate us from one another. Personally, however, I purposely avoid making a grand production out of telling people about my sexuality. The concept of "coming out" implies placing a new definition on one's sexuality. Definition implies boundaries. Boundaries mean limitations. And I refuse to limit myself by squeezing my sexuality into a one-word definition.

I will not "come out" to anyone by saying "Guess what... " Come out of what? Out of a closet that shouldn't exist in the first place. Out of an oppression that we as a community must strive to erase, not re-emphasize. Instead I choose to act as if my sexuality is just as valid as anyone else's. In order to ignore those artificial boundaries, I simply don't comply with the traditional rules of the game, which mandate that I choose a label and make a point of telling people about it.

I decided that acting naturally about my sexual preferences will help others to see my choices as natural; the agenda of my personal revolution therefore begins by being myself. People who know me will come to understand my connection to women as they see the development of my political ideals, career, personal life, and spiritual identity. Likewise, they will see that I sometimes have wonderful friends and lovers who are men. At first they may be confused, but my hope is (and my experience has shown) that they see my affections for women and men as the natural fulfillment of my fascination with people in general, or as proof of the fine lines between friendship, sensuality, and sexuality.

If someone asks me directly about my sexual orientation, I certainly don't shy away from the question. I tell them, whether or not I use the word "bisexual," that I am proud of being able to express my feelings toward a person, regardless of gender, in whatever way I desire. If such openness must have a label — for the sake of visibility within the lesbian and gay communities and heterosexual world, for the sake of giving strength and support to others who don't fit into either category — then I suppose bisexuality is as good a word as any.

I relate bisexuality to openness. It is, for me, a willingness to acknowledge feelings, despite prevailing taboos, and to break down the prefabricated barriers that our culture instills within us. In this light, my bisexual identity is one of recognition of each individual's potential to contribute in some way to my life, whether as friend, lover, acquaintance, or otherwise. So I try to be as open as possible toward people of all types — of all sexualities, cultures, races, ages, abilities, lifestyles, and personalities — and look for what is unique in each, as long as they're not oppressive to others.

Bisexuality can be a unifying force in the world. But we must be careful not to make the mistakes of some of our lesbian sisters who profess sexual acceptance and demand to have their sexuality valued positively in the eyes of the world, while, in a blatant act of fear-driven hypocrisy, invalidate bisexuality as an orientation. If we are to be a voice of acceptance, we must continually re-examine our own homophobia, biphobia, and heterosexism. If we claim self-definition for ourselves, then we must accord that right to others. We have no right to tell a lesbian she's really bi because she occasionally sleeps with men or to tell a woman she's not bi because she has only slept with men. As a bisexual movement we can create a community where it is safe for everyone to comfortably express their sexuality without fear of judgment.

Dajenya

Sisterhood crosses gender preference lines[1]

I must respond to Marilyn Murphy's article "The Gay–Straight Split Revisited," which appeared in the Fall 1989 *Lesbian Contradictions*. While much of what she says has merit, I am unable to ignore some of her grosser accusations and overgeneralizations, such as "[bisexual women] are sexual with our oppressors [men]" and "Women who relate to men suffer physical, mental, emotional, and spiritual abuse regularly. Even those 'special' men we hear about drain a woman's energy, insult her intelligence, and expect her to serve them as their 'privileged domestic.'" I am a woman, and this statement insults my intelligence.

I have been female all my life. My maternal ancestors are Jews from Russia and my paternal ancestors probably come from West Africa. I was raised by a single working mother and I continue to live below the poverty level today. I was raised politically and was involved throughout my life with the civil rights movement, the anti-war movement, the socialist movement, the gay movement, the feminist movement, and the lesbian community. I am, by nature, bisexual.

Throughout my life I have discovered some people who had very appealing qualities such as kindness, intelligence, sensitivity, compassion, open-mindedness, creativity, responsibility, awareness, the ability to communicate, etc. Some of these people were female and some were male (born that way). Some were black, some white, some other. Most of the people that I've befriended in my adulthood have been lesbian, gay, or bisexual, but I've known some great heterosexual people as well.

My mixed racial and gender "preference" backgrounds allow and force me to see things from more perspectives than most people care to. I have often observed that leftists, feminists, lesbians, and African

Americans are just as fond as anyone else of dividing the world up into simplified categories of "us and them," "the good guys and the bad guys," "black and white," "right and wrong," "female and male," "rich and poor," "gay and straight," "for or against," "friend or enemy."

Each oppressed group tends to wear its oppression like a badge of honor, of proof that "we are more oppressed than anyone else," with the implication that this somehow makes us better than anyone else. Black-power enthusiasts are just as capable of proving how black people are more oppressed than anyone else as lesbians are of proving that lesbians are more oppressed (and thus the vanguard of "the revolution").

Some of us get caught in the middle of this competition for the title of "more oppressed than thou," and it is easy to resent the fact that most people feel only their own individual oppression and ignore, or merely pay lip service to, everyone else's cause.

If I were to try to escape the often scathing judgment of separatists by carefully arranging my life to suit all their theories, I would not only deprive myself of the enjoyment I get from knowing and relating to certain individual men, I would also have to deprive myself of the enjoyment I get relating to individual white women, including white lesbians. Racism is just as oppressive as sexism, so why stop at one category? Believe me, black separatists can be just as angry and judgmental as any white lesbian separatist. And, of course, if I'm going to be really fair in cutting off all privileged classes, I must never associate with people who, unlike myself, have incomes above the poverty level.

Would my isolation from everyone in the world except black bisexual or lesbian women living below the poverty level change the world for the better? No. Would it improve my own life? Definitely not. Would it satisfy the separatists? Maybe. But why bother? There's always someone to put you down no matter what you do. So ultimately you have to base your choices on your own experiences and beliefs as well as on the deep feeling and inner needs which influence each person's beliefs.

I don't believe that every individual who is in some way or another (race, gender, able-bodiedness, etc.) more privileged than someone else is thereby necessarily an oppressor. I judge people by their actions and statements, not by whether their genitals or skin color or sexual orientation is awarded privileges in an oppressive society.

Almost everyone alive in the U.S. today is more materially privileged (even myself on AFDC) than most of the people in the world throughout history and today. I do not choose the imperialist foreign policy of the U.S. government, any more (maybe less) than you choose for black people to suffer the effects of racism. If you are white, you are not creating and supporting racism by the very "act" of being white. Likewise, a man is not automatically supporting the patriarchy by the very "act" of being male. Nor does a heterosexual or bisexual necessarily support the patriarchy just because the person she or he loves is of the opposite gender.

I am not "consorting with the enemy" if my friend or lover is white or male, unless their actions are oppressive. Incidentally, both black people *and* lesbians are capable of being quite as oppressive within a relationship as anyone else. (Haven't you heard of lesbian battering?)

Not all men are oppressive. Not all women are not. You don't have to believe me, but that is my experience, not theory. Actually, to be more accurate, I find we all have oppressive tendencies to greater and lesser degrees. Unfortunately it is generally the most power-hungry and oppressive of us humans that get ourselves into positions of power and perpetuate systems that oppress us all, to greater and lesser degrees.

But scapegoating anyone with any privilege or focusing only on men and straight or bisexual women as being "the enemy" doesn't do anything to promote a better system. It is limited to venting rage, to letting off steam — endless steam

Don't get me wrong; I think every separatist has as much right to her lifestyle and beliefs as anyone else. If she has a personal need or desire to avoid, as much as possible, contact with anyone who is not a lesbian, then that's probably what she should do. She certainly has every right to. If she feels that associating only with lesbians will create a better world, she's entitled to her beliefs. But that doesn't mean that any woman who makes other choices is supporting the patriarchy.

As a bisexual, I have been more "out" in the straight world than in the lesbian community. In a deliberate attempt to avoid being seen as better than "real" lesbians by the straight world, I have been out as a lesbian rather than bisexual to the straight world. Because of the extreme biphobia in the lesbian community, and because the lesbian and gay community is one I have always admired, related to, and identified with, it has been much more difficult to be out as bisexual in the lesbian community than to be out as lesbian in the straight world.

As a bisexual, I have been exposed to the same homophobic oppression as any lesbian. I never "left a woman for a man," but like most lesbians over thirty, I have had more than one relationship in my life. When I was with a female lover, my inherent bisexuality ("bisexual privilege?") did not protect me, any more than it protected my lover from being literally stoned by a group of six teenagers when we walked hand in hand through a park.

At another time in my life, when I broke up with the father of my children, I was exposed to the same sword hanging over my head of losing custody of my children for being a lesbian. My ex knew I would not deny my lesbianism in court even at the risk of losing my beloved children who mean the world to me, nor try to "soften the charge" by pleading bisexuality. Judges don't tend to see bisexual mothers as being more fit than lesbians anyway. Some judges consider bisexuality worse.

Furthermore I discovered while researching custody issues that the commonly held belief that heterosexual women usually win custody battles is a myth. I have read that in 63 percent of cases, if a father really wants custody, he usually gets it, even if the mother is as straight as apple pie. The automatic right to custody of her children is one "heterosexual privilege" that heterosexual mothers just don't really have.[2]

To lose or be threatened by the loss of one's life, one's children, one's livelihood, one's self-respect is indeed oppressive — much more oppressive than "not being invited to a party." Of course. However:

1. All the oppressions listed in the preceding paragraph are not unique to lesbians. Black people (including straight black men) as well as Native Americans have been oppressed in the same genocidal ways as lesbians have.

2. This oppression and genocide is not caused by individuals choosing heterosexual relationships; all individual heterosexuals should not be blamed for the atrocities of patriarchy any more than all white people should be blamed for the atrocities of racism and white exploitation and control of the world.

3. The lesbian community grossly underestimates its own value and impact when it refuses to acknowledge the tremendous loss and isolation a woman feels when she is exiled from the lesbian community for admitting her bisexuality or choosing a partner of the "wrong" gender. Just because lesbians don't have the power (and most don't have the inclination) to starve, jail, or kill anyone they don't like or disagree with does not render insignificant the enormous pain a woman feels when she is ostracized and isolated from the only community she identifies with and loves. It is not a question of being excluded from a few parties and lesbian events.

The lesbian community, much as we fail to appreciate it, is a support system in whose relatively tight-knit fabric many lives are woven. Many lesbians' entire lives are intricately involved in, and dependent on, the lifestyle, politics, belief systems, affection, communication, and support that the lesbian community provides and represents. Identifying as a lesbian is more than who is sleeping in your bed, as any unpartnered lesbian can tell you.

If someone who so totally identifies as a lesbian one day meets an individual who touches her psyche in a place that's never been reached before, or meets a deep and complex need in her that no one else has ever come close to, or has a deeper spiritual kinship with her than she has ever felt with anyone else, or simply treats her better than anyone else ever has, and this person happens to be a male, then it's not a simple matter for her of "exchanging lesbian oppression for heterosexual privilege." It is an enormous trauma to be forced by this world of dichotomy, labels, and judgment to choose between (a) the person who fills a deep affectional and spiritual, not just sexual, need in her and (b) the world (lesbian community) in which her whole life and identity are intricately entwined.

Finally, I want to reiterate that no one has a monopoly on pain, anguish, and human suffering or on the ways in which oppression severely harms us all.

I am aware that appropriately applied anger can be extremely effective and valuable. It is also true that extremists challenge us all to re-examine our beliefs, values, and behavior, and sometimes point in the direction we need to head even if some extremists go further in that direction than we might want to go.

Still, I want to remind all who read this that love and compassion, which includes tolerance of differences, is the ultimate goal.

Notes

1. This article was previously published in *Lesbian Contradictions* 29, Winter 1990.

2. Marianne Takas, *Child Custody: A Complete Guide for Concerned Mothers*, Harper & Row, 1987, p. 2.

Rebecca Gorlin

The voice of a wandering Jewish bisexual

When I think of being bisexual, I am reminded of my Jewish ancestors who, kicked out of different countries, tried to find a place to call home. I, too, have wandered, in the gay and straight worlds, Jewish and not, feeling kicked out and alienated.

We've both built our own communities, straddled several worlds, and survived enormous oppression. Nazi concentration camps killed millions of Jews, lesbians, and gay men; bisexuals must have died there, too. In the last twenty years, many more bisexual and gay men, and fewer bisexual and lesbian women, have died of AIDS.

Whether or not we like it, most of us are very successful at passing, because being Jewish or bisexual is not something that can be seen just by looking at us. If I am walking down the street with my boyfriend, I am automatically assumed by gays and heterosexuals alike to be heterosexual. If I were to walk with a girlfriend, everyone would think I'm a lesbian. By the same token everyone assumes I am Christian.

Over the last eight years, I have done plenty of soul-searching. I am beginning to understand what being a Jew means to me and to gain a sense of Jewish pride. I had no Jewish education growing up and have been wanting to learn more about Jewish history, rituals, and customs. I've been reading about Jewish women and feminism. For four years I have sung with the Zamir Chorale of Boston and learned about Jewish music. I am a member of Am Tikva, a lesbian and gay Jewish group. The more I learn, the more at home I feel as a Jew. As bisexuals, we too must go through a learning process in order to feel at home and to gain bisexual pride and visibility and power for ourselves and as a community.

This eight-year search includes my struggle to develop a proud lesbian, then bisexual, identity. Identifying as a lesbian for seven years made me see how much I love women and began my awareness of homophobia and heterosexism. When I came out as a bisexual, I realized that men are important to me, too. Being with a man again I had to deal with male–female differences, sexism, and heterosexual privilege. Fortunately, I have been able to talk about these issues in a lesbian-to-bisexual support group called the Hasbians.

What I want most is to integrate my bisexual and Jewish identities. This has not been easy because, as a bisexual I feel alienated from both the heterosexual and homosexual Jewish communities. I don't go to certain straight Jewish functions to avoid getting sucked into a very sexist and heterosexist community that will only accept me if I'm with a man and don't discuss my "other side."

Am Tikva works on the issues of sexism and heterosexism, but not much on biphobia. There are other bisexuals in Am Tikva, and except for a token topic in an occasional discussion group, our issues are never addressed. The group is very gay and lesbian oriented.

When we are in Jewish circles, we have got to come out whenever possible. San Francisco's Ahavat Shalom states that it is for lesbian, gay, and bisexual Jews. Am Tikva and other gay and lesbian oriented Jewish groups need to recognize our presence and be inclusive. Lesbians and gay men have worked hard for recognition in heterosexual Jewish groups; they should understand our situation as bisexuals and Jews.

Lilith, a Jewish feminist magazine, had in their Summer 1989 issue an article about the particular difficulties experienced by Jewish lesbians and gay men coming out to their families because of the Jewish traditions of family and having children. I was very annoyed to find no mention of Jewish bisexuals. We, too, face homophobia when we come out to our families. Like lesbians and gays we are often seen as never having children if we have a same-sex partner. In addition, there are the heterosexual assumptions. Our opposite-gender partners are celebrated, and our same-sex partners are usually denied. If we have children with a man, we're seen as a traditional Jewish family when in fact we are not. We have to speak out in either case.

Recognition takes a strong and united bisexual front; it won't happen unless we demand it. In non-Jewish circles, be they bisexual, gay, lesbian, or heterosexual, we have to come out and challenge any anti-Semitism. As bisexuals, we have to come out and challenge biphobic stereotypes and attitudes whenever we experience them. If we don't, biphobia and anti-Semitism will go on, and we will be invisible. We must stand up and be proud of our Jewish bisexual selves. Then we will find a place to call home.

Roland Glenn

Proud father
of a bisexual son

T he letter arrived just when we were expecting it. It notified me that I was being drafted into the U.S. Army on August 24, 1943. I was eighteen. The instructions were short and clear. I was to report at 4 p.m. in front of the Ligonier, Pennsylvania, movie theater with nothing but a tooth-brush and sweater. I had two weeks to prepare myself. My parents promised they'd care for my dog and the 1935 Chevy sedan that my dad had bought me with his $300 World War I government bonus. I would miss chasing the girls who were most easily persuaded into the back seat of my car.

On the twenty-fourth, Mom prepared a stuffed turkey dinner with all the trimmings, and the whole family gathered to give me a proper send-off. The cooking and preparation kept Mom busy all day. She probably planned that as her way of dealing with the pain of our impending separation. My baby sister, Doris, was too young to know about war, but she knew I was leaving and clung to me. We both cried.

After that great meal, we left the old Victorian house where I had spent many years of my youth and walked together down North Main Street and through "The Diamond," which to this day is one of the most beautifully preserved public squares anywhere. A block further on and there we were in front of the movie house.

We, the future soldiers and defenders of freedom, were met by Ligonier's mayor and members of the draft board. The color guards of the American Legion and the Veterans of Foreign Wars were already in position to lead the parade. The high school band was playing patriotic songs. I had once been a member of that band and played the euphonium. All of our families lined the sidewalks as we draftees lined up behind the band. This was a big deal and was one of those moments when I was supposed to become a man. At the very least, I was trying my best to act like one. The mayor launched into a speech about how proud he was of those of us who were about to leave. It was painful just standing there. I wished that he would get it over with so that we could make our exit. A trumpeter sounded a fanfare, and the band struck up a Sousa march. The parade finally began. Our families and friends walked along the sidewalks waving small American flags.

Unexpectedly, my father stepped out of the crowd and was there marching beside me. This was not a time when public displays of affection between men, even fathers and sons, were common. But this loving man had his own ways of showing support. He said, "Cappy, I want to make this march with you," and I felt his arm slip around my back. So I got a free hug or two. We marched together the remaining blocks to the Ligonier railroad station. Before I boarded the train, we hugged each other again and whispered, "I love you." That was a very special moment between us.

Pride Day

Today is Pride Day, June 19, 1989, forty-six years later. How have those years slipped by so fast? I have been looking forward to this day for some time. That earlier march to the train, with my dad by my side, has recently been on my mind. I have told the story to my wife, Carol, many times and said, "I want to do that with my son and to have the same experience, as a father, that my own dad had with me forty-six years ago. Let's march on Pride Day. We will not be sending our son off to war but supporting him in another important cause." It was not yet clear to me how much I would be doing for myself by stepping out of the crowd and being there with him.

We didn't know what to expect other than the fact that we both would be marching within the bisexual contingent. How many people would there be? How many groups? Would there be a band? Would people line the sidewalks? Would we see anyone we knew or who knew us? What would they think? Would we show up on the evening news?

As we headed across town, I felt nervous about the whole thing. I could have easily used my health problems as an excuse for not getting involved. I might have said, "We will think about doing it next year." But it began to dawn on us that we were also the beneficiaries of making this march when we showed up at the brunch for the Bisexual Women's and Men's Networks. Each person passed us along to others who gave us a hug and said things like, "We have been so eager to meet you." It felt like a large family reunion. There were soon about one hundred individuals in the room enjoying this warm beginning of a very important day. I was probably the oldest dude in the room, but that didn't seem to matter. I knew that I had made the right decision.

Liz suggested that we make signs to carry. The two of us old troopers were soon down on the floor with magic markers. The message was easy: PROUD PARENTS OF A BISEXUAL SON.

While I am not a total stranger to marching for causes, I didn't fully anticipate what would happen next after we loaded ourselves onto the Green Line and headed for Government Center. Emerging from the station into that mass of people reminded me of an earlier day, in Washington, when some friends and I had marched on the South African Embassy with four thousand members of the Urban League. This crowd was many times larger.

Alan Hamilton spoke on stage as the representative of the bisexual community and highlighted the many injustices which our society still imposes upon individuals who have chosen gay, lesbian, or bisexual lifestyles.

Suddenly a young man stepped up and said, "Thank you for being here supporting all of us. I wish that my parents were with me today." As I moved through the crowd toward our place in the line of march, a number of individuals made similar comments. When the parade was about to begin, I could not see either the beginning or the end of the thousands of marchers. The sheer size of this demonstration of pride was beyond any of my expectations. I was breathless with excitement and was also deeply affected by the numerous reminders of concern for the people with AIDS.

Finally the column began to move. I didn't notice it at first but it soon became apparent that cheers and applause were being directed at us from people observing the three of us walking together and the message on our signs. We had not lost sight of the original purpose which had led to our choosing this particular action of demonstrating our support for Woody. But it became more obvious that the message on our signs was conveying something more important — "parental support of children." As the march progressed, Woody and I were interviewed by a local radio station, which presented an excellent opportunity to explain what it meant to me to be there with my son. The most poignant moment came when a young man stepped out of the crowd and asked, "Would you consider adopting another child?" Carol quickly replied, *"Yes."* There were also a number of sad moments when young women and men approached us and said, "I lost my own mother or father because of my sexual preference." We both thought how impossible it would be for us to lose one of our children because they had chosen a lifestyle different than our own.

Carol and I walked home slowly and silently. I was trying to assimilate this experience, feeling tired but just fine. This was the longest distance

I had attempted to walk since my operation. I had done something which I had really wanted to do, and Carol had joined me, as she has done throughout our lives together when we faced important issues.

Alan, Pepper, and Woody came over in the evening. We went out together for dinner and made plans to spend the Fourth of July together at the Cape. It felt so very good to be together at the conclusion of this day. After dinner we walked slowly home, as if trying to stretch out this important day of expressing our pride in one another. There were hugs and plenty of kisses all around.

When Woody and I hugged each other, I said, "You know, I think that we did something special for each other today." He agreed. I don't think that he realized that I was also thinking of the hug that my dad gave me forty-six years earlier at the Ligonier railroad station. Fortunately, I have not lost a son because of war or arguments. Woody and I will have plenty of opportunities to share our memories. I hope there will be more marching parents next year.

Dolores Bishop

Another senseless loss

*In the early summer of 1987, seven people, all strangers, met in
an empty storefront in San Francisco's Castro District. With a few
portable sewing machines and a growing cadre of volunteers,
they began to document lives they feared history would neglect.
Names and dates were not enough for this memorial; the symbols
and souvenirs of a lifetime were also added, stitched onto fabric
panels measuring 3'x 6'. Each panel remembered one person.
Later panels would be sewn together and displayed as a quilt.*

*Today the AIDS Memorial Quilt continues to grow. Every day
panels arrive at the NAMES Project workshop, where volunteers
stitch them into the Quilt.*[1]

In July 1987, I walked into the NAMES Project storefront with my first
panel in memory of my friend Jack Natkin. I put it on the front desk,
filled out their information card, and looked at the panels hanging on
the walls. I stood there weeping; somehow I just couldn't leave. Someone
gave me a slow hug and a tissue, and inquired about my panel, asking
if I had made it. When I said yes, I was asked if I would like to help sew.
I called my dentist to cancel an appointment, sat down at a machine, and
didn't leave until midnight. That was my first midnight of many, helping
to sew the Quilt together.

The Quilt has helped me get myself together, too. I had seen my
mother through a painful losing battle with cancer. She died a few
years ago at eighty-six. We had our battles, but I still miss her. My
father and husband are gone, too. They are not coming back and
that's that. Screaming and kicking the floor seems useless as a rational
method of dealing with it. That's the crux of it; it's emotionally hard
to let it all out.

This is how the Quilt has helped me personally, as it has the bisexual
and gay communities who have been hardest hit by AIDS. Out of this
very public, highly visible, multimedia AIDS memorial many feelings have
surfaced — loss, fear, anger, frustration, and also pure hatred toward
those in our government who are doing nothing to fight AIDS. This
hideous catastrophe is spreading around the planet and nothing is
forthcoming, not even any concern, and surely not policy or money. The

Quilt's message to the world tells of red tape, stalled committees, homophobia, delayed funds, and a constipation of the spirit.

I'm better now with how I deal with my own pain and the loss of so many friends to this epidemic. Especially now, I can do the "sixty-second hour," helping someone like myself who is standing in the doorway, often in tears, panel in hand or wanting to create one. Inspiring, heart-rending, this somber litany in cloth is an incredible mountain of love, a tribute to the loss we all have suffered by the untimely death of those we love.

When Alan Rockway died of AIDS in November 1987, our bisexual community lost one of its key leaders. His was another senseless loss. Alan, a founding member of BiPOL, had been very active as a gay-identified bisexual organizer. He co-authored the controversial Gay Rights Ordinance in Dade County, Florida, which spurred Anita Bryant's Save Our Children Campaign. It was only fitting that his treasured political t-shirts would make up his panel for the Quilt. Members of BiPOL met to design and sew the panel in his honor. We gathered his well-worn and most favorite t-shirts — "Anita Sucks," "A Day Without Human Rights Is Like A Day Without Sunshine," "Hurricane Anita," "Anita you're the pits!" These were pieced together with other special t-shirts that captured Alan's essence. An original "Rocky Horror Picture Show," "The Great 'BI' Centennial," a "Bisexual Center — Love Spans the Spectrum," and a flashy Rio de Janeiro rounded out his story. When we chose the glitzy red-silver cloth to spell out his name we knew he was smiling down on us. His panel hung on display in the front window of Moscone Convention Center during the Christmas showing. He would have loved it.

I'm proud of everything I've done: finding that certain cloth or trim, stitching letters onto the panel, making something shorter or longer, cutting, sorting, stacking, folding, dragging bundles around from here to there and back again, pinning, repairing, painting, and giving lessons on the sewing machines. The sewing bee is an important support system that provides a way for people to express their love, pride, anger, frustration, and pain.

And the panels are such expressions of love! Decorated with everything from a Barbie doll, cremation ashes, stuffed animals, jockstraps, racing silks, ballet slippers, condoms, cock rings, and photos, to sequins, beads, lace, leather, feathers, fur, merit badges, tuxedos, gowns, rhinestones, pearls, and glitter, glitter, glitter.

After a successful 1988 national summer tour the Quilt returned to Washington, D.C., in October on the ellipse between the White House and the Washington Monument. It had grown to the size of seven football fields, and represented over 8,000 names of those who had been lost to the AIDS epidemic.

At dawn our San Francisco crew was stunned into near silence by the 1,000 volunteers who showed up from all over the country. With the unfolding crews in place, we began to open the Quilt bundles into their squares on the grass, while readers began to recite the list of 8,000-plus names over the loud speakers. When the entire quilt had been opened, the crews and onlookers stood holding hands around the edges of the Quilt for a silent tribute; many of us were in tears. The reading of the names went on all day. Mr. Reagan made sure not to see this patchwork of protests. He made a very public exit from the White House by helicopter when we were setting up the day before.

At 5:30 p.m., we began folding the bundles for the night and taking them to the trucks. By 7 p.m., I joined 20,000 people in the Candlelight Walk spearheaded by parents carrying pictures of their children who had died. We walked with our candles past the White House, around the reflecting pool, and to the Lincoln Memorial for a service. It was a quiet crowd, prideful, and determined. Many candles were set adrift on the pool. I got in at 10 p.m., the exact moment the news aired their coverage of the Quilt. After a twenty-hour day I felt energized, renewed, proud, and complete with my efforts.

While the NAMES Project claims not to be political, it has certainly inspired political action. It has broken down barriers, assisted the grieving process, and inspired diverse communities to work together to fight the AIDS epidemic.

Note

1. The NAMES Project brochure, 1989.

ben e factory

"out"line of one man's polymorphic liberation

Not born on the Fourth of July (rather the ninth), 1961, in Des Moines, Iowa, United States of Alienation. The folks who chanced to cause my birth were the kids of immigrants — wood and textile workers, machinists, and, of course, unpaid domestic laborers (moms). Living next to the railroad and the river, i dreamed of the unknown places i might venture off to on a boxcar or a raft, escaping the regime of school, bed-making, lawn-mowing, and big brothers. Alas, this existential jail-break took years to pull off.

"Scientifically" speaking, i can't say whether i got queer by designer genes or if my environment "polluted" me; no one can say till we unpollute our social ecology and stop living like grandiose paranoid lap dogs.

Baths with my brothers, father, and boyhood friends are reminiscences of shameless fun and male bonding. Showers in the company of other boys in the gym and at religious camps and retreats helped expose our young bodies and souls to each other's curious comparisons and unspoken desires.

"Playing doctor" and skinny-dipping were favorite thought-crimes shared with both girls and boys. I was more fascinated with dicks till the girls got breasts and pubic hair. Assholes were, of course, always a universal mecca of taboo delight.

"Dressing up" as and playing roles of both grown-up men and wimmin was a frequent bit of early switch-hitting drag. Both sets of roles seemed accessible and expressible to me; the either/or hadn't sunk in yet. I also partook of both stereotypical girl stuff and boy stuff: cooking and construction, sewing and mowing, folk dancing and football.

Particularly vivid images stick with me: Dad in his lavender jumpsuit (Mom's favorite color!?); watching an older man masturbate after he lured me out of a chess game and up to his room in the YMCA; me at six 69ing with my sixteen-year-old brother. I didn't then see this as manipulation, which is now apparent in view of his wanton objectification and exploitation.

Puberty had its highlights. Before i became conscious of or came out as "bisexual," i had feelings which i didn't really distinguish as other than "normal." Socially and sexually, i was caught up in the compulsory heterosexual attractions to the gals. Yet, socially and emotionally i felt closer to guys.

Viewing and being viewed in the locker room was "in-F-ably" tantalizing. I'll never forget Doug's comment admiring my sweaty semi-engorged cock, though being sized up as poorly or well hung i now find to be a meat-headed cliché. Drawing in art class and viewing nudes in books, i saw both sexes as aesthetic. I fortunately didn't get stuck in acquiring, possessing, and gender stereotyping the people to whom i was attracted. This was reflected in my early poetry which was often "romantic" in the sense of being both idealistic and focused on emotional and sexual relations.

Becoming conscious of my sexuality and finally coming out began with my involvement in religious youth activities: Summer camp, retreats, and then conferences turned out to be hotbeds of hetero- and homo-eroticism with all of the multibunk rooms, open showers, hand-holding partner-switching folk dancing, and those quiet wandering paths.

Topeka, Kansas, 1974, is, believe it or not, where and when i first touched another naked male and felt that sexual "thang." A religious youth conference brought us to Topeka, where several of us somehow ended up in a gym or health club. There in a steamy steam room, i discovered myself leisurely lounging about with a few chums, all of us naked. We filled this little room with our contacts — visual, verbal, and physical (shoulder to shoulder, rubbing elbows, and knocking knees). This was the first time i was conscious of wanting to touch another boy in a sexual way.

At fourteen i found myself signed up for compulsory Heterosexual Monogamy 101: Dating, kissing girls, then caressing and massaging their backs, breasts, legs, and buttocks. I noticed compulsory heterosexuality caused me to become stiff. I began to developed my male character armor. Checking out Mom's *Playgirl* magazines, i oozed desire for real emotional and sexual relations with other boys, something unavailable in this course.

Sweeeeet sixteen ... mm-hmm. Right after graduating from high school, i smoked pot for the first time with my best friend, Andy, then felt relaxed enough to finally tell him that i loved him and would like to physically express my affection with him. He said he loved me too, but wasn't into sex with guys. Frustrated in my unrequited love, but not feeling rejected, i went off to the University of Iowa. There i met Karen, who accepted my love and my "bisexuality" (i finally knew that Elton John and i were not alone in the world). Karen and i joined the Socialist Party USA and several other campus and community activist groups, learning more about heterosexism and liberation as we grew together.

The summer of 1978, i roomed with Bill, a friend from high school. He was the first male to accept my offer to share forbidden fruits. Sixty-nine revisited, this time with a peer and an informed consensuality. We continued off and on for a couple of years till he moved back to Kansas City. "Sex, drugs, and rock 'n' roll," we took a walk on the wild side and began to free ourselves from the domestication and colonization which caged and collared us. Being with him, i experienced a marvelous insight: We could really listen to each other, feel each other to be intimate equals, and we began to see through our male conditioning. When Karen returned at the end of the summer, i heard her in a new way, as an equal with whom i struggled toward mutual liberation.

The autumn of 1978, i came out as bisexual to three of my brothers. The two older ones had been on the fringes of the New Left (Weather Underground, Black Panthers, etc.) and accepted my radical sexuality without batting an eyelash. My younger brother, at that time a neo-*laissez-faire* liberal, loosened his bow tie to extend his pro-choice anti-sexism to include support for freedom to experiment with and choose one's affectional orientation in the face of a repressive heterosexism.

Mom, Dad, and Grandma Koko found out about my bisexuality in the summer of 1980. We were sitting in a restaurant in Iowa City right after i'd gotten a scholarship to go study at the United Nations in New York City. My folks were elated. The waitron came swishing up to the table to welcome us and give us glasses of water. After he left, Mom queried, "I wonder whether people like that ever live happy normal lives...?" A long silence fell. I replied, "Seems to me that happiness is abnormal, statistically speaking, since most people live pretty miserable lives." "What do you mean by that?" she asked. "Well," i said, "if he's gay, as you're supposing, he may, in fact, be happy or at least as happy as anyone else on the average. Knowing a fair number of gays, lesbians, and bisexuals, i feel that happiness and misery are common to everyone." The waitron sauntered on back, and the topic was dropped as we all gobbled.

The next day, Mom and Koko and i were sitting in the kitchen back home in Des Moines peeling potatoes. Mom joked that all of her boys (five living, no sisters) are such capable cooks and will make so many fine husbands for working women. I said, "I like cooking for myself, and once a week for my co-op housemates and our visitors, but i wouldn't want to be a house-husband, or for that matter, any kind of husband." Mom said, "You'll be lonely if you don't get married, and with your opinions, people will think you're gay." Grandma Koko, seeing the worry on her daughter's face, chimed in, "Jacque, we both know from experience that cooking is usually more satisfying than marriage. We both have married friends who are plenty lonely. And i have close friends who aren't married, some straight, some gay, who are happier being independent; even so, they have families of friends and lovers." Not quite what Mom wanted to hear. Koko continued, "I've loved a few men, all with problems, and I've always counted on other women for warmth and support. You can understand that. You've always had close girlfriends, some who you love a lot."

Then i decided to tell them: "Even though Karen and i feel love and commitment for each other, we don't want to be married. Being married and straight aren't the only ways of being happy. And whatever problems i may have with women, sex isn't one of them; the same goes for men. Regardless of what people may think, i'm not gay, i'm bisexual. I can love people based on who they are, instead of what sex they are."

Koko once again added her perspective, "Having lived in California, i know that lots of people have some experience with or desire for both sexes. There isn't really a line between being straight or gay, it's often a more or less kind of thing." Mom didn't say anything just then, or for the next seven years, about my sexuality. Dad found out from Mom. All he said at the time was "Watch out for your health" — a practical suggestion, since AIDS was just becoming known.

Men's anti-sexist discussion and action groups in the Socialist Party and in the Progressive Student Network (PSN) were seminal, so to speak, in the development of my critical and practical approaches to realizing the vision of egalitarian and mutually supportive relations between wimmin and men, and among men. In the PSN, i met John, and we organized the bisexual support group using the lessons we'd learned in the network and in left anti-sexist struggles. We were soon joined by a woman organizer from the River City Housing Cooperatives and in addition to support work, began to do outreach, education, and political action to make bisexuals visible and recognized activists in the "queer liberation" movement. We worked on four main areas:

1. creating a bisexual liberation community — we met and got to know one another, developed a sense of who we were as a group, and what we all wanted ... without making a scene for cruising or meat-marketing;
2. supporting each other in coming out and in challenging internalized oppressions — while we did a certain amount of peer and group

counseling, and personal healing and growth work, we did not engage in "therapeutic" interventions or psychological advising;

3. educating ourselves and the community — we shared various articles and books, had presentations and discussions, and put out literature on bisexuality and its relationship to sexism, monogamy, AIDS hysteria, etc.; and

4. politicizing and mobilizing bisexuals — helping to make the connections between liberation struggles around gender, sexuality, race, class, empire, ecology, boredom, etc.

Shortly after i got to Seattle, i contacted a bisexual group composed of wimmin and men; it turned out to have just folded. The gals pulled through though and kept developing the Seattle Bisexual Women's Network (SBWN).

In late 1988 and early 1989, i worked with the SBWN in pulling together a "men's auxiliary" from contacts in my previous attempt and a few new guys. In June 1989, at Seattle's Pride March and Freedom Day Rally, the SBWN had a picnic at which the men's auxiliary started getting in gear.

Our first men's group meeting happened in late August 1989: Half a dozen guys and a couple SBWNers got together in a quiet little dive, plotted the sexual revolution, and drank a fair amount of beer and java. The Seattle Bisexual Men's Union began meeting regularly in late September 1989 and doing effective outreach through the Seattle Gay News, in addition to posting and word of mouth. As of February 1990, there are about two dozen men who've come to our group activities, and we're seeing new people at every meeting. Yeaaah!

So ... to rap up, i feel that my coming out and my organizing efforts have been linked very closely with my struggle to liberate myself from the effects of sexism, propertarianism, and authoritarianism, and, of course, ismism. ("All we are saying is, 'Give chance a piece.'") Humor, poetry, listening, constructive self-criticism, experimental weirdness, and partying with the masses have been key in unlocking the door that tight-assed moralism has slammed in my face.

Rebecca Shuster

Beyond defense

Considering next steps for
bisexual liberation[1]

As bisexual people, we are united in the goal and dream of ending the oppression of bisexuals,[2] and a wider vision of eradicating all oppression. As we move toward the establishment of an organized constituency, taking this early opportunity to review the current state of bisexual liberation and the strong and the weak points in our efforts to date can assist us to formulate the most effective strategies for the next period. We can then develop and act on a liberation program that will, piece by piece, dismantle institutionalized oppression, individual participation in oppression, and the effects of internalized oppression on our lives and our organizations.

Reason for pride

We have done well. Individually and collectively, we have made great strides. Bisexual organizations have germinated nationally and internationally, initiating support groups, newsletters, dances, lesbian and gay pride march contingents, and conferences. Those who have folded newsletters, convened the first daring support groups, told their stories in the lesbian, gay, and mainstream press, etc., deserve praise and thanks. These political, social, and textual meeting places provided forums to heal, to think, to forge vital redefinitions of societal[3] concepts of closeness and sexual identity, and to take action. There we have learned about the mechanics of bisexual and lesbian and gay oppression and the resulting injury of all people: bisexuals, lesbians and gay men, and heterosexuals.[4]

Within and outside our organizations, bisexuals play a pivotal role toward flexibility of sexual choice and identity. Many bisexuals understand and courageously act on the knowledge that identity is useful as a tool for personal and world evolution but not as a limitation on any human being. We are increasingly able to set up the broad strokes and passing moments of our lives without the imposition of those constructs. We speak out against sexual harassment in our workplaces, where we are often assumed to be heterosexual. We volunteer in AIDS hospices, often assumed to be lesbians and gay men.

In addition, many bisexuals understand and act on the importance of building a wide range of close relationships, sexual or not, with both women and men. Many bisexuals aim to bar societal assumptions about gender from bearing on our love, and our lives are outstanding models for weaving networks of tender, committed relationships.

These wise, creative, bold decisions to seek to define ourselves and sculpt closeness free of the prescribed restrictions on women, men, affection, and sexuality have given us a particular willingness to hold out a vision of human potential, do independent thinking, respect others with diverse life choices, and be liberation leaders for many social change movements.

We can be proud and pleased.

Remaining challenges

The mainstream media sometimes lists bisexuals among populations battling AIDS, and some lesbian and gay organizations have added the word "bisexual" to their names. But we cannot mistake the visibility we have gained for genuine advances in our liberation any more than saying civil rights laws which guarantee the rights of people of color can be celebrated as an end to racism. Misconceptions about and intolerance toward bisexuals remain rampant in heterosexual, lesbian, and gay cultures. Bisexuals continue to be considered profiteers of heterosexual privilege, indecisive, untrustworthy, exotic, incapable of committed relationships, promiscuous, and responsible for the spread of AIDS. Bisexuals face vicious, systematic mistreatment, enforced with violence and threats of violence. That oppression, in all its glaring and hidden forms, is largely internalized, leaving bisexuals with a distorted self-image that prevents us from flourishing and hinders leadership development.

To eradicate bisexuals' internalized oppression, we must begin to identify the forms it can take:

♦ *Political and personal homelessness:* Repeated rejection in the lesbian, gay, and heterosexual communities leaves bisexuals feeling as though we are not welcome anywhere and do not fit anywhere. As a result, we are often suspicious, defensively "covering all our bases" as if attack can come from any corner at any time, and skeptically testing out those we meet to somehow determine if they can be trusted.

◆ *Marginalization:* Bisexuals often internalize the accusation that we are odd or strange and accept a place outside of all that is established, "mainstream," or usual. This view leads us to political errors, confusing potential allies for "the enemy."

◆ *Hiding (in the closet):* Bisexuals often conceal who we are — our assets as well as our difficulties — in the hopes of protecting ourselves from intolerance. Thus, we often act on pretense, losing the ability to detect the actual degree of safety in each specific situation.

◆ *Refusal to choose:* Because we long to reach our full potentials, we often feel that deciding to commit ourselves to one person, one career, etc. is inherently limiting or suffocating. Profound vows to maintain open options often underlie our identities as bisexuals, sometimes rooted in past experiences in which we were forced to make unnecessary and emotionally costly choices. Those vows can leave us unwilling to close any door, even to do what is right. We may be overdiversified and spread thin, attempting to substitute "equal opportunity" and a lack of affiliation for genuinely ending oppression.

◆ *Gender confusion:* Bisexuals sometimes do not feel or define themselves as wholly male or female. In our earnest desire to dissolve gender roles, we may pretend to achieve androgyny, as if women's and men's liberation can be accomplished without the arduous and powerful work of unraveling the effects of this oppression and realizing liberation for all women and men.

◆ *Superiority:* Because we have been forced to defend ourselves again and again, bisexuals often justify our difficulties not only as strengths, but as preferred lifestyle. Bisexuality is not better than any other sexual identity, and to act as if this were the case keeps us gravely divided from lesbians, gay men, and heterosexuals.

In particular, bisexuals often defend our sexual practices as superior to those of heterosexuals, lesbians, and gay men. While bisexuals are often leaders toward sexual freedom, selecting partners of both genders is not by itself equivalent to liberation. All young people raised in this culture absorb debilitating mythology about sexuality, and far more frequently than we have yet acknowledged or documented, are the victims of sexual abuse. These experiences impede the ability to intelligently choose sexual partners and activities, regardless of sexual identity. Since bisexuals are not raised differently from the rest of the culture, we therefore act on the same kinds of sexual compulsion, inhibition, and confusion as our heterosexual, lesbian, and gay friends.

The task before us is to design a strategy which will most rapidly eliminate any oppression and internalized oppression that hinders bisexuals' lives. There is much work to be done.

Bisexual liberation and lesbian and gay liberation

Where bisexuals have begun to become visible and build organizations, a division between bisexuals and lesbians and gay men has often been created that is a key barrier to our success. As a starting point, bisexuals must understand that those who are labeled or identify as bisexual are subject to the identical mistreatment as lesbians and gay men to the degree to which we challenge gender-based stereotypes. If we review the content of the oppression and internalized oppression of bisexuals listed above, it becomes clear that our experience is simply a form of lesbian and gay oppression, not a separate oppression. When a lesbian, gay man, or bisexual is perpetuating a bisexual's oppression, she or he is acting out of internalized oppression. When a heterosexual plays that role, she or he is acting as an agent of the oppression.

Because the oppression of bisexuals is lesbian and gay oppression, bisexuals are, in part, a constituency *within* lesbian and gay liberation. To define bisexuals' oppression as distinct from lesbian and gay oppression is divisive and slows the fulfillment of our goals. Like sections of the working class, we cannot permit ourselves to be pitted against one another but instead must unite against our common oppression.

At the same time, bisexuals are a constituency within heterosexuality. When we are assumed to be heterosexual and participate in heterosexual relationships, activities, and institutions, we reap the benefits and sustain the limitations of heterosexuality. To deny this part of our lives is vain and as destructive as denying the inextricable connection between bisexuals' oppression and lesbian and gay oppression.

A bisexual is, then, 100 percent lesbian or gay *and* 100 percent heterosexual. Like someone of mixed racial or ethnic heritage, we are simultaneous, full members of both groups. No activity or belief secures our standing; we can stop searching for hospitality. Every place is our home. Each aspect of being a lesbian, gay man, or heterosexual fully applies to every bisexual: We can reclaim all the richness of each community as our own, and we can name and recover from every injury we have withstood as members of both groups. If we attempt a detour around complete pride or healing, we are settling for less than becoming our whole selves.

A bisexual identity brings with it all the components of lesbian, gay, and heterosexual identity, plus the distinctive results of blending both experiences. The oppression and internalized oppression of a bisexual has particular twists and emphasis. For example, gay men and lesbians may be labeled "deviant," while bisexuals may be labeled "exotic." Bisexuals, gay men, and lesbians all generally internalize "not feeling safe" in the world, which may, for example, produce overdiversification for bisexuals: taking on multiple careers, social change projects, etc. For lesbians and gay men, this segment may produce a different version of the same unsure stance, a constriction of life options: accepting narrow, limited possibilities for careers, social change projects, etc. Bisexuals can play the fullest role possible by claiming every portion of our identity and leading in the subversion of oppression wherever we go and with each person with whom we come into contact. Just as someone with one Israeli parent and one Palestinian parent has a profound potential role with Israelis, with Palestinians, and with others of the same mixed background, an immense opportunity awaits us as bisexuals.

Bisexual liberation and women's liberation
All oppressions operate in complex relationship to one another, each insuring the perpetuation of the other. Because the oppression of bisexuals, like all lesbian and gay oppression, is used to reinforce sexism in our society by creating a penalty for challenging gender roles, our liberation is particularly tied to women's liberation. Any liberation work we undertake as bisexuals must incorporate a commitment to ending sexism. To assert that our liberation could be considered separate from feminism would create the same kind of false and destructive division as considering our liberation separate from lesbian and gay liberation. Bisexual women's organizations have consistently backed feminist policies and activities, and bisexual women generally conceive their identities in the context of women's liberation. Bisexual women's continued dedication to women's liberation and the dissolution of gender roles, the continued advancement of bisexual men's understanding of and participation in this same effort, and joint work on the elimination of sexism in mixed-gender bisexual groups is essential to the success of bisexual liberation.

Constructing a program for bisexual liberation
We are emerging from the initial stages of bisexual liberation work and have a unique opportunity to devise a strategy based on the victories and errors of past and current liberation movements. By delineating two distinct and substantially disparate programs for bisexual liberation, I hope to help frame a discussion of a full range of possible strategies.

1. *Build a bisexual liberation movement by founding and building local, regional, national, and international bisexual organizations.*
Many bisexuals advocate forging a bisexual movement that aims to create visibility, spread information about bisexuality, draw as many people as possible into the identity, offer a safe place for anyone who takes on the identity, organize social events for bisexuals, take political action against bisexual oppression, and continually grow in membership. This plan, modeled on many other liberation movements, could inspire a ground

swell of bisexual comings out, bring the term "bisexual" into common usage and raise bisexuality into routine recognition as a sexual identity, foster personal and collective pride among bisexuals, and document and address instances of mistreatment of bisexuals by heterosexuals and lesbians and gay men. Through this plan, large numbers of people could be exposed to the concept of a third option for sexual identity, sexual activity, and affection.

Central to this strategy is an assumption that many people will take on a bisexual identity as the identity becomes more visible and less stigmatized, and that drawing people into the identity is desirable and furthers our liberation. Currently, very small numbers of people label themselves "bisexual," though large numbers of people have sexual feelings or fantasies about or contact with both women and men at some point in their lives. As we chart the course of our work, we must ask ourselves if selecting this plan and thereby proliferating the identity among this latter group would assist in the elimination of the oppression or simply offer us the feeling of comfort that we are not isolated in our experience. We must learn to distinguish between a personal and political belief that all people are capable of emotional, physical, and sexual closeness with both genders, and chauvinism that places bisexuality over other sexual identities.

To organize separately as bisexuals may imply an acceptance of the societal assumption that "heterosexual" and "lesbian and gay" are *real* categories of human beings, that we need a third such category in order to assert our own brand of hegemony. Bisexuals could meet in organizations and only commiserate about feelings of marginalization and homelessness, while simultaneously touting our "superiority," leaving us caught in internalized oppression and playing a role that helps to perpetuate lesbian and gay oppression. The current system relies on the segregation of heterosexuals and lesbians and gay men. If we proceed with a plan which asserts a hegemonous third category, we risk trivialization, division from the other two, and further ghettoizing our efforts.

In addition, to identify bisexuality as discrete from heterosexuality and homosexuality may lead to the misinterpretation that sexual closeness with both women and men is relegated to bisexuals only. If it is assumed that only heterosexuals are free to get close to a member of the other gender, and lesbians and gay men are the only ones who are free to get close to a member of the same gender, then forming a bisexual movement could compound these absurd divisions.

On the other hand, if bisexuality is defined as the potential to have sexual relationships with women and/or men, then ubiquitously offering the identity and welcoming all people into it could unleash the full continuum of human possibilities. Given the weight of lesbian and gay oppression, that process could be quite lengthy. But by slowly bringing everyone into one identity that holds infinite options, the whole system of identification and oppression would inevitably collapse.

The key difficulty of this strategy appears to be the potential for divisiveness between those who identify as bisexuals and those who do not, while the key strength may be the achievement of visibility of the identity.

2. *Build bisexual organizations for the sole purpose of generating small support groups and take political action against the oppression of bisexuals only as a constituency within the lesbian and gay liberation movement.*

Support group meeting topics could include what has been good and what has been hard about being bisexual, coming-out stories, specific aspects of internalized oppression, setting goals for our lives and leadership, and visions of a future without oppression. There, bisexuals would reclaim pride, tell stories, and give voice to the pain of mistreatment in an atmosphere of warmth and safety. Support groups generally work best when a leader assists participants to take turns talking about their lives, and when there is an agreement to meet for a specified number of weeks or months.

In addition, group members could discuss their experiences as lesbians and gay men and as heterosexuals. Meetings might then address what's been good and hard about being lesbian and gay and heterosexual, and specific topics such as "handling sexism in relationships with members of the other gender," or "how lesbian and gay oppression effects us at work." If support groups remain focused on "bisexual oppression," we may not wholly dismantle our internalized oppression. By examining all the interlocking parts of our oppression, we could begin to imagine coming into our real selves outside all oppression, no longer inside the box of any identity.

These support groups would welcome anyone who identifies as bisexual. No one would be "recruited" to a group or to the identity based on a sexual attraction they "once had." Thus, support groups would be designed for the relatively small number of people who identify themselves as bisexuals and have experienced the accompanying oppression and internalization of oppression.

If bisexual political and social activities were narrowed to the formation of support groups, bisexuals could isolate themselves within the sanctuary of their groups without ever taking on liberation work. As long as lesbian, gay, and bisexual oppression exists, we may be pulled to withdraw into corners and closets that appear to be safe.

Political leadership would include working in lesbian and gay organizations to quash lesbian, gay, and bisexual oppression, and founding and building heterosexual organizations which fight to end that oppression (such as Parents and Friends of Lesbians and Gays). A bisexual could select either approach based on her or his history with identity, relationships, community, and social change work. Bolstered by our participation in support groups, bisexual activists could make personal decisions about where and when to come out based not on shame or fear but on her or his best thinking about how to be most influential and self-respecting in each situation. This plan requires that bisexuals bar internalized oppression from bearing on those decisions but risks burying bisexuals in lesbian, gay, and heterosexual organizations where they may never feel safe in assuming a proud stance as these organizations' rightful leaders.

Underlying this plan is an assumption that bisexuals' political energies are more strategically useful if applied to the lesbian and gay liberation movement than to an independent bisexual movement. If this assumption is correct, then people with, for instance, one Asian parent and one white parent would best caucus in support groups with other Amer-Asians to find pride in and empathy for their unique experience. Then, rooted in that identity, they would choose to be activists on behalf of the elimination of racism in organizations of Asians, of people of color, and of white people, rather than creating a Amer-Asian liberation movement.

In addition, by emphasizing lesbian and gay liberation, this strategy aims to expose a continuum of sexuality and affection, instead of making a third sexual identity more available by centering on bisexual visibility. As we gradually dismantled internalized oppression through support groups, bisexuals could become models of the flexible use of identity. And as we gradually put an end to lesbian and gay oppression, each sexual identity could be eliminated one by one and replaced with acceptance of our infinite human diversity. In the meantime, handling mistreatment in lesbian and gay and heterosexual groups would be difficult for many of us. Bisexuals' internalized oppression could turn this vision into an excuse for publicly and privately denying who we are.

This strategy could give bisexuals access to the affirmation and healing we need to prepare to claim our homes among lesbians and gay men and heterosexuals and rapidly take our place with them as powerful leaders of all people. By establishing the whole of bisexual liberation work within lesbian and gay liberation and heterosexual organizations, the joint power of the resulting coalition could exert tremendous force against the oppression.

The key difficulty of this strategy appears to be the potential for bisexuals to remain hidden out of fear, while the key strength may be a unified coalition on behalf of lesbian, gay, and bisexual liberation.

Conclusion

Appraising the accuracy of the theoretical underpinnings of these two programs, and their likely strengths and difficulties in practice, is a demanding and complex task. Just as difficult is imagining and deliberating on every potential option before us. Our challenge is to take into account every aspect of the current state of bisexual liberation, every piece of information we can assemble about what has worked and what has not in this and all liberation struggles, and every implication of selecting each possible program for action. This work calls us to transcend the oppression and internalized oppression that can easily sabotage our thinking and our actions.

We must constantly re-evaluate what is most effective to liberate bisexuals, and standing on that foundation, we will successfully abolish all oppression based on sexual identity and gender.

Notes

1. I am grateful to Josephine Dombrowski, Maggie Gladstone, Loraine Hutchins, David Jernigan, Lani Kaahumanu, Bill Mack, Alizza Maggid, and Clare Thompson for their contributions to and assistance with this article.

2. I define "bisexuals" here as anyone who has privately or publicly chosen this identity based on her or his personal definition of that identity.

3. The use of the terms like "society" or "this culture" are intended here to refer to the United States, though some statements accurately describe other cultures as well.

4. Like men, white people, able-bodied people, etc., heterosexuals profit from existing economic and political structures and are mistreated in order to insure their cooperation with that system. Through these structures and other forms of societal conditioning and norms, heterosexuals are coerced to, for example, participate in the oppression of lesbians, gay men, and bisexuals; to accept inflexible roles in relationships; to enlist in the oppressive institution of marriage; and are immediately targeted with lesbian/gay oppression if they defy narrow rules for behavior as women and men, such as showing closeness with a member of the same gender.

Ann Schneider

Guilt politics

For me, bisexuality is the pride of being open-minded, but it is also the struggle of reconciling my desires with my feminist consciousness. Finding a bisexual community of men and women helped me find the strength to stop justifying my sexual practices and instead see the oppressiveness of the politics that made me feel guilty for sleeping with men.

I've always felt that making love is an important form of self-expression. It has been a source of power and inspiration in my life for the work of remaking society. As the French students said in 1968, "The more I revolt, the more I want to make love. The more I make love, the more I want to revolt."[1]

I became a feminist only when I started living with a man and began seeing how he had more power socially than I did: more self-confidence, more friends, more certainty about what he wanted and was entitled to. I can't imagine my life without a commitment to social justice and to empowering the oppressed of the world. I don't rank the issue of the oppression of bisexuals on the same level as genocide, for example, but my sexual freedom is integral to my independence, my identity, and why I fight for everything else.

Feminism is what gives my idea of sexual freedom definition. My awareness of sexism and determination not to be controlled by it dictates my behavior in relation to men. Because of the thousands of years of the sexual double standard, for instance, I can never bring myself to promise fidelity to a man. The unfettered right to choose my sexual partner, when and how, to me is the *sine qua non* of women's liberation. While the greatest threat to this freedom is violence against women and all the more subtle forms of male domination, we likewise cannot allow feminist theory to constrict our scope of choice.

There is a tendency among lesbian-feminists to denigrate women who do not sleep exclusively with women as less feminist than themselves. While not all women who identify as lesbian-feminists act or feel this way, to speak about sexual orientation only as a political issue tends to encourage judgments about people on the basis of their sexual preference. The mistake is often made of equating an individual's deepest sexual desires with the expression of an intellectual, moral, or political alignment. To the extent lesbian-feminism as a philosophy encourages this intolerance, I reject it.

Bisexual feminists confront the prevailing prejudices of both the heterosexual and gay and lesbian communities. We recognize that bisexual women can pass among heterosexuals and reap the benefits of male-conferred status, usually including a degree of social comfort as well as the class advantage and greater financial security that men usually have over women. As a feminist, I have always opposed that these privileges are given only to nonlesbians. I represent the lesbian point of view in my interactions with the straight world, forcing it to acknowledge feminist existence and thereby building bridges between the straight and gay worlds.

Nonetheless, no bi woman I know has escaped the pain of being ostracized by some elements of the lesbian community. But this personal pain is not the only harm of lesbian chauvinism. In fact, I believe the equation of sexual preference with one's side in the way against patriarchy ultimately plays into the hands of the oppressor.

Lesbians often assume that bisexual and heterosexual women are male-identified and that when push comes to shove, we will always desert the feminist cause to protect our relationships with men. Some circumspection is certainly justified given the number of times lesbians have been disappointed with the loss of a friend or a lover to unchallenged heterosexuality. But the phenomenon of women going back to behaviors like wearing makeup, seeking refuge in the nuclear family, once considered strictly unfeminist, is not restricted to lesbian women. Women are withdrawing in droves from the difficult, everyday, tiresome struggle of challenging sexism wherever it rears its head.[2]

Nonetheless, commitment to feminism endures in many gay, straight, and bisexual women. The contributions of thousands of straight and bi women in the past decade alone to the women's movement must be acknowledged.

To make assumptions about a person on the basis of the sex of her partner's sex mimics the trashing of lesbians and gay men by homophobes. Lesbian-baiting should be a familiar enough experience to all feminists to know that such tactics are simply a way of avoiding the real issue. In the same way, the charge of being "male-identified" used against nonlesbian feminists can also be a form of baiting, substituting for a real examination of differences in strategy. Sleeping with women by itself no more confers clarity of analysis or leadership than does being born female. There are a great many power-hungry, racist, unsisterly lesbians in the world.

Sleeping with women effects political change only on the level of exemplifying that women can find intellectual, social, and sexual happiness without men, but simply adopting a politically correct lifestyle doesn't affect the larger political, social, and economic systems that keep women poor and powerless. Many politically active feminists work for gay and lesbian rights and reproductive rights, against military intervention, and for a variety of other issues. Loving men does not make our feminist work any less valuable or effective.

Sexual expression is a value in itself which we must defend by increasing women's power of sexual choice. Lesbians expand the options for all women, but our focus as feminists must be on the freedom to choose. For women who choose to love and be sexual with men, the demands of lesbian-feminism collapse into guilt politics, asking us to give up the pleasures and privileges we receive in return for feminist validation. Creating guilt about choosing men as lovers is no way to organize women. Instead, we must build women's consciousness of their oppression as a class or caste so that they can imagine a world free from sexual violence and degradation. Only a positivist approach as opposed to one which criticizes women for receiving privileges from men can provide a motive for joining the lifelong struggle to liberate women.

This struggle has to include building models for nonexploitative, nonoppressive relationships between men and women, not only because men and women will always exist, and not only because there will always be bisexual and heterosexual women, but also because men must learn to treat all women with respect, a lesson that begins at home. Moreover, (lesbian) feminists can't dismiss the concerns of bisexual and heterosexual women without damaging the movement. Women's liberation cannot succeed unless it is supported and identified with by millions of women.

Lesbian vanguardism has harmed the movement by dividing women working for the same goal. Organizations have been split by using strict lesbianism as a litmus test, forcing bisexuals out, while continuing to work with closeted bis who present themselves as lesbian. Intense concern with sexual practices tends to heighten personal antagonisms where there is enough political unity otherwise to work productively. Charges of homophobia are easily made but difficult to refute. Such fights have lead to burnout and have caused activists to drop out. Moreover, the silencing that results from the demand, "feminism is the theory, lesbianism is the practice," has stunted the development of a critique of sexuality and has allowed a retreat to the belief that all sexual preference is innate.

This essay is not a plea for acceptance into the lesbian community. Instead, I hope to encourage some re-evaluation of the harsh effects of a politic that places too much emphasis on one's choice of lovers. Sexuality is far too subjective and unpredictable a part of our psychological makeup to be restricted to intellectual theory. Perhaps some of us can consciously reshape our sexuality to an extent, but to impose rigid expectations on sexual behavior hardly seems conducive to reaching a deeper understanding of how sexuality is culturally shaped. As a bisexual feminist, I believe exploring all aspects of sexuality is important in enabling us to theorize about the role sexuality plays both in perpetuating our oppression and in helping us visualize our liberation. Ultimately, I think we want to show women how the patriarchal ideology shapes women's view of their own sexuality so that they can see how such behavior can be unlearned. This approach teaches women that it is within their power to determine their sexual preference and that many of the things that seemed natural about women's subjugation are not. After all, to borrow a phrase from Karl Marx, speaking about philosophers who theorize about the world, "The point is to change it!"

Notes

1. "May 1968 Uprising Wall Slogan," *Redstockings Feminist Revolution,* Random House, 1975, p. 129.

2. Barbara Haber, "Is Personal Life Still a Political Issue?," *Feminist Studies* 5, no. 3 (Fall 1979).

Elise Krueger

My pet peeves

1. **W**orkshops on "Lesbians and Straight Women Working Together" that ignore the tremendous amount of potential contributions (and work already done) by bisexual women.

2. Comments that include the phrase "a stage" as a devaluation. Since when is a woman going through any kind of life-passage or questioning less worthy of respect? That one *really* pisses me off, almost as much as the assumption that bisexuality itself is a phase. For some people it is, for some it isn't, and there is no way to tell.

3. The assumption that "everyone is bisexual," which I've heard said with the sugary smugness usually found in fundamentalists or other forms of politically correct purists. No evidence has convinced me of this; furthermore, it's not on my agenda to make sure everybody is like me.

4. The assumption that women are less likely to hurt women than men. I've been sexually assaulted by both and emotionally devastated by both. I remain unconvinced of the inherent superiority of either gender.

5. Lesbians who say "women's" when they would like to say "lesbian." Bi women who say *anything else* when they would like to say bisexual. *Anybody who says "women's" when they don't include* all *women*, whether they are lesbian, bi, straight, asexual, or transitional; whether they are monogamous, celibate, nonmonogamous; whether they are old, young, white, African American, Latina, Asian, Native American, abled, differently abled...

6. People from the straight press who insist on characterizing bisexual women as bored suburbanites or indiscriminate party girls. People from the lesbian press who, when they talk about bisexuals at all, depict us as pitiable wanna-bes who are all probable carriers of AIDS ... *the bisexual as the "Typhoid Mary"* of the lesbian community. This makes me almost as angry as finding myself faced with the need to do Safe Sex 101 yet again with anyone from any community — we must educate ourselves. We must not panic.

7. People who assume that my male lover doesn't know about my identification ... or that my female lovers haven't known.

8. The lack of bisexual armbands in the pile next to the lesbian armbands at Take Back the Night rallies. Fixing this omission was our first bi-radical act a couple of years ago.

9. The fear in the voices of the professors and lesbian community leaders who come out to me in secret as bi. I grieve for the loss of our sisters' voices; we cannot afford to silence any of us!

10. ANYONE WHO LETS SOMEONE ELSE DO THE WORK OF FREEDOM.

Lenore Norrgard

Can bisexuals be monogamous?

"**B**ut, can bisexuals be monogamous?" It's a question we often hear. Some bisexuals — often the monogamous ones — are offended by the inquiry. This is understandable, since many people stereotype us as sexually ravenous creatures who are indiscriminately sexual with people of both genders, hopping into bed with anyone at the drop of a hat.

I've heard many bisexuals answer the question blithely: "Of course. Just like a straight woman can be attracted to more than one man and be sexual with only one, a bisexual can be attracted to more than one person and be sexual with only one."

The answer is accurate — in describing some bisexuals. Bisexuals who live a monogamous lifestyle are evidence that at least some bisexuals can be monogamous. But can all of us be so? Is there any difference between our choices and those that lesbian and gay or straight people make?

I think there is a difference.

I personally find that being sexual with women is qualitatively different from being sexual with men. Part of the difference is biological, part is sexual socialization, part is emotional and spiritual. In my conversations with women who have had sex with people of both genders, I've heard my own experience echoed. What we each experience as the distinct qualities of sex with each gender may be different but for most women the distinctions exist.

Some bisexual women find it more important to have a sexually exclusive relationship than to satisfy the different sexual hungers felt for women and men. However, I think it's also true that it's very difficult to be sexually active with a woman and a man at the same time because of the pressure in our society to choose between what are presented as mutually exclusive opposites. Many bisexual women spend their social time in the lesbian community when they're with a woman, and in the straight community when they're with a man; this gets a bit hectic and even more intensely disorienting when one is involved with both a woman and a man at the same time!

It's difficult enough to persuade people to accept us as individuals who have made a "both/and" choice, refusing the "either/or" pressure of our culture. To choose to be in a sexual relationship with only one gender at a time makes the "both/and" choice a bit less apparent and therefore a bit more palatable to nonbis.

I have met bisexuals who feel the need to have a relationship with both a man and a woman most of the time. Most of those whom I've met have separate relationships with the two partners; some choose to combine them in a true triangular relationship, in which all three share sexual and romantic bonding. When I placed an ad in the weekly looking for a woman lover, I didn't identify myself as bi, yet I received responses from women partnered with men who were seeking special, sexual friendships with a woman. These letters were not rude or offensive but seemed to be quite honest and candid and were respectful in expressing the diverse needs and interests of the writers.

Certainly there are bisexual women who desire sexually exclusive relationships who are content to be sexual with only one partner. Some of them have a clear preference for one gender, and when they're with the preferred gender, they experience no pressing urge to be with the other. Others find that having a sexual relationship with someone of either gender quite satisfactory and sufficient.

As for myself, when I've been in an intimate ongoing relationship with a woman, my sexual interest in men tends to wane. However, when I'm in a similar relationship with a man, I still hunger for women. A few years ago I fell in love with a man with whom I enjoyed a good sexual relationship. After two months I felt compelled to tell him that while I could imagine staying with him for years, I could not imagine going without a woman lover for a long time.

Different strokes for different folks. I don't think that any particular style is superior to any other. All should be acknowledged, respected, and valued for their uniqueness. As bisexuals, we are a radical sexual minority. I'd like to see our bisexual community take a more honest look at ourselves and embrace our diversity. We've owned up to some of our other differences — such as different degrees of bisexuality and different kinds of bisexual identities. We've even acknowledged that some of us feel more comfortable with monogamy, while some of us are more comfortable with nonmonogamy.

However, I believe that by answering the question "Can bisexuals be monogamous?" with a blithe "Sure!" we're not acknowledging that this is true for only a portion of us, and that bisexual orientation casts a different light on the monogamy question. It would be more accurate to answer, "Some of us are, some of us aren't. Some of us enjoy sexually exclusive relationships. Some of us like to have both a woman (or women) and a man (men) in our lives when we can."

I think that the easy "Sure!" answer is offered up in a plea, unconscious though it may be, to nonbis to accept us as "just folks," to make them believe that we're just like them. To ward off the uncomfortable realization that the choices we make in how we live our sexuality are different from those that exclusively lesbian or exclusively straight people make. It's uncomfortable to be different, and it's all too easy to camouflage our differences, hoping to be accepted by those who are ill at ease with our nonconformist, "both/and" orientation.

It's crucial that we own up to who we are and take pride in all the ways there are to be bisexual. Our reticence at admitting that some bisexuals indeed cannot be monogamous reminds me of the conservatism that set into some sectors of the gay rights movement after its early radical years and could be just as dangerous.

It was drag queens, bulldykes, and gays of color who rioted at the Stonewall gay bar twenty years ago[1] and launched the modern, radical gay rights movement that paved the way for bi pride. After a few years the white, middle-class males who dubbed themselves gay "leaders" sought to jettison the "undesirable" nonconformists from the ranks of the movement, seeking to convince middle-class America that gays are just like straight people — our men don't wear dresses and our women don't wear tuxedos, we're "just folks."

If we examine how this strategy played out over the last fifteen years, we can see that it led to a single-issue orientation that left lesbians, gays of color, and anyone else who didn't fit into white, middle-class America's vision of "normal" out in the cold. We had splitting along sex, race, and class lines, and only in the last few years have we begun to have limited success in uniting across these divisions to fight the onslaught of the right wing. How much further ahead we could be now if from the beginning we had embraced all sectors of the sexual minority community into one radical movement for liberation! We probably wouldn't even need a bi movement, because bis could have been included.

We should take to heart the hard lesson the gay movement taught us through trying to present gays as "normal." Our salvation lies in taking pride in who we are, in our diversity, and in educating the nonbi public as honestly and proudly as we can. In this way the acceptance we gain will be real and deep, not superficial. We can gain acceptance — and our rights — by truly reaching out, person to person, to strangers, and introducing ourselves honestly.

Time has shown that we probably will not win the Mormon Church to our side — but we probably can develop mutual understanding with feminists, people of color, unionists, and the lesbian and gay community. Yes, we are human beings like all the rest; we have thoughts and feelings, difficulties and joys — it's important to communicate the full breadth of our humanity to others. We can enrich the lives of others, not only our own, by honestly sharing our similarities and differences and learning to also treasure the ways that others are different from ourselves.

Note

1. The riots at Stonewall tavern took place in New York, June 1969, and are commemorated each year with Lesbian and Gay Pride Week.

Lucy Friedland & Liz A. Highleyman

The fine art of labeling
The convergence of anarchism, feminism, and bisexuality

We are two bisexual women who get a kick out of trying to define ourselves in relation to our communities and the world at large. The world is a huge place, and sometimes we wonder how human beings, much less bisexuals, manage to connect at all. Our trick? It's in the labels. We found each other through a Boston anarchist group called Black Rose. Soon we discovered that we were both bisexual. What fun! From there we found that our ideas about feminism diverged. Some feminists say that Liz is "male-identified" (whatever *that* means); some call Lucy a "man-hater" (whatever *that* means). We formed an anarcha-feminist group with other women to discuss anarchism and feminism and how they figure into our politics and relationships.

As a bisexual activist, Lucy finds it frustrating to be at a conference or some other event and to hear bisexuals give a litany of reasons why they don't want to call themselves bisexual. For her, coming out as a bisexual feels like one of the most important steps one can take to change the world for the better. Liz thinks that this is too judgmental, and that it is fine for people to call themselves, or not call themselves, whatever they wish. On the other hand, she finds it important in certain circumstances that people see her as an anarchist, a bisexual, a sex radical, or all three.

We have each found some labels that feel right for us. Lucy is an anarcha-feminist bisexual, and Liz is a bisexual anarchist. The distinction may appear to be a fine one, but the order of the words, and the context in which they are delivered, matter a lot. These labels, these tidbits of self-knowledge, which are always under scrutiny and subject to change, publicize a great deal about who we are and what (and who) we get passionate about. In this piece, we'd like to explore the issues of anarchism, feminism, and bisexuality, locate some points of convergence, and maybe, in the process, get to the bottom of this labeling business.

The urge to label

Most people in our society feel the need to sort people and things into categories and to give those categories labels: male and female, homosexual and heterosexual, progressive and conservative. This compulsion to classify is a natural part of the human thought process; we are constantly bombarded with so much input that we must have some way to organize it in order to understand our experience. As natural as this tendency is, it also presents a danger. We should be cautious that the categories we construct are not overly confining or resistant to change, and that the labels we use are not degrading or judgmental. Categories and labels are useful tools, but we should regard them as tools only and not as ends in themselves. We must not be afraid to revise or abolish a classification scheme or a set of labels when it has become more harmful than beneficial.

One of the most common features of the classification systems we use is the division of things into dualistic "all or nothing" categories. This causes us to sort the people we encounter and the things we experience into one or the other of two mutually exclusive sets. The existence of bisexuality challenges this process. We are taught to think of people as either heterosexual (normal) or homosexual (deviant). When faced with bisexuality, an option which does not fit within either of the accepted categories, most people react with discomfort — their stable way of viewing the world is shaken. This is why so many insist on viewing bisexual people as "really homosexual" or "really heterosexual," as being in transition between one pole and the other, or as being "part homosexual and part heterosexual," rather than "all bisexual."[1]

The anarchist philosophy

Like bisexuality, anarchism poses a challenge to the categorical way we think. Anarchism as a political philosophy places a high value on diversity, individuality, and self-identification. The main principle of anarchism is that hierarchical authority, including the state, the church, and economic elites, is not only unnecessary but harmful. Anarchists believe that people can only realize their full human potential when they are free. Anarchism is more than a political program; it is a set of values and a way of life that encompasses political theory and practice and personal experience. Anarchism does not have a specific party line; the details of the anarchist vision and how to achieve it have varied widely with time and place, as indeed they must if they are to have relevance beyond specific era and locale. Anarchists believe that a just and organized society can be achieved in a nonhierarchical and participatory manner based on voluntary, cooperative, decentralized groups.[2]

Anarchism is unique in its openness to new ideas. In order to remain relevant and fresh, it must absorb new viewpoints and integrate new groups. This openness to change makes anarchism a natural framework for feminists, bisexual people, lesbians and gay men, and others who have been excluded from traditional politics and ignored or despised by many so-called "radical" groups. The use of direct democracy, affinity groups, and nonhierarchical organizations, which have been an important part of the feminist and gay movements, are also integral to anarchist practice. The struggle of bisexuals, gay men and lesbians, and other sex radicals to be free of the constraints of traditional heterosexist norms is inherent in the anarchist goal of achieving the freedom to live as one chooses while respecting the rights of others and attaining equality in all relationships.

There is some debate among anarchists regarding the usefulness of categorization. Some believe that schemes of classification that allow us to view a person primarily as a member of a group, and thus as a recipient of the stereotypes associated with that group, is detrimental to the ideal of viewing everyone as an individual. Others find classifications beneficial because they allow members of certain groups, usually oppressed groups, to find solidarity and to celebrate and reclaim their group identity as a positive rather than a negative feature. Through the strength of the group as a united entity, they may find it easier to resist oppression. While it may be possible to rid ourselves of such classification schemes when all people are free and equal, in the meantime the ability to proudly claim and find strength in a group identity is an important means of self-empowerment and can be a valuable tool in the struggle for liberation.

Why anarcha-feminism?
If anarchism is based on the elimination of all hierarchies, why do we need a separate category of anarcha-feminism? Some anarchists believe that anarcha-feminism is redundant, since anarchism *per se* addresses sexism and heterosexism as forms of domination that we want to eradicate. Many feminist anarchists (mostly women) disagree. They prefer the label "anarcha-feminist" in order to emphasize feminist concerns. Historically, feminist values have gotten lost or been obscured within revolutionary politics. Women, who have been instrumental in social change movements, have often seen new regimes come into power and revert to old sexist ways.[3] Unlike other revolutionary movements, anarchists do not wish to replace one group of leaders with another, but anarcha-feminists hope that by keeping "feminism" up front, the values represented by this word will infuse anarchist organizing, process, and goals. Part of the anarcha-feminist vision is to construct a world where

women's voices and accomplishments are as valued as men's, and part of that process may involve women devoting their time and energy only to women. If this were a perfect world, this might not be necessary, but for many women, a women-only environment feels nurturing and self-affirming. We hope that even in an anarchist utopia women would find reasons to spend time with one another, and that this would not be seen as occurring at the expense of men.

Feminism is a concept that is understood in as many different ways as is anarchism. Ask a feminist what makes her or him a feminist, and you will get as many answers as the number of people you ask. One definition of feminism involves the establishment of a matriarchy to replace the current patriarchy — that is, giving women authority over men instead of the other way around. This particular definition is antithetical to anarcha-feminism. Grounded in anarchism, anarcha-feminism advocates the elimination of "power over" in favor of individual and collective empowerment that allows everyone — men, women, and children — to have control over their own lives.[4]

Anarcha-feminist values were embodied in the second wave of feminism in the United States in the early seventies.[5] Only since the eighties have some of these values been eroded in favor of a less inclusive "pragmatism" that sacrifices process for results. On the other hand, some feminists seem more committed than ever to creating a feminism that includes underrepresented groups such as working-class women, women of color, women with disabilities, and men. Feminists' interest in building ties with other women internationally is a particularly propitious development. The connections made across national boundaries by feminists can be especially important in improving the quality of life for women worldwide.

The sexual/political connection

Some people's sexual orientation evolves through exposure to feminism or some other political ideology. For many others, politics do not shape their preferences. To what extent do our sexuality and our political views influence each other? While many regard these two spheres as separate, others find that their sexual and political identities interact strongly in ways that affect many aspects of their lives.

There appear to be two tendencies in the way people experience the connection between politics and sexuality. The first is for people to become politically aware as a result of their sexuality. In our society, people whose sexual orientations and choices fall outside of the norm (bisexuals, lesbians and gay men, the nonmonogamous, and other sex and gender radicals) are subject to misunderstanding and prejudice and in many cases outright oppression. This situation often leads these people to fight for rights they are denied, and this struggle may take on a political character. Those who are oppressed on the basis of their sexuality may be especially sensitive to the oppression of others, whether on the basis of race, religion, nationality, or any of the arbitrary distinctions that the powers-that-be have used to retain their control. This empathy may lead those with nonnormative sexual orientations and practices to an awareness of the interconnections among various forms of oppression and to take part in the struggle to gain rights and respect for everyone. Having a nonnormative sexual identity may also lead one to question the patriarchal, heterosexist assumptions and practices that allow a certain segment of the population to attain power and wealth at the expense of the rest. As a result of this process, one's overall outlook may take on an explicitly political hue.

The second tendency is somewhat opposite. By studying political philosophy, engaging in political action, and developing an awareness of injustice, people may begin to question the basic values they have been taught. This may lead to the realization that they can refuse to adhere to the hierarchical, sexist, heterosexist, and sex-phobic tenets they grew up with, and they may begin to explore a variety of social and sexual alternatives. An awareness of anarchism and feminism seems especially likely to encourage people to question their assumptions about sexuality and relationships. The critique of the patriarchal power structure, traditional sex roles, the mandated nuclear family, and forced reproduction has led many proponents of anarchism and feminism to adopt a style of living and loving that is more in keeping with their beliefs.

In reality, of course, these descriptions more closely represent ends of a spectrum rather than two distinct models. There is not necessarily a cause-and-effect relationship between sexuality and politics or vice versa. The development of sexual and political identities is a highly personal and evolutionary process. Most people experience a comingling of the various factors contributing to their sexual and political growth.

Liz's experience is closer to the second tendency described above: I held anti-authoritarian views while growing up, long before I had ever heard of anarchism. I often rebelled against my parents and teachers and legal and religious authorities, and I resented being told what to do. I believed that only I knew what was right for me. While I found both men and women attractive, I held the usual assumptions about the appropriateness of heterosexual relationships. Since I was generally happy in my relationships with boys and men, I was comfortable with a heterosexual identity. At the same time, I rejected most of the anti-sex and "pro-family" views that I was exposed to in Catholic school and the sexism of the Southern culture.

When I went away to college in the early eighties, I met people who identified as anarchists, and realized that the views I held had a name. I read everything I could about anarchist philosophy and was especially influenced by the writings of Emma Goldman, including her alternative views on the role of women, sexuality, and relationships.[6] It was also in my early college years that I was exposed to feminism and began to meet people who openly identified as gay or lesbian. Many of my friends were interested in exploring alternative sexual and relationship options.

Although I had decided at an early age that the traditional female role and the nuclear family were not for me, it was not until I became familiar with anarchist philosophy and alternative sexuality that this sense of self evolved from being a personal lifestyle choice into a basis for political action. I did much of my questioning of sexuality within a community of pro-sex gay men, and within this context, I first came out as a politically active bisexual. I spend a lot of time talking with others, individually, in workshops, and in computer discussion forums, about politics and sexuality and how they interact. I make a point of being identifiable as an anarchist, a bisexual, and a sex radical in order to meet others who share my ideas and to provide people with the opportunity to question me, as well as their own assumptions. I hope that by being open and active I can encourage people to explore their own options and to accept and respect the diversity of sexual choices that people make.

Coming out: Putting your best label forward
Whether people become politicized through their sexual orientation, change their sexual practices because of a political philosophy, or some amalgamation of both, the next step is coming out, either privately or publicly. Coming out as an anarchist is like coming out as bisexual. Just as "avowed bisexuals" are often not taken seriously, people who adopt the "anarchist" label commonly find themselves subject to misunderstanding, bigotry, and ridicule. The word "anarchy" is used interchangeably with "chaos," especially by the mainstream media. People typically think of anarchists as irresponsible at best and violent at worst. People often laugh when we tell them about an anarchist event: "An anarchist conference? Ha, Ha, that means everyone shows up at different times in different cities." "An anarchist organization? Don't you mean an anarchist *dis*organization?" A common caricature of an anarchist depicts a grinning little man in a black coat holding a bomb.

In addition to facing incredulity and scorn, in some cases your job may be at risk. Employers might think that you'll undermine a business given the chance (we might), that you'll put your political commitments before your employer's interests (we do), or that you're willing to break the law to get what you want (we might be). Being known publicly as an anarchist may mean that you are denied entry to certain countries. For example, both anarchists and homosexuals are explicitly forbidden by law to enter the United States. Many anarchists, like members of sexual minorities, are not willing to put themselves at risk by coming out publicly.

For some people, anarchism is a theory or a set of ideals that they do not choose to live by on a day-to-day basis because a completely anarchistic lifestyle can be rough going in present-day America. Such a lifestyle would involve resisting the institutions that suck us into dependency, ranging from agribusiness, to utility companies, to the IRS. Many anarchists find ingenious ways to subvert "the system," living out their political ideals in an unaccommodating society. There is a wide range of ways to circumvent the establishment, and some people are willing to go to greater lengths than others. Some spray-paint graffiti and break minor laws. Others use office supplies and resources for their personal and political work. Some find ways of working under the table to avoid paying taxes. "Dumpster diving" is a means of recycling adopted by some anarchists, even as a way of getting food, to avoid buying into the consumerist, ecologically harmful patterns encouraged by the capitalist system. Although not everyone wants to live in an unheated squat to avoid the real estate racket, we admire those who do. Anarchists who are open and vocal about their choices are particularly brave souls, willing to create a lifestyle for themselves that feels harmonious with their political convictions.

Lucy's story says a lot about the coming-out process and how we choose our labels: As an anarchist bisexual, I'm more vocal about my bisexuality than my anarchism. Right now I am particularly compelled to make an issue of my bisexuality and to make sure people know I'm bisexual, not heterosexual or lesbian. I feel beholden to all bisexuals to try and make their lives a little easier by being visible, just as other bisexual women have done and continue to do for me. I feel less identification with anarchists. It's not that I have more in common with bisexuals as a group. Bisexuals have no more inherently in common with each other than anarchists do. Both groups are very heterogeneous. My decision to identify more closely with bisexuals than with anarchists is mainly due to the absence of a cohesive community of anarchists in Boston which would provide momentum. For me, the love and encouragement of other bisexuals in Boston and elsewhere is what keeps me going, what keeps me inspired.

I adopted the bisexual label first. In 1981, before I knew what feminism was, I had my first sexual involvement with a woman. Neither of us called ourselves gay or bisexual at the time. Mary and I found each other at a (heterosexual) Halloween party, and the pheromones flew. We stayed together for about a year, and during that time I didn't consider myself a lesbian. The potential to be sexual with a man again seemed pretty strong, and taking on a lesbian label seemed to deny that possibility. I would have felt like an imposter. In addition, I had never known any lesbians before, and the ones I met through Mary seemed very different from me. When she moved away, I took up with men again, but with a difference: I no longer felt like a heterosexual.

The only associations I had with the word "bisexual" were from *Playboy* and *Penthouse*. By age twelve, I had become a porn aficionado, since the couple for whom I babysat and my older brother kept copies of the magazines around. I must say that I came in touch with my bisexuality, or with my bisexual feelings, through men's pornography. When I later heard of the Boston Bisexual Women's Network, I thought, "Okay, that's for me, because I'm a bisexual woman." At one of the first events I attended, women were eating bagels and talking about sexism. I didn't have a clue what they meant by "sexism," but I figured I'd better bone up on the subject if I was going to fit in with these women (or get them into bed).

The bisexual label brought me not only more sexual opportunities, but also some accompanying philosophies. Until that time, feminism and gay and bisexual liberation had never been part of my education or associations, even though I was living in a "progressive" city jam-packed with academics. Suddenly, a whole new subculture opened up to me that had been absolutely invisible before.

About a year later, I drifted into the Black Rose anarchist group. Gradually I adopted a set of anarchist values which dovetailed with the new worldview I'd gained from my exposure to feminism and gay and bisexual politics. What still bewilders me is how we can go on for years living in the mainstream culture without ever knowing about these other worlds. In contrast to Liz's experience, for me the road to politics was paved with sexual intentions. I'm forever grateful to those influential bisexual women and lesbians who showed me the way.

Fashioning an anarcha-feminist future

While some people carry on their lives within alternative subcultures, we as anarchist activists are committed to changing society as a whole and creating a more equitable world where diversity is accepted and cele-brated. What do we mean by anarchist change? Given that the overthrow of the government does not seem imminent, how can we go about fashioning an anarcha-feminist future? How can we bring anarcha-feminist values in line with present-day political realities (or vice versa)? As bisexual anarcha-feminists, we want to look at our own movements critically. How can the bisexual, lesbian and gay, and other sexual liberation movements incorporate anarcha-feminist values?

There are many ways to build social change movements. Some of these are more inherently anarchistic than others. Anarchists have ideas about political activism that differ from those of most liberals and leftists. Anarchists generally do not believe in petitioning the state for alleviation of their grievances, nor do they view restrictive legislation (such as the censorship of pornography) as the way to achieve their goals.

Many bisexual and gay activists focus on reforming the system. Reform-minded types (including some anarchist sympathizers) work within the system because they want the immediate benefits that gay-positive and woman-positive legislation may bring. People want a gay rights bill in order to make our lives better right now. However, most anarchists think that legislative and judicial change will not sufficiently redress the damage caused by patriarchal, money-dominated forms of government and by prejudicial attitudes. Anarchists believe that the system must be radically altered or undermined in order to bring about a more profound and lasting liberation. The long-term, and even the short-term, benefits of legislative change often prove temporary and insufficient. A law that activists have slaved over for months, even years (for example, the recently enacted Massachusetts gay rights law took seventeen years to pass) can later be repealed or weakened depending upon the prevailing political climate.

Reform-oriented activists tend to rely heavily on the media to present their case. Many demonstrations and actions are primarily performances for the TV cameras. Anarchists tend to emphasize direct action rather than attempting to sway opinion through secondary means. It is rare for anti-establishment causes to get factual, balanced coverage in the mainstream media, which prefer sensationalism and simplicity in their reporting.

An anarcha-feminist strategy for social change would include finding ways to build strength and diversity by organizing locally from the grass roots, rather than centralizing power at the top. Attention to collective process is crucial. Anarcha-feminists hate to have one person representing different people with different perspectives. Ideally, equal consideration and respect should be given to every opinion, regardless of whether it is a majority or a minority view. For this reason, anarcha-feminist process, which emphasizes consensus decision making, is often seen as slow and laborious. However, many anarcha-feminists are unwilling to turn over their decision making to an elected representative unless that person is directly accountable to and recallable by the constituency. Anarcha-feminists generally do not support strategies such as the "Feminization of Power" campaign initiated by the National Organization for Women, which seeks to get women elected to positions of power within the U.S. government. It's true that women have been underrepresented in government for too long, but an anarchist's choice would be to eliminate the government rather than increase women's role in it.

An anarcha-feminist strategy also emphasizes education, both of group members and the public, and the exploration of creative and novel tactics. We must devise ways to avoid the despair that often comes from confronting the mammoth state establishment. It is important that our methods promote a sense of empowerment, and even fun, for the participants. We have had the opportunity to participate in many political events, both of the reformist and the anti-authoritarian type. We hope that by describing some of these experiences we can give a better idea of what we mean by anarcha-feminist activism.

Although most bisexuals do not call themselves anarchists, there is a high degree of acceptance of anarcha-feminist practice and of the goal of fostering a society that values equality and diversity. In order to be politically effective, we must develop a sense of our own identity and pride in our communities, whether we define ourselves as bisexuals, anarchists, feminists, people of color, or members of some other group. Coalition work can be very valuable, but we must have a clear sense of who *we* are and what *our* goals are before we can ally with others.

The Fifth Annual East Coast Bisexual Network Conference, held in Cambridge in May 1989, was a part of this process for us as bisexuals. The presence of over two hundred bisexual people in one place created an extraordinary level of energy and sense of community. Bisexuals of varying ages, races, religions, abilities, and sexual and political proclivities were present. Some were just beginning to acknowledge their bisexuality, while others were out and active as bisexuals. Some identified primarily as gay men or lesbians, while others considered themselves primarily heterosexual. Some were married, some were involved in alternative relationships, and others were blissfully playing the field. Although we were diverse, a sense of solidarity came from sharing the bisexual label. While our associations with lesbians and gay men are important, bisexual people must form our own community and organizations and engage in political activism as open bisexuals.

For many people, demonstrations are an important means of political activism. Although they may be useful, protests and demonstrations are only one of many possible tactics. Our experience with political demonstrations has been varied. Some are centralized and media-focused and do not allow for the important person-to-person contact that may be the main benefit of such activities. Others are decentralized with an emphasis on education and on the empowerment and enjoyment of the participants. Some demonstrations succeed by directly interfering with "business as usual." The ongoing wave of militant demonstrations conducted by AIDS activist groups such as ACT UP have been remarkably effective in changing public attitudes and compelling government agencies and corporations to make positive changes.

Another type of demonstration is exemplified by gay, lesbian, and bisexual pride celebrations. These events, characterized by socializing and networking, theatrics and fun, are proactive affirmations of who we are, rather than reactive protests against specific actions of the power structure. Although it may be scary to reveal one's identity to a hostile public, the presence of many others acting in solidarity provides support and validation. At pride events we can get a taste of what the world would be like if everyone could be open about and accepted for who they are.

The 1989 march in D.C. for women's equality and women's lives sponsored by the National Organization for Women showed how one event can embody both reformist and subversive elements. Liz was part of an anarchist contingent made up of various genders, ages, and sexualities. It was an opportunity to connect with anarchists from around the country, many of whom rarely see each other. There was rowdy singing and dancing. We had banners proclaiming our demand for sexual freedom, of which reproductive freedom is only one aspect. We passed out pamphlets we had written about self-help abortion techniques, and we talked to people in the crowd about ways that we can take our lives into our own hands when the state works against us. I found the march positive and empowering. On the other hand, many other participants felt lost in the huge mass of demonstrators, hemmed in by the organizers' attempts at crowd control, and dismayed at the focus on celebrities and the lack of radical political analysis on the part of the speakers. Even within the same demonstration, people can have widely differing experiences depending upon their expectations and the tactics they choose.

Creating alternative structures
The issue of reproductive freedom is one that is currently receiving a great deal of attention. It is an example of how legislative reform is not powerful enough to ensure our rights. After the *Roe vs. Wade* case was decided by the Supreme Court in 1973, public opinion in favor of abortion rights steadily eroded, in part due to the efforts of the religious right and political conservatives. In the past year, as the courts have begun to place increasing restrictions on abortion, the political climate is shifting again, this time in favor of the right to choose as the extremism of the anti-feminist, anti-sex, and anti-abortion faction has become too blatant to ignore.

There are various strategies we can use in our fight for reproductive freedom. We can try to influence legislators by letter-writing and electoral campaigns, we can concentrate on changing public opinion by mass demonstrations and the press, and we can develop alternatives that will ensure our freedom of choice even when the state tries to take it away. While all these methods may be part of a successful effort, an anarcha-feminist strategy would focus on the latter. This may involve rebuilding the network of feminist health centers that flourished in the early seventies. We can teach one another safe and effective abortion methods, since we cannot, and should not have to, rely on the government and the medical establishment to take care of us.

Another step is to rediscover alternative abortion and contraceptive methods used by traditional women healers, while also working to develop new, safer, and more effective options. This kind of strategy has been developed in the wake of the AIDS crisis. While the government has denied funding to combat the disease, people with AIDS (PWAs) and other activists have built an independent network of alternative testing sites, community research initiatives, treatment facilities, and hospices. PWAs are seeking out a variety of treatment options, including herbal and holistic methods, creating alternative channels for obtaining drugs that are mired in the red tape of the FDA approval and testing process. The rate of AIDS transmission has decreased dramatically among gay men due to safer sex education programs that have been developed and implemented by members of the gay community, even as government officials sat on their hands afraid to utter the word "condom."

Bisexual and gay people have been active in both AIDS and reproductive rights issues. This momentum has come, in part, from an ingrained hatred of the government telling us how to live our lives. We resent the powers-that-be for legislating what we can do in bed and for encroaching upon our right to make other choices concerning our bodies. Hopefully, alliances will continue to be made between gay men, lesbians, bisexuals, feminists, PWAs, people of color, and others so that the knowledge and resources developed in the fight against AIDS can be used in the struggle for reproductive freedom. Bisexuals are in an advantageous position to help build some of these bridges.

To label or not to label: A conclusion
This article, rife with labels, has explored some of those that we have taken on as activists. The reader may be asking why some people are likely to adopt, and even seek out labels, while others shy away from them. People take on labels for a variety of reasons. Probably the most powerful reason is that the label acknowledges an important, and perhaps inescapable, truth about themselves. Other incentives are positive associations with a label and admiration for those who wear it and the existence of a community of people who share the label and can provide solidarity and support. Labels may be used as political tools, as a way to make a statement, or to make connections with others. Some people choose certain labels explicitly in order to avoid other labels that do not fit. Why do some people reject labels? Specific labels may be rejected because of the lack of positive associations, role models, or communities. Another powerful discouragement is the fear of coming out in the face of a hostile society; this is especially true when considering labels that are likely to provoke a negative response. Still another reason

is that labels may lead to false alliances — for example, the idea that those who share a label should always support one another, even though they may have conflicting political views and agendas. We should take care not to reject potential friends and allies because we do not have enough labels in common. Some people reject the very idea of labeling. They refuse labels on principle as too simplistic and because labels allow us to view others as collections of traits and stereotypes rather than as complex and unique human beings.

As bisexual anarcha-feminist activists, what do we hope to achieve by the use of labels? Accepting a label that is widely despised can be an empowering experience. It is a means of claiming an identity and displaying it proudly. By adopting a label, we may encourage others to come out of their own closets and to take pride in who they are. Openly identifying with a label can be a good way to meet others with similar ideas and goals. Finally, wearing a label is an important means of education. Many people fear or dislike those associated with certain labels because they are different, "abnormal," or "deviant." If more of us openly acknowledged our unpopular labels, it would become apparent just how common some forms of "deviance" really are!

We have identified areas of commonality between anarchism, feminism, and bisexuality. Both anarchism and feminism advocate the end of domination of men over women. Some forms of feminism, like anarcha-feminism, share with anarchism the desire to end all hierarchies be they government over individuals, white people over people of color, or heterosexuals over nonheterosexuals. Anarchism and bisexuality both challenge established categories and encourage us to view the world as fluid rather than compartmentalized. Bisexuality and feminism both challenge traditional sex roles and notions of gender.

The belief that the personal is political, which originated with feminism, is also embodied in anarchism and bisexual liberation politics. All three emphasize individual control over our lives and bodies. This includes the right to love whom we choose, the ability to create alternative relationship and family structures, and the power to make our own decisions about reproduction. The three philosophies embrace a politic of acceptance which aims to make the world a better place, a world in which the label issue will have lost its urgency.

Anarchism, feminism, and bisexual liberation are complementary. We do not find ourselves pulled in three directions by clashing points of view. Rather, we find that our experience of each value system enriches and deepens the other two. The three philosophies provide a coherent and meaningful framework for understanding our interactions with other people and for interpreting our experience of the world.

Notes

1. Rebecca Shuster, "Sexuality as a Continuum: The Bisexual Identity," in *Lesbian Psychologies,* ed. Boston Lesbian Psychologies Collective, University of Illinois Press, 1987, pp. 57–71.

2. For example, see Alexander Berkman, *ABC of Anarchism,* London: Freedom Press, 1987; and Colin Ward, *Anarchy in Action,* Harper & Row, 1973.

3. Sheila Rowbotham, a socialist feminist, has documented this historical phenomenon in her book *Women, Resistance, and Revolution: A History of Women and Revolution in the Modern World,* Vintage Books, 1974.

4. A good introduction to anarcha-feminism is Susan Brown's "Why Anarcha-Feminism?," *Kick It Over,* Special Issue on Anarcha-Feminism, Spring 1987. (P.O. Box 5811, Station A, Toronto, Ontario, Canada M42 1P2.)

5. For an overview on anarcha-feminist thinking in the early seventies, see *Quiet Rumors: An Anarcha-Feminist Anthology,* London: Aldgate Press.

6. For example, Emma Goldman, *Anarchism and Other Essays,* Dover, 1969.

Sheilah Mabry

Conflicts

I.

He said I wear
my sexuality
like a badge of honor
A statement
questioning
himself

For if his identity is
tied up
in heterosexual privilege
and I parade my bisexuality
he's lost

She wants me
to tell her
that I hate men
I can't cuz I don't

Not simply because
they are
my brothers, cousins,
uncles, fathers, and
friends

I like the way
they feel

inside
like I like
the way
she feels
inside

and

I'm
not "choosing"   .
cuz
I won't
cuz I can't see

not

loving a woman
loving a man
loving a woman
cuz I can't see

II.

Walking down a street
near Ebenezer Baptist Church
in Atlanta
holding hands
with my bruthalover

I, dressed in loose-fitting cotton shirt
unisex
men's brown leather bomber jacket
short hair
earringless
unisex
men's black shoes and socks

Heads turn
fingers pointing
They think
We're two "fags" together
        He no longer wants to hold hands

Walking down a store-lit street
Newbury Street
in Boston
holding hands
with my sistahlover
Mass. Avenue
near the Auditorium "T" stop
We turn
Nobody notices

I "look like a dude"
and she's "femmed out"
this night

We take a chance
a few yards away from the
Boylston Street fire station
where
gay-bashing
took place

We take a chance
    in the evening

III.

In a group of heterosexual women
they talk
about their men
I talk
about mine
I do not tell them that my
formerlover
is a woman

In a group of homosexual men and women
they talk
about their lovers
I talk about mine
I do not tell them that my
presentlover
is a man

HETERO/HOMO/SEXUAL
                ASSUMPTIONS
ABOUT WHO
                I AM

I am
not a lesbian
although I may
love one

I am
not a heterosexual
although
I may
love one

and

I'm not "choosing"
cuz
I won't
cuz I can't see

not

loving a woman
loving a man
loving a woman
loving
cuz I can't see

Rich Aranow

Potential lovers

The first time I came out, I came out as a bisexual. I had just graduated from college, and I was living on a Quaker-based farm in a community of thirty people. Along with the hard work of running a farm, there was a strong commitment to group process and helping each others' personal growth. In this supportive environment, I began to admit to myself that I had erotic feelings for men. I only told a few people and continued identifying as a straight man to the rest of the community.

At a weekly meeting of the men in the community, I remember a good friend of mine saying that he enjoyed being in men-only space because it was free of "potential lovers." Other men agreed with him immediately. I felt as if I had been punched in the stomach. I didn't speak again for the rest of the meeting, feeling isolated and afraid to say this was not the case for me. Afterwards I went down to the lake and cried. I felt the acute pain of not fitting into a world where it's assumed what erotic responses you will have and which you won't have. I had denied my feelings for men for so long because of the fear of rejection and not fitting in, and now my fears were being realized.

Retelling this story I am struck with anger at a world creating so much unnecessary pain from something as wonderful as sex and love. Soon after leaving the farm I began identifying as bisexual. I believe I did this for a number of reasons. The fact that I had strong erotic feelings for women was crucial, but I also identified as bi because a gay identity was too scary for me.

My family, friends, and society had told me in numerous spoken and unspoken ways that it was not okay to be gay, so to say I was bisexual allowed me to have erotic feelings for men and avoid the "g" label. I'm

• 303 •

not saying identifying as bi was free of societal reprobation, but for me it was an easier label to wear. I could have sex and relationships with men, but I could still relate to my straight male friends in a way that didn't exclude me from my understanding of what society called "male."

As time progressed, I got romantically involved with different women and men and became more and more comfortable with my homoerotic feelings. I began to admit that my feelings for men were stronger than my feelings for women. About four years after my initial coming out as bisexual, I began to identify as gay. I discovered the gay community to be a vibrant, supportive place where my homoerotic feelings were not merely accepted but celebrated. I felt safe, supported, and free to experience and explore homoeroticism with joy and pride. I cannot stress how important the gay community is to me. I believe it to have an important role in the health of the world. I moved in with my male lover and got a job working at a gay community center doing AIDS prevention work.

My lover and I attended a gay and lesbian health conference with a number of gay friends. At one of the breaks some of us attended a showing of safer sex videos in one of the hotel suites. They were highly erotic videos of people being very sexual in safe, responsible ways. During the scenes which involved heterosexual or lesbian coupling, I noticed my lover was uncomfortable. He looked over to me and rolled his eyes as if to say, "How boring." I, however, was having a very different response. I was turned on by the scenes and was enjoying the erotic feelings they were invoking in me. My lover sensed the difference in our responses and immediately looked over to one of our friends who joined him in eye rolling and quiet expressions of disinterest.

After we left one of them remarked how uncomfortable he felt watching the straight and lesbian scenes, and the others agreed with him. Suddenly I felt alienated from the group in much the same way I felt many years earlier at my men's group on the farm. It was an unstated assumption that none of us "gay" men would respond erotically to the "straight" videos. It was automatically assumed which erotic feelings I had and which ones I didn't have. I was afraid of ostracism and disapproval so I didn't assert myself. And although I discussed my feelings with my lover afterwards as we walked with the group of gay men, I didn't have the courage to label myself as different.

Although the oppression I felt at that moment was similar to the oppression I sometimes feel as a gay man in straight company, I would like to emphasize that in no way do I feel the oppressions are the same. I have never feared for my physical safety walking arm-in-arm with a woman in a gay neighborhood the way I have feared walking with my gay lover in straight neighborhoods. The institutionalized homophobia of our society in the media, schools, courts, religions, medicine, etc., gives the oppression of gays an enormity that cannot be compared to the oppression I sometimes feel from the gay community for my bisexuality. I strongly believe that homophobia is the bottom-line oppression. Biphobia and heterophobia are only products of it. As bisexuals, we need to be in the forefront in the fight against homophobia, and this can best be demonstrated by our actions.

Since my experience at the health conference, I have begun to make love with a woman friend of mine on a regular basis. I have told most of my friends (gay, straight, bi, and nonaligned), and the response has been supportive. Some gay acquaintances have come out to me saying that they also are "gay-identified bisexuals," which has been a surprising and validating consequence.

I sometimes feel my gay friends need to be assured that I am not abandoning them or my gay identity. I find I am primarily attracted to men, and I feel that my primary romantic relationships will probably be with men throughout my life. I get tremendous support and security from the gay community, and I hope to celebrate my homoeroticism and gayness more and more as I learn about and define myself. However, I enjoy occasional sex with women, and I do not see why I have to eliminate it from my life in order to fit into a gay identity.

Lani Kaahumanu

Hapa haole wahine[1]

> *In order to feel safe I need to feel known ... Is visibility safety?*
> *Complex questions. Uncomfortable, uneasy answers, stirring up*
> *old hurts, old angers, old fears ... Why is the possibility of "pass-*
> *ing so insistently viewed as a great privilege ... and not under-*
> *stood as a terrible degradation and denial?*
> —Evelyn Torton Beck, *Nice Jewish Girls*[2]

I grew up
not quite fitting in
and not understanding why

I was raised
with menehunes[3]
and leprechauns
sushi and corned beef
flower leis and Ikebana
kimono and aloha shirts
chopsticks and silverware
miso and tuna casserole

My mother
born in Japan
grew up
in Kobe and Waikiki
the traditional hula
her most prideful
gift of grace to the world

Ikebana
the Japanese art
of flower arranging
my great Aunty Madge
one of thirteen Masters

in the world
(at that time)

My father
a proud
St. Paddy's
County Cork
Irishman
singing
too ra loo ra loo ra
whose mother
my only living grandparent
spoke a little Yiddish
and
would whisper
in my ear
"marry a nice Jewish man
they take care of their wives..."
she was sincere
and steady
in this advice

all this
growing up
in a Catholic family

I was
conceived in Hawai'i
born in Canada
October 5, 1943
during WWII
named Lani
which means heavenly

then on to Denver
for several months
where
my great Uncle Harry
a successful
California businessman
had been "sent"
to run a chicken ranch
when the relocation camps
were in full swing

he and my Aunty Madge
were the first
to give vitamins
to hens
to fortify eggs

recently I learned
it was a cover
for a CIA radio relay station
my great Uncle Harry
proud to be
General MacArthur's right-hand man
during the mid-to-late forties

common stories
while I was growing up
except for the CIA
            and relocation camps

1949 St. Bruno's
first grade
Sister Theophane
told me...
"Lani is a heathen name"
it was unacceptable
the Christian middle name Marjorie
would have to do
for eight years
in grammar school

I didn't throw the ball
like a girl
I hit home runs
over the fence
before and after school
the only times
I was allowed
on the better fields
to play with the boys

I didn't enjoy
playing house
so I was the dad
and went outside

to "work"
to be one of the boys

I was told
I was lucky
to have the golden skin
it meant
I didn't have to hide
from the sun
for fear of getting too dark

for fear of being called
pickaninny
like my sister

I danced the hula
every year
in the talent show
when we studied Japan and Hawai'i
I brought nori seaweed
to eat
kimonos to try on
talked about King Kamehameha
my great great great great great uncle
told the Japanese children's story
of the "peach boy"
dombororo koko sukoko
I took pride
in my multicultural
        multiracial
        girlchild self

Coming home from school
shoes all over the porch
I knew family and friends
from faraway lands
had arrived
leis, poi, fresh pineapple
ukelele, muumuus, love and laughter

Friends would secretly ask
if my Aunty Madge and Uncle Harry
were really related to me
were really in my family

"Are they Chinese or what?"

I was told
never to ask
why their eyes were slanted
I knew why
and couldn't figure out
why anyone would
ask such a thing

In high school
I talked with the girls
about the boys
we had crushes on
and
I talked with the boys
about the girls
we had crushes on

and
even though
I asked
time and again
I was never allowed
to work
because I was a girl
and
"would have a husband
to take care of me
someday"

It was even
a struggle
getting permission
to earn money
babysitting
but once convinced
it would prepare me
for my role in life
I was allowed

For me
there was no college prep
I took

typing, shorthand
business machines
so I
"would have a skill
in case
my husband died
and I was left
to raise the children"

In my junior year
I fell in love
went steady with
the captain of the football team
two years after high school
we were married
in the church
but
outside the communion rail
he was not Catholic

My father died of a heart attack at age 46
protecting and supporting
a wife and four daughters
that he lovingly
and conscientiously
placed on pedestals
built on
lost potential
his, and ours

for me
the certificate would have read
underlying cause of death ... sexism

Five years later
I was 26 years old
my husband taught
at the high school
where we met
we had a son, a daughter
and a home in the suburbs

I was not your everyday
full-time suburban housewife mother

following my conscience
I left the church
joined Another Mother for Peace
was an anti-Vietnam, anti-nuke peace activist
collected food for the Black Panther breakfast program
supported Ceasar Chavez's UFW organizing and the grape boycott
was a Little League mom, never missed the game show "Jeopardy"
ran the art corner on Fridays, was recess lady on Wednesdays
a field trip driver, watched "Days of Our Lives" faithfully
and was a budding gourmet cook

I began reading
about women's lib, burning bras, no make-up
my best friend stopped shaving her legs
and wore shorts in the summer
it was very radical!

I smoked marijuana
wore peasant dresses
had granny glasses
drove a VW van
picked up hitchhikers
fell in love
with "Working Class Hero"
John Lennon

read Baba Ram Dass
"Be Here Now"
spent a weekend
at an Enlightenment Intensive
asking "Who am I?"
18 hours a day

dropped acid
saw Mao Tse Tung
in my bathroom mirror
and realized
"A Separate Reality"

I grew by leaps and bounds
my consciousness raced
it was a rush to follow
u n d e r s t a n d i n g
for the first time

in my life
I had never
determined
what I wanted
what I needed
what was real for me

I was crying all the time
my husband and closest friend
figured it out
"you need to leave," he said
"you've never had a chance to explore,"
"you've never been out in the world,"
"you've never had a life of your own."
as soon as I heard it
I knew he was right
he wanted the children
saying there was no way
for me to do what I needed to do
and he didn't want to be alone
I trusted him and felt his love and support

We had grown up
fourteen years later
to be very different people
fourteen years later
we let go, and cried
remained friends and struggled
with the pain and confusion
of our two young children

I moved to San Francisco
nine months later, 1975
began to keep a journal
got involved with establishing
the Women Studies program
at San Francisco State
a hotbed of feminism
a hotbed of lesbianism
I came home to myself
as a woman
a powerful primal connection
that had been denied

I wrote papers for classes
and discovered
I was a woman-loving woman
I was a feminist
I was a radical
I was a lesbian
I was a leader
I was a poet
discovered I was a writer
and came out

I spoke out publicly
as a lesbian mother
marched in the
Gay Freedom Day Parade
"2-4-6-8 are you sure
your mother's straight?"
came out to my children
my ex-husband, my friends
my sister, my mother

But because I slept with men
three times in four years
I discovered I was a lesbian
who had "unfinished business"
who had "some issues" to work out
there were no bisexual
role models
women's sexuality
was
lesbian sexuality
or nothing

There was a lesbian-feminist movement
with strong lesbian role models
with strong lesbian voices
with strong lesbian visions
who inspired me to be all I could be
and to trust my woman-loving woman
feelings and experience

the personal was political
and fundamentally correct
unless you slept with men

I graduated with honors
travelled to Hawai'i
lived in Maui for nine months
felt my roots
grow deep into the earth
through the soles
of my feet
grounded solid
Lani my heathen name
visible everywhere
street signs, newspapers
on the tips of people's tongues
I belonged
my heart was home.

In 1980
I was a public lesbian
who fell from grace.

I met a kindred spirit
a soulmate
a bisexual man
who met me
eye to eye
heart to heart
politic to politic
psyche to psyche
sex to sex.

We met
as feminists
as organizers
as writers
as thinkers
as theoreticians
as lovers
as best friends.

There seemed to be
no limits or boundaries.

To deny
or keep

such an experience
hidden
in a lesbian closet
was impossible
unthinkable
to me.

When I returned to San Francisco
to my lesbian family of friends
saying I was a bisexual
saying I was in love with a man
saying I refused to be kicked out
I believed and trusted
that even if I was with a man
the personal is indeed political
I knew I wasn't the enemy
I also knew I wasn't alone
I would find others
like myself who refused
to be in the lesbian/gay closet

Nine years later
I travelled to Japan
with my daughter, Dannielle
stepping off the plane
walking in the streets
I immediately sensed a coming home
welcomed by the
familiar ties
familiar eyes
I felt at peace
with myself, with my identity.

I pass for white
struggle for visibility
in a sea of white faces
a barometer for prejudice.

I pass for white
self-doubting my place
in the people of color
community.

I passed for white

even to myself
for a while,
got lost in the dominant culture
slipped over the edge
fingers barely grasping
self-acceptance

self-hate and sabotage
powerful words of denial and shame
a simmering
constant pattern
in my life.

I have always felt
alienated from words
attacked by them
silenced by them
ignored by them
made invisible by them
words have never been fast friends.

I listen to the voices
that come from my heart
and scream from my guts
I am more
than what you see
I say this only to myself
sure no one will listen
and terrified everyone will...

Sitting with
17 lesbians of color
in a dis-assimilation workshop
at a conference on racism
each spoke to the pain
of being invisible
erased in a white world
of trying to fit in, of trying to pass
r e a l i z i n g
they never would
they never could
l i s t e n i n g
to their anger
to their rage

r e c l a i m i n g
racial and cultural pride
I sat
i n v i s i b l e
hardly able to breathe
tears streaming down my cheeks
a lump in my throat
as big as the shame
my white skin affords me
s i l e n c e d   i n   f e a r
I could not speak
I began to cry, and cry, and cry
from a place so deep, so old, so long denied
e x p o s i n g   t h e   p a i n
of having given up, of having given in
of having been beaten down
to a white pulp
my guilt, my shame, my sense of exhaustion
my love, my pride, my sense of family connection
laid bare

With their arms around me
my words came slowly

I belong and am disowned
by one and the other
I have silenced myself
many times not speaking out
terrified of exposure
terrified people would see
would realize
I don't belong
I am not really
who I appear to be

My voice comes
in the form
of the written word
safe on paper, in print
people "hear" but don't see me.
I struggle
still not trusting
the words
that have betrayed me

that have been used against me
that have limited me
that have denied my existence
that have been an oppressive tool.

The medium
I am comfortable with
is food
the colors, the shapes
the textures, the aromas
the taste combinations
the work and play
and consumption of food
nurtures me
it is familiar
    safe
    acceptable

I have a clear sense
because I know
I have been trained
to be a good cook/mother/wife
it was my role in life

But, do I know
I am a good writer?

not really

I still
have to reread
the stuff I've written
the stuff I've published even
to reassure myself
like I can't believe
like I can't trust
the words are mine
came from me
were created
strung together
molded to fit
my thinking
my experience.

When I share
my racial and cultural roots
people scoff
"you can't be!"
"you're kidding!"
"no you're not!"
then proceed to tell me
then proceed to define me
then proceed to invalidate
what is really real for me.

What gives anyone
the right
to tell me who and what I am?

I never want to hear
that I don't look Hawaiian
that I don't look Japanese
that I'm lucky I don't look my age
that I can't be, that I couldn't be
Why make such a big deal about it?
Why is it so important?

I never want to hear
that I am not a bisexual
that there is no such thing
that if I haven't been with a man for a while,
I should call myself a lesbian
that I am hurting lesbians
that I am confusing
an already confusing situation for heterosexual society

Why make such a fuss?
Why don't I just keep it quiet?
Why is it so important?

Don't tell me who I am
Don't tell me what my experience is or has been
Don't tell me my personal is not political
Don't ask me why it is important or what's the big deal

I won't be silenced
I will make a fuss
and I will tell you why it is so important

but only once...

Don't talk to me
unless you are willing
to listen

Don't talk to me
unless you are willing
to face yourself

I am brown
I am yellow
I am white
I am a proud, visible, and vocal mixed-race multicultural woman.
I claim it all and have no shame for it is the truth.

I am a middle-aged woman. I appreciate my 47 years of experience.
This is what it looks like. My face and body are a map of my life.
I don't want to be younger. I enjoy growing older and wiser.

I am a brazen radical bisexual feminist woman.
I love women as fiercely and passionately as *any* woman can.
I am a woman loving women: bisexual/lesbian/heterosexual/asexual.
I love and trust the men who are my allies,
struggling side by side doing the necessary work
of dismantling the shame of patriarchy in their lives
and who are taking emotional responsibility for loving themselves
and each other.

VISIBLE VOCAL PROUD AND STRONG

Mixed-race people threaten the core of a racist society.

VISIBLE VOCAL PROUD AND STRONG

Bisexuals jeopardize the foundation of a heterosexist monosexual culture.

VISIBLE VOCAL PROUD AND STRONG

Aging women (no matter how old we are) break the back of ageism.

VISIBLE VOCAL PROUD AND STRONG

Lesbians and women-loving women cut to the heart of sexism.

It is time to nurture the organic radical integration[4] process.
Differences recognized and appreciated give a sense of the whole.

I am sick and tired of lesbians who love lesbians, not women.[5]
I will not allow lesbian chauvinism to silence me one more time.
I am angered by unexamined and unacknowledged internalized
misogyny, homophobia, biphobia and heterophobia wherever it exists,
but especially in my lesbian, gay, and bisexual communities.
I am pissed at politically conscious people
who do the work of liberation but don't recognize
sexism, racism, and classism as the tap root of all oppressions.

Assimilation is a lie.
It is spiritual erasure.[6]
We must proceed with mutual responsibility and respect.
We must give words to the silence behind the lies.
We must listen to ourselves and to each other.
If we take the time to recognize the fact
that we are already in it together
this revolution is truly ours,
all of ours
and it is here, now
in *our* midst.
We have to be wise enough
and patient enough
to trust ourselves
and each other
and the solutions
we will create.
That is feminism.
That is revolution.

Notes

1. *Hapa haole* is Hawaiian for half or mixed Hawaiian and white. *Wahine* means woman.

2. Evelyn Torton Beck, *Nice Jewish Girls: A Lesbian Anthology,* rev. ed., Boston: Beacon Press, 1989, pp. xvi–xxvi.

3. *Menehune:* "Legendary race of small people (in Hawai'i) who worked at night building fishponds, roads, temples." Pukui, Elbert, and Mookini, *The Pocket Hawaiian Dictionary,* Honolulu: University of Hawai'i Press, 1975.

4. This is a term Robin Morgan coined in *The Anatomy of Freedom, Feminism, Physics, and Global Politics,* Anchor/Doubleday, 1984.

5. I want to thank Hester Lox for her thinking on this point.

6. I want to thank Jane Litwoman for this concept.

Beth Elliott

Bisexuality

The best thing that ever happened to lesbian-feminism?

"**A**ny woman can be a lesbian," says the song. "Feminism is the theory, lesbianism is the practice," goes the slogan. And, to many women, the "women's community" is a lesbian community. The lesbian-feminist message is clear: Addressing one's romantic and sexual energies to women rather than men offers women a better, more liberated life with more resources for self-actualization.

One would think lesbian-feminists would have a vested interest in encouraging as many women as possible to explore loving women and in making it easier for women to identify as lesbians and to become romantically and sexually involved with other women. How ironic, then, that lesbian-feminists are putting so much energy into narrowing the qualifications for acceptance as a lesbian and in making it more difficult for women to join the ranks of woman-loving women.

In their pioneering work *Lesbian/Woman,* Del Martin and Phyllis Lyon described a lesbian as any woman whose "*primary* erotic, psychological, emotional, and social interest is in a member of her own sex, even though that interest may not be overtly expressed" (emphasis added). This was the first woman-identified definition of lesbianism because it recognized factors beyond sexual expression as the key elements in women's love for one another.

Martin and Lyon specifically rejected patriarchal definitions of lesbianism, which seem to have been based on wishful thinking: the hope that most women's lesbianism might be explained away. By the phrase "may not be overtly expressed," they factored out cultural differences between men and women in reported homosexual activity. And, by using the word "primary," they specifically rejected the notion that exclusivity of preference was essential to a lesbian identity — snubbing the male hope that "if she could do it once [with a man], she can do it again."

Lesbian/Woman was published in 1972, about the time that a great number of radical feminists were discovering that lesbianism might make for an attractive metaphor for women living lives independent of patriarchal values and uncompromised by a male partner's slow or reluctant adjustment to a less sexist way of life. At this time lesbianism as one form of love and attraction began to be eclipsed by lesbianism the political statement. By the end of that decade, the going definition, as promoted by lesbian-feminists, went something like this: "A lesbian woman is a woman-identified woman whose needs are most completely satisfied with other women *only*" (emphasis added).

This definition is taken from *A Lesbian Primer* by Liz Diamond, a book that has been adopted for use in colleges throughout the United States, including Harvard. Other pronouncements in that book also reflect the shift in emphasis from loving women to women-only. Among these is a quote from an unnamed lesbian who defines "lesbian" as "a woman-identified woman who does not sleep with men." The author also "educates" her readers with stereotyped claims about bisexual women that have no basis in fact. She says that "bisexual women generally do not identify themselves as lesbians," that bisexuality is "usually more a sexual preference than a lifestyle," and that because bisexual women "relate to men sexually, [they] do not experience the same oppression as lesbians."

It is apparent from the rigorous specifications a woman must meet before she dare call herself a lesbian that the freedoms proclaimed in the early days of women's liberation have now become tyrannies of their own. Though it was once a breakthrough to affirm that a woman need not wear skirts and nylons, makeup and long hair, those "you need nots" have become "thou shalt nots," which seems to miss the point. And, much more specifically, with lesbianism now being defined less by whom you love than by with whom you do not sleep, a woman can now be accused of letting down the side and be socially ostracized for any deviation from the standard women's community dyke profile, whether in dress, attitude, vocabulary, political slant, or sexual behavior. And to think it used to be straight men who had the vested interest in denying that any given woman was "really" a lesbian!

What's the point of discouraging women from exploring their options and widening their horizons by loving other women? What's the point of saying that only certain women may love other women and only under certain circumstances? And, if this rigid codification is its essence, what's the point of lesbian-feminism at all?

As lesbian and bisexual feminist activism continues to promote and enhance our freedom to love women, it is inevitable that more and more women will find a comfortable place for themselves somewhere along the bisexual continuum, if for no other reason than the nature of human sexuality.

Historically, we are just beginning to emerge from an age in which lesbianism has had to be hidden for the sake of survival. Only within the past generation has it been possible to be out of the closet with any modicum of safety anywhere. Twenty to thirty-five years ago, the only way one could act on a desire to love a woman was usually to find and join an underground community and to adopt its ways in total no matter how rigid they might be.

Today, thanks to the progress we have made over the years, a woman need not leave her entire life behind and adopt a new one in order to be involved with another woman. Many women today are coming out wherever they happen to be, sometimes in the midst of their heterosexual friends. Having more options, women coming out today are making a wide range of choices of their own, not just that one hard choice between totally straight and conforming to the mainstream or totally gay and conforming to the subculture.

As a result, more women are more free to love more women than ever before. So what's the problem? If lesbian-feminists truly wish to promote women's freedom to love, sleep with, and bond with other women, they should support women who choose that freedom. They should be deliriously happy that the barriers are breaking down and that fewer women are feeling compelled to avoid their feelings for other women. They should not deter women from loving women by harassing them for not loving a woman in the official, approved lesbian-feminist community manner.

But they do. They want so much to believe in the universal efficacy of the stock lesbian-feminist identity and behavior package that they react to the thought of any woman declining to adopt it as her own — or, perish the thought, customizing it to fit her own tastes and standards — as though such deviation could somehow threaten the continued existence of lesbianism and the lesbian community. Therefore, they try to herd out any nonstandard lesbian, or any bisexual feminist, because she is "not really a lesbian." Their motives are grounded in the belief that society cannot be changed unless it is changed all at once, and that this can be done only by persuading enough women to join this standardized community, adopting the approved model of identity and politics, to achieve critical mass for an amazon explosion. As for other avenues for change, the belief is that any alternative can only be a competing, counterproductive one.

In thinking this way, doctrinaire lesbian-feminists are missing out on the golden opportunity for societal transformation that bisexual liberation presents. Because they think only in terms of a classic overthrow of The

System, they haven't noticed that bisexuality can set the stage for a situation in which, to paraphrase Wavy Gravy, The System just sort of gets lost in the shuffle.

Bisexuality could be the best thing that has ever happened to lesbian feminism. It delivers the benefits of loving women — and the freedom to do so — to more women. Moreover, it ensures the proliferation of lesbian-feminist values into the mainstream, rather than allowing them to be cordoned off within a subculture which does the mainstream the favor of removing its members and values therefrom.

Every woman deserves the benefits of loving women, and we cannot afford not to make those benefits accessible to more women. This notion of lesbian "purity" defeats the basic purpose of feminism, which is to make women's lives better. We should be making it "OK" for more women to love each other without having to stake out one side of any mythological "fence," because freedom cannot result from restriction.

The freedom to be bisexual can make alternatives to compulsory heterosexuality less the avant garde phenomenon or radical choice and more something within the range of choices the average woman feels comfortable taking for granted as viable.

When women feel no pressure to make an all-or-nothing choice about sexuality, lesbians are less likely to get burned in that stereotypical situation of the "fence-sitter" or "experimenter" who runs back to heterosexual life when the chips are down. And straight women will be less reluctant to acknowledge what they know, deep down inside, to be the benefits of lesbianism: relationships based on women's values and sisterly affection that combine the best features of love and friendship.

Changes such as these are already taking place. In a 1980 survey done at the University of California at San Francisco, 28 percent of the women responding said they would consider bisexuality (i.e., a relationship with a woman) as a viable option should they not be able to establish a satisfactory relationship with a man. Note that the women in these surveys would identify themselves as bisexual rather than lesbian: They are looking for a satisfying relationship, not an entire lifestyle, and they may not consider their heterosexual background to be the burdensome hindrance many lesbians have felt it to be in their own lives.

Quite clearly, lesbian purists are setting themselves up to be victims of their own success. Because lesbian *and* bisexual feminists have made it easier to choose to love women, one's lesbianism need no longer be an all-consuming identity factor, or even a central one. Many lesbian and bisexual women are identifying more with other peer groups: family, ethnic groups, friends or schoolmates, industry, locale, spiritual path, or even those who share a particular avocation. Meanwhile, a portion of the lesbian community has forgotten that this state of affairs was long the goal of the lesbian movement: to make sexual orientation irrelevant in terms of acceptance wherever one desires to be accepted and appreciated.

Some lesbians have found it better to choose lovers and friends on the basis of who they are as people rather than by their sex or orientation. Becoming socially adept in both heterosexual and lesbian worlds, these women have achieved a bisocial or bicultural way of life. They have found that "heterosexuality as a second language" can afford them a wider, more interesting, and more satisfying range of experiences, whether or not they ever have heterosexual experiences themselves.

Sex, of course, is the big bugaboo. Some lesbian writers have tried to explain away the embarrassing number of women who have ceased caring about exclusivity in their lesbianism. In doing so, they have created a bisexual stereotype: the lesbian who has casual sex with men because it's easier to score a heterosexual one-night stand. This, of course, is not unknown. More often, though, lesbians who end up doing what some call a "sport fuck" with a man have been in a situation, such as travel, in which a good time with a kindred spirit just happened along. Sometimes, when companionship is appreciated, it doesn't make sense to stand on ceremony and refuse the lagniappe of a night shared with an interesting person.

I could counter-stereotype by claiming that sophistication has its own rewards, pointing out that my own identity affords me a broader community of friends and the means to bond with them through experiences or capabilities in common. My concern, though, is that the lesbian community's indulgence in exaggerated, institutionalized biphobia will throw away the opportunity to transform mainstream values in a way that will make them more compatible with lesbian-feminism. Validating feminist bisexuality will enable heterosexual women to bond with lesbians through experiences or capabilities in common — and to be in an excellent position to promote within the heterosexual community a positive attitude toward lesbian relationships.

If lesbian-feminism truly desires to liberate women and transform society's concepts of gender and sexuality, then we must tear down the fence between straight and gay. That division is as artificial and unnatural as patriarchal sex roles.

For the good of all women, woman-identified lesbian values must be made accessible to more women. That will not happen if women must fear ostracism for not being lesbian enough, if women must take a loyalty oath in order to have the opportunity to explore coming out in a lesbian community. For the good of all women, lesbian biphobia must end, and bisexuality must be accepted as a viable feminist way of life.

Given the chance to show results, feminist bisexuality could prove to be the best thing that ever happened to the lesbian-feminist movement.

Karen Klassen

Talking about sex, gender, and desire*

Dear Loraine,   *September 1989*

Hi. I got your address from Tasha. I'm living in Halifax, one of the grayest, foggiest, rainiest places I've ever experienced, while I study feeding and movement patterns in tadpoles. Probably I'll be here another year or so. I haven't gotten really involved in the Halifax women's community. The people I'm close to here are all somehow involved with school, mainly the biology department. I've been lovers with a man, a Portuguese Ph.D. student, Rui, since last fall. I've often felt strange and ambiguous about the relationship — not about him as a person, but about the gender and sexual orientation aspects of it. It's something I need to talk about, and I thought you would be exactly the right person to contact.

Last fall I told Tasha I felt like "a lesbian involved with a man, not really bi." Now it's getting hard to make this kind of distinction. I am more open to men than I used to be. But at the same time, my connections with men are so different from those with women. There are parts of myself, ways of being, which I just don't experience with men. And I still want the things in my life that I feel and that I am with women, both on a personal, emotional, and sexual level, and in terms of participation in women's community.

---

* *Editors' note:* The following letters were sent to Loraine by Karen Klassen, from Halifax, Canada. We thought her unique perceptions on sex, gender, and desire and her description of a woman coming out of a lesbian identity and into bisexuality were important to include in the book. Therefore we've published them, as is, with permission from the author.

There are issues I'd like to discuss, but it seems difficult to find women who want to talk openly about sex, politics, society, and how these things come together in their lives. I have some practical questions: How can I best maintain my integrity as a person who is not straight, while living in a world which sees me with a man and assumes I'm straight? It's a different situation than being in the straight world as a lesbian, with women and not with any man. In some ways it's easier to come out in reference to a present relationship with a woman, easier when I'm not known as involved with a man. (At first, when I was more ambiguous about my relationship with Rui, I tried to keep it private, but I found this difficult. People are very good at noticing het relationships, even with all my "closetedness.") Also, people take what I tell them about my lesbian relationships differently now, less seriously. And lying through silence has a different feel now — in a sense I'm less comfortable with it.

I am also unsure of my place in lesbian society. My close friends have been mostly okay with me seeing a man, but I have gotten some clear negative reactions and done some walking on eggs, nervously, around it.

❖

October 1989

Dear Loraine,

I've been thinking a lot about "lesbians involved with men" vs. "really bi" women. In many ways it's a moot point, but I think it's a question of identity and behavior, which makes me lesbian-identified but functionally bisexual, at least now. It relates to what Lani said,[1] in that my experience and perspective have been shaped by living as a lesbian. Basically, I prefer to explain rather than label, but there are elements in others and in myself that seek some kind of "canned" identity. This becomes less realistic as complexities surface in our lives. I'm much different from when I was bi at eighteen years old, one label is inadequate to describe both who I was then and who I am now. Whether I can claim any sort of stable sexual identity is debatable, except that I'm not straight and never really was.

Another element of sexual identity has to do with the interaction of gender and desire. Since I discovered it was possible, I've always felt a clear desire for women, in a way that I never have for men. This desire brought me through a year of isolation, desperately seeking women of like mind, into a basically straight part of the women's movement, into various less than ideal sexual situations, because they gave me access to women and finally, into lesbian circles.

Since my "lesbian adolescence," I've learned that there is more to attraction and compatibility, sexually and otherwise, than gender and sexual orientation. I've become more selective in some ways, and less in others. However, I still feel something with women in general, even with many women with whom I would not be sexually compatible. I've never had this kind of generalized, gender-specific desire for men.

I have a desire for sexuality which can in some ways be filled by men, and has been at times, but it is not specific to men as elements of my desire are specific to women. My recent involvements with men are based on particular individual connections, with a background of wanting sex and intimacy, but not of wanting men, *per se.*

Deborah Gregory, at the 1985 women's sex conference in Toronto, said that we tend to talk about sexual identity and preference only in terms of the gender of our partners — and that there are other important aspects of sexual orientation which get less press. Some of these are more visible now, particularly S/M stuff, but there is a lot we never talk about. I think these unarticulated elements of sexual style are a big part of what make people compatible or not, as lovers and they're not all gender associated.

I have a lot of questions revolving around sex. For instance, what part of the difference I feel between being with men and with women is general, and what is particular to me? How do straight women feel with men? How do clearly bi-identified women feel with women and with men? And what about other lesbians who have been involved with men? (I know these women exist, though we seldom hear of it.)

When I started being sexual with men again last summer, I had a lot of trepidation. I didn't really know where to go with it. It's been very interesting, very different for me than my sexuality with men before I came out. I know my sexual self much better now. But I also know more of what is possible for me with women than with men. I don't mean particular sexual acts, but ways of feeling, ways of experiencing a lover and myself, and the flow of energy between us. There are particular states of being which I associate with certain acts, but I don't think that they are exclusively linked. I just don't know how else to create those feelings, how to create them with a man.

Probably some of these states are woman-specific, and I should forget even trying to experience them with a man. Other states I associate with women are places I could perhaps also go with men, if I knew how. And probably there are states, perhaps states I'd like, that I could experience only with men, but I haven't developed my sexuality with men to that point.

In thinking specifically about sexual experiences, and what I have and haven't experienced with men of the realm I know is possible with women, I run into a vocabulary problem. We barely have words for the most concrete, physical elements of our sexuality, let alone the mental, emotional, and spiritual elements of it.

One experience I've had only with women is associated with fisting, in a context where it went both ways in the relationship. (Non-reciprocal fisting feels different for me, even with women.) At times, this has been much beyond a bodily experience, transcendent perhaps. From a "bottom" perspective, I have sometimes moved through the physical sensations, letting them go, and traveled to another plane of consciousness. From a "top" perspective I have moved through fucking a woman with very conscious care to a place where my body did it, without thought, but closely in tune with her and feeling what she felt. To a certain extent I was also in tune with her on the other dimension, not going with her so much as seeing where she went. Probably some form of transcendent sex is possible with men, but I haven't experienced it, and I imagine it would be quite different.

I think some lesbian-specific facets of sexuality are about making love with someone with a body like my own. This allows me to understand what she feels, and to be understood, in a much clearer, more immediate way than is possible in much of heterosexuality. This kind of knowing is particularly strong with women whose sexuality is like my own. There are other, more specific elements. The feelings of being very inside someone, of that kind of openness in a woman lover, and of being enclosed is something I like a lot and don't have with men. I feel men open to me, but in a different way, and I never really feel enclosed by them.

Another lesbian-specific feeling has to do with being a woman wanting a woman, and the amazement which stays with me, even when I know she wants me, that she wants *me*. Subconsciously I think I'm still affected by the social messages that women want men, and therefore, women don't want me. In a sense it still surprises me when they do. It doesn't surprise me that men want me. I've been conditioned all my life to expect it.

These are things I feel are fundamentally different with men and women. There is also quite a bit that I think is not necessarily exclusive to one or the other gender, but in practical terms usually is.

One dimension of sexuality I have explored with men, but not with women, is taking the position of "top" for my own pleasure. I have played with clearly defined sexual roles with women, but as "top" when I have taken a woman, it has always been with a focus on her pleasure, and my own has come secondarily through pleasing her. With men I have sometimes taken a position of absolute control for my own pleasure.

The most extreme instance was my first sex with a man since I came out. It was an affair at a conference which I began very ambiguously, unsure of whether I could get what I wanted sexually from a man. Once I decided that I wanted him, I also decided that the responsibility for my pleasure was my own. I took him, and I had my pleasure with him. In later discussions with lesbian friends I was asked whether I didn't think I had "used" him. I feel clearly that I did not. It was something that he wanted and enjoyed, and, though my focus was on my own pleasure, I wasn't insensitive to him. He was responsive to me, and gave freely what I demanded. He had his pleasure through mine. I can't really imagine having this kind of sex with a woman, though I'm sure it's possible, and that women do it. I think it would be a delicate thing, psychologically, but with this man it was easy.

My experience of role dynamics, in both explicit and unacknowledged forms, is very different, in sex with men and women. I would like to hear from gay men who have started being sexual with women in relation to this. I have also found it very different making love with "straight" women, or women who are accustomed to sex with straight men, and with "lesbians," or women used to sex with women. And this is not only a question of knowledge or technique, but also of the perspective with which women come to sexuality.

For the last year I have been sexual a lot, mainly with a man whose sexuality has been shaped by making love with straight women, while mine has been shaped by making love with lesbians. We've both changed. Some of these changes are good in our relationship, but some of them don't work for me.

Have you ever been with a person of one sex and wanted something impossible with that combination of bodies? I had that feeling a fair bit with Rui, earlier (and always what I wanted was to be inside him, in ways I couldn't be.) It was not easy. Now my sexuality, at least the part on the surface, has changed. In some ways it's easier with him now, but I also feel disconnected from parts of myself through these changes. And I think it makes me less present in sex, and perhaps other ways, with him.

November 1989

Dear Loraine,

I've been through a sort of crisis in my sexuality this fall, upon realizing that it hasn't been as intense as I'm used to, and that I haven't been all there. Rui has noticed this less than I. It's not that the sex is bad, i.e. negative, for me. It is good in some ways, but I don't get all that I could from it. In many ways it is emotionally based and symbolic of the loving between us, rather than a strongly sexual experience. I say this even though I often, perhaps usually, have orgasms — they're just not that intense, the whole experience is not that sexually intense for me.

I think part of it is related to how often we have sex, which is pretty much every day when we're together. And I have no objections to so much sex. In fact in some ways I want it, especially since I know I'll have these long dry spells when we're apart. In other ways it doesn't really allow me to miss it, which is related to a particular kind of wanting it, which I think would make it more intense. Another factor may be the certainty and security of it all. I never feel that I might not be able to have sex if I wanted it, that he might not want me. Which in a way makes it too easy. I don't have to work for it. I also don't have to work in it; if I want to I can determine the action, but if I don't take the initiative he will do all the "work" for me. I think this makes me less present. With him, I've become more "femme," and not in the Joan Nestle[2] sense of the word, but in the "passive"-receptive sense, which relates to this lack of intensity and lack of focus. I think there are several lesbian-specific aspects of sexuality which make me more present, force me to focus in ways that I don't have to with a man. This doesn't mean I can't be fully present with a man, only that it's easier to slide away from the experience.

I know that a certain degree of insecurity heightens the sexual edge for me. Imbalanced power dynamics can create insecurity and that sexual edge in a big way. But even in my balanced, secure relationships with women, I have never had the sense of guaranteed sexual response that I feel with men. Men seem more predictable in wanting me. Some of this is, I think, real and some may come from my conditioning that men want women, thus me, and women want men, therefore not me.

Perhaps another factor is that sex between women doesn't have the socially or biologically set patterns that it does with men. This is not to say that het sex necessarily goes by those patterns, though I find often it does — perhaps it's laziness on my part. But with women I don't have the option of falling back to a set pattern. And even if I get stuck in a sexual rut of my own making, it still doesn't allow the kind of passivity that intercourse with men does. I'm forced to be more active, to pay more attention.

Going through these letters for the book, I've been thinking of so much more I'd like to discuss about sex and the development of desire. These letters are a part of the continuing development of my thoughts on sexuality. This conversation is ongoing.

Notes

1. Lani Farrell Kaahumanu, "Biphobic: Some of My Best Friends Are," *Plexus 9*, no. 4 (1982): 15.

2. Joan Nestle, "Butch–Femme Relationships: Sexual Courage in the 1950s," *Restricted Country,* Firebrand Books, 1987, pp. 100–109.

Love that kink

My roots

Call me kinky, I don't mind. I *am* kinky — if you mean different from the lie we're sold as the norm. At forty-two, I'm celebrating a quarter-century of making love with many different people, many different ways. I don't want children or marriage. I have fur on my upper lip and legs. When not forced to wear secretarial drag, I don fishnet shirts with bike tights, lace glitter shoestrings on my tennis shoes. Even growing up as a fat girl with glasses, saddle shoes, plaid skirts, and vests, I knew I was different. I traveled, as a white teenager during the civil rights movement, between my black, inner-city church friends in Washington, D.C., and my white, mostly Jewish, friends in the suburbs. From my black friends I learned that I could choose whether or not I dealt with racism, while they faced it every day. Many of my white friends were Red Diaper babies, children whose parents' lives were ruined by the McCarthy era. Downplay differences, I was taught, avoid discussions of religion, politics, or sex. But I learned that it was more interesting to explore differences than to run from them. As I watched laws being challenged and people fighting to be free, I felt a new sense of hope and identification with everybody different from the mainstream. I began to push back the limits around me.

I was excited whenever I saw people's eyes spark, eyebrows raise, and the murmurs of conflict start. These surface clashes, I found, often signal deeper issues underneath, points of difference that make us each unique. Later I learned to calm myself and observe for a beat, rather than to spontaneously react — because when I followed my instincts, and only later sorted out the feelings intellectually, my passion would often draw me too fast into something I barely understood.

I mention all this as background. What I want to discuss is AIDS, its impact upon me, and how all this relates to what society labels kinky, or not, normal or different, right or wrong. AIDS has illumined connections between race, sexual orientation, gender differences, and class which I never saw before, and has caused me to identify even more with those our society ostracizes. AIDS and sex are connected in our imagination now, but society's fear and distrust of sex stems from much farther back. But because people with AIDS often get accused of having kinky sex (whether or not it's true), I decided to investigate kinky as a term.

Origins of *kinky*

Most dictionaries define *kinky* two ways. The first is "full of kinks, tightly curled hair." The second definition is "weird, eccentric; specifically sexually abnormal or perverse."[1] But what's kinky to me may not be abnormal to you. And when many people get excited, they'll joke about "getting kinky," indicating, not something negative, but something especially pleasurable and arousing that they relish. Why is kinky something we claim only in an altered, heightened state?

Twenty years ago I first experienced the kinky label from straight people when I openly expressed my attraction to women. Then lesbians also rejected me for not denying my attraction to gay and straight men. I began to identify as bi, someone the world displaces their sexual fantasies — both positive and negative — upon, and someone belonging to neither group, an outlaw.

I looked for others like me whenever I could. I made love in groups, often with co-workers and friends. After much trial and error, I learned how to tell when the circumstances for group sex were right, and when they weren't. The exhilaration of creating a group creature that begins with cuddling like kittens and intensifies as the pulse and rapture coursing through the group builds is an exhilarating experience of camaraderie that leaves me touched and honored each flight.

Interracial sex also blessed me. I love black men! This does not mean I don't love others. I do. And, I *really* love black men. It's scary to admit that, though. I feel like I get hit from all sides — by people who think I'm racist even admitting this attraction to people who think I'm not racist enough.

Acting on all these desires expands my self-confidence and pleasure immensely. I've learned I can live communally or alone, and that, even with all my wonderful friends and lovers, I am still best lover to myself.

But how did kinky *hair* get associated with abnormal sexuality? Is straight hair more normal? ("Oh, Loraine," some of my friends said, "now you're going too far, there isn't political meaning in everything." But I don't believe in linguistic coincidence. Root origins and evolving word meanings often reveal important history. Just look at all the derogatory terms used for woman and what their original meanings were. It's an education in itself.[2])

There is a link between the "unusualness" of the sex act and the "differentness" of the people labeled kinky. Difference itself is seen as bad, and feared — the dreaded Other. What is feared also is eroticized. And, *not* coincidentally, it's the minorities, the people with the least power, who get labeled as Other, labeled as kinky, more often than not.

The late 1800s was when "kinky" began to be used as a synonym for "weird," sometimes being associated with male or female homosexuals, and nonheterosexual intercourse, sadomasochism, and group sex. Starting around the turn of the century in the United States and Great Britain, "kinky-head" and "kinky-nob" also became derogatory terms for African Americans in white colloquial speech.[3]

After slavery was abolished, the white man's fear of free black sexuality (as opposed to his own sexual enjoyment of black women he'd been acting on, consensually or not, for years) was expressed colloquially. Kinky became both the term for black people *and* for deviant sex. Language now divided society into white and nonwhite, like us or different — i.e., kinky.

To understand further how cultural differences are both denigrated and sensationalized just look at any point where sex and race converge. The oppression of sexual and racial minorities connects, for instance, in how mixed-racial couples are described in pornography — even heterosexual sex is "kinky," if it's interracial. These stereotypes have erotic power, precisely because they are different than the majority, and thus, taboo. The places where most power differences and eroticized images come together in our society — between women and men, whites and people of color, adults and children — are all relationships of dominance and submission, of inequality.

What's the point in relation to AIDS? Since AIDS affects sexual and racial minorities disproportionately, and since it's often transmitted through sex, the power differences among us are exacerbated by its spread, its neglect, and our efforts to "control" it.

One sexual minority most labeled kinky is the S&M community.[4] Does this have anything to do with the fact that they acknowledge and act out the extremes of power differences to the point of parody? S&M is seen as the ultimate form of kink. However, only certain kinds of sm get classified this way. Women are thoroughly trained to be masochists in this society, men are trained to be dominant. That's hardly considered kinky. It's only when the roles are reversed, or exaggerated; as when a submissive man waits on his mistress, or someone is led around on a leash, that it's considered "kinky."

AIDS makes perfect sense

We live in an age
when "natural sex" has become
deadly
and the only lovemaking
deemed "safe"
is like the water—
filtered through chemicals;
or driven underground.

In some parts of Africa
No blood supply is safe.
Death now more than ever inextricably links with love.
Numbers become faces.
Death screams your own name.
Nothing will ever be the same!

As nothing else could, AIDS challenged my assumptions about sex. Since AIDS, things have become even more polarized between heterosexuals and gays, between monogamous and nonmonogamous types, between "clean-livers" and drug users, whites and people of color; especially since the disease seems to target these latter groups. I began thinking a lot more about sex; what was safe, what was not, what was kinky, what was straight. Lo and behold, old distinctions didn't hold. What was straight could be unsafe, what was kinky could be safe. Extremes met in the middle.

AIDS defies boundaries. The AIDS crisis has brought discussion of private practices out into the open. Conditions of sexuality, poverty, and drug addiction that people used to conceal are now revealed, often in the most painful ways. And as the AIDS statistics both here and abroad show, the boundaries between gay and straight, kinky and normal do not exist. This disease can strike anyone, but it disproportionately affects the least powerful among us, increasingly decimating people of color, women, poor and homeless people, youth, and drug addicts, as well as gay and bisexual men. As the populations where this disease is spreading are those with less access to health care and insurance than the groups that first suffered, the contradictions in our society are increasingly being exposed. Class differences, for instance, are quite explicit. The rich live longer on AZT. The poor die undiagnosed in a matter of days. "It's not who you do, it's what you do," the safe sex trainers say; "there are no risk groups, only risk behaviors among us all." A whole new approach to sexual honesty, among everyone, is necessary to prevent this disease.

Yes, AIDS makes perfect sense in a world gone mad, a world that attacks itself with pollution and misuse of precious life resources. From the dioxin-tainted earth, air, and water of Love Canal, New York, to the radiation-devastated land around the nuclear plant at Chernobyl in the Soviet Union and the ongoing deaths caused by the chemical factory spill at Bhopal, India — environmental disasters that assault our own and the planet's immune systems are growing. After studying what is known about the origins of AIDS in an attempt to silence my paranoia, I decided it didn't matter whether AIDS was accidentally or purposely designed to attack minorities or not. What matters is that it *acts* that way, the effect is the same.

Several friends with AIDS died while I edited this book. Feeling connected with other people's pain has changed me in ways I never expected. My feminist assumptions about how we'll achieve equality and get beyond objectification and roles have been questioned profoundly.

I'm angry angry angry
that my freedom to express my love and passion
is cramped.
I'm angry my friends are dying young.
I'm ashamed that I'm resistant to safe sex.
I'm afraid it's a choice
between people I'm attracted to
(who don't play safe)
and people I'm *not* attracted to who do.
I'm afraid of my own death wishes, too.

The intrusive way people questioned me
about what John and I did in bed
infuriated me.
I could take it when I felt they were trying
to learn, vicariously, through me,
what to do if and when they themselves
loved or touched someone with AIDS.
But when they started making judgments
from their own celibate or monogamous boxes
about what risks I took—
"You *did* it with a rubber?"
"You kissed? how deep? how could you?"—
I felt ripped apart.
I didn't trust their concern.

This exhibitionist who loves to flaunt
finally understood
how voyeurism offends.
Because it was mostly in the "concern"

that came out after he died,
friends asking me not to be so "promiscuous,"
asking me to be careful 'cause they cared about me.
All very well you might say,
but what I *felt* was: you people, *you* aren't my lovers,
my lovers are *dying,* or already dead.
I don't want to be left here with this fear and this distrust
between people who pair off into little exclusive bonds
and no longer touch in large groups
or touch me.
I felt their resentment and vengeance too —
"See, that's what your behavior causes—
we're so glad *we* controlled *our*selves."

With John
I started
pushing through my own fears,
offering to massage
his achy back and shoulders,
using a needle on him
to help dig out an ingrown hair,
looking in wonder at the blood on that needle,
carefully throwing it away
and washing my hands.
And snuggling close to him
while I could still savor his warmth,
before the horrible disease
left him cold.

Somehow as AIDS changed me—
watching friends die,
fearing my own death and antibody status—
my sexuality transformed too.

Soft, sweet, egalitarian lovemaking isn't enough now. The dance I
want to dance calls for suspense and the sharp edge of tensions and
polarities, the roles and rituals choreographed under our control this time
since they cannot be ignored. I am drawn to lush, erotic media, jack- and
jill-off parties centered around safe-sex masturbation, and the sensual
touch of leather, latex, and lace, now that exchange of bodily fluids is
taboo. I've found these props can be used to create fantasies, to play-act
dramas that release some of the fear, desire, stress, rage, and pain that
overload us.

After working hard for sexual and social equality for twenty years
I suddenly didn't know how soon I'd die,
which dreams would shatter next.
Impatient with my sex-phobic feminist sisters,
I decided to discover why porn and sm
still held such a charge,
how I could test the limits to center myself.

People in sm groups accepted me as a bisexual woman.
I found camaraderie among these transvestites, dominant women,
submissive men.
I wanted to see why and how
powerful straight white men
submit to dominant women,
to explore what of myself
is ready to be dominant,
wants to be submissive,
and how I can learn
about equalizing roles from this.

I learn now from the roles I rejected,
both femme and butch extremes.
I learn about negotiation and consent,
practices developed in the sm world
that have very real application
for the world of all safe sex.
What seemed a world of rigid opposites from afar
is fertile with dialogue and ambiguities within.
Boundaries and roles become fluid.
Some switchable folk even explore both dominant and submissive
within themselves.
Feels a lot like being bisexual, to me...

I investigated the swinging scene,
to find out what it was like
to see if safe sex or genuine bisexuality
had touched the male double standard—
men enjoy watching women touch, they don't touch each other.
Except for my small circle of friends,
I felt alone. Swingers had hang-ups too.

So I sought out other feminist artists
experimenting radically with sex,

and found they were all
bisexual, big surprise!
I came out as sex radical—
performed in a women's masturbation film,
read group-sex erotica in public,
became known as a promoter
of lesbian-made porn.

After my feminist, anti-porn beginnings
enjoying porn was something I never expected.
I watched my friends, the new lesbian-feminist video producers.
They made films that were erotic, funny, thought-provoking.
I saw that video has potential
as a safe-sex teaching vehicle
better than any guilt-tripping poster, class, or pamphlet
ever will.
I come from a liberate-the-media
community-organizing background
so to me,
taking control of the production of sexually explicit material:
    (1) to teach people about lovemaking, and
    (2) to teach people about safe sex,
is the most natural thing in the world.

There's nothing I'd rather do.

Express yourself!
"Save Sex!" they say, when someone admonishes about the need for safe
sex. It's not contradiction, it's affirmation. Kinky sex, that is, *all* sex but
a very narrowly proscribed kind in this sex-phobic world, seems
threatened. In this age of AIDS it takes imagination to keep hope and
love alive. And as more of us are labeled kinky, the term loses meaning.
But that time has not yet come.

    Neither AIDS nor the power imbalances and injustices between us
will disappear overnight. I still want to realize our feminist dream of
equality, and of eroticizing equality (not power imbalances) too. I long
for the time when there is only power-from-within, and power-over is
gone. We won't get there until we work out more of this power shit first,
though. The "charge" of power-over will not be deactivated or willed
away. It may partly be defused through responsible explorations that
demystify dominance and submission, by ritualizing and choreographing
them to extremes. It's all interesting to me. And none of it, as long as it's
consensual and caring, is taboo.

AIDS showed me more about connections between folks. What affects each, affects all. What's kink is irrelevant.

Notes

1. *Webster's New Collegiate Dictionary,* Springfield, Mass.: Merriam, 1977.

2. See Judy Grahn's *Another Mother Tongue: Gay Words, Gay Worlds,* Boston: Beacon Press, 1984; and Barbara G. Walker's *The Woman's Encyclopedia of Myths and Secrets,* Harper & Row, 1983, for instance.

3. Richard A. Spears, *Slang and Euphemism,* New American Library, 1981.

4. S&M is shorthand for any form of consensual sexual play invoking the acting out of fantasies, feelings, and roles involving dominance and submission and the exchange of power and trust. Feminists into dominant/submissive sex-play have changed the term from S&M to S/M or s/m or sm — to denote the fluid, exchanging nature of these power poles, rather than their separateness.

Michael Ambrosino

Choosing not to

Coming-out stories can have a particular eloquence to them. Purposeful and frightening, coming out begins an awkward journey. Filled with courage, scrutiny, humor, and hatred, many eventually celebrate, having absorbed the power reclaimed by finally owning oneself. I've read about and watched men and women finally embrace their sexual preferences and then carry on with what seems to be an endless task of informing friends, family, and acquaintances. There's a clarity here, a purpose sustained by the individual's emerging sense of self and the support the lesbian and gay community offers those who dare to reach for it.

Comparatively speaking, my own emergence was vague and ambiguous; a private affair full of disappointments and a klutzy sense of trial and error. Because of an uncertainty about bisexuality, friends and family blinked nervously, shrugging in their minds and hearts, not quite understanding what kind of animal I was declaring myself to be. Lesbians and gay men also experience the litany of annoying questions, stupefying attitudes, and sentiments born of ignorance that, via violence and discrimination, literally kills so many women and men. Many whom I told about my bisexuality saw only the possibility of my becoming infected with the HIV virus. Some cried uncontrollably, seeing my life racing toward a final countdown.

Most responded with glibness, confusion, or anger fueled by stereotypes of bisexuals as traitors to one pole or another, misfits, or sexual dyslexics — people who can't make up their minds. For many I was the first "real" bisexual they had ever known. "But you're so happy!" "Do you ever have successful relationships?" Twisted facial expressions accompanied those questions about what my sexual preference entailed. Most people were disbelieving, very skeptical, checking for change, and constantly thinking some day I would "straighten out" or "queer up."

I knew very few bisexuals, landmarks found in most lesbian and gay communities do not exist for us. So it was off to the gay bars with a naive vision of brotherhood, which, I quickly learned, translated into a feast of hands and not much more. Gay men have enriched my life; in a world all too tolerant of violent, insensitive, shortsighted males, gay men have provided me with a refuge. For much of my initial coming out, the choices were few. Searching for the words to convey my feeling of being "home" among gay men, I recall mostly the images: so many rounds of laughter, so many stories of suffering, so many men who, against the constant chant of "faggot," evolved into some of the wisest, human, and resourceful men I know. That we do not honor these men, that this world refuses to see the peace implicit in their ideals disgusts me. With AIDS, the patriarchy has finally found a cure for the challenges gay and bisexual men have thrown in their faces: quietly kill them.

Finding a balance between those masculine traditions of our upbringing that have merit and those we develop in resistance toward the more absurd and often deadly values of the patriarchy is often a confusing and lonely journey. In my search for self, gay men have always been primary role models, examples of an alternate grace and beauty. I've seen carnivals of perseverance in the face of a society that merits the killing of gay culture (while tapping into its profitability), their emotional and political gifts to the world, and even the men themselves. Unfortunately, when it comes to supporting my bisexuality, many have failed, even to the point of being unwilling to talk about it.

After ten years of struggling to find myself within this strange psycho-sexual soup, only in the last year and a half have I felt at home with my bisexuality: accepting it thoroughly, giving myself the space to live with the imperfections, fears, and delights of being emotionally, physically, and sexually open to both men and women. I'm out in as many situations as possible, standing up against biphobia in my communities as I work for an AIDS social services agency staffed overwhelmingly by lesbians and gay men.

My emergence as a bisexual man has consisted of three definite stages: (1) acknowledging my attraction to men and then acting upon it; (2) realizing that I was bisexual and actively trying to define and learn more about myself as a bisexual man; and (3) realizing that I could be in a relationship with either a man or woman, and yet still consider myself bisexual. In other words, I didn't have to prove the "legitimacy" of my bisexuality to anyone.

Bisexuals have just begun to establish themselves as unique, as different and alike as any other established group, yet with their own public and private idiosyncrasies. Countless times I find myself turning to bi men or women, knowing their experiences will provide me with a more understanding and constructive critical platform with which to discuss my life, politics, and sexuality. We die, get beaten up, are discriminated against (especially by lovers, straight or gay), passed over (omitted from countless so-called liberation day parades), and blatantly discounted and misunderstood even as our numbers increase, diversifying what is now beginning to be known as the community of sexual minorities. Upending traditions along the way, paving our acceptance by solidly pointing out the limits placed on loving, sexuality, sexual pleasure, and sexual experimentation in both cultures, bisexuals now are helping to set a new agenda for the lesbian and gay community.

Acknowledging only the "heterosexual" side, bisexuals are perceived by gays as being immune from the discrimination and violence that face all sexual minorities. Our "heterosexual privilege" somehow outweighs those times we get chased from bars, beaten in parks, infected with HIV, or are rejected by our biphobic lovers. Three acquaintances have committed suicide because of the confusion and anger their bisexuality created in their lives. Obviously, biphobia has devastating consequences on the ability of bisexuals to lead healthy lives.

Scared and unaware of any possible alternatives, many "gay" men refuse to explore either a resurging urge to have sexual relationships with women or the heterosexuality they might have felt all along. It's just too difficult to deal with a shifting sexual vocabulary. They take the words they know and use them in a community that provides many of them the only safety and comfort in their lives. Without adequate support systems, to leap into what is initially perceived to be a confusing, ambiguous void seems all the more dangerous. Straddling lives, pulling taut the lines of communication between two very different worlds, finding rare and often claustrophobic pockets of acceptance is what awaits bisexuals who come out.

True, there are more pressing issues facing humanity than the fate of bisexuals, our history, our sense of culture and community. But if we are to stand for the liberation of all peoples, carefully listing the "isms" as they come and go in our lives, then we must acknowledge biphobia: the fear of bisexuals, bisexuality, and our rightful place in straight, gay, and lesbian environments.

Without a sense of purpose, without a clearly defined perspective many bisexuals fail to recognize the political implications of their sexual preference. Lack of awareness, lethargy, and the fact that the diversity of our population is tremendously hard to organize have all contributed to the slow-forming sense that a bisexual community exists. Cutting across all social strata, bisexuality thrives, potentially comprising the largest pocket of the sexual minority community. But organizing bisexuals has been one of the most frustrating and least productive endeavors in my political experience. Our inability to organize, build our own resource centers, periodicals, and political action groups has often been a reflection of our limited sense of ourselves. Nonetheless, we continue to prosper, primarily because so many bisexual women have plunged in pioneering the formation of small groups that have slowly emerged across the country.

Lagging behind our sisters, bisexual men have been slow to act on organizing ourselves into a productive coalition. For men wishing to find and sustain supportive environments in which we can begin to realize some sense of being other than the models this country dictates, the search brings few results. Is it impossible to claim those abilities of men that cultivate our strengths and still be feminist and gay and lesbian positive? Must so many men either attack feminists for realizing their power or completely subordinate themselves to feminist philosophy, not recognizing the desperate need for us to take responsibility in creating our own systems of progressive principles? Within our own circles, I feel we can develop alternatives to those aspects of being male that we dislike most, working out the misogyny within the tradition of masculinity, realizing our responsibility to each other in ways in which we have rarely dealt.

I flip-flopped for years about how men can address these issues. I've grown simultaneously weary of coalitions among men and respectful of those willing to work together toward the recognition of how our behavior both betrays and sustains us. Central to the ability of men to organize around our common struggles is the ability of men to surmount and overcome internalized homophobia.

I see my vision of love between men as incredibly subjective; men do love each other traditionally and untraditionally all over the planet, whether or not we choose to express and share these complex feelings in healthy or constructive ways. In my experience, the most intimate relationships I've seen between men have been those of gay or bisexual men. Still, in the four cities I have lived in over the last decade, bisexual men have been far more apathetic or lethargic in terms of defining our needs and working together to satisfy them.

Any struggle toward a finer recognition of ourselves will be a slow, arduous task. Years of covering up — falling back on cultural norms that allow us leniency toward our natural response to pain, confusion, and sorrow — is one reason we flinch when offered the opportunity to grow. My own record of rejecting those who would have helped me overcome some of these obstacles is dismal, and I recognize the man in me and other men who only works for change when desperation forces us to do so. Denial — working through issues around rape, violence, and the patterns ingrained after years of attempted recruitment into a society that discards those not white, male, and middle class — is a battle in which we must temporarily give up a need to control, trusting that other men might help provide a new sense of love and direction.

AIDS statistics have plunged bisexual men into an unprecedented limelight. Each month the Centers for Disease Control reports on the growing number of bisexual men living with and dying of AIDS. At the height of AIDS hysteria, bisexual men, along with gay men, Haitians, and prostitutes, became the expendable scapegoats with which to bait the American public. Portrayed as promiscuous and irresponsible, bisexual men were the dangerous infectors, living a veiled life of sexual conquests, spreading the disease by keeping secret the reality of the "other half" of their sexuality.

Positioning us as statistics, the push in AIDS educational materials has hardly focused on bisexual male behavior, leaving us adrift along with people of color, lesbians, and adolescents as to what we can do to protect ourselves. Slowly bisexual men are being integrated in the literature aimed at preventing the spread of AIDS. While acknowledging that a good portion of the anonymous sexual activity in any given metropolitan area is among men who either do not identify as gay or who have sexual relationships with both women and men, HIV educational programs specifically designed for these men have been slow in coming. Given this, bisexual male invisibility increases while the number of bisexual men dying from the disease increases exponentially.

While gay men have fought to uncover and chronicle the voices of gay PWAs, the histories of bisexual men afflicted with the disease are much less common. Where are these men? Dying in the cities? Closeted in gay ghettos? If anything it is a testament to the general invisibility of bisexual men, our personal histories, and the contributions we have made. Here again, lacking political clout, with few organized channels, bisexuals must create their own arenas with which to challenge those who stereotype or omit us from important historical periods. Our history is huge but scrambled; the books that really represent us have yet to be written.

Men will always offer me a brand of love and affection that is different but complimentary to the love of women. To have been able to experience both in a lifetime has been a gift and a guiding force in many of my ideals. To have never been able to experience both, holding these thin threads together, would have deprived me of a greater sense of love and life. Growing as a bisexual has been frustrating. Sometimes I begin to wonder what the big deal is, resenting the middle ground I'm forced to represent in a bitter fight between two warring opponents. Too often lives are on the line and, if forced to choose, my heart easily sides with the lesbians and gay men who have shared so much of themselves with me. It is within their vision that I find a healthier state of being. But it is among bisexuals and those who would support us that I feel most comfortable, most productive, and most free to express the full range of my personhood. The fact that bisexuals are beginning to band together to represent ourselves is the most positive element I've seen among bisexuals in many years.

Until bisexuals believe that they have as much right to exist and to prosper, that our position in a sexually segregated society is a vitally important alternative, then we will remain a silent majority, the ineffective middle ground. As bisexuals we can offer such a variety of progressive alternatives to the mainstream. Building upon what has already been accomplished, confronting skeptics and bigots alike, we envision the day when bisexuality is not the least understood of sexual preferences, when it becomes comfortably approached as a norm.

There are certainly some who have encompassed my bisexuality in wonderful ways. They remain a minority, though, and it is usually with a personal reaction of disgust and a practical application of patience and consistency that I have gained the trust in those suspicious of how my bisexuality might taint my priorities or intentions. In affirming our bisexuality, we honor our individual experiences, holding dear those graceful and clumsy selves who represent the achievement of having forged a unique person in the context of a society of rigid alternatives. We choose not to.

Amanda Udis-Kessler

Present tense

Biphobia as a crisis of meaning[1]

The lesbian and gay reaction to bisexuals has tended to veer between "You don't exist" and "Go form your own community; you're not welcome in ours," while the heterosexual reaction has tended to veer between "You don't exist" and "I hate all you queers." God knows we've heard enough of these sentiments, and I don't enjoy repeating them, but this particular set holds value for us if we consider the fear behind the anger. The denial of bisexuality by both straights and gays is common, as is our rejection from lesbian and gay communities and our designation as "homos" by heterosexuals. I believe that this biphobia has arisen as a result of American sexual discourse, the ways in which Americans understand sex and sexuality.

Specifically, I think it can be argued that a good deal of biphobia is the expression of a crisis of meaning posed by bisexuals which affects heterosexuals and homosexuals differently and which needs to be dealt with differently in the two cases. In each case, a collective myth is threatened, raising questions about the lesbian and gay past and the heterosexual future.[2] To appreciate the strength (and fragility) of these collective myths, we need to consider the uses they have in our society.

Sexuality is, of course, a biological aspect of our humanity, but it is also very much culturally constructed. Specific sexual practices, symbols, meanings, values, and power connections are located in concrete historical societies and vary over time and from culture to culture. For example, sexual object choice is managed differently in different societies; a Native American, Pacific Islander, or African may engage in same-sex behavior without in any way having a lesbian or gay identity. The collective myth behind American sexual discourse includes two facets that lead directly to biphobia. First, we consider sexuality to be an essence, an unchanging core identity, and the way that lesbian and gay communities have adopted this view (which can be called essentialism) has led to a great deal of lesbian and gay biphobia. Second, we are still suffering the effects of a sex-negative cultural history which contributes greatly to homophobia and heterosexual biphobia.[3]

The extent to which sexuality is biologically or culturally determined is the subject of a debate between essentialists and constructionists. I indicated above that essentialism is the view that one's sexual orientation is an unchanging essence, which involves a transhistorical and transcultural identity. I also indicated that essentialism is not a universally accepted understanding of sexuality. An opposing view, constructionism, posits that categories of sexual identity are constructed and that human sexuality is wider in scope than the categories we assign it. This is to say that categories create, rather than reveal, social types. The essentialist versus constructionist debate has arisen as a result of changes in Western sexual discourse.

Before 1869, everyone was heterosexual and no one was heterosexual. By this I mean that all people were believed to be biologically oriented toward people of the opposite sex, there was no need for a word or category "heterosexual" since there was no opposite or conflicting category "homosexual." Certainly there were homosexual *acts,* homosexual *behavior,* but no homosexual people and no word "homosexuality." The fact that there could be behavior contrary to what was understood as natural did not cause anyone to rethink their concepts of the natural; rather, they simply labelled same-sex acts unnatural. Biblical injunctions against homosexual behavior must be seen in this light.

In 1869, the word "homosexuality" was coined and the concept — and category — of "the homosexual" came into existence, requiring the "discovery" of the heterosexual as well. I don't mean to suggest that heterosexuality was thought of as anything other than normative, or that homosexuality was taken seriously as a biological entity at that point. Physical and psychological understandings of homosexuality competed, but the constant which is of interest to us here is the depth of the homosexual identity which was brought to light. Sexuality was not simply a matter of acts. It involved an essence which did not change easily if at all. At the end of the nineteenth century, there were two identities to match sexual acts where none had been before, two categories of person: heterosexual and homosexual.

If we jump ahead a century to Stonewall, we notice a dramatic change in the *meaning* of the homosexual identity. The early gay liberation movement, revolting from decades of assimilationism à la Mattachine Society and Daughters of Bilitis, took on an ethnic model of oppression and counterculture. In doing so, it maintained pre-Stonewall essentialism while adding a separatist politics. In this model, lesbians and gay men, drawing on the civil rights movement, defined themselves as an ethnic minority with sexuality rather than skin color the determining factor and with homophobia rather than racism the oppression.

Lesbian and gay activists had long taken the insight of experiencing sexuality as beyond choice and considering this proof that it was a natural part of their sex drive.[4] Interestingly enough, while this approach would seem to require a straightforward correlation between sexual behavior and core identity, such a correlation was not made. Many lesbians and gay men came out after being heterosexually active, and some of these people had enjoyed their heterosexuality; they simply enjoyed homosexuality more. Lesbian and gay essentialists simply switched the heterosexual assumption of prior ages and claimed that these people were essentially gay, regardless of their sexual behavior. Thus, a woman who came out at forty had really been a lesbian all along but had not been in touch with her true sexuality.

The acceptance of essentialism was not universal, however. Some psychologists and sexologists raised troubling questions about this conception which could invalidate forty years of a woman's life. They asked whether the experience of sexuality as beyond chosenness necessarily meant that it was biologically grounded. They asked why sexual identity appeared in such different forms in different cultures, and whether essentialism didn't carry with it a certain cultural imperialism. These constructionists posited that the categories of homosexuality and heterosexuality were *constructed* rather than *discovered* a hundred years ago, created because changing social circumstances dictated a need for such categories. Without denying the place of nature in our lives, they pointed out that socialization affects us tremendously, including the extent to which we think nature shapes us. They argued that sexuality is not simply the unfolding of one's natural essence. Rather, sexuality is learned, relational, contingent, and unpredictable; sexuality *is* as sexuality *does*. There are sexual scripts within every society and there are variations on those scripts in every society.

As we may imagine, the constructionist view of sexuality, with its fluidity and its connotation of choice, threatened lesbians and gay men as soon as it was proposed. Constructionism challenged the "oppressed ethnic minority" approach by arguing that sexuality could not be compared to skin color as a natural phenomenon. The response of lesbian and gay communities was understandably fierce; as Steven Epstein notes, "people who base their claims to social rights on the basis of a group identity will not appreciate being told that that identity is just a social construct."[5] Constructionism could not offer a sound political replacement for essentialism. "[O]nce we have deconstructed identity," so the fear went, "we will have nothing ... which is stable and secure upon which to base a politics."[6] The upshot of this thinking was that sexual theorists continued the essentialist versus constructionist debate in academic journals and other settings, but it had little impact upon community members and their separatist culture and politics. This has remained true since the early days of gay liberation, with Steven Epstein noting in 1987 that "while constructionist theorists have been preaching the gospel that the hetero–homosexual distinction is a social fiction, gays and lesbians, in everyday life and in political action, have been busy hardening the categories."[7]

What does this have to do with bisexuality? Consider a lesbian who has gone through a traumatic coming-out process with loss of family and friends, but who is finally secure with a lesbian identity in a supportive community. Or consider a gay man who has spent his life being harassed and hurt for being gay, who knows personally that oppression means having one's choices removed but who has been able to rebuild his sense of having choices and his sense of humor within an urban gay male culture. Sexual essentialists are secure in their assertion that these two people may have had to suffer but that now they are home and able to build and love and fight back. But what if this man or this woman falls in love with someone of the opposite sex? What, then, was their pain and suffering about? Do the experiences which shaped them mean nothing? Was there an easier way? And should they have taken it? What is the connection of their pasts to a new and surprising present? Both of these people have come through tremendous soul-searching to reach their lesbian and gay identities, which provide them with a myth by which to structure their lives, offering social and political meaning to their personal histories. Is the myth that fragile? Is their sexuality that fragile? How are they to be true to themselves and what does being true to themselves mean in this situation?

The larger lesbian and gay community carries a great deal of shared pain; indeed it is built on it. Stonewall would not have happened without a bunch of drag queens and some diesel dykes being sick and tired of being sick and tired. When lesbians and gay men who are deeply connected to their communities ask the questions above, the whole community feels the effect. If enough people ask them, the collective myth — and the community — are in danger. For both can only remain intact if the pain which built the community was in some way the inevitable product of being oneself in a heterosexist society. This brings us back to the essentialist verses constructionist debate, but with a clearer sense of the urgency behind the response to constructionism. Just as bisexuality would threaten the gay man and lesbian described above, the fluidity and connotation of choice within constructionism would seem to challenge both the history and the future of lesbian and gay communities.

Now we are in a position to see the leap of logic which has accounted for so much lesbian and gay biphobia: it is a leap which connects bisexuality and bisexuals to sexual constructionism and both to a crisis of meaning which may be both personal and communal. Lesbians and gay men, protective of the essentialist view of sexuality, equate the fluidity and apparent choice-making of bisexuality with that of constructionism and feel a tremor in the structure underlying their lives and identities.[8] No matter if, unlike the examples above, they do not experience bisexual feelings themselves, constructionism claims that the potential is always there, and that is enough of a threat.

When bisexuality equals constructionism, bisexuals become walking reminders of the potential crisis of meaning for lesbians and gay men, posing a threat to identity and community far greater than the one posed by heterosexuals. Lesbians and gay men have been able to define themselves as other than heterosexual; bisexuals challenge that definition regardless of our intention to do so. Behind the painful lesbian and gay biphobia which we have experienced is a poignant cry for a self; "you don't exist" means "I do exist." And, too, the rejection as a group ("go form your own communities; you're not welcome in ours") is a way for lesbians and gay men to claim a group identity, to say "*we* exist, not just as individuals but as a community." This fragility may be hidden beneath flippancy, sarcasm, culture, and camp, but any bisexuality education which does not keep it in mind will not open barriers where it counts: in the heart.

What, then, about heterosexual biphobia? Is there, strictly speaking, such a thing? And if so, from whence does it come? Taking these questions seriously requires looking at some of the sexually problematic messages heterosexuals have internalized *without having to challenge them as lesbians and gay men do*. These messages basically revolve around the interface of sex negativity and dualistic thinking that permeates our culture.

Sex negativity comes down to us from Hellenistic idealism, gnosticism, and Christianity. For the equation of sex with sin we may thank Saint Paul and the mystery cults of his day, the early Church fathers, and the Puritans. This is a powerful history, and we feel its effects in our body hatred and our experience of sex as sick, shameful, and dirty, something done secretly and furtively. Sex negativity is visible in traditional Christian views on sexuality, in sodomy laws, in sexual dysfunction, and in the nonexistent or inadequate sex education in much of America.[9] The latter would be amusing if it did not lead directly to sexually transmitted diseases, unwanted pregnancies, and AIDS deaths, as well as indirectly fostering sex roles which contribute to rape.[10]

Sex negativity has always been closely related to hierarchical dualistic thinking. Philosophers from Plato to Descartes have held that the mind or spirit is superior to the body, that culture is superior to nature, and that men are superior to women. These various hierarchies are interconnected; the primary shapers of our culture have symbolically desexualized men, associating them with culture and the spirit, while women have been appointed representatives of sex, nature, and the body. This is not just an excuse for keeping women in their place, as we might imagine, but part of a collective myth used to manage men's fears of chaos and death (since neither culture nor the spirit die). With the discovery or creation of "the homosexual," lesbians and gay men were assigned the lowest place in the linkage of women, sexuality, and nature. They came to stand for sex as sin and to serve as the repository of America's deepest fears about sex and the body, representing lust out of control, promiscuity, dirtiness, and death. The fact that same-sex sex cannot produce a child only aggravated this symbolism, while the recent presence of AIDS brought these fears to a conscious level.

Bisexuals play an interesting role in this dynamic. We have been much less visible to mainstream America than lesbians and gay men, due primarily to our lack of a formal movement with significant numbers to capture the attention of the press. The onetime phrase of the sexual revolution, "everyone's really bisexual," has failed to have either accuracy or impact. Yet we do have a symbolic meaning for mainstream Americans who encounter us: We bring them closer to homosexuality and therefore to their deepest fears about being embodied creatures. As with lesbians and gay men, we bring about a personal and potentially collective crisis of meaning, though one oriented toward the future rather than the past.

Bisexuality can provoke this crisis of meaning for a heterosexual by casting her or his sexual future into doubt. Consider a woman who has always known herself to be heterosexual, who recognizes genuine attractions to men. She is quite clear that she is not a lesbian, but what happens on the day when she finds herself attracted to a woman? What does this mean about her sexual future? As with the lesbian and gay examples above, what might being true to herself mean in this situation? In a dualistic culture where nonheterosexuality is demonized and heterosexuality is made to represent all that is good and right and pure, this woman may have to face gremlins which society has tried very hard to keep hidden.

The essentialist-versus-constructionist debate about sexuality has not reached the American mainstream enough to be very troubling, but the challenge to categories posed by both constructionism and bisexuality would be a problem for any culture which uses categories as ours does to scapegoat some people in return for offering the rest peace of mind.

For if lesbians and gay men find the otherness of heterosexuals useful in defining themselves, consider how useful the otherness of homosexuals is in maintaining the American collective myth. There is a group upon which to project all of one's fears about being embodied, sexual, mortal, about having physical urges which sometimes seem out of control. Moreover, gay men and lesbians can represent godlessness, evil, and the decline of culture, which is the only way some parts of mainstream America can understand the social and sexual changes of the last twenty-five years. In order for this collective myth to work, however, the use of sexual categories must be thoroughly ingrained; they must not be seen as a useful if incomplete way of describing reality but rather as the truth, the whole truth, and nothing but the truth.

Bisexuality threatens this unconscious acceptance of good and evil, us and them dualism by throwing some grey in with the black and white, by representing a continuum. Once it is possible for a person to be both heterosexual and homosexual, than perhaps it is possible for a person to be both good and evil, mind and body, culture and nature. If this possibility creeps into the all-or-nothing dualism still used today to manage the fear of death and chaos, the collective myth is in danger. Bisexuality has not had the impact on the heterosexual culture that it has had on lesbian and gay communities, but it has the potential to challenge the meaning of heterosexuality as an experience and an institution. Here, too, the comment "you don't exist" really means something else, namely "I'm not gay," while "I hate all you queers" means "gays are other," roughly translated as "I'm not gay." From this perspective, both the lesbian and gay and the heterosexual reactions to bisexuals center not around bisexuality as such, but around homosexuality. The heterosexual reaction to the bisexual is "I'm not gay." The lesbian and gay reaction to the bisexual is "I *am* gay."

The title of this paper, "Present Tense," has a double meaning. It refers to the challenge to the lesbian and gay past and the heterosexual future posed unintentionally by bisexuals, and it refers to the way that challenge takes place.[11] If bisexuality is a passing phase, a transitional period only, the lesbian and gay past and the heterosexual future retain their meaning and the present need not be tense for them. Yet if bisexuality is its own legitimate sexual identity as we know it to be, if we are not just confused or fence-sitting or in closets with revolving doors, if we live our bisexuality *in the present tense,* we will inevitably pose crises of meaning in American culture. We raise that dangerous question raised also by constructionism: to whom are we really similar and from whom are we really different? Who is our real enemy? Do we have one?[12]

How can this way of thinking about biphobia affect the educational work we do? First, I think it is extremely important when educating heterosexuals to work from their homophobia and do some education that may seem tedious or not in our best interest. If their crisis of meaning is based around a fear of homosexuality which has been driven into them since they were born, they need some of the same information and encouragement that lesbians, gay men, and bisexuals need; their biphobia may simply be homophobia in drag. From this perspective, once homosexuality is less threatening to them, bisexuality will be merely confusing rather than troublesome; we know very well how to educate in response to confusion.

It will be more difficult to educate in response to the lesbian and gay crisis of meaning without seeming to diminish its importance, but I suspect that there are two steps. First, we must be actively involved in lesbian and gay liberation, both because it is our liberation and because lesbians and gay men need to know that we are really with them. We need to grapple with the reality of heterosexual privilege and its links to sex and class stratification. Until we do this, we will never convince lesbians and gay men that we won't simply abandon them in hard times. Second, we must raise the essentialist versus constructionist question again with the aim of considering the strengths and weaknesses of both positions and moving beyond a one-or-the-other dichotomy.[13] We will want to raise questions about the common role of lesbians, gay men, and bisexuals in the future of sexual justice (not just sexual freedom) in America and elsewhere.

Just as lesbians and gay men do not personally choose to represent the worst aspects of embodiment, bisexuals do not personally choose to threaten the meaning systems by which lesbians, gay men, and heterosexuals live. But if we have this effect, we have all the more reason to work against the homophobia which injures and limits people of all sexualities and all the more reason to make the connections between homophobia and other supremacist systems which keep us alienated, disempowered, and afraid. We are not fence-sitters. Let us strive to be bridge-builders.

Notes

1. This paper draws extensively on an earlier paper, "Bisexuality in an Essentialist World," which appears in Tom Geller, ed., *Bisexuality: A Reader and Sourcebook,* Times Change Press, 1990.

2. There are, of course, more tangible issues present as well: Lesbian biphobia includes painful experiences around heterosexual privilege, while both lesbians and gay men have fears based in experience of abandonment by bisexuals, both as sexual partners and as partners in the struggle for liberation.

3. Clearly, sexual messages are transmitted and received differently depending on race and class, and different language is used to consider these problems. I can only speak out of my own experience as a white, middle-class, able-bodied, and college-educated woman. I offer this perspective with the confidence that people of many other backgrounds are asking these questions in ways most appropriate to them.

4. Ironically, the period around Stonewall is also the point at which some radical feminists began to choose political lesbianism and to publicize that choice; the question of choice in essentialist versus constructionist debates (and between bisexual and homosexual people) is double-edged, depending on one's politics.

5. Steven Epstein, "Gay Politics, Ethnic Identity: The Limits of Social Constructionism," *Socialist Review* 93, no. 4 (May–August 1987): 22.

6. Diana Fuss, *Essentially Speaking: Feminism, Nature, and Differences*, Routledge, 1989, p. 104.

7. Epstein, "Gay Politics, Ethnic Identity," p. 12.

8. There are certain links between constructionism and bisexuality, but they are not as substantial as they have been made to seem. It is as possible to be a bisexual essentialist, for example, as it is to be a lesbian Republican.

9. For excellent and thorough examinations of American body hatred, see James Nelson's *Embodiment: An Approach to Sexuality and Christian Theology*, Augsburg Publishing House, 1978; and Ernest Becker's *The Denial of Death*, Free Press, 1973. Some sections of Mary Douglas's *Purity and Danger*, Frederick Praeger, 1966, are also relevant.

10. There is another major discourse which has arisen in response to sex negativity and sex as sin, which can be called sex compulsivity and sex as salvation. *Embodiment* (ibid.) discusses some of its attributes, while Edwin Schur's *The Americanization of Sex*, Temple University Press, 1988, is primarily an extended discussion of the subject.

11. Incidentally, bisexuality also challenges lesbian and gay "eschatologies" (e.g., "someday the whole world will come out" or "someday we will have a society just of women") as well as an individual's exclusively heterosexual past by raising the question of moments of same-sex desire denied, distorted, or projected safely away.

12. For a discussion of the limits of the ethnic minority and separatist community approach, see Geller, pp. 61–62. Jana Sawicki offers a provocative thought along lines similar to my own: "Only if feminists democratize their struggles by giving equal respect to the claims of other oppressed minorities will they avoid ... destructive Gemeinschaft [which] refers to the ... sense of community in which conflict is experienced as an all or nothing contest ... for the right to have one's feelings. Individuals involved in such conflicts sometimes become preoccupied more with bolstering their own identities than with their political goals. [This is] self-defeating insofar as it often leads to internal struggles over who really belongs to the community" (in Irene Diamond and Quinby Lee, eds., *Feminism and Foucault: Reflections on Resistance*, Northeastern University Press, 1988, p. 187). Once lesbian and gay struggles are linked to international struggles of race, class, and gender, what is the logic of excluding bisexuals?

13. See Geller, pp. 60–61; Fuss, especially chapter 6, and Epstein are extremely useful as well.

Political activism

A brief history

The roots of the current bisexual community and movement have been visible and growing since the mid-seventies. In larger cities, where the Sexual Freedom League and naturists of the sixties, the Gay Liberation Front and Women's Movement of the seventies made their mark, bisexual social, support, and educational groups formed. It is difficult to present an accurate account of our roots when we are just becoming visible to ourselves.

The isolation has been broken now in a number of major urban areas, and there is a growing sense of history being made. Within that sense of history is a desire to know what and who has come before. The voices in this book only begin to present our "bistory." We cannot include the activities of the bisexual communities and movements in Canada, Europe, the Netherlands, New Zealand, or other eastern and southern hemisphere countries we are just learning about. Nor do we pretend that what we do include here is complete. What follows is but a beginning for others to expand upon.

The earliest and most visibly organized groups were in Chicago, New York, Washington, D.C., and San Francisco. The first meeting of Chicago's Bi-Ways was held in December 1978. They held regular activities and produced a newsletter. Chicago's Action Bi-Women, a feminist-oriented group, was formed in the early eighties out of Bi-Ways.[1] Over the years the Chicago bi community, like many groups, has gone through periods of inactivity. Presently both groups are active, have a newsletter, and report that the University of Chicago has a social and support group for bisexuals.

The Bisexual Forum of New York began as "a social, educational, and support group seeking to encourage awareness of bisexual issues in a nonthreatening and nonjudgmental environment"[2] in 1975. By 1977, a newsletter was being published, and workshops, lectures, and other activities carried the forum into the eighties. The organization peaked in 1980 with over two hundred active members, and a mailing list of several thousand. Because of the general burnout, changes in life circumstances, and lack of new leadership, the last official meeting took place in 1983. The New York Area Bisexual Network (NYABN) has been active since the mid-eighties, and the Bisexual Political Action Committee (BIPAC) of the NYABN organized in the mid- to late eighties. In 1990 BIPAC mobilized a successful national writing campaign against Hetrick-Martin Institute (Harvey Milk High School), which had offered an offensive workshop called "Bisexual Men: Fact or Fiction?" — a clearly biphobic description.

In the early eighties, social, support, and educational groups for bis were organized in more major cities and towns. Bisexuals within the lesbian, gay, and feminist communities began to speak up and identify themselves. The years 1983 and 1984 seem to be when numerous bisexuals independently and sychronistically organized worldwide.

♦ The Boston Bisexual Women's Network, which was founded in 1983, came out of a meeting called by women in a support group called the BiVocals. It is still one of the most active groups providing a lifeline for over eight hundred people internationally with its newsletter. Robyn Ochs's story in the Community Section documents the excitement of that historic first meeting and shares the history of that group. The Boston Bisexual Men's Network formed shortly after BBWN as a support, social group and also has a newsletter. The political group BICEP — Bisexual Community Engaging in Politics — was founded by Lucy Friedland in Boston in 1988. BICEP keeps a media watch, writes letters to the editor, protests, and educates. Their loud and visible presence protested Governor Dukakis's homophobic foster parent policy, which not only bars lesbian and gays but also bisexuals from being foster parents. This was a clear reminder that homophobia is a bisexual issue. In a historic move the BBWN and BBMN recently rented office space in the Lesbian Gay Center sharing an office with the East Coast Bisexual Network and New England Lesbian, Gay, and Bisexual Veterans.

♦ The East Coast Bisexual Network is a regional umbrella group that was founded in 1985 to facilitate communication between people and groups. The steering committee has members representing Maine, New Hampshire, Massachusetts, Vermont, Connecticut, Rhode Island, New York, New Jersey, Pennsylvania, and Washington, D.C. Yearly conferences or retreats are held drawing 150 to 250 bisexuals from all over the U.S. In 1989 they incorporated and are now working on getting funding. This regional network is a unique model for the rest of the country.

♦ Washington, D.C., formed Bi-Ways, a social and support group that was a reincarnation of the seventies group there. In 1988, a separate women's group within Bi-Ways formed. A new group, the Bi-Women's (and Men's) Network, was also established in 1989, as a support and social group for more traditionally oriented bis into monogamous or duogamous relationships only.

◆ Seattle women attending a mixed support group that met in the mid-eighties wanted a group that would address specific feminist women's issues. They formed the Seattle Women's Bisexual Network in 1985. Their social, support, and highly visible community education efforts, as well as the newsletter *North Bi Northwest,* have attracted positive attention for bisexuals in this region. SBWN networks with Vancouver, Canada's Bi-Focus group across the border and also holds a yearly open house for the community at large. The Seattle Bisexual Men's Union holds support groups and has social functions as well.

◆ Bisexual groups in England, Scotland, and Amsterdam were also organizing in the late seventies and throughout the eighties.

Bisexuals have been active in Long Beach and Los Angeles, California; Baltimore, Maryland; Rochester, Ithaca, and Albany, New York; Philadelphia, Pennsylvania; Portland, Maine; New Haven, Middletown, and New London, Connecticut; Cincinnati and Cleveland, Ohio; Northampton, Amherst, and Marlboro, Massachusetts; Kahului, Maui, Hawai'i; Miami, Florida; St. Louis, Missouri; Portland, Oregon; Dallas, Texas; and St. Paul and Minneapolis, Minnesota. And lesbian and gay student groups in colleges around the country are changing their names to include bisexual people. The times are changing.

One city's story

San Francisco is a unique city. The lesbian and gay communities are a respected and viable part of the city because of the incredible risk-taking of the many people who came from all over to join in building a community. Many bisexuals have actively supported and been a part of this community since the late seventies. On June 30, 1977, the San Francisco Bisexual Center, which opened in 1976 offering social and counseling services, held its first press conference to speak out against Anita Bryant and State Senator John Briggs's efforts to bar homosexuals from employment as schoolteachers in the California school system. It emphasized that gay concerns were also bisexual concerns. (Several contributors to this anthology, including Arlene Krantz, document the importance of the center in people's lives.)

BiPOL, a bisexual, lesbian, and gay feminist political action group, was founded in the spring of 1983 by a small band of highly visible bisexual political activists within the lesbian and gay communities. As the reality of the "gay cancer," or AIDS, was dawning, Dr. Alan Rockway, Lani Kaahumanu, Bill Mack, Autumn Courtney, Arlene Krantz, Dr. Maggi Rubenstein, and Dr. David Lourea shared the same sense of urgency —

visibility was the key. That summer one of the first AIDS demonstrations in San Francisco was organized by BiPOL outside the Haitian Embassy protesting that government's AIDS-phobic arrest of fifty-six gay and bi men.

AIDS awareness and education programs were developed in the early eighties by bisexual activists. The programs stressed:

 ◆ the use of "bisexual" in all literature referring to AIDS and gay men;
 ◆ recognizing women as a potential risk group; and
 ◆ using a sex-positive approach as opposed to fear tactics.

These issues and programs were presented at conferences, at the bathhouses, before Mayor Feinstein's AIDS Education Advisory Committee, at the first "Sex in the Age of AIDS" workshop offered by the city to the San Francisco Public Health Department, and at the Cauldron. Most of what the programs stressed was incorporated in what was to become the internationally renowned "San Francisco Model" for cities and communities responding to the AIDS epidemic. But what was completely ignored by everyone was the importance of the use of "bisexual" in all AIDS education and prevention literature.

In California the Lesbian/Gay Freedom Day Parade is second only to the famous Rose Bowl Parade in Los Angeles. BiPOL's 1984 contingent made the front page of the *San Francisco Chronicle,* and won the lesbian and gay communities' coveted "Most Outrageous Contingent" award. The theme was "Unity Is Our Bi-Word." "Mayor Bi-Anne Feinstein" and a very pregnant "Princess Bi" holding a little sign pointing to her "Bi-son," rode on top of a red 1972 convertible, the bumper banner welcoming one and all to "The San Francisco Bi Area." Prancing behind the car were large white molar-shaped cardboard "Bi-cuspids" holding "We are everywhere" signs, a Bi-valve for human rights, Bi-ceps, and a Bi-detector that scanned the cheering crowds.

One week later the Democratic Convention was scheduled to arrive. BiPOL decided to take advantage of the national media in town. A press conference was called to nominate Lani Kaahumanu for vice president to run with Walter Mondale. As an ex-housewife mother of two from San Mateo, a mixed-race, multicultural lesbian-identified bisexual feminist, she would vie with Geraldine Ferraro and then-mayor Dianne Feinstein. With her campaign slogan — "Tippicanoe and Kaahumanu too" — she would be the first out bisexual Hawaiian running for a major office. The purpose would be to get as much bisexual visibility as possible.

That same week BiPOL's street theatre crew staged a rowdy press-attended "Stop the 1984 Falwellian Agenda: 'La Cage Aufalwell'" sexual healing of the Moral Majority. They sprinkled "fairy dust" on the sidewalks outside the downtown Holiday Inn where Jerry Falwell was holding his "Brotherhood Family Forum." The first bisexual rights rally was held the following day on the stage in front of Moscone Convention Center. BiPOL got media coverage in *Newsweek,* and in newspapers in Los Angeles, Chicago, San Francisco, and New York.

In 1984, in its eighth year, board president Autumn Courtney announced that the Bisexual Center would close its doors. Fighting the AIDS epidemic took its toll in time and energy, and the lack of new leadership brought an end to this internationally known counseling and service center.

Bisexuals continued to be overwhelmed with AIDS and ARC. The San Francisco Department of Public Health (SFDPH) became a major battlefield. As an AIDS educator, activist, and therapist, David Lourea repeatedly went to the SFDPH to demand that bisexual statistics be made visible, that it was gay *and bisexual* men who were dying — "How do we educate bisexual people if we are ignored?" Because of his persistence, this then became the token mention of bisexuality (dropped after the first sentence) in most news stories.

In 1985 Maggi Rubenstein was the first out bisexual invited to speak at the Lesbian/Gay Freedom Day Parade Celebration.

BiPOL's close-knit family was stunned when Alan Rockway was diagnosed with AIDS. Alan's press releases and "biphobic and bipositive" media watch and response slowed considerably.

In 1986 Autumn Courtney, who had worked long and hard for several years on the Lesbian/Gay Freedom Day Parade Committee and had served on its board of directors, earned the right to run for co-chair of the parade. An easy target, she met the challenge at an open, standing-room-only community meeting. She fielded the biphobic questions and won the position. As an out bisexual, she represented the largest lesbian and gay community in the world, traveling to many cities across the nation giving speeches about lesbian, gay, and bisexual rights.

Ann Justi, inspired by the East Coast Bisexual Network, began to organize what would become the Bay Area Bisexual Network (BABN). BABN has grown to include a bi-monthly newsletter and a speaker's bureau, and sponsors monthly community forums, socials, and weekly support groups.

BiPOL political activist Alan Rockway, Ph.D., died of AIDS in his home in November 1987. In 1976, as an out gay-identified bisexual, Alan co-authored the Dade County, Florida, gay rights ordinance —the very first successful popular vote gay ordinance. Outraged, Anita Bryant and right-wing fundamentalists launched a national anti-gay "Save Our Children" crusade that eventually overturned the ordinance. Alan spearheaded a nationwide "gay-cott" of Florida orange juice, which was so successful that Anita Bryant lost her lucrative Minute Maid orange juice celebrity-rep contract. Alan was a relentless politico, known for his chuzpah and his flare for orchestrating the most audacious media capers. His astute political sense, analysis, and inclusive feminist ideals are built into the foundation of the San Francisco bisexual movement and community.

Conference participants, First National Bisexual Conference,
San Francisco, June 1990, Mission High School steps.

National Bisexual Network

The 1987 National March on Washington for Lesbian and Gay Rights became the ideal opportunity for bisexual people to organize nationally.

Lucy Friedland and Liz Nania from the Boston Bisexual Women's Network organized a national contingent for the march. Loraine Hutchins worked with the D.C. march office to make sure bisexuals were included in the contingent lineup, and Lani Kaahumanu wrote an article that became part of the Civil Disobedience Handbook. As Liz and Lucy worked on the National Bisexual Network contingent banner, representing bisexuals who were coming from all over the United States to march, they wondered — how can we have a banner without a network? They contacted Autumn and Lani to use BiPOL's post office box number for the flyer "Are you ready for a National Bisexual Network?," asking BiPOL to handle the response to the flyer.

What follow are excerpts from:

◆ the "Call to Bisexuals" flyer,
◆ chants from the actual march,
◆ a *Gay Community News* story written after the march, and
◆ the results of the "Are we ready?" flyer.

❖

A call to bisexuals: March on Washington!
by Liz Nania and Lucy Friedland

On Columbus Day weekend, tens, maybe hundreds of thousands of supporters of lesbian and gay civil rights are going to demonstrate in Washington, D.C.

The National March on Washington for Lesbian and Gay Rights is going to be the most impressive display of lesbian and gay pride and solidarity ever seen in this country. As bisexuals, can we afford to sit back and watch this event unfold on national tv? Not a chance. At last May's conference in New York, the East Coast Bisexual Network (ECBN) Steering Committee unanimously voted to sponsor a National Bisexual Contingent.

These are dangerous times for bisexuals. Nearly every day we are treated to some nasty biphobic media coverage of bisexuals and AIDS ... Bi's are equally threatened by the anti-choice and anti-sex agenda of the Reagan Administration as are lesbians and gays. We confront the same hostilities, the same discriminations. The pending appointment of another ultra-conservative judge to the Supreme Court can do us no good...

Even though bisexual issues overlap with those of our gay and lesbian friends, they aren't identical. We can't let gays represent us in D.C. We have to go there ourselves, as bisexuals, to speak openly and vociferously as a separate and vital contingent. We must achieve some visibility on our own terms instead of passing as heterosexuals or gays. It's a matter of pride, and survival. Why travel to D.C. and melt into a homosexual affinity group or organization when you aren't gay or lesbian? Once we begin to publicly claim our bisexual identities, we will no longer go unacknowledged or left out. The very fact that the March wasn't called "The Lesbian, Gay, and Bisexual March on Washington" is problematic, but only by organizing locally, regionally, and nationally can we expect to see our bisexual rights protected and promoted...

Witness the birth of a national bisexual movement in Washington on October 11th! Whatever size of the Bisexual Contingent, it will be a *proud* contingent. You can count on it. We'll be waiting for you!

Chants for bis!
by Sharla of the Boston Bisexual Women's Network

> We are bis, we're not confused!
> We love whomever we choose!
>
> Lezzies 'n' faggots 'n' bis, oh my!
> Lezzies 'n' faggots 'n' bis, oh my!

A momentous event:
The national gathering of bisexuals at the march on Washington[3]
by Liz Nania

This was surely one of the finest moments in bisexual history. Gutsy bisexuals from about twenty states, women and men with the courage and conviction to affirm their identity before more than half a million lesbians, gays, and gay-rights advocates...

Sunday morning marked the beginning of the first ever gathering of bisexual women and men from all over the country! Our meeting place was almost as grand as the occasion — the Mayflower Hotel ... The feeling of electricity could have lit up the whole hotel! We made friends and compared experiences of our community (or lack thereof) nationwide; we wore red and black and made red satin sashes with our own bi slogans emblazoned in gold; ... we pinned on "Bisexual Pride" and "Bi-phobia Shield" buttons; we talked about founding a National Bisexual Network. From there, the hundred participants marched to the Ellipse where we gathered our signs, our banners and our strength...

When the March began we hoisted beautiful, glittery signs proclaiming, "We're Not Fence Sitters, We're Bridge Builders," "Bisexuality is a Viable Option," and the ever-popular, "Equal Opportunity Lover."...

The rally after the March proved at least as exciting as the March itself. I witnessed hundreds of thousands of us joining together in one massive euphoric gathering. I felt completely welcomed as a bisexual. Although most of the speakers and entertainers were top-notch, many of us were aware that the word "bisexual" was largely conspicuous by its absence from the stage and the literature. But, hey, it's only 1987! Give us a few years and about a million hours of consciousness-raising, okay? We're up to the task; that's why we were there...

Are we ready?

Within four months after the March on Washington, BiPOL received over 150 inquiries and over $500 to cover copying and mailing costs of the responses to "Are we ready for a National Bisexual Network?" The answer was obviously *yes!* But the grass roots organizing was focused locally. Those interested in networking nationally were for the most part isolated and separated by long distances. BiPOL sponsored the June 1990 National Bisexual Conference in San Francisco as a practical solution for not only organizing the National Bisexual Network, but for bisexual people to "Educate, Advocate, Agitate, and Celebrate!" BiPol's Bisexual People of Color Caucus was formed to foster visible and diverse leadership in the bisexual movement. The Conference was held during Lesbian/Gay Pride Week and attracted over 400 people from around the world. The San Francisco Board of Supervisors officially proclaimed June 23 as Bisexual Pride Day. The National Bisexual Network is growing. The bisexual movement has come of age.

Notes

1. George Barr, "Chicago Bi-Ways: An Informal History," *Bisexualities: Theory and Research Journal of Homosexuality* 11, nos. 1, 2 (ed. Klein and Wolf): 231–234, Haworth Press, 1985.

2. Chuck Misaan, "The Bisexual Scene in New York City," ibid., pp. 223, 224.

3. Excerpted from "Speaking Out," *Gay Community News,* December 1987.

Resources

The North American Multicultural Bisexual Network
584 Castro Street, #441
San Francisco, CA 94114

Bisexual People of Color Caucus/BiPOL
584 Castro Street, #422
San Francisco, CA 94114
(415) 775-1990

Gay, Lesbian, & Bisexual Veterans of America
Attn: Miriam ben-Shalom
National Chairperson
1350 North 37th Place
Milwaukee, WI 53208

East Coast Bisexual Network (ECBN)
c/o Boston Lesbian/Gay Service Center
338 Newbury Street, 2nd floor
Boston, MA 02115
(617) 247-6683

International Directory of Bisexual Groups *
(obtainable through the Boston Bisexual Women's Network
c/o Boston Lesbian/Gay Service Center
338 Newbury Street, 2nd floor
Boston, MA 02115)

---

* See this directory for all other groups.

Glossary

biphobia : the fear of intimacy and closeness to people who don't identify with either the hetero- or homosexual orientation, manifested as homophobia in the heterosexual community and heterophobia in the homosexual community.

bisexual : people who have erotic, affectionate, romantic feelings for, fantasies of, and experiences with women and men, and/or who self-identify as bisexual.

gay-identified bisexual : a man whose main experience and identification is within the gay community. Many times there has been a gay-identified period before realizing bisexual identity. Also a woman who identifies with the general umbrella term gay, which is inclusive of all homosexual women and men, not just the male homosexual community.

heterophobia : the fear of closeness and/or intimacy with those of the other sex; the fear of being perceived as opposite-sex oriented.

heterosexism : the assumption that being heterosexual is inherently better or more moral than being lesbian, gay, or bisexual. Like racism, sexism, and other forms of oppression, heterosexism awards power to members of the dominant group (heterosexuals) and denies it to members of the subordinate group (lesbians, gay men, and bisexual women and men).[1]

heterosexual-identified bisexual : a woman or man who may have same-sex lovers, but whose main experience and identification is within the heterosexual community. This includes married people as well as single people, celibates as well as swingers.

heterosexual privilege : the benefit of basic civil rights and familial recognition heterosexuals accord themselves as the "norm" — e.g., marriage, job security, tax breaks, parental rights, foster parenting, visitation, and inheritance rights. For women, such privilege often also means the material and physical security of being with a man who has more access to earning power (financial security) and who can protect her from other men. For men it can mean protection from homophobic "faggot" attacks by other men and benefiting from women's free labor in patriarchy — for example, in the forms of housework, cooking, child rearing, and emotional nurturing. This varies depending on race, class, culture, age, and physical abilities.

homophobia : the irrational fear of closeness and intimacy with others of your gender, which manifests itself in hatred, revulsion, disgust, and culturally sanctioned prejudice and violence (homosexual-panic defense).

internalized oppression : the process by which people come to believe the stereotypes and misinformation the dominant culture communicates about them and other people. Internalizing these negative assumptions denies oneself and perpetuates the stereotype (a self-fulfilling prophecy).

Kinsey scale : This scale is an equal-interval scale with continuous graduations between heterosexuality and homosexuality. An individual rating is based on relative amounts of heterosexual and homosexual response. Kinsey used the scale to rate individuals on overt experiences and psychological reactions. The ratings are as follows:

    (0) Exclusively heterosexual
    (1) Predominantly heterosexual, only incidentally homosexual
    (2) Predominantly heterosexual, but more than incidentally heterosexual
    (3) Equally heterosexual and homosexual
    (4) Predominantly homosexual, but more than incidentally heterosexual
    (5) Predominantly homosexual, only incidentally heterosexual
    (6) Exclusively homosexual[2]

Klein Sexual Orientation Grid : This grid was developed to measure a person's sexual orientation as a dynamic multivariable process. The grid was designed to extend the scope of the Kinsey scale by including attraction, behavior, fantasy, social and emotional preference, self-identification, and lifestyle. These characteristics are also measured in the past, in the present, and as an ideal. The Klein grid provides a framework for understanding sexual orientation on a theoretical level. On a practical level it enables the researcher to separate groups more precisely, to focus on the individual while noting some of the common configurations.[3]

lesbian-identified bisexual : a woman whose main experience and identification is within the lesbian community. Many times women experience a lesbian-identified period before realizing a bisexual identity.

monosexual : a term used for both heterosexuals and homosexuals — i.e., all people who love only one gender and take for granted the sexual dichotomy set up by the patriarchy. Bisexuality calls this system of categories and divisions into question.

patriarchy : the power of the fathers: a familial-social, ideological, political system in which men — by force, direct pressure, or through ritual, tradition, law, language, customs, etiquette, education, and the division of labor — determine what part women shall or shall not play, and in which the female is everywhere subsumed under the male.[4]

sexism : the institutionalized belief system of the "innate" or the "natural" superiority of men over women, based in misogyny (the fear and hatred of women) and maintained by a state of personal privilege for men in a hierarchy depending on race, class, culture, age, and physical abilities within an androcentric (male-centered) patriarchal framework — i.e., religion, capitalism, medicine, nuclear family, etc.

sex radical : someone working for sexual civil liberties among consenting adults, for whom free and liberated sex is a political act as well as an art form. A term formed in reaction to right-wing backlash against women and sexual minorities.

sex worker : someone who makes their living in the sex industry, whether as a producer or performer of pornography, as a prostitute, a phone-sex worker, etc.

sm : any form of consensual sexual play involving the acting out of fantasies, feelings, and roles involving dominance and submission, and the exchange of power and trust. Originally based on the terms *sadist* and *masochist*, feminists have changed the term from S&M to s/m or sm, to denote the fluid, exchanging nature of these power poles, rather than their separateness.

swingers : sometimes described as the most domesticated sexual adventurers — for their proclivity to share their assignations with their spouses, not conceal them — these people usually operate in heterosexual couples and temporarily swap partners or engage in various forms of group sex.

transperson : the umbrella term for many different sexual minorities who identify with the opposite physical sex and gender than the body in which they were born. A *transsexual* can be either pre-op, or post-op, that is, they may choose to dress as the sex they identify as, without ever getting an operation to change their genitals, or they may opt for the operation. And, regardless of their gender identification, their sexual orientation may be heterosexual, homosexual, bisexual, or whatever they define it as. A *transvestite* is someone who cross-dresses. They may be heterosexual, bi, or gay. *Gender-fuck* is a term for people who cross-dress or mix and match sex-role-identified clothing with no attempt to conceal their gender — a bearded man wearing a dress, for instance.

Notes

1. "The Campaign to End Homophobia" (brochure), 1990.

2. Klein, Sepekoff, and Wolf, "Sexual Orientation: A Multi-Variable Dynamic Process," *Bisexualities: Theory and Research,* no. 11 of the book series *Research on Homosexuality,* ed. Fritz Klein and Timothy J. Wolf, Haworth Press, 1985, p. 37.

3. Ibid., pp. 38–48.

4. Adrienne Rich, *Of Woman Born: Motherhood as Experience and Institution,* Norton, 1976, pp. 57–58.

Contributors

CHRIS ALEXANDER was born in Salt Lake City, was raised as a Mormon, and is about to be licensed as a clinical psychologist. He shares his Oakland home with three rabbits and two birds and has worked at the San Francisco AIDS Foundation for three and a half years.

MICHAEL AMBROSINO is currently searching for a working engine for his 1968 International 1000. He is an AIDS outreach worker, writer, and graphic artist in Portland, Oregon.

RICH ARANOW is a proud sexual adventurer who works in San Francisco AIDS prevention and treatment.

CLIFF ARNESEN, president of the New England Gay, Lesbian, & Bisexual Veterans, has testified twice before congressional subcommittees as an out bisexual for the rights of lesbian, gay, and bi veterans. He works at the Veterans Administration.

C.J. BARRAGAN III, born November 6, 1958, hibernated the first seventeen years of his life in the San Fernando Valley. B.A., 1980, in Political Science, from the University of San Francisco. He currently works in human resources for a law firm and has found the love of his life, but still wants a house in San Francisco, political involvement, and a big white Samoyed named Spock.

RICHARD SUSAN BASSEIN lives in Berkeley, California, and has been a math professor at a women's college for thirteen years. The acceptance and support of his children, friends, colleagues, and neighbors have enabled him to be open about his lifestyle. He co-founded East Bay Bi-Friendly — a social group for bi women and men inspired by and modeled on BiFriendly San Francisco.

DOLORES BISHOP, Master of Human Sexuality. SWF, blonde, thirty-nine forever. An Oakland resident, abortion counselor, healer, massage junky, peripatetic scribbler, and producer of Bay Area Safe-Sex Parties. She is polymorphous perverse, ambi-handrous, a card-carrying bi-sensual, and a party animal. Yeah.

BRENDA BLASINGAME, born into an Army family in the Midwest, has moved a lot, enjoys music, dance, travel, film, friends, and lots of physical closeness. For five years she has directed programs to end violence against women and children. Because she is a black, Jewish, bisexual woman she is committed to fighting all oppression and carries this out by conducting workshops on these issues.

JANET BOHAC received her B.A. from the University of Miami, where she received the Ila Rosenbaum Award for Scriptwriting. She also attended the American Film Institute in Los Angeles as a Screenwriting Fellow and graduated from Western Michigan University with an M.F.A. in writing. Her work has recently appeared in *Phoebe* and *Anima*.

MICHAEL BREWER is an artist, a writer, and a Long Island boy. He currently resides in Switzerland with his family and is working on a science fiction novel.

NATE BROWN, fifty-two, was born in California and has spent most of his life there. He's done many workshops, primarily with the Human Awareness Institute, San Francisco Sex Information, and I.A.S.H.S. Self-employed as a classical music archivist, his hobbies include being with his friends, hosting groups in his home, and classic movies.

WAYNE BRYANT is a programmer, writer, dowser, and cartoonist. When not on the road he lives in the Boston area with his two cats and occasionally members of the Cornerstone Theater Company, including his lover of seventeen years. He has been a member of the Boston Bisexual Men's Network since 1986 and is currently co-editor of its newsletter and representative to the East Coast Bisexual Network.

SUSAN CARLTON's pet name for her sexual identity is "polymorphously perverse," but she has been organizing around bisexuality for a few years at the University of California Berkeley campus, where she spends most of her time hastening the revolution that will liberate everyone (not just everybodyexcept-you). Her bed has three pillows and three comforters, and, true to a stereotype in this case, she is happiest as the filling in a human sandwich.

SHARON HWANG COLLIGAN, born 1969 in Boston, is a student at the College of Public and Community Service, University of Massachusetts. A child rape survivor, she is lonely and struggling to resist the multiple oppressions that attack our powers to touch deeply and to write out loud and clear.

DAJENYA is an undiscovered poet living in the San Francisco East Bay. She has waited fifteen years to see some of her writing published in a book. A full-time mother and a full-time psychology student. Three years sober, she finds each day she is feeling more alive, happy, joyous, and free.

BETH ELLIOT, onetime gifted child suitably warped in a minor-league prep school, is a San Francisco Bay Area writer who is proud to be a Celt and a third-generation native Californian. Also being an ace softball player, she rather enjoys being referred to as a switch hitter.

ben e factory, an average guy from Iowa, now lives with two friends in Seattle, Washington, where he plays with his ten-year-old friend Al, drinks Siberian ginseng tea nonstop, eats macrobiotic vegan junk food, dances to ska and rai music, works as a community organizer with the homestead cooperative land trust, and foments safe orgiastic social revolutionary fun.

C.K. FERRIER is a published poet and has also written for the *Boston Phoenix* and *Providence Journal Bulletin*. She is currently doing graduate work in North American religious history and is working on a book about religious and racial intolerance.

ANN FOX is a psychologist working in a college counseling center and private practice, with long-standing involvements in feminist, psychology, and personal growth activities. Her clinical work includes individual, group, and couples therapy. Her speciality is working with women.

LUCY FRIEDLAND is an anarcha-feminist bisexual activist (phew!). With Liz Nania she organized the National Bisexual Contingent for the 1987 March on Washington for Lesbian and Gay Rights and initiated the National Bisexual Network. In June 1988 she founded the Bisexual Committee Engaged in Politics (BiCEP) to increase the awareness and visibility of bisexuals through direct action politics.

CHRIS GIRARD, of French descent, is forty years old, is the parent of two children, and works in international development. He loves challenges, games, renovating old houses, and is enjoying the new triad with Billy and Art.

ROLAND GLENN is a retired educator and public service professional who lives in the seaside wilderness of Cape Cod. As a bisexual writer of essays, he relates his life's varied experiences and tells about his developing sexuality, which he considers to be a loving and never-ending process.

REBECCA GORLIN, born in New York in 1961, came to Boston in 1980 for college and has lived there ever since. Her major activities include singing, composing, writing literature, and political activism as a bisexual-identified bisexual. She lives with her boyfriend, Andy, and Sally and Garfield, two crazy cats.

CHANDINI GOSWAMI is: Indian. U.S. American. Feminist of color. South Asian American Activist. Asian American organizer. Bisexual lesbian. Daughter. Student. She is all of these identities. Has yet to find a functioning way to bring them all together. Is not even sure that would be the best idea.

PAUL HAUT escaped from Southern California and has lived in the Bay Area since 1982. He invaded the city of San Francisco in 1988, and has vowed never to leave. He enjoys the hell out of writing songs, walking, singing, exploring, his friends, and chocolate.

LIZ A. HIGHLEYMAN is an activist involved with ACT UP/Boston, BiCEP (the Bisexual Committee Engaging in Politics), Black Rose (a Boston anarchist group), the North American anarchist community, and the women's self-help movement. She works at the MIT Artificial Intelligence Laboratory and enjoys computer networking and photography.

JOHN HORNE died at thirty-three of AIDS, 1989. Interior designer, AIDS activist. Married to Madie, of Connecticut and Tucson, for eleven years.

KAREN HURLEY is a member of BiUnity and the Philadelphia Bisexual Network, and celebrates chaos with her coven, Twisted Sisters. ("'Tis an ill wind that blows no minds.") Doctoral student, clinical psychology, Temple University.

LORAINE HUTCHINS sleeps every night with her cat Lover Chops between her legs, in an old house in a tree-shaded area of Washington, D.C. She has worked as an activist for twenty years in the youth advocacy, feminism, peace, and tenants' rights movements. She now serves on the East Coast Bisexual Network Steering Committee and bicycles everywhere. She is a D.C. native, Taurus with Cancer rising, Aquarius moon.

LAURA JOHNSON calls herself Laura Wildwoman, artist and maker of magic. Her birth certificate says she was born in 1941, but she doesn't really know how old she is. She's thoroughly politically incorrect, doesn't fit categories too well, and by the time you read this something else will be happening.

A. BILLY S. and PEACHES JONES, father and daughter, both live in Washington, D.C. Peaches is a sophomore math major at Howard University. Formerly director of minority affairs at the National AIDS Network, Billy is now a senior associate in health and human services at MACRO Systems, and has been a gay activist, both nationally and locally, for many years.

LANI KAAHUMANU represents the bisexual community on the Lesbian/Gay Advisory Committee to the Human Rights Commission for the city and county of San Francisco, is on the Bay Area Bisexual Network Board, and co-chairs BiPOL's People of Color Caucus. She is on the editorial board of *Empathy*, a new interdisciplinary journal, and writes and performs with Mothertongue Feminist Theater Collective. An aging hippy and a member of Asian Pacifica Sisters, she has a 26-year-old son and a 24-year-old daughter and works for National Gay Rights Advocates.

BOBBI KEPPEL trained as a marriage and family therapist and has been working as a substance abuse counselor. She is a part-time fiber artist specializing in quilts and quilted clothing. She has played, sung, and supported folk music enthusiastically for almost fifty years. In June 1990, she moved from Maine to Canada to live with Helen.

MATTIE KEY came out as a writer, and as an erotic writer, while writing this story. When not pursuing fantasies, she spends her time working a very responsible, vanilla job. Claiming her bisexuality has been a sensual liberation; her goal is to keep the flame burning high.

KAREN KLASSEN, a 27-year-old second-generation Canadian of Mennonite origin, has been a naturalist and conservation educator, now studying herpetological ecology. Straight by default until seventeen, then bi three years, lesbian six years; now, it seems, bi again.

ARLENE KRANTZ is a successful businesswoman and a proud new grandmother. She is a founding member of BiPOL.

ELISE KRUEGER shares a St. Paul house with her sweetie, her hearing aids, an artist friend, three cats, and a variable number of computers. A vocal, out bisexual, she believes passionately in sushi, folk music, vampire novels, and the quest for the perfect rummage sale. She wants to be a curmudgeon when she grows up.

MATT LeGRANT is a 33-year-old city planner. He likes being a generalist in a society increasingly dominated by specialists. If any characteristic can describe his interests, it is variety — in food, music, reading material, and people. He loves the San Francisco Bay Area, and is a California native.

OBIE LEYVA was born in Mexico and moved to Hayward, California, where he was raised. He attends the University of California, Berkeley, where he confronts racism, discrimination, and biphobia as a political activist and AIDS educator.

DAVID LOUREA, a radical revolting sexologist from hell, founded and directed Bisexual Counseling Services in San Francisco and helped develop the Eroticizing Safe-Sex Process — viewed today as the most comprehensive safe-sex program available. He has written and taught extensively on safe sex and human sexuality and works as a preschool instructor, teacher, and administrator.

SHEILAH MABRY was born and raised in the Hell's Kitchen section of New York City. She graduated from the University of Massachusetts, Boston, with a degree in English. A bisexual who seeks to liberate herself from both the heterosexual and homosexual communities, she wants to start a bi newsletter for people of color.

DAVID MATTESON teaches family therapy and couples therapy at Governors State University, south of Chicago, has a private practice, and has been working as a psychotherapist and professor for over twenty years. One of the initial members of the National Organization of Men Against Sexism, a founding member of the Campaign to End Homophobia, and currently on the editorial board of *Empathy,* a new interdisciplinary journal about homophobia education.

NEIL MacLEAN has read only two autobiographies in his life — Wilheim Reich's and Tim Leary's. Mostly it doesn't interest him.

NACHAMA has spent her fifty years trying to figure out the best road to sanity — on the East Coast, in the Midwest, and presently in the West. Her joys in life stem from relationships with friends, family, lover, and her bi-breed, Chipper.

LANEY NELSON is a nineteen-year-old avid basketball fan and a participant in the sport. She is a P.E. major at California State, San Francisco.

LENORE NORRGARD has been a rights activist since high school days in Iowa, where she started with youth rights and anti-war work and developed consciousness around racism and sexism. Active in lesbian and gay rights and feminism since she moved to the Northwest in 1975. A founding editor of *North Bi Northwest,* the Seattle Bisexual Women's Network newsletter. Writes fiction and articles on contemporary China.

ROBYN OCHS, an escapee from New York City now living in Cambridge,

Massachusetts, is a not-so-mild-mannered university administrator. She helped found and is an active member of the Boston Bisexual Women's Network and the East Coast Bisexual Network. She is a member of both BBWN's speaker's bureau and Boston's Gay, Lesbian, and Bisexual Speaker's Bureau.

LISA ORLANDO is a recovering East Coast cynic who practices bi-celibacy and Jungian feminist witchcraft in Berkeley, California. She currently makes her living by contributing theatrical complexity and interesting verbs to a collaborative writing project on "green" psychology. She dreams about finding (or founding) a religious–therapeutic community in the woods where people can write theory and poetry, engage in intensive soul making, and create both a stable base for social change work and a model for ecological living.

CAROL A. QUEEN, a San Francisco writer and sex educator and activist who works within the lesbian, gay, bisexual, and AIDS activist communities, is currently most fascinated by radical sex–gender play, power, and the sex industry. She experiences sex as profoundly interesting and empowering, and wishes everyone else did, too. She is working on a novel.

RIFKA REICHLER is a 25-year-old bisexual woman who lives in South Dakota with her husband and is expecting her first child in September 1990. She enjoys laughing, reading, writing, and spending time with family and friends.

JOE RIOS is a graduate student at the University of California, Berkeley.

BETSY ROSE is a singer, songwriter, and daughter and granddaughter of ministers. She voices the connections between spirituality, creativity, and feminism. Recently she has been working with Buddhist peace monk Thich Nhat Hanh, with Vietnam veterans, and in AIDS hospices.

KARLA ROSSI, born in Karlsruhe, Germany, in a Volkswagen on the autobahn, at a speed of eighty miles an hour, grew up in a small midwestern town near Toledo, Ohio. That wasn't fast enough for her, so she relocated to San Francisco and purchased a Volkswagen so that she could live life in the fast lane, once again.

MAGGI RUBENSTEIN is dean of students at the Institute for the Advanced Study of Human Sexuality and maintains a private therapy practice. She appears regularly on "Electric City," a gay cable television program in San Francisco, and has been active in the Lesbian, Gay, and Bisexual Voters Project.

ANN SCHNEIDER, a 31-year-old union-sponsored legal services attorney, lives collectively with five women and men in Brooklyn and is active with a local anti-gentrification group. She enjoys going to women-only dances, marching in Gay Pride parades, and being in a two-year, nonmonogamous relationship with a man.

MARCY SHEINER is a free-lance writer whose work has appeared in *Mother Jones,* the *San Francisco Chronicle,* and the *San Francisco Bay Guardian.* She's currently working on a novel.

REBECCA SHUSTER is a Boston-based psychotherapist, consultant, teacher, writer, and support group leader. Author of "Sexuality as a Continuum: The Bisexual Identity" (*Lesbian Psychologies*, University of Illinois Press, 1987), she is now at work on an autobiographical narrative about the inner life of a young child.

SHU WEI CHEN — ANDY was born in Buenos Aires, Argentina, to a Chinese immigrant family. He recently graduated from San Jose State University, and has a very strong interest in the visual arts.

ALAN SILVER is a forty-year-old black man who is a proud parent and emerging bisexual, actively involved in various community organizing projects.

RONDA SLATER has been performing her poetry, songs, comedy, and theater pieces since 1974. Since 1984 she's been touring the U.S. and Canada with her one-woman play "...A Name You Never Got," the true story of her reunion with the daughter she gave up for adoption in college. She resides in Oakland, California.

ANNIE SPRINKLE is a Manhattan-based performance artist, photographer, sex educator, and ex-porn star and prostitute. She is currently touring internationally with her one-woman show, "Annie Sprinkle — Post Porn Modernist," and has created two post-porn videos, *Rites of Passion* (about tantric lovemaking), and *Linda/Les & Annie* (about her lover Les Nichols, a female-to-male transsexual and hermaphrodite).

SHARON FORMAN SUMPTER is a redheaded "recovering actress" and fairy practicing healing arts, sex education, and activism in Hollywood. She works with survivors of abuse, institutionalization, and sexual oppression. She has been published in *Sinister Wisdom,* and loves to read, be in nature, lie in bed, and be in touch with the Goddess.

SUZANNE specialized in adolescent development psychology, with a separate major in political science. After twelve stressful years in the health field, she recently resigned to write and paint full-time.

HAP STEWART lives in Marin County, California, and recently went to the Mojave Desert on a vision quest. He receives loving support from his daughters, Rachel and Evangeline, and is learning to give love to his son, Glenn. Special thanks to Dave Martin, Tamayo Sato, Steve Egri, Sheila Brooke, Carole Russell, Suzanne Thompson, Irene Smith, and Rick, a bisexual friend who died in 1989.

ELLEN TERRIS was an active member of the Boston Bisexual Women's Network, serving as its treasurer. She helped plan and run the 1989 East Coast Bisexual Network Conference and now resides in Seattle, where she is a member of the Seattle Bisexual Women's Network.

LEONARD TIRADO is an Albany, New York, psychotherapist and activist, resolutely deviant and devotedly Buddhist, his life inspirations being Jean Genet and Thich Nhat Hanh.

NAOMI TUCKER is a feminist bisexual activist in San Francisco who works with battered women. She is a member of the Bay Area Bisexual Network, BiPOL, and the Boston Bisexual Women's Network.

AMANDA UDIS-KESSLER's past includes les/bi/gay activism and education, lots of music, HIV-test counseling, and worship-leading at a local Boston congregation. Her present and future are less clear, but seem likely to include more music, radical sociology, cats, and frozen yogurt.

KEI UWANO was born and raised in northern Japan. In the early seventies she and four other radical lesbian-feminists opened a women's center in Tokyo. She moved to the U.S. ten years ago and is currently attending acupuncture school.

CORNELIUS UTZ was born on a midwestern farm in 1909, the youngest of eleven children. After thirty-nine years of social work practice and volunteering with senior citizens, he began working as a textile artist, doing macrame, weaving, lace making, and fabric dying. Avid bridge player, active member of a Unitarian-Universalist church.

ELIZABETH REBA WEISE, a Seattle bisexual activist, is one of the founders of the Seattle Bisexual Women's Network. She is currently editing *The Bisexual Feminist: Essays on Feminism and Sexual Identity,* a Seal Press anthology. She tries to catch "Star Trek" with the Seattle Bisexual Star Trek Affinity Group whenever she can.

SELENA JULIE WHANG is working on her master's thesis, combining women's studies, Asian American studies, and interdisciplinary arts, at San Francisco State University.

VICTORIA (TORI) WOODARD grew up on a Colorado ranch, is a graduate of Antioch University's feminist therapy program, and teaches women's studies at Contra Costa College. She lives in Berkeley and is interested in peace, cnvironmcntal, cthnic, gay, and womcn's issucs.

IRENE WOLT is a feminist and radical writer and activist who left the East Coast for the Los Angeles area almost twenty years ago. Since writing the poem she has been in a relationship with a woman, with whom she plans to live happily ever after.

AMANDA YOSHIZAKI, an educator, potter, and reformer who lives in San Francisco, hangs out with her bi-husband and bi-cats. She has passions for chocolate, poetry, and bubble baths.

LISA YOST is a short-story writer and toxicologist. She is transplanted from the Midwest and Washington, D.C., to Seattle, where she is reveling in the long sunny days of summer. Her writing has been published in *Backbone, Common Lives/Lesbian Lives,* and *West Wind Review,* and has received honorable mention in a national contest and in a contest for Washington, D.C., area writers.

Other books of interest from
ALYSON PUBLICATIONS

LAVENDER LISTS, by Lynne Y. Fletcher and Adrien Saks, $9.00. This all-new collection of lists captures many entertaining, informative, and little-known aspects of gay and lesbian lore: 5 planned gay communities that never happened, 10 lesbian nuns, 15 cases of censorship where no sex was involved, 10 out-of-the-closet law enforcement officers, and much more.

IN THE LIFE, edited by Joseph Beam, $9.00. When writer and activist Joseph Beam became frustrated that so little gay literature spoke to him as a black gay man, he did something about it: The result was *In the Life,* an anthology which takes its name from a black slang expression for "gay." Here, thirty-three writers and artists explore what it means to be doubly different — black and gay — in modern America. Their stories, essays, poetry, and artwork voice the concerns and aspirations of an often silent minority.

THE TROUBLE WITH HARRY HAY, by Stuart Timmons, cloth, $20.00. This complete biography of Harry Hay, known as the father of gay liberation, sweeps through forty years of the gay movement and nearly eighty years of a colorful and original American life. Hay went from a pampered childhood through a Hollywood acting career and a stint in the Communist Party before starting his life's work in 1950, when he founded the Mattachine Society, the forerunner of today's gay movement.

GAYS IN UNIFORM, edited by Kate Dyer, introduction by Congressman Gerry Studds, $7.00. Why doesn't the Pentagon want you to read this book? When two studies by a research arm of the Pentagon concluded that there was no justification for keeping gay people out of the military, the generals deep-sixed the reports. Those reports are now available, in book form, to the public at large. Find out for yourself what the Pentagon doesn't want you to know about gays in the military.

WORLDS APART, edited by Camilla Decarnin, Eric Garber, and Lyn Paleo, $8.00. The world of science fiction allows writers to freely explore alternative sexualities. These eleven stories take full advantage of that opportunity with characters ranging from a black lesbian vampire to a gay psychodroid. Here are adventure, romance, and excitement — and perhaps some genuine alternatives for our future.

THE GAY BOOK OF LISTS, by Leigh Rutledge, $8.00. Rutledge has compiled a fascinating and informative collection of lists. His subject matter ranges from history (6 gay popes) to politics (9 perfectly disgusting reactions to AIDS) to entertainment (12 examples of gays on network television) to humor (9 Victorian "cures" for masturbation). Learning about gay culture and history has never been so much fun.

LESBIAN LISTS, by Dell Richards, $9.00. Lesbian holy days is just one of the hundreds of lists of clever and enlightening lesbian trivia compiled by columnist Dell Richards. Fun facts like uppity women who were called lesbians (but probably weren't), banned lesbian books, lesbians who've passed as men, herbal aphrodisiacs, black lesbian entertainers, and switch-hitters are sure to amuse and make *Lesbian Lists* a great gift.

LONG TIME PASSING, edited by Marcy Adelman, $8.00. Here, in their own words, women talk about age-related concerns: the fear of losing a lover, the experience of being a lesbian in the 1940s and '50s, the issues of loneliness and community. Most contributors are older lesbians, but several younger voices are represented.

THE ALYSON ALMANAC, by Alyson Publications staff, $9.00. Almanacs have been popular sources of information since "Poor Richard" first put his thoughts on paper and Yankee farmers started forecasting the weather. Here is an almanac for gay and lesbian readers that follows these traditions. You'll find the voting records of members of Congress on gay issues, practical tips on financial planning for same-sex couples, an outline of the five stages of a gay relationship, and much, much more.

MACHO SLUTS, by Pat Califia, $10.00. Pat Califia, the prolific lesbian author, has put together a stunning collection of her best erotic short fiction. She explores sexual fantasy and adventure in previously taboo territory — incest, sex with a thirteen-year-old girl, a lesbian's encounter with two cops, a gay man who loves to dominate dominant men, as well as various S/M and "vanilla" scenes.

THE BEST MAN, by Paul Reidinger, $8.00. Ross is an attractive, blond-haired, well-built law student at Stanford ... and he's made it quite obvious to David that he'd like them to spend more time together. That's the good news. The bad news is that Ross is already involved with David's best friend, Katherine. What's a boy to do?

CRUSH, by Jane Futcher, $8.00. It wasn't easy fitting in at an exclusive girls' school like Huntington Hill. But in her senior year, Jinx finally felt as if she belonged. Lexie — beautiful, popular Lexie — wanted her for a friend. Jinx knew she had a big crush on Lexie, and she knew she had to do something to make it go away. But Lexie had other plans. And Lexie always got her way.

DADDY'S ROOMMATE, by Michael Willhoite, cloth, $15.00. This is the first book written for the children of gay men. In thirty-two pages a young boy, his father, and the father's lover take part in activities familiar to all kinds of families: cleaning the house, shopping, playing games, fighting, and making up. The drawings, by popular caricaturist Michael Willhoite, are simple and colorful, and the binding is sturdy — perfect for children aged two to five.

Ask for these titles in your favorite bookstore. Or, to order by mail, use this coupon or a photocopy.

— — — — — — — — — — — —

Enclosed is $_____ for the following books. (Add $1.00 postage when ordering just one book. If you order two or more, we'll pay the postage.)

1. _____

2. _____

3. _____

4. _____

name: _____ address: _____

city: _____ state: _____ zip: _____

ALYSON PUBLICATIONS
Dept. H-74, 40 Plympton St., Boston, MA 02118

After June 30, 1992, please write for current catalog.